Cognitive Development and the Ageing Process

In the World Library of Psychologists series, international experts present career-long collections of what they judge to be their most interesting publications – extracts from books, key articles, research findings, practical and theoretical contributions.

Professor Patrick Rabbitt has been a prominent contributor to knowledge of cognitive performance and cognitive ageing for over half a century. He has made a range of significant contributions to geronotological research, from the development of information processing theories in the 19650s and 1960s to a new understanding of decision making and the ageing process in subsequent decades.

This collection of his research articles represents a review of how work in cognitive performance and cognitive ageing has developed in the past 50 years. Whilst the nature of scientific research means that some of the questions posed have since been answered, Rabbitt adds introductory sections to articles which contextualise its place in the subject area and offer a personal view on the evolution of the field.

This book is important because it provides a perspective on the development of cognitive research and the ageing process through the work of an active researcher in the field. It will interest all students and researchers interested in cognitive development and gerontology.

Patrick Rabbitt was a member of scientific staff at the MRC Applied Psychology unit at the University of Cambridge, UK, from 1962 to 1967; worked for the University of Oxford, UK, as a lecturer in psychology (1968–1982); the University of Durham, UK, as Professor of Psychology and head of department (1982–1983); and the University of Manchester, UK, as the Research Chair in Gerontology and Cognitive Psychology and Director of the Age and Cognitive Performance Research Centre (1983–2004). He is currently Associated Researcher at the Department of Experimental Psychology, University of Oxford, UK.

World Library of Psychologists

The *World Library of Psychologists* series celebrates the important contributions to psychology made by leading experts in their individual fields of study. Each scholar has compiled a career-long collection of what they consider to be their finest pieces: extracts from books, journals, articles, major theoretical and practical contributions, and salient research findings.

For the first time ever the work of each contributor is presented in a single volume so readers can follow the themes and progress of their work and identify the contributions made to, and the development of, the fields themselves.

Each book in the series features a specially written introduction by the contributor giving an overview of their career, contextualizing their selection within the development of the field, and showing how their thinking developed over time.

Thinking Developmentally from Constructivism to Neuroconstructivism
Selected Works of Annette Karmiloff-Smith
Annette Karmiloff-Smith

Acquired Language Disorders in Adulthood and Childhood
Selected Works of Elaine Funnell
Edited by Nicola Pitchford, Andrew W Ellis

Exploring Working Memory
Selected works of Alan Baddeley
Alan Baddeley

Cognitive Development and the Ageing Process
Selected works of Patrick Rabbitt
Patrick Rabbitt

For more information about this series, please visit: https://www.routledge.com

Cognitive Development and the Ageing Process

Selected works of Patrick Rabbitt

Patrick Rabbitt

Routledge
Taylor & Francis Group
LONDON AND NEW YORK

First published 2019
by Routledge
4 Park Square, Milton Park, Abingdon, Oxon OX14 4RN

and by Routledge
605 Third Avenue, New York, NY 10017

First issued in paperback 2022

Routledge is an imprint of the Taylor & Francis Group, an informa business

Publisher's Note
The publisher has gone to great lengths to ensure the quality of this reprint but points out that some imperfections in the original copies may be apparent.

British Library Cataloguing-in-Publication Data
A catalogue record for this book is available from the British Library

Library of Congress Cataloging-in-Publication Data
Names: Rabbitt, Patrick, author.
Title: Cognitive development and the ageing process : selected works of Patrick Rabbitt / Patrick Rabbitt.
Other titles: Selections
Description: First Edition. | New York, NY : Routledge, 2019. | Series: World library of psychologists | Includes bibliographical references and index.
Identifiers: LCCN 2018061198 (print) | LCCN 2019022058 (ebook) | ISBN 9781315621142 (Ebook) | ISBN 9781848723702 (hardback : alk. paper)
Subjects: LCSH: Cognition—Age factors. | Ability, Influence of age on. | Developmental psychology.
Classification: LCC BF724.55.C63 (ebook) |
LCC BF724.55.C63 R333 2019 (print) | DDC 155.67/13—dc23
LC record available at https://lccn.loc.gov/2018061198

ISBN 13: 978-1-03-247550-9 (pbk)
ISBN 13: 978-1-84872-370-2 (hbk)
ISBN 13: 978-1-315-62114-2 (ebk)

DOI: 10.4324/9781315621142

Typeset in Bembo
by codeMantra

For Adrian, Helen and Jenny, and in memory of Joy, a poor explanation of what I was up to when I was not with them.

Contents

Preface

It is uneasy to realise that I have been writing journal articles for 60 years and queasy to find myself re-printing 16 of them with annotations. Any that my colleagues have found useful have served their purpose and those that they did not have earned obscurity. This preface is an attempt to spin an act of deluded vanity as an opportunity to express gratitude. First to those who introduced me to a job in which I have been as happy as it was possible to be for the last 60 years: Donald Broadbent, who supervised my first attempts at research and then R. (do not ask) Conrad, who ably taught me to publish it; Christopher Poulton, the first senior scientist to take time to tell me that he thought that what I was trying to do was useful; Alan Welford, whose warmth and humanity made his encouragement believable and whose great learning made it reliable and useful; Jim Birren, an equal source of great kindness, practical help and scientific insight, who introduced me to an excitingly wider, and friendlier, view of Psychology than I had previously known; Paul Bertelson, who helped me to laugh at my work and my colleagues and to enjoy some of both. I have been extraordinarily fortunate with mentors.

Equally with collaborators: Subhash Vyas, an excellent research assistant and friend; Geoff Cumming, greatly gifted with intelligence, patience and practical and mathematical skills; Elizabeth Maylor, whose remarkable intelligence, integrity, cheerfulness and refusal to be patient with my failings enhanced my life; Ian Stuart-Hamilton, who taught me far more than he realized or than I ever admitted; Vicky Abson, who first recruited the Newcastle longitudinal panel and kept it, and me going; Nuala Bent, Lynn McInnes, Pip Brown and Maureen Jones, who really ran the whole show for almost 20 years while also (Nuala and Lynn) making their own studies and independent intellectual contributions; Brian Stollery, who did his best to educate me. Also too many research students who taught me before and after they became distinguished professors. None are forgotten, I was lucky in all and am very grateful to them, but must especially boast of the achievements of John Duncan, Stephen Monsell, Tim Perfect (now Hollins) and Louise Phillips, who all tactfully put up with my failings and far transcended my limited interests. My greatest debt is to Mary Lunn, a gifted statistician whose analyses taught me to see questions and answers in 20 years of accumulated longitudinal data that I could never have recognised without her patient collaboration.

This annotated collection was suggested to me as a retirement project by Russell George, Commissioning Editor at Routledge. For six years he prodded me to begin with all of the massive patience with procrastination that his profession requires. I began to write a year ago and am now grateful that I did so. The task of deliberately re-living fragments of a very long past became much more interesting than I thought it could be, and the moment I realised that I had actually finished was exquisite. That this arrived is an achievement for Charlotte (Lottie) Mapp, who tolerated tedious and ingenious vacillations and, beyond the call of her duties, obtained all necessary permissions from publishers. The result seems as shocking a waste of verdant trees as might be *A Walker's Guide to Industrial Spoilage Along the Canals of Northern England* but Russell, Lottie and I at least have the joy of knowing that the task is over.

Works reprinted

Patrick Rabbitt (1965). An age-decrement in the ability to ignore irrelevant information. *Journal of Gerontology, 20*(2), 233–238.

Patrick M. Rabbitt (1967). Learning to ignore irrelevant information. *The American Journal of Psychology, 80*(1), 1–13.

Patrick Rabbitt, Geoffrey Cumming & Subhash Vyas (1979). Modulation of selective attention by sequential effects in visual search tasks. *Quarterly Journal of Experimental Psychology, 31*, 305–317.

Patrick Rabbitt (1978). Hand dominance, attention and the choice between responses. *Quarterly Journal of Experimental Psychology, 30*, 407–416.

P.M.A. Rabbitt & S. M. Vyas (1974). Interference between binary classification judgments and some repetition effects in a serial choice reaction time task. *Journal of Experimental Psychology, 103*(6), 1181–1190.

Patrick Rabbitt, Paul Osman, Belinda Moore & Brian Stollery (2001). There are stable individual differences in performance variability, both from moment to moment and from day to day. *The Quarterly Journal of Experimental Psychology: Section A, 54*(4), 981–1003.

Patrick Rabbitt, Geoffrey Cumming & Subhash Vyas (1978). Some errors of perceptual analysis in visual search can be detected and corrected. *The Quarterly Journal of Experimental Psychology, 30*(2), 319–332

Patrick Rabbitt & Subhash Vyas (1981). Processing a display even after you make a response to it. How perceptual errors can be corrected. *The Quarterly Journal of Experimental Psychology: Section A, 33*(3), 223–239.

Patrick Rabbitt (2002). Consciousness is slower than you think. *The Quarterly Journal of Experimental Psychology: Section A, 55*(4), 1081–1092.

Patrick Rabbitt (1993). Does it all go together when it goes? The Nineteenth Bartlett Memorial Lecture. *The Quarterly Journal of Experimental Psychology: Section A, 46*(3), 385–434.

P.M.A. Rabbitt, L. McInnes, P. Diggle, F. Holland, N. Bent, V. Abson, N. Pendleton & M. Horan (2004). The University of Manchester longitudinal study of cognition in normal healthy old age, 1983 through 2003. *Aging Neuropsychology and Cognition, 11*(2–3), 245–279.

Patrick Rabbitt, Mary Lunn & Danny Wong (2008). Death, dropout, and longitudinal measurements of cognitive change in old age. *Journal of Gerontology, Series B: Psychological Sciences, 63*(5), P271–P278.

P. M. Rabbitt, M. Scott, N. Thacker, C. Lowe, M. Horan, N. Pendleton, C. Hutchinson & A. Jackson (2006). Balance marks cognitive changes in old age because it reflects global brain atrophy and cerebro-arterial blood-flow. *Neuropsychologia*, *44*(10), 1978–1983.

Patrick Rabbitt, Said Ibrahim, Mary Lunn, Marietta Scott, Neil Thacker, Charles Hutchinson, Michael Horan, Neil Pendleton & Alan Jackson (2008). Age-associated losses of brain volume predict longitudinal cognitive declines over 8 to 20 Years. *Neuropsychology*, *22*(1), 3–9.

Patrick Rabbitt, Marietta Scott, Mary Lunn, Neil Thacker, Christine Lowe, Neil Pendleton, Mike Horan & Alan Jackson (2007). White matter lesions account for all age-related declines in speed but not in intelligence. *Neuropsychology*, *21*(3), 363–370.

Patrick Rabbitt, Oemetse Mogapi, Marietta Scott, Neil Thacker, Christine Lowe, Mike Horan, Neil Pendleton, Alan Jackson & Dan Lunn (2007). Effects of global atrophy, white matter lesions, and cerebral blood flow on age-related changes in speed, memory, intelligence, vocabulary, and frontal function. *Neuropsychology*, *21*(6), 684–695.

Commentary

Discriminating between groups of things

In 1949 Shannon and Weaver published a mathematical theory of communication showing that the information value of signals can be computed as the amount by which they reduce uncertainty as to which of several possible messages has been sent. Applied human experimental psychologists, who had worked with communications engineers on defence research projects during the Second World War, realized that this metric allowed them to quantify the effects of increasing items held in short-term memory (Miller, 1956) and the difficulty of decisions as the complexity of choices increased. Hick (1952) showed that Choice Reaction Times (CRTs) to signals increase with their information value expressed by the information transmission formula $CRT = K(\log_2 N + 1)$, where N is the number of signals and associated responses to them and K is an empirically derived constant. Hyman (1953) also showed that CRTs to individual signals vary with their different, independent probabilities and Pierce and Karlin (1957) found a similar relationship between reading speed and the number of different random words to be read. In all these cases participants made a different response to each signal they were given so that the information value of signals and of responses was the same. This questioned whether variations in signal and response information load have equal or different effects on decision times. Perhaps this seemed too dull and formal a project for most investigators to pursue but, in 1958, Donald Broadbent realized that it was a key to resolve current debates as to whether we can obtain some information from words that we see so briefly that we cannot completely identify them.

Bruner and Postman (1947) and Goldiamond (1958) had found that people need longer tachistoscopic exposures to recognize emotionally challenging words than neutral words. They might have asked whether this could be explained by differences in the frequency of the written usage of the words that they compared but preferred a more thrilling speculation that it was evidence for what they termed "Discrimination without awareness", "Subception" or "Subliminal Perception". Following Freud's claim that recall of emotionally challenging memories can be inhibited, or "blocked", from conscious awareness they suggested that conscious recognition of challenging words might similarly be delayed until they had appeared for so long that they became impossible to ignore. Neutral words were not blocked and so could be recognized at briefer exposures.

In 1958 Donald Broadbent took me on as a research student and, very generously, set me, as a research project, his excellent question whether words or symbols might be recognized as members of classes such as "disturbing" or "neutral" faster than as particular items.

Richard Gregory very kindly designed and built for me an ingenious and functionally temperamental tachistoscope. I spent five tedious months failing to find recognition thresholds for learned sets of neutral symbols. Donald suspected egregious idleness and threatened to end my support. Given this boost to motivation I thought to turn the question around and to time how long volunteers took to distinguish between arbitrary learned sets of letters when the number of sets, and of symbols in each set, were varied. That is, how CRTs to sets of symbols are affected by independent variations in signal and response information loads. The only previous study of CRTs for distinctions between classes rather than unique items had been Donders' (1868) "c" reaction experiment which had used a Go/No Go task in which volunteers responded to only one of five different possible signals and not to any of the other four. This did not address my question because Reaction Times (RTs) to the class of "No Go" responses could not be measured. I used a stopwatch to time people sorting cards printed with single letters into two, four and eight arbitrary sets of one to N symbols. When young adults discriminated between two sets of signals their CRTs were faster for stimulus sets of one than for sets of two but thereafter remained constant as set sizes increased from two to 12. In contrast, RTs in the four- and eight-set tasks increased as a multiplicative function of the number of response sets and of the number of letters in each of these sets (Rabbitt, 1959). It was hard to find volunteers for these tedious experiments so I persuaded some patient and compliant late-middle-aged persons to help, on the naively expedient assumption that though they might be slower than young adults they would show the same pattern of variations in RTs across all conditions of signal and response information loads. I was surprised that even in the two-set condition older adults' sorting times increased with the number of items in each response set and that, for them, the multiplicative effects of signal and response choices seemed to be more marked than for young adults. Contradicting my assumption that old and young would differ only in terms of their average CRTs, this seemed new evidence that ageing brings about not only quantitative but qualitative changes in information processing. This conclusion turned out to be sadly misleading but began the perplexity about cognitive changes in old age that has consumed the rest of my working life.

Donald seemed mollified by these results but I puzzled how to maintain an uneasy truce. Possibly the most common everyday situation in which we must distinguish between classes of more than one item is when we visually search a crowd for members of a class of "targets", such as friends, scattered among an indeterminately large "background" class of strangers. This is an instance of a two-set choice task in which vocabularies of different target and background items vary independently. When I tried to check this, I found that, consistently with my CRT experiment (Rabbitt, 1959), volunteers' scanning times increased as a multiplicative function of the number of different targets for which they searched and the number of different symbols in the target sets and in the background sets (Rabbitt, 1962; 1964; 1965). Shepherd (1964) also reported similar findings. A new discovery was that while young adults could process several spatially adjacent letters simultaneously, older adults could do this only for smaller clusters (Rabbitt, 1965). Also, consistent with the Rabbitt (1959) results, increasing the number of letters in the vocabulary of background letters slowed the old more than the young. I reported to Donald, who remarked that I was "getting on like a house on fire". This seemed uncomfortably ambiguous because our relationship was uneasy and the idiom was unfamiliar to an Anglo-Indian, but, reassuringly, he continued my apprenticeship.

While carrying on visual search people must distinguish all target items from each other and from all background items but, logically, they need not distinguish background items from each other. Rabbitt's (1962; 1965) and Shepherd's (1964) results confirmed that they do not do this. Although the total potential vocabulary of relevant plus irrelevant letters remained the same in all conditions (i.e. 26), young adults' search times increased with the number of different target letters more sharply than with the number of different background letters. If people scanned displays to identify each individual letter in turn their search speeds would vary with the total number of relevant plus irrelevant letters rather than, as it did, with the ratio of relevant to irrelevant letters. Target letters had to be completely identified because a different response was required to each but, in accordance with the logic of task demands, background letters were not distinguished from each other. Consistent with Rabbitt's (1959) findings, in a CRT categorization task older volunteers were slowed more than young adults by increases in the sizes of the sets of letters for which they searched. The paper reproduced below discusses these results.

References

Bruner, J. S., & Postman, L. (1947). Emotional selectivity in perception and reaction. *Journal of Personality, 16*(1), 69–77.

Donders, F. C. (1868). Die schnelligkeit psychischer processe: Erster artikel. *Archiv für Anatomie, Physiologie und wissenschaftliche Medicin*, 657–681.

Goldiamond, I. (1958). Indicators of perception: I. Subliminal perception, subception, unconscious perception: An analysis in terms of psychophysical indicator methodology. *Psychological Bulletin, 55*(6), 373.

Hick, W. E. (1952). On the rate of gain of information. *Quarterly Journal of Experimental Psychology, 4*(1), 11–26.

Hyman, R. (1953). Stimulus information as a determinant of reaction time. *Journal of Experimental Psychology, 45*(3), 188.

Miller, G. A. (1956). The magical number seven, plus or minus two: Some limits on our capacity for processing information. *Psychological Review, 63*(2), 81.

Pierce, J. R., & Karlin, J. E. (1957). Reading rates and the information rate of a human channel. *Bell Labs Technical Journal, 36*(2), 497–516.

Rabbitt, P.M.A. (1959). Effects of independent variations in stimulus and response probability. *Nature, 183*(4669), 1212–1212.

Rabbitt, P.M.A (1962). Discriminations between signals and choices between responses. Unpublished Ph.D. thesis, University of Cambridge.

Rabbitt, P. (1965). An age-decrement in the ability to ignore irrelevant information. *Journal of Gerontology, 20*(2), 233–238.

Shannon, C. E., & Weaver, W. (1949). *The Mathematical Theory of Communication*. Urbana, IL: University of Illinois Press, Urbana.

Shepherd, R. D. (1964). Classification time and class complexity in inspection tasks, *Occupational Psychology, 38*(2), 87–97.

1 An age-decrement in the ability to ignore irrelevant information

P.M.A. Rabbitt[1]

Responses made by human beings typically concern circumscribed aspects of their environments, and so are based upon a small fraction of the information simultaneously made available by their sense organs. This selectivity is a condition of survival, since urgent responses may be slowed by the consideration of irrelevant information.

Irrelevant perceptual input can be ignored by selecting between modalities. We may look or listen (Broadbent & Gregory, 1961). Recent experiments have concerned selection between receptors in the same modality, particularly the ears (Broadbent, 1954; Treisman, 1961). Such selection is clearly central, and perhaps most interesting, when discriminations are made between members of a set of complex stimuli which are all of the same kind. The example most frequently investigated has been the "cocktail-party experiment" (Cherry & Taylor, 1953) in which *S*s are required to discriminate between competing monologs, usually by repeating one aloud and ignoring the other.

Analogous situations occur in visual search, as when a crowd is scanned for a friend or when a particular word is sought in a dictionary. Techniques for investigating performance in visual search allow the investigator to measure the time taken to ignore irrelevant items (Archer, 1954; Gregg, 1954; Hodge, 1959) and so to quantify results in terms of transmitted information and to make estimates of channel-capacity in this type of task.

Results on young *S*s (Rabbitt, 1964a) suggest that selection between relevant and irrelevant items on a visual display may be considered as an example of a more general type of task in which the same response is made to each member of one set of items, while different responses are made to members of other similar sets (Rabbitt, 1959; Broadbent & Gregory, 1962; Pollack 1963). *S*s searching a display for relevant items among irrelevant items may be considered to make the responses "relevant_1, relevant_2, relevant_3 . . . relevant_N" to each of N items for which search is conducted and to make the response "irrelevant" to all items in the "irrelevant" set. The response-times of young people are unaffected (Broadbent & Gregory, 1962) or only slightly affected (Rabbitt, 1959; Pollack, 1963) by increases in the number of items in each of the sets between which they discriminate. In contrast, the response-times of old people increase sharply with the number of different items in each set discriminated (Rabbitt, 1964c). If an analogy exists between stimulus categorization tasks and visual search tasks it should follow that the difficulty of discriminating between relevant and irrelevant information increases with age. The experiment described below was made to examine this prediction.

Materials and methods

Materials

Eight packs of 48 visiting card blanks measuring 2¼" × 3½" were made up, 4 for each of 2 experimental conditions.

Condition 1

Half the cards in each pack were stencilled with the letter A and half with the letter B. These letters were capitals, 5 mm. high, stencilled in india ink. The A or B on each card might be stencilled in any one of nine possible locations (Figure 1.1, iv.) Each pack was made up so that the relevant letter (A or B) appeared, as far as possible, equally often in each of these nine locations. *S*s were required to sort these packs into 2 piles, by separating cards marked with A from cards marked with B. The four packs provided displays with four conditions of irrelevant information:

Pack 1: Only the relevant letter A or B appeared on each card. (Figure 1.1, i).

Pack 2: Besides the relevant letter A or B, one other letter of the alphabet appeared on each card. These (irrelevant) letters were stencilled in the same size, ink, and type face as the relevant letters. All letters of the alphabet from C—Z were used in turn as irrelevant letters. An irrelevant letter might appear in any of the nine possible locations on the face of a card, and all locations were used in rotation, so that the relative positions of the relevant and irrelevant letters on the face of each card were effectively randomized (Figure 1.1, ii).

Pack 3: Besides the relevant letter A or B, four irrelevant letters appeared on each card. All letters of the alphabet from C—Z were used in turn as irrelevant letters. All four irrelevant letters on each card were always different. Irrelevant letters were located at random among the nine possible locations on the face of each card (Figure 1.1, iii).

Pack 4: Besides the relevant letter A or B, eight irrelevant letters appeared on each card. The constraints on selection and location were as described for Packs 2 and 3 (Figure 1.1, iv).

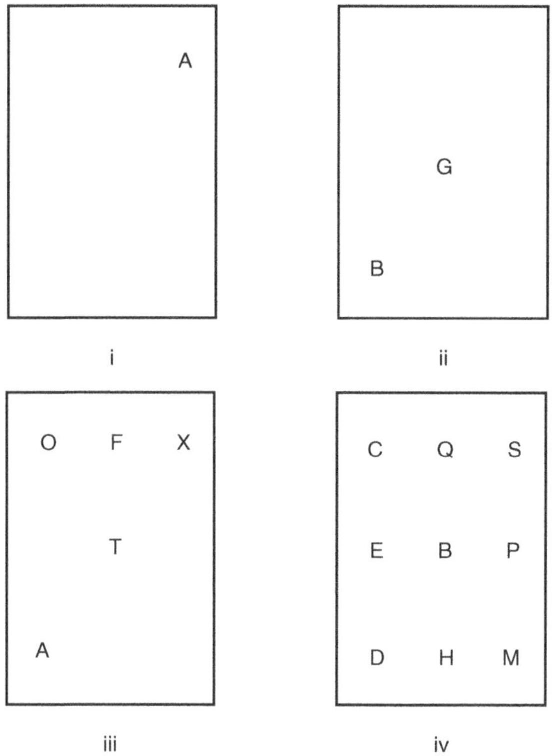

Figure 1.1 Displays used to vary number of irrelevant symbols in Conditions 1 and 2.

Condition 2

Four packs of 48 cards were made up, in which equal numbers of cards in each pack were stencilled with one of the eight relevant letters A, B, C, D, E, F, G, or H. The four conditions of irrelevancy described in Condition 1 were duplicated. Cards in Pack 1 each bore one of these eight relevant letters, but no other symbol; Cards in Pack 2 each bore one relevant and one irrelevant letter; Cards in Pack 3 each bore one relevant and four irrelevant letters, and cards in Pack 4 each bore one relevant and eight irrelevant letters. Irrelevant letters were drawn from the vocabulary of letters I—Z, and were stencilled in the same size, ink, and type face as the relevant letters. Constraints on their selection and location were precisely as described in Condition 1, and the displays were again as illustrated in Figure 1.1, i—iv.

It will be noted that the total *vocabulary* of relevant and irrelevant letters employed was the same in each condition: that is, the 26 letters of the alphabet A—Z.

Subjects

Two groups of *Ss* were tested; Group 1 consisted of 11 young people, 3 men and 8 women aged from 17–24 years (mean age 19.0); 5 were women students at a teacher's training college, 3 were sales personnel at a Cambridge department store, and 3 were undergraduates at the University of Cambridge, England. All volunteered to serve without payment. Group 2 consisted of 11 old *Ss* aged from 65—74 years (mean age 67.4 years); 2 were men and nine were women. (These *Ss* were tested at the Section on Aging, N.I.M.H., N.I.H., Besthesda, Md., to which the writer's thanks are due.) All were members of a retired civil servants' club in Washington, D.C., U.S.A., and had held very senior positions during their working lives. Most members of this group were university graduates. Although test scores were not available, these *Ss* were at least the intellectual equals of the young group on any socio-economic criterion.

Procedure

Half the *Ss* in each group were first tested on Condition 1 and then, on another day, were tested on Condition 2. The remaining *Ss* reversed the order of practice. *Ss* were instructed to deal the cards as fast and accurately as possible into the number of piles appropriate to their condition. Packs in each condition were presented in random order until each had been sorted ten times. *Ss* held the packs face-downwards in their non-dominant hands. Cards were turned and dealt with their dominant hands. This was done to ensure that *Ss* could not overlap the act of dealing each card with an examination of its successor. Over-all sorting times for each pack were recorded by *E* with a stopwatch. Each pack was thoroughly shuffled by *E* before each sorting to randomize the order in which the relevant symbols were encountered.

Results

Errors

Ss in the old group committed errors on 0.012% of their responses when sorting packs in Condition 1 and on 0.014% of their responses in Condition 2. Young *Ss* committed errors on 0.15% of their responses in Condition 1 and on 0.17% of their responses in Condition 2. Differences between age-groups and Conditions were not significant.

Sorting times

Means and standard deviations of sorting times recorded for each group are given in Table 1.1.

An analysis of variance was carried out on the combined data for the two groups. The details of this analysis are set out in Table 1.2.

Table 1.1 Mean Times (in Seconds) to Sort Packs of 48 Cards into 2 Piles (Condition 1) or 8 Piles (Condition 2) Under Four Conditions of Irrelevant Information.

	N	*Pack 1 (0 Irrelevant)*		*Pack 2 (1 Irrelevant)*		*Pack 3 (4 Irrelevant)*		*Pack 4 (8 Irrelevant)*	
Condition 1 (2 Relevant)		Mn (Sec.)	σ (Sec.)	Mn (Sec.)	σ (Sec.)	Mn (Sec.)	σ (Sec.)	Mn (Sec.)	σ (Sec.)
Young *Ss*	11	18.2	3.01	26.4	4.48	30.6	4.37	31.2	4.12
Old *Ss*	11	30.4	9.33	33.0	9.53	48.0	10.57	55.6	14.17
Condition 2 (8 Relevant)									
Young *Ss*	11	32.3	2.78	38.0	5.03	41.8	5.24	49.4	4.98
Old *Ss*	11	44.6	8.83	55.4	15.32	60.4	16.1	64.4	19.4

The main point of interest is whether the sorting-times of the young and old *Ss* were differently affected by an increase in the number of symbols for which they had to search (Conditions) or by variations in the number of irrelevant symbols on the display (Packs). Table 1.2 shows that the interaction term for Conditions x Age was not significant ($P > 0.25$). It seems that as the number of relevant symbols was increased from two to eight the increase in sorting time was much the same for old and young people. However, the interaction term for Packs x Age was significant ($P < 0.01$), which indicates that the sorting times of the old *Ss* increased more sharply than those of the young with the number of irrelevant letters on a display (Table 1.1). The significant Packs x Conditions interaction ($P < 0.001$) confirms that increases in the number of irrelevant letters on display affect sorting time more in Condition 2 than in Condition 1. It is particularly interesting that the third order interaction term for Packs x Conditions x Age was also significant ($P < 0.01$), since this indicates (Table 1.1) that the interaction between Packs and Conditions was more marked for the young group than for the old.

The remaining terms of the analysis listed in Table 1.2 simply confirm that *Ss* take longer to sort cards into eight piles than into two piles (Conditions $P < 0.001$), that sorting is slowed by the addition of irrelevant symbols to displays (Packs, $P < 0.001$) and that the old *Ss* sort cards more slowly than the young (Age, $P < 0.001$).

Discussion

The main finding of this experiment is that the speed with which *Ss* ignore irrelevant symbols on a visual display varies with the number of relevant items for which they are set to search. This result has been discussed in other contexts (Rabbitt, 1962, 1964a). Discussion of the present data turns on the interpretation of the age differences observed in the efficiency with which irrelevant symbols can be ignored.

It is known that young people can simultaneously process several symbols or words when scanning a visual display (Mackworth & Mackworth, 1958)

Table 1.2 Analysis of Variance on Mean Sorting-Times Obtained for Old and Young Groups of Subjects in Both Experimental Conditions.

Source of Variation	*Degree of Freedom*	*Sum of Squares*	*Mean Square*	*Variance Ratio*
Packs	3	8,860.10	2,953.37	92.37**
Conditions	1	8,747.64	8,747.64	93.24**
Age	1	10,571.00	10,571.00	17.99**
S/age	20	11,747.99	587.40	
Packs/conditions	3	156.59	52.20	6.61**
Packs/age	3	514.41	171.47	5.36*
Conditions/age	1	4.98	4.98	0.63
Packs/conditions/age	3	569.75	189.92	24.04**
Packs/*Ss*/age	60	1,918.02	31.97	
Conditions/*Ss*/age	20	1,876.40	93.82	
Packs/conditions/*Ss*/age	60	473.85	7.90	

*$P < 0.01$.
**$P < 0.001$.

or when reading (Morton, 1964). It has been further suggested that the size of the perceptual sample may vary with the amount of information which a *S* is required to process (Rabbitt, 1962; 1964a; Morton, 1964). It is possible that when young *Ss* search for two relevant letters they ignore irrelevant symbols more quickly because they process them in larger groups than when they search for eight relevant letters. The significant interaction-terms obtained for Age vs. Packs and for Age vs. Packs vs. Conditions could therefore be explained on the assumption that old *Ss* cannot sample letters on a display in large groups in either condition. It is not a new finding that *Ss* process items on a display in groups. The interest of the present data lies in the suggestion that the size of such groups varies with the number of items for which search is conducted, and with the age of the *S*.

In the majority of the population visual acuity deteriorates considerably with advancing age (Weiss, 1959). While no *S* in the present experiment suffered from any serious visual defect, and all who needed correcting lenses wore them, it can be assumed that the old *Ss* had poorer acuity than the young. The difference might imply that old *Ss* would take longer to discriminate between relevant and irrelevant symbols on displays. However, marked increases in discrimination-time with age have been demonstrated in situations in which visual acuity does not seem to have been a limiting factor (Birren & Botwinick, 1955; Botwinick, Brinley & Robbin, 1958; Rabbitt, 1964c). Moreover, recent models to account for age-decrements in the discrimination of brightness and contrast (Gregory & Cane, 1955) suggest that differences in the performance of populations of old and young people are better explained by models which assume changes in central perceptual processes than by deterioration in the peripheral receptors.

Decrements in central perceptual processes probably also compel old people to take longer than young to discriminate between letters of the alphabet, but it is unlikely that the results of the present experiment are corollaries of the demonstrations mentioned above. (Birren & Botwinick 1955; Botwinick, Brinley & Robbin, 1958.) Discriminations between letters of the alphabet cannot be treated in the same way as discriminations to which psychophysical functions and quantification in j.n.ds are directly applicable. Letters are complex stimuli and vary along many continua of difference (they may be rounded or angular, with or without a vertical or a cross-bar, etc.) *Ss* discriminating between letters may use any of these numerous points of difference as cues. Fitts, Weinstein, Rappaport, Anderson, and Leonard (1956) and Attneave (1954) have shown that *Ss* discriminating between complex stimuli improve their performance as they learn to use some optimal set of cues and to disregard others as misleading or redundant. This demonstration of an increase with age in the time required to discriminate between complex stimuli may not only reflect changes in discrimination processes (Gregory & Cane, 1955; Birren and Botwinick, 1955), but may also represent a failure to learn or to employ optimal, non-redundant cue systems (Rabbitt, 1964b).

The suggestion that old people probably sample fewer letters together, as a group, than do young people has no parallel in experiments in which *Ss* are required to discriminate between pairs of simultaneously presented stimuli. Young people show a similar contraction in perceptual span when they search for eight rather than for two relevant letters. Moreover, Morton (1964) has shown that the perceptual span contracts with increases in the information load of material which *Ss* are given to read. It is plausible to regard such effects as caused by the necessity to employ a wide range of cues to discriminate between complex stimuli (whether words or letters) as stimulus uncertainty increases. In such tasks "Information-load" is properly calculated from the vocabulary of *cues* between which *Ss* are required to select rather than from the vocabulary of complex symbols to be discriminated from each other. The perceptual sample may thus represent a constant limit to the number of cues which can be simultaneously considered. When it is necessary to use a wide range of cues to discriminate between letters, the number of letters which can be simultaneously processed may be correspondingly reduced. It would be consistent with this hypothesis that old *Ss* might seem to take smaller perceptual samples than young people because they base their discrimination between letters on a wider and more redundant range of cues than the young.

Finally, discriminations made in the present experiment represent a special case in that *Ss* do not identify every relevant or irrelevant symbol in the display as a particular letter of the alphabet. If they did, the time taken to discriminate between letters could vary only as a function of the total vocabulary of relevant + irrelevant letters. This was kept constant at 26 items, the English alphabet, in both conditions. Differences in the time taken to discriminate between relevant and irrelevant letters vary with the ratio of relevant to irrelevant items within this common vocabulary (i.e., 2: 24 and 8: 18).

Relevant letters must be discriminated from each other and from irrelevant letters. Irrelevant letters need not be discriminated from each other.

The results suggest that indeed they are not, but are ignored as members of an undifferentiated subset of stimuli. This task may therefore be compared to other situations in which *S*s have been required to make the same response to all members of one group of stimuli and to make other differentiating responses to members of other similar groups; (Rabbitt, 1959; 1962; Broadbent & Gregory, 1962; Pollack, 1963). In a task of this type the response times of old *S*s were found to be more affected than those of the young by increases in the number of stimuli in each group to which they made a response (Rabbitt, 1964c). The present data are thus also consistent with this earlier finding that old people are less efficient than the young at separating a vocabulary of stimuli into sub-classes, when a different response is appropriate to each sub-class.

These results illustrate a series of interrelated perceptual changes which accompany old age. The most important question, that of the relative contributions of such changes to the effect described, awaits further work. A useful practical outcome of such work will be improvements in the design of visual displays to increase the safety and convenience of an aging population. Meanwhile, the present results may have some value both in drawing attention to the problem and in discouraging any simple model for its resolution.

Summary

Groups of old and young *S*s were timed at a card-sorting task in which they searched either for two or for eight letters of the alphabet among varying numbers of irrelevant letters. Old *S*s took longer than young to discriminate between relevant and irrelevant letters in both conditions. Results suggest that young people process several letters simultaneously as a group when searching for only two items (Condition 1), but sample letters in smaller groups when searching for eight items. The performance of old *S*s suggests that they sample letters in smaller groups than do young people. If the size of the perceptual sample-space diminishes with increasing age, it may be assumed that old people are at a disadvantage in a wide range of perceptual skills, for example, probably in reading. The possible contributions to this effect made by three different types of decrement in perceptual function are discussed.

Acknowledgements

The writer owes thanks to Mr. D. E. Broadbent and to Dr. R. Conrad, who respectively supervised the work, and criticized the manuscript.

Note

1 Medical Research Council Applied Psychology Research Unit, Cambridge, England.

References

Archer, E. J.: Identification, of visual patterns as a function of information-load. *J. exp. Psychol., 48:* 313–318, 1954.

Attneave, F.: Some informational aspects of visual perception. *Psychol. Rev., 61:* 183–204, 1954.

Birren, J. E., and J. Botwinick: Speed of response as a function of perceptual difficulty and age. *J. Geront., 10*: 433–436, 1955.

Botwinick, J., J. F. Brinley, and J. S. Robbin: The interaction effects of perceptual difficulty and stimulus exposure-time on age-differences in speed and accuracy of performance. *Gerontologia, 2:* 1–10, 1958.

Broadbent, D. E.: The role of auditory localisation in attention and memory-span. *J. exp. Psychol., 47:* 191–196, 1954.

Broadbent, D. E., and M. L. Gregory: On the recall of stimuli presented alternately to two sense-organs. *Quart. J. Psychol., 13:* 103–109, 1961.

Broadbent, D. E., and M. L. Gregory: Human responses to classes of stimuli. *Nature, Lond., 193:* 1313, 1962.

Cherry, E. C., and W. K. Taylor: Some further experiments upon the recognition of speech with one and with two ears. *J. acoust. Soc. Amer., 26:* 554–559, 1953.

Fitts, P. M., M. Weinstein, M. Rappaport, N. Anderson, and J. A. Leonard: *Stimulus correlates of pattern recognition: A probability approach.* Off. Naval Res., Washington, 1956, Nav. R.-495 (02), 151 pp.

Gregg, L. W.: The effect of stimulus complexity on discriminative responses. *J. exp. Psychol., 48*: 289–294, 1954.

Gregory, R. L., V. Cane: A statistical information theory of visual thresholds. *Nature, Lond., 176:* 1272, 1955.

Hodge, M. H.: The influence of irrelevant information upon complex visual discrimination. *J. exp. Psychol., 57:* 1–5, 1959.

Mackworth, N. H., and J. F. Mackworth: Eye-fixation recorded on changing visual scenes by the television eye-marker. *J. opt. Soc. Amer., 48*: 439–445, 1958.

Morton, J.: The effect of context upon speed of reading, eye-movements, and eye-voice span. *Quart. J. exp. Psychol., Camhr., 16:* 340–354, 1964.

Pollack, I.: Speed of classification of words into super-ordinate categories. *J. verb. Learn. & verb. Behav., 2:* 159–165, 1963.

Rabbitt, P. M. A.: Effects of independent variations in stimulus and response probability. *Nature, Lond., 183:* 1212, 1959.

Rabbitt, P. M. A.: Perceptual discrimination and the choice of responses. Univ. of Cambridge, Cambridge, Eng., 1962, Unpubl. Ph.D. Thesis. 260 pp.

Rabbitt, P. M. A.: Ignoring irrelevant information. *Brit. J. Psychol., 55:* 403–414, 1964. (a)

Rabbitt, P. M. A.: Grouping of stimuli in pattern recognition as a function of age. *Quart. J. exp. Psychol., Cambr. 76:* 172–176, 1964.(b)

Rabbitt, P. M. A.: Age and time for choice between stimuli and between responses. *J. Geront., 19:* 307–312, 1964.(c)

Triesman, A.: *Attention and speech.* Univ. of Oxford, Oxford, 1961, Ph.D. Thesis, 207 pp.

Weiss, A. D.: Sensory functions. *In:* J. E. Birren (Editor), *Handbook of Aging and the Individual.* Univ. Chicago Press, Chicago, 1959, pp. 503–536.

Finding what you are looking for

In 1965 it seemed to me that when people carry out categorization tasks (Rabbitt, 1959) or make logically equivalent decisions between target and background items in visual search (Rabbitt, 1962; 1965; Shepherd, 1964), increases in signal information load affect decision times much less than do increases in response information load. I also thought that the effects of signal information load were modified by two sources of individual differences between people: their ages and how much they had been practised. Consequently I still interpreted my results on symbol categorization (Rabbitt, 1959) as evidence that interactions between signal and response information loads are significantly greater for old than for young adults. In spite of some growing evidence to the contrary I continued to believe that age-slowing reflects qualitative rather than simply quantitative changes in information processing efficiency. On the second issue, practice, Neisser (1963) had found that if young adults are trained long enough they learn to scan as fast for 12 as for two different target letters. Rabbitt (1962) had also found that if target and background items belong to different, over-learned classes of symbols, such as letters and digits, even unpractised young adults are not slowed by increases in the numbers of different symbols for which they search. Brand (1971) later convincingly replicated and extended this unpublished result.

From 1955 until at least 1980 (e.g. Birren, Woods & Williams, 1980), a core belief among cognitive gerontologists was that slowing of performance in all cognitive tasks is the most sensitive and easily measured behavioural index of differences in mental abilities between young and older people. Birren and Botwinick (1955a) found that the absolute difference in the times that younger and older people need to make line-length discriminations becomes greater as discriminations become harder. Simple explanations for age-related slowing were tested and dismissed. Birren and Botwinick (1955b) found no differences in speed of nerve conduction as behaviourally estimated by Helmoltz's technique of comparing Reaction Times (RTs) to touches on the foot and jaw. Direct electrophysiological measurements later confirmed that age does slow neural transmission rates, but so very slightly that this cannot account for the much greater observed increases in behaviourally measured Choice RTs (CRTs) (e.g. Dorfman & Bosley, 1979). Birren's results showed that age-slowing is not caused by degenerative changes in muscles and joints and so must reflect slowing of the central nervous system because it was too marked to be explained in terms of nerve-conduction rates.

Hick (1952) had found that the CRTs of his single (then) young(ish) volunteer, Richard Gregory, increased with the number of signal and response alternatives and were fitted by a formula for information transmission ($CRT = K \times \log_2 N - 1$) where N is the number of different signals and responses and K is a constant. Welford (1959) used Hick's apparatus to repeat his experiment on elderly volunteers and found that the same formula (i.e. $CRT = K \times \log_2 N - 1$) described increases in their average CRTs. Thus the finding that increases in the number of signal and response alternatives slow older adults proportionally more than younger adults is completely explained by an increase in the single term, K. In other words, across all conditions of information load, CRTs of older adults can be estimated by multiplying CRTs of young adults by the same number. Welford's result was initially overlooked as merely another confirmation of the everyday cliché, "old and slow" and taken as further evidence that age-related slowing must be due to changes in the functional efficiency of the brain rather than the peripheral nervous system.

Joe Brinley (1965) and Botwinick, Robbin and Brinley (1960) first formally tested and confirmed that as the number of signal and response alternatives increases, the mean CRTs of groups of older adults can be accurately estimated by multiplying the mean CRTs for younger adults by an empirically derived constant. Nevertheless, heedless of this mounting evidence, I continued to believe that greater age-related slowing as signal entropy increased must reflect qualitative rather than merely quantitative changes in the efficiency with which signals are recognized and responses to them are chosen and made. At a meeting in Carmel, California, some 20 years after Brinley's widely publicized discovery, Tim Salthouse trenchantly revealed my error by reporting a re-analysis of my published results (Rabbitt, 1959; 1965) showing that, across all signal set sizes as well as response set sizes, older adults' CRTs can be accurately estimated by multiplying young adults' CRTs by the same constant. In spite of wide acceptance and discussion of John Cerella's (1985) meta-analysis of published results from 114 different experiments showing that age-related increases in average decision times remain proportionally identical across a wide range of task demands and levels of difficulty, I remained querulous and obstinately unenlightened until about 1990. Verhaegen's (2015) masterly meta-analysis now shows that this is true of all published results comparing mean decision times of old and young adults in nearly all tasks for which published data are available. Verhaegen's meta-analyses specifically include data from all published age comparisons on visual search and even on clinical tests on which slowing is known to be a sensitive diagnostic index of frontal brain damage (see also Verhaegen & de Meersmann,1998; Shilling, Chetwynd & Rabbitt, 2002). Note that these analyses cannot challenge the existence of phenomena such as negative priming, distractibility, or the possibility that age changes are related to earlier and more severe changes in fronto-parietal brain areas. They do show that comparisons of decision times of old and young adults on neuro-clinical diagnostic indices are not evidence for absolute rather than proportional age-slowing in tasks in which frontal brain areas are involved.

This striking proportional constancy of decision times across all behavioural tasks is not just a methodological caveat against some interpretations of age-related slowing of visual discriminations. Across a range of tasks of different kinds and levels of difficulty the slower mean decision times for groups of individuals with lower intelligence test scores can be accurately estimated by multiplying the faster means for individuals with higher intelligence test scores by a simple constant (Rabbitt, 1996). Linear scaling also accurately predicts the extent of CRT slowing due to alcohol ingestion, and of speeding after prolonged practice. Like age, alcohol and practice linearly transform the entire distributions, as well as the means, of CRTs (Maylor et al., 1992). In serial self-paced CRT tasks, distributions of the relatively fast CRTs obtained when identical signals and responses are immediately repeated (the "repetition effect", Bertelson,1961) also turn out to be linearly scaled down versions of the slower distributions of decision times when successive signals and responses are different (Rabbitt, 1992). This remarkable generality of proportional scaling effects, both between and within individuals and between task demands, suggests that the cognitive effects of individual differences, subject states and differences between task conditions are mainly modulated by global rather than local changes in the brain.

A different reason why Rabbitt's (1959; 1965) results only partially reflect the independent effects of variations in signal and response information load is that they were collected only early in practice. Neisser (1963) found that when young adults are sufficiently practiced, they learn to search as rapidly for 12 as for two different targets. Following Green and Anderson (1956) Rabbitt (1962) had also found that when target symbols were distinguished from background symbols by colour, increasing the numbers of different background items makes no difference to search speed and that this is also what happens if target and background symbols are from different, over-learned sets, such as letters and digits, with which people have become familiar over a lifetime. Brand (1971) convincingly replicated and extended these results. Apart from their familiarity as different learned classes of symbols, a plausible reason why changes in the numbers of different letters and digits used in a search task have little or no effect on scanning times is that their distinctive micro-features identify them as members of different sets of symbols. The capital letters used in Rabbitt's (1965) and Brand's (1971) experiments are derived from a Roman alphabet designed to be incised with a stylus on a tablet or with a chisel on stone. The critical features to discriminate between letters are the angles and orientations of straight lines. Digits are derived from Arabic numerals designed to be drawn with brush strokes and the critical points of difference between them are the positions and placements of curved lines, making it much easier to discriminate between, rather than within these classes of over-familiar symbols. It is misleading to quantify the difficulty of discriminations between sets of symbols as a function of the sizes of the vocabularies from which they are drawn. For example, finding rounded target letters such as D or P is easy if they are embedded among background letters made up entirely of straight lines, such as H, I, X, or M and harder if they are embedded among other rounded letters like B, C, G and R. It follows that difficulties of discriminating between letters cannot be quantified in terms of the number of different *symbols* between which we choose, but rather in terms of the *least number of different critical features* we need to distinguish them – which, of course, is only rarely the same thing. It is useful to apply the information metric to estimate the relative difficulty of discriminating between larger or smaller vocabularies of complex symbols only if we can precisely specify the range of critical features that volunteers must use to make the discriminations that we ask of them.

A way to track volunteers' gradual discovery and use of the least number of effective cues that distinguish between target and background symbols is to practice them on discriminations between one set of target and background items and then measure how much they are slowed if the background items are changed so that the efficient cues that they have learned are no longer valid. This method also allows us to compare the efficiency with which older and younger adults learn and use the critical distinctions necessary to distinguish between sets of targets and background items. The next paper reproduced describes what happens.

References

Bertelson, P. (1961). Sequential redundancy and speed in a serial two-choice responding task. *Quarterly Journal of Experimental Psychology, 13*(2), 90–102.

Birren, J. E., & Botwinick, J. (1955a). Speed of response as a function of perceptual difficulty and age. *Journal of Gerontology, 10*, 433–436.

Birren, J. E., & Botwinick, J. (1955b). Age differences in finger, jaw, and foot reaction time to auditory stimuli. *Journal of Gerontology, 10*(4), 429–432.

Birren, J. E., Woods, A. M., & Williams, M. V. (1980). Behavioral slowing with age: Causes, organization, and consequences. In L. W. Poon (Ed.), *Aging in the 1980s: Psychological Issues* (pp. 293–308). Washington, DC: American Psychological Association.

Botwinick, J., Robbin, J. S., & Brinley, J. F. (1960). Age differences in card-sorting performance in relation to task difficulty, task set and practice. *Journal of Experimental Psychology, 59*, 10–18.

Brand, J. (1971). Classification without identification in visual search. *Quarterly Journal of Experimental Psychology, 23*(2), 178–186.

Brinley, J. F. (1965). Cognitive sets, speed and accuracy of performance in the elderly. In A. T. Welford & J. E. Birren (Eds), *Behavior, Aging and the Nervous System* (pp. 114–149). Springfield, IL: Thomas.

Cerella, J. (1985). Information processing rates in the elderly. *Psychological Bulletin, 98*(1), 67–83.

Dorfman, L. J., & Bosley, T. M. (1979). Age-related changes in peripheral and central nerve conduction in man. *Neurology, 29*(1), 38–38.

Green, B. F., & Anderson, L. K. (1956). Color coding in a visual search task. *Journal of Experimental Psychology, 51*(1), 19–24.

Hick, W. E. (1952). On the rate of gain of information. *Quarterly Journal of Experimental Psychology, 4*(1), 11–26.

Maylor, E. A., Rabbitt, P. M. A., James, G. H., & Kerr, S. A. (1992). Effects of alcohol, practice, and task complexity on reaction time distributions. *Quarterly Journal of Experimental Psychology Section A, 44*(1), 119–139.

Neisser, U. (1963). Decision-time without reaction-time: Experiments in visual scanning. *The American Journal of Psychology, 76*(3), 376–385.

Rabbitt, P. M. A. (1959). Effects of independent variations in stimulus and response probability. *Nature, 183*(4669), 1212.

Rabbitt, P. M. A. (1962). Discriminations between signals and choices between responses. Ph.D. thesis, University of Cambridge.

Rabbitt, P. M. A. (1965). An age-decrement in the ability to ignore irrelevant information. *Journal of Gerontology, 20*(2), 233.

Rabbitt, P. (1992). Many happy repetitions: A celebration of the "Bertelson Repetition Effect" 1961–1991. In J. Alegria, D. Holender, J. Junca de Morais, & M. Radeau (Eds). *Analytic Approaches to Human Cognition* (pp. 313–330). Oxford: North-Holland.

Rabbitt, P. (1996). Do individual differences in speed reflect "global" or "local" differences in mental abilities? *Intelligence, 22*(1), 69–88.

Shepherd, R. D. (1964). Classification time and class complexity in inspection tasks, *Occupational Psychology, 38*(2), 87–97.

Shilling, V. M., Chetwynd, A., & Rabbitt, P. M. A. (2002). Individual inconsistency across measures of inhibition: An investigation of the construct validity of inhibition in older adults. *Neuropsychologia, 40*(6), 605–619.

Verhaegen, P. (2015). *The Elements of Cognitive Ageing.* Oxford: Oxford University Press.

Verhaegen, P., & De Meersman, L. (1998). Aging and the Stroop effect: A meta-analysis. *Psychology and Aging, 13*(1), 120–126.

Welford, A. T. (1959). Psychomotor performance. In J. E. Birren (Ed.), *Handbook of Aging and the Individual* (pp. 562–613). Oxford: University of Chicago Press.

2 Learning to ignore irrelevant information

P.M.A. Rabbitt

In most tasks of choice-response, the time taken to discriminate between members of a set of stimuli varies with the size of the set, *i.e.* with information-load. Exceptions to this rule occur in visual search.

For example, in tasks in which subjects (*S*s) searched for varying numbers of letters of the alphabet on displays containing all 26 letters. Shepherd,[1] and, in a different experimental situation, Rabbitt[2] found that the time taken to discriminate between relevant and irrelevant letters increased with the number of letters for which the *S*s searched, although the total vocabulary of relevant plus irrelevant letters was always the same (*i.e.* 26). It follows that the *S*s could not have scanned displays to identify each symbol in turn as a particular letter of the alphabet, responding appropriately only when they encountered a relevant letter. If they had, discrimination-time could only have varied with the total number of relevant plus irrelevant letters, and not with the ratio of relevant to irrelevant items, as was in fact observed. The results suggest that while the *S*s had to discriminate relevant from irrelevant letters they did not discriminate irrelevant items from other irrelevant items. The usual assumptions of information-theory must therefore be modified before they can be applied to visual search.

Rabbitt suggested that visual search might be treated as a particular example of a more general range of tasks in which the *S*s make the same response to all members of one group of stimuli and make different responses to members of other groups.[3] For example, in Shepherd's experiment the *S*s cancelled all relevant letters and ignored all irrelevant letters.[4]

Unfortunately, differences in the times taken to discriminate between various sub-sets of relevant and irrelevant items may be unreliable indices of the relative amounts of information which the *S*s have to transmit. There is now some doubt as to whether any association between choice-response time and the number of S-R alternatives is observed after extended practice.[5] In the specific situation of visual search Neisser reports that the *S*s scanning columns of symbols take no longer to locate a member of a set of 10 different relevant items than to locate a single relevant item.[6] It is doubtful whether the discrepancy between Neisser's results, on the one hand, and Rabbitt's and Shepherd's findings, on the other, can be reconciled by experiments based on comparisons between response-times obtained in different situations, since all such comparisons can be criticised on the grounds that they do not represent some hypothetical limiting level of performance attained after extended practice.[7]

Letters are complex stimuli which may be discriminated from each other in terms of the presence or absence of a wide range of characteristics. Fitts *et al.* have shown that *S*s learning to discriminate between complex patterns improve their performance by identifying and using a range of critical cues and by ignoring other details as misleading or redundant.[8] The process of discriminating relevant from irrelevant letters would clearly be most economical if the *S*s used the minimal number of cues. This minimal number might be expected to vary with the ratio of relevant to irrelevant items rather than directly with the total vocabulary of items on a display. We might also expect that the number of cues which *S* must consider (and so, possibly, also his decision-time) would increase with the number of items in the relevant set.

It has been suggested that improvement in speed of visual search with practice depends partly on the learning of a cue-system which is optimal for discriminations between specific sets of relevant and irrelevant items.[9] If this is so, substitution of a new set of irrelevant items would slow search. In this case the slowing of search on transfer from one display of irrelevant symbols to another will be an index of the extent to which previous improvement with practice has been due to learning of a specific cue-system.

Emperiment I: two or eight relevant stimuli

This index is used in Experiment I to compare the relation of improvement with practice to learning of a specific, relevant-irrelevant cue-system as the number of relevant stimuli is increased from two to eight.

Material

Two packs of 48 cards measuring $2^1/_4 \times 3^1/_2$ in. were made up for each of two conditions.

Condition 1

Half the cards in each of these two packs were stencilled, in India ink, with the letter A and half with the letter B. Letters were block-capitals 6 mm. high. These were the relevant letters for which the *S*s searched, sorting the packs to separate A and B cards. The relevant letter on each card was imbedded in a 9-letter nonsense-word centered on the card. The other (irrelevant) letters making up this word were eight letters of the alphabet stencilled in the same ink, size and style as the relevant letter. All cards within each of these two packs bore the same irrelevant letters. In Pack 1 these were R, V, N, Q, Z, O, T, and J. In Pack 2 they were Z, M, S, I, U, P, W, and L. The positions of the irrelevant letters were so varied that every card bore a different nonsense-word. The position of the relevant letter was also systematically varied so that, as far as possible, A and B appeared equally often in each of the nine possible letter-positions.

Condition 2

Six cards in each pack were stencilled with one of the eight relevant letters, A, B, C, D, E, F, G, and H. *Ss* sorted these packs into two piles to separate cards marked with A, B, C, or D from cards marked with E, F, G, or H. The relevant letter on each card was embedded in a 9-letter nonsense-word as in Condition 1. The two packs featured the same sets of irrelevant letters in used Condition 1. The same precautions were taken to randomize the positions of relevant and irrelevant letters within each pack.

Procedure

Each *S* was given one of the two packs in his condition and asked to sort it into two piles on the scheme described. He might be required to sort the same pack 1, 3, 6, 9, or 12 times, depending on the group to which he was assigned. After these training trials he was given the other pack in the same condition, without comment on the exchange, and asked to sort it as fast as possible.

Five groups of 18 *Ss*, in each of the conditions, each experienced one of the 5 levels of practice described (*i.e.* 1, 3, 6, 9, or 12 practice sorts before transfer). *E* thoroughly shuffled each pack before it was sorted and timed every sort with a stop-watch. The *Ss* were urged to sort as fast and accurately as possible; improvement was praised and errors were recorded and admonished. Packs of cards were held face-down for sorting, cards being turned over one at a time for inspection to prevent preview of sequent displays. Half the *Ss* in each group of 18 were trained on one pack in the condition while the remainder reversed this order of practice. All *Ss* were tested individually.

Subjects

One hundred and eighty *Ss* were tested. Ninety were unpaid volunteer Royal Navy "ratings" aged 17–31 yr. (mean 21.7), and 90 were paid housewives aged 22–48 yr. (mean age 39.2).

The *Ss* were divided into 10 groups of 18 (5 groups per condition) with 9 'ratings' and 9 housewives in each group. The 'ratings' form an unusually homo geneous population and a random allocation resulted in groups closely matched for age and *I.Q.* The housewives were also allocated at random, with precautions to match groups as closely as possible for age.

All the *Ss* were free of gross visual defects and wore any correcting lenses prescribed for them.

Results

(1) Errors. No groups in either condition made errors on more than *0.3%* of responses. This incidence was too small to allow valid comparisons.

(2) Sorting-time. Mean sorting-times are set out in Table 2.1.

Homogeneity of populations. Comparison between groups of *Ss* brought to different levels of practice within each condition involves the assumption that the

Table 2.1 Mean sorting-times per pack on training- and transfer-trials

Groups		*Practice Trials*												*Transfer*
		1	*2*	*3*	*4*	*5*	*6*	*7*	*8*	*9*	*10*	*11*	*12*	
Searching for 2 relevent items	$\bar{X}$ sec.	91.0	81.2	77.3	76.4	71.1	73.9	73.4	72.8	70.1	68.9	67.3	68.5	80.1
	σ	18.1	20.2	17.4	18.1	15.2	14.3	13.3	18.2	12.4	14.2	12.4	12.2	14.3
	$\bar{X}$	89.0	80.4	78.6	75.6	72.7	72.8	72.2	71.1	68.4				79.1
	σ	20.5	21.4	27.6	16.9	15.9	16.7	15.6	16.2	18.2				15.4
	$\bar{X}$	78.0	78.1	78.2	74.5	71.8	71.9							80.9
	σ	19.7	16.9	15.4	13.2	15.4	13.4							14.6
	$\bar{X}$	93.0	80.8	78.7										83.2
	σ	14.9	17.2	14.9										15.2
	$\bar{X}$	86.0												83.7
	σ	14.1												14.7
Searching for 8 relevent items	$\bar{X}$	150.9	133.0	116.4	114.0	109.7	107.2	98.4	98.5	95.2	96.4	95.8	95.4	114.9
	σ	34.4	30.2	24.1	20.1	23.4	22.1	23.4	18.2	18.0	17.1	17.4	17.0	20.2
	$\bar{X}$	152.6	137.5	118.3	115.3	107.6	105.4	97.9	98.1	94.0				113.5
	σ	31.4	29.3	28.3	28.6	21.2	23.4	19.6	22.0	18.8				23.8
	$\bar{X}$	151.8	131.2	117.6	111.5	107.1	99.8							114.0
	σ	31.7	25.4	24.2	24.0	19.6	17.6							19.7
	$\bar{X}$	154.3	132.0	119.3										116.0
	σ	41.6	29.5	20.5										19.6
	$\bar{X}$	149.8												131.4
	σ	21.4												19.4

groups are appropriately matched. To test this, analyses of variance were made on scores for the first practice trial over all five groups, over the first three trials for the four groups, over the first six practice-trials for three groups, and over the first nine practice trials for two groups. None of these analyses showed any significant difference between groups. While no similar check could be made between the *S*s in Conditions 1 and 2, the large numbers involved, and the consistency within each sample, make homogeneity a reasonable assumption.

(3) Decrement on transfer to a different irrelevant set. Mean sorting times for the last practice and the transfer-trial were compared by *t*-test at each level of practice within each condition. In Condition 1 (2-relevant), sorting-times on the transfer trial were not significantly different from sorting-times for the first trial on the practice-pack ($p > 0.1$). Times for transfer-packs were significantly longer, however, than for the terminal trial when this was the 3rd ($p < 0.01$), the 6th ($p < 0.001$), the 9th ($p < 0.001$) or the 12th ($p < 0.001$) practice-trial. In Conditions 2 (8 relevant), the mean sorting time on transfer was significantly *faster* 1 practice-trial ($p < 0.01$), and there was no significant difference after 3 practice-trials ($p > 0.1$). Sorting-times for transfer-packs were significantly longer for the final trial after 6 ($p < 0.01$) after 9 ($p < 0.001$) and after 12 ($p < 0.001$) practice-trials.

Mean difference-scores (terminal practice-transfer-trial) for each group are plotted in Figure 2.1 as a function of practice in both conditions. Negative values indicate that the transfer-packs were sorted faster than the practice-packs.

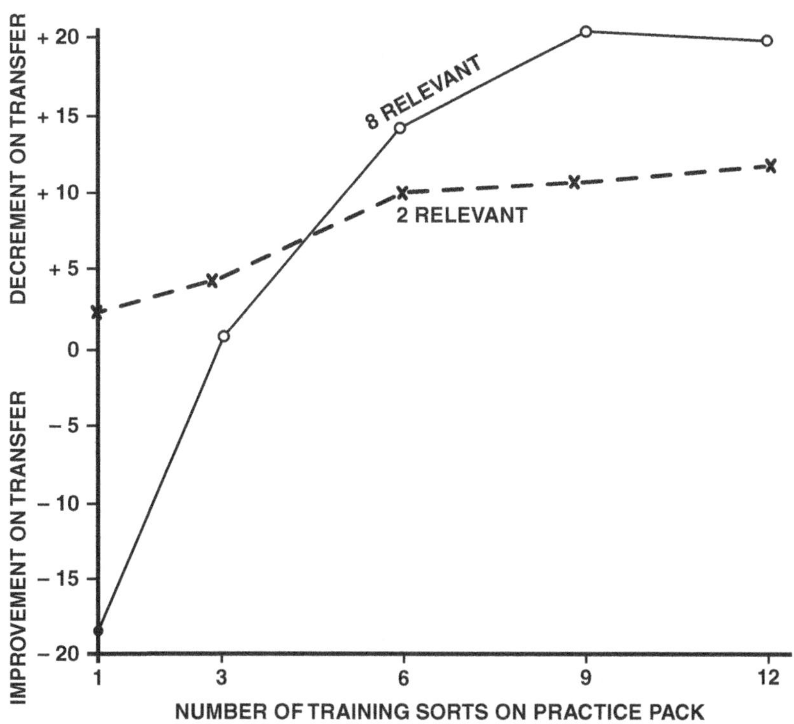

Figure 2.1 Mean difference-score, transfer-trials, last practice trial (sec.)

The S^2 statistic (studentized range statistics), was calculated for the mean difference scores over all groups.[10] In Condition 1 (2-relevant), mean decrement on transfer was significantly greater after 3 training-trials than after 1 training-trial ($p < 0.01$), and greater after 6 training-trials than after 3 training-trials ($p < 0.01$). The decrement differences between 9 and 12 practice-trials were not significant ($p > 0.1$). In Condition 2 (8-relevant) differences between 1, 3, 6, and 9 practice-trials were all significant at the ($p < 0.01$) level. The difference-scores for 9 and 12 practice-trials were not significant. Using S^2 it was also possible to compare decrement-scores between conditions at equivalent levels of practice. After one practice trial, decrement in the 2-relevant condition was significantly greater than in the 8-relevant condition ($p < 0.01$). There was no difference between conditions after three trials ($p > 0.25$), and decrement scores were significantly greater in the 8-relevant condition that in the 2-relevant condition after six ($p < 0.01$) nine ($p < 0.001$) and twelve trials ($p < 0.001$).

Discussion

Decrements in speed on transfer show that improvement with practice is partly due to specific learning of a particular set of irrelevant letters. It is reasonable to use these decrements as indices to compare the improvements due to such specific learning for different levels of practice and conditions. Although curves for this specific learning cannot be directly obtained, the curves showing decrements in transfer as a function of practice in each condition (Figure 2.1) may be considered analogs of these functions.

On this analogy, we see from Figure 2.1 that *S*s searching for only relevant symbols show rapid specific learning between one and six training trials. At this point the curve appears to reach an asymptote and there is no suggestion that decrement increases with further practice. In contrast, *S*s searching for 8 relevant items show continuing learning until the 9th training trial, and it is not until the 9th-12th training trials that there are signs that learning is completed. The decrement on transfer varies significantly, moreover, between conditions. After 1 training trial decrement is greater in the 2-relevant than in the 8-relevant task, after 3 training trials decrement is the same in both the tasks but after 6, 9 or 12 trials decrement on transfer is uniformly greater in the 8-relevant task.

The data thus fit the hypothesis that the *S*s have to learn more cues to discriminate between eight relevant and eight irrelevant symbols than to discriminate between two relevant and eight irrelevant symbols. It is consistent with this hypothesis that if the cue-system required to discriminate eight relevant letters is more elaborate it should take longer to learn. Again, because it is more elaborate, once it is learned, its loss on transfer might well imply correspondingly greater reduction in efficiency. The results of Experiment I therefore fit the general hypothesis that the difficulty of discriminations between two sets of items varies with the ratio in which items are distributed between the sets.

Letters of the alphabet are complex symbols and the range of cues required to discriminate between them may vary between wide upper and lower limits which can only be roughly fixed by the number of symbols in each set. Although Experiment I suggests that the information transmitted in discriminating between sets of symbols does, in general, vary with the number of symbols to be discriminated, nevertheless the of number necessary cues may vary with the particular physical characteristics of different sub-sets. Variations in the number of items in the sets to be discriminated may prove only roughly correlated with changes in the amount of information which the subject transmits.

Experiment II: variations in cue-system

Experiment II was made to provide a practical demonstration of this point as a basis for further discussion, and also as a further test of the sensitivity of the technique used in Experiment I.

Material

Three packs of 50 cards were made up, as described for Experiment I. Half the cards in each pack each bore the relevant letter C and the other half the relevant letter O. In all packs, these relevant letters were embedded, among sets of seven irrelevant letters forming with them an 8-letter nonsense-word centered on each card. In Pack 1, irrelevant letters contained no curved lines (A, E, F, H, I, K, and L). The same was true of Pack 2, in which the irrelevant letters were M, N, T, V, W, X, and Y. In Pack 3 the rounded relevant letters C and O were embedded among other letters contained curved lines (B, D, G, J, P, Q, and S). The same precautions described for Experiment I were taken to randomize the locations of relevant and irrelevant letters on the displays.

Procedure

Two groups of 24 *S*s were tested. Half the *S*s in each group sorted Pack 1 six times; the remainder sorted Pack 2 six times. After this initial training, all the *S*s in Group 1 were transferred to Pack 3. In Group 2, the *S*s practiced on Pack 1 were transferred to Pack 2 and vice-versa. This tested the extent to which training on discriminations between rounded and angular letters transferred when a new set of angular letters was used.

The procedure for administering and timing the packs was the same as in Experiment I.

Subjects

Twelve *S*s in each group were R.N. ratings aged from 17–24 yr. (mean age 19.8). The remaining 12 *S*s in each group were housewives aged from 32–46 yr. (mean age 38.2). Groups were matched for age as closely as possible.

Results

Mean sorting times for each group on each practice trial and on the transfer-trial are set out in Table 2.2

Table 2.2 mean sorting-times per pack on training and transfer trials

		Transfer to pack 1	*Transfer to pack 2*	*Transfer to pack 3*
Pack 1	66.2 (σ = 4.9)		67.1 (σ = 5.4)	79.4 (σ = 8.2)
Pack 2	65.1 (σ = 4.2)	66.4 (σ = 5.0)		78.4 (σ = 9.0)

Sorting times on the six practice trials are closely similar for each group, analysis of variance shows no significant difference between them. The *S*s in Group 1 show marked decrement on transfer from discriminations between rounded and angular letters to discriminations between rounded letters and other rounded letters ($p < 0.001$). In contrast, the *S*s in Group 2 show no significant decrement on transfer to a new set of irrelevant letters ($p > 0.1$). We must conclude that while the same cue system is used to discriminate round from angular letters in Packs 1 and 2, different cue-systems are required to discriminate relevant from irrelevant letters in Packs 1 and 2 on the one hand and in Pack 3 on the other.

Discussion

As far as we can deduce from Experiment II, the same cue-system was used to discriminate the letters C and O from either of the two sets of angular irrelevant letters, *i.e.* the same cue-system was appropriate for both sub-sets of 7 out of 14 angular letters. Thus, under these circumstances, variation in the vocabulary of irrelevant letters is seen to be a less critical determinant of choice-time than variation in the physical characteristics of the particular relevant and irrelevant items.

The results of Experiments I and II throw some light on discrepancies in the results of earlier investigations on visual search; Shepherd and Rabbitt found that the time taken to discriminate relevant from irrelevant stimuli on a display increased with the number of relevant stimuli for which their *S*s searched.[11] In contrast, Neisser reports that the *S*s scanning columns of symbols take no longer to locate any one of a set of 10 different items than to locate a single relevant item.[12]

The task of discriminating all members of a set of relevant items from all members of a set of irrelevant items is, logically, a particular example of the general situation in which the *S*s must make one response to all members of one set of stimuli and another response to all members of another similar set. It is not therefore surprising that discrepancies in results with visual search should be paralleled in the literature on stimulus-categorization tasks. Nickerson and Feehrer found that the time taken to identify stimuli as members of one of two categories increased as a linear function of the number of stimuli in each category.[13] In another task of this kind, however, Pollack reports that while choice time rises sharply as the number of stimuli in each of 2 categories is increased from 1 to 2, further increases in stimulus-entropy have markedly less effect.[14] Rabbitt also found that *S*s choosing between

2 classes of stimuli showed a sharp increase in response-time as the number of stimuli in each class increased from 1 to 2 items, but that further increases from 2 to 12 items resulted in no detectable change in response-time.[15] Finally, in contrast to all these other results, Broadbent and Gregory found no change in response-time as the number of stimuli in each of 4 response-classes was increased from 1 to 8 items.[16]

Comparisons between these four sets of data are confounded by important differences in the tasks from which they were obtained. Nevertheless, it is probable that an important variable was the amount of practice which the *S*s received. For example Nickerson and Feehrer gave their *S*s less practice than did any other investigator quoted,[17] while Broadbent and Gregory investigated a task in which the *S*s were aided by their life-experience in reading.[18] Broadbent and Gregory's *S*s separated cards marked with the name of one British town from cards marked with the names of others. Stimulus-entropy was varied within each class by printing these town names in different combinations of upper and lower case letters. Thus the speed with which *S* identified, say, the combination bOITOn and BoltOn as members of the same class related to a lifetime's experience at reading meaningful combinations of letters. A training study by Rabbitt directly makes the point that some interactions between stimulus-entropy and response-time may disappear with extended practice.[19]

The analogy between search and categorization suggests that discrepancies between Neisser's, Shepherd's and Rabbitt's results may also be due to differences in practice.[20] This explanation must be treated with caution, because Shepherd's and Rabbitt's *S*s were highly trained in their tasks. There are, moreover, wide differences in the tasks investigated by the three authors, and at least two general reasons why we cannot be sure that Neisser's results described a limiting level of performance which can be attained in *all* tasks of visual search.

(1) Experiment I shows that improvement with practice requires the learning of a system of cues which is optimal for discriminations between a particular set of relevant and a particular set of irrelevant symbols. It is also apparent that though the *S*s may, with practice, reduce the range of critical cues which they consider in order to make their discriminations, the number of cues which they must use is likely to increase with the number of relevant symbols for which they search. Experiment II suggests that the vocabulary of *cues* that the *S*s use may be independent of very wide variations in the vocabulary of irrelevant symbols amongst which they search. Neither Neisser nor Broadbent and Gregory suggests that the time taken to distinguish between any two or four classes of symbols is independent of *all* possible variations in the range of cues which *S*s must consider—whether such variations are associated with the number or with the *complexity* of symbols to be discriminated. A similar point has been made by Conrad—discussing his finding that short-term memory capacity for letters of the alphabet is limited by their acoustic confusability rather than by their information load as conventionally calculated.[21]

(2) Neisser's and Shepherd's tasks represent special cases of visual search in which their *S*s made the same response to all relevant stimuli. In contrast, *S*s in Experiment I above and in earlier studies made one response to all stimuli in one relevant sub-set (*e.g.* the letters A, B, C, or D) and another response to all stimuli in a different relevant sub-set (*e.g.*, the letters E, F, G, or H). This implies that they discriminated between three rather than between two categories of stimuli (Relevant_1/Relevant_2/Irrelevant).

The results of previous experiments in which the *S*s have discriminated between more than two categories of stimuli suggest that response-time is a multiplicative function of the number of categories and of the number of stimuli in each such category. For example, an increase in the total stimulus ensemble from 12 to 16 items may cause little or no increase in response time when the *S*s discriminate them into four response-classes, but may bring about considerable increases in response-time when they discriminate them into six or more classes.[22] In visual search we might therefore also expect that the time taken to distinguish relevant from irrelevant stimuli would vary with the number of different categories into which the set of relevant stimuli must be separated.

It is obviously important to find some means of comparing the (various) amounts of information transmitted by the *S*s undertaking different search- or categorization-tasks. Unfortunately there are at least six objections to the conventional use of variation of choice-response time as an index for this purpose:

(1) Functions predicting changes in rate of gain of information must be based on comparisons among a wide range of situations in which populations of stimuli are divided into different numbers of equal and unequal sub-sets. The available data suggest that discrimination-times depend on some interaction between the level of practice, the number of stimuli involved, the number of sub-sets into which stimuli must be divided and the relative sizes of these different sub-sets. Empirical determinations of rates of gain of information in different categorizations therefore require the slippery decision as to when a "limiting level of performance after extended practice" is attained for each of a large number of different tasks.

(2) The relative sizes of the vocabularies of items between which the *S*s discriminate may be a very coarse index of vocabularies of *cues* which they use, and consequently also of the information which they transmit. (Experiment II above). The features employed as cues must vary with practice, with the number of items in the particular sub-sets of items involved and, among other factors, with the relative perceptual "obviousness" of the various different available cue-systems.[23]

While it is indifferent to the calculation of transmitted information what particular features of complex stimuli are employed as cues, variations in the discriminability of different sets of potential cues must confound the use of choice-time as an index of the relative amounts of information transmitted in different situations. (See also Conrad for a discussion of this point in relation to the limits set to short-term memory capacity by confusability of items stored.)[24]

(3) It may be theoretically possible to calculate how the optimal range of cues needed to discriminate between given sets of stimuli will vary as the principles of categorization are altered. It is unlikely, however, that *Ss* use *optimal* sets of cues. We only know that they reduce the range of cues they use as far as they are able.

(4) The existing data do not suggest that the time taken to discriminate between categories of items varies continuously with the range of cues which the *Ss* must consider. The majority of experiments on stimulus categorization suggest some discontinuities in the relationship between stimulus-information and choice response time.[25]

(5) As an extension of *(4),* information transmitted in categorizing complex stimuli depends not on the principles of classification *required* of the *S* but rather on the strategy of classification which he actually *uses.* For example, a theoretically optimum strategy to discriminate the 8 letters, A, B, C, D, E, F, G, H, into the 4 sets A,B/C,D/E,F/G,H would use only such cues as are necessary to distinguish letters within each set from letters in other sets *(i.e.* the letter A need only be distinguished from the letters C, D, E, F, G, H but not from the letter B and so on). Cues which distinguish letters from others in the same set are theoretically redundant, and need not be considered. The *Ss* may, however, perform this task in a sub-optimal way, and identify each letter as a particular one of a set of eight possible items and then assign it to its response-category. We know that Ss do not adopt this sub-optimal strategy in some visual tasks, but we do not yet know the limiting range of cues within which such economical strategies are possible.

These five arguments also emphasize that comparisons of performance under various principles of stimulus-categorization (Broadbent and Gregory, Pollack, Nickerson, Feehrer & Rabbitt) provide very unreliable indices of the relative amounts of information processed in different situations.[26] An additional difficulty is specific to conditions encountered in visual search experiments:

(6) Where many symbols are simultaneously present on a display, *Ss* are known to process them in groups of two or more spatially-adjacent items rather than one at a time.[27] Rabbitt has suggested that details of differences in the time taken to search for two and for eight relevant items can only be explained on the assumption that *Ss* can process several adjacent symbols together when searching for two items, but may not be able to do so when searching for as many as eight.[28] Similarly, Morton has shown that eye-voice span in reading (and also the number of symbols on a printed page considered at a single fixation) varies inversely with the information-load of the material read.[29] The trade-off between eye-voice span and information load which masks differences in reading speed with various materials may also be expected to operate in visual search.

The experiments described offer examples of a technique which may be useful in the investigation of the cue-systems which *S*s recognize and adopt in visual search tasks. The development of similar techniques must become increasingly important, since experiments to investigate perceptual discriminations between complex stimuli are of very limited value unless they are designed to reveal which of the very complex series of options available to them *S*s actually learn and use.

Summary

Two experiments used a training-transfer paradigm to investigate learning of irrelevant symbols in visual search tasks. Groups of *S*s were practiced at locating members of particular sets of relevant letters embedded among restricted vocabularies of irrelevant letters. Search-time reduced with practice, but increased when *S*s were transfered to displays incorporating a new irrelevant vocabulary. This increase in search-time on transfer provided an index of the extent to which improvement related to learning of cues was specific to discriminations between particular relevant and irrelevant sets.

The results of Experiment I suggest that the number of cues used to discriminate relevant from irrelevant letters increases with the number of relevant letters for which the *S* is required to search. Experiment II suggested that search time is less affected by the relative sizes of the relevant and irrelevant vocabularies than by the particular physical characteristics of symbols in the relevant and irrelevant sets. These results are discussed in the context of recent experiments investigating the time taken to discriminate between classes of signals.

Notes

1 R. D. Shepherd, Classification time and class complexity in inspection tasks, *Occ. Psychol.*, 38, 1964, 86–89.
2 P. M. A. Rabbitt, Ignoring irrelevant information, *Brit. J. Psychol.*, 55, 1964, 403–414.
3 Rabbitt, *op. cit.*, 411.
4 Shepherd, *op. cit.*, 88.
5 E. H. Mowbray and M. V. Rhoades, On the reduction of choice-response times with practice, *Quart. J. exp. Psychol.*, 11, 1959, 16–24.
6 Ulric Neisser, Decision-times without reaction-time: Experiments in visual scanning, JOURNAL, 76, 1963, 376–385.
7 Neisser, Visual search, *Scient. Amer.*, 210, 1964, 94–102.
8 P. M. Fitts, Meyer Weinstein, Maurice Rappaport, Nancy Anderson and J. A. Leonard, Stimulus correlates of visual pattern-recognition, *J. exp. Psychol.*, 51, 1956, 1–11.
9 Rabbitt, *op. cit.*, 410 f.
10 B. J. Wimer, *Statistical principles in experimental design*, 1962, 72.
11 Rabbitt, *op. cit.*, 406 ff.; Shepherd, *op. cit.*, 87–97.
12 Neisser, *op. cit., Scient. Amer.*, 94–102.
13 R. S. Nickerson and C. E. Feehrer, Stimulus categorisation and response-time, *Percep. mot. Skills*, 18, 1964, 785–793.

14 Irving Pollack, Speed of classification of words into superordinate categories, *J. verb. Learn, verb. Behav.*, 2, 1963, 159–165.
15 Rabbitt, Effects of independent variations in stimulus and response probability, *Nature*, 183, 1959, 1212.
16 D. E. Broadbent and Margaret Gregory, Human responses to classes of stimuli, *Nature*, 192, 1962, 1315 f.
17 Nickerson and Feehrer, *op. cit.*, 785–793.
18 Broadbent and Gregory, *op. cit.*, 1315 f.
19 Rabbitt, Perceptual discrimination and the choice of responses. Unpublished Doctoral dissertation, University of Cambridge, 1962, 2.47 f.
20 Niesser, *op. cit.*, this JOURNAL, 376–385; Shepherd, *op. cit.*, 87–97; Rabbitt, *op. cit.*, 403–414.
21 R. Conrad, Acoustic confusions in immediate memory, *Brit. J. Psychol.*, 55, 1964, 75–84.
22 Pollack, *op. cit.*, 159–165; Rabbitt, *op. cit.*, Nature, 183, 1959, 1212 f.
23 Rabbitt, Stimulus information load and discriminability, *Nature*, 197, 1963, 726 f.
24 Conrad, *op. cit.*, 75–84.
25 Broadbent and Gregory, *op. cit., Nature*, 192, 1962, 1315 f., Neisser, *op. cit.*, this JOURNAL, 76, 1963, 376–385; Pollack, *op. cit., J. verb. Learn. verb. Behav.*, 2, 1963, 159–165; Rabbitt, *op. cit., Nature*, 183, 1959, 1212.
26 Broadbent and Gregory, *op. cit.*, 1315; Pollack, *op. cit.*, 159 ff. Nickerson and Feehrer, *op. cit.*, 785 ff.; Rabbitt, *op. cit., Nature*, 1212 f.
27 N. H. Mackworth and J. F. Mackworth, Eye fixations recorded on changing visual scenes by the television eye-marker, *J. opt. Soc. Amer.* 48, 1958, 439–445.
28 Rabbitt, *op. cit., Brit. J. Psychol.*, 55, 1964, 406 ff.
29 John Morton, The effects of context upon speed of reading, eye-movements, and eye-voice span, *Quart. J. exp. Psychol.*, 16, 1964, 340–354.

Visual search between 1967 and 2007

Neisser's (1963) finding that young adults can eventually learn to search as fast for 12 as for two letters may be explained as their gradual discovery and use of the minimum number of cues needed to make discriminations rather than as improvement at wholistic comparisons between complex symbols. Rabbitt's (1962; 1965; 1967) experiments suggest that as people age they become less efficient at finding and using optimal sets of cues. We do not yet know whether, given enough practice, older people may also achieve parallel processing, if only for a smaller vocabulary of targets. Early in practice, older people use more than the necessary minimum of cues or features but we do not know whether this handicap is permanent or, with practice, can reduce to the young adult norm. If there are indeed individual differences in the maximum number of cues or features that people can simultaneously process, these may be termed their individual "cue-bandwidths" and these may vary with their ages and their levels of intelligence.

Plude, Hoyer and Lazar (1982) found that when the number of targets is varied between experiments, young adults' search times initially increase with the number of targets they seek, but also that long practice with the same set of targets reduces this effect. They suggested that at least two functionally distinct kinds of processes may be used to discriminate between signals early and late in practice, and that age might affect these differently. Context for this suggestion had been provided by Schneider and Shiffrin (1977) and Shiffrin and Schneider (1977) who showed that the general finding that the times that young adults need to distinguish between letters in a CRT task increase with the number of different symbols between which they must distinguish is true only early in practice. After long practice the effects of signal and response set sizes reduce and, eventually, disappear and performance is unaffected by concurrent secondary tasks. Shiffrin and Schneider suggested that practice allows a gradual transition from a mode of processing controlled, from the "bottom up", by information that, while it is novel, must be held in immediate memory – a system that is vulnerable to distraction from concurrently presented information – to a different, "top down", mode in which input is "automatically" referred to representations that are permanently held in long-term memory in which they can be directly accessed in parallel. Fisk and Rogers (1991) and Fisk, Rogers, Cooper and Gilbert (1997) found that this narrative also fits results obtained from young adults practiced on a visual search task. Madden and Nebes (1980) also found that when target and background set sizes are held constant, practice markedly reduces but does not entirely remove age differences in search speed. Their results raise questions that remain unanswered: whether brain ageing makes "parallel", or "automatic" processing impossible, or just slower to achieve, and whether age permanently reduces the "bandwidth" of different cues for which people can simultaneously test.

Saul Sternberg (1966) was the first to study search for matches against representations held in immediate memory. He asked young adults to remember lists of from two to six different digits and then to decide, as fast as possible, whether a subsequent single probe digit had, or had not been one of them. "Yes" decisions were faster than "No" decisions and times for both "Yes" and "No" increased linearly with the number of items in remembered lists. Sternberg argued that that each probe digit is compared successively against internal representations of each member of the target set. Thus "Yes" decisions can be made as soon as a match occurs but "No" decisions must be delayed because they are made by default after all comparisons have failed. Consequently, while signals are still unfamiliar, decision times will increase linearly with their number. Anders, Fozard and Lillyquist (1972) found that the Sternberg memory search functions obtained from old adults have both slower intercepts and steeper slopes than those from the young and argued that this explains why increases in target set sizes initially affect older more than younger adults. So, from the mid-1960s to the 1980s the standard model was that improvement at signal categorization tasks involves gradual transition from slow decisions actively controlled by reference to information transiently held in working memory ("bottom up" processing") to much faster decisions made by reference to learned information permanently held in long-term memory.

Until the 1990s we had no way to directly relate age changes in hypothetical system performance characteristics such as "top down" (i.e. working memory driven) or "bottom up" (i.e. long-term store driven) processes to neurophysiological and neuroanatomical changes in the brain. Experimenters could only make the expedient assumption that all individuals free of brain damage or pathologies experience the same patterns, and rates, of age-related brain changes. This unlikely assumption rationalized comparisons involving very small groups of young and old persons (in at least one widely cited study a critical comparison between sub-conditions was between N's of two young and two elderly people). To believe that we can generalize about age changes from tiny samples misses the point thoroughly documented (e.g. by Raz et al., 2010), that even healthy high-functioning older individuals markedly vary in terms of the patterns and amounts of age-related brain changes that they have experienced and that inter-individual brain variability markedly increases with the average age of the population sampled. Psychologists of all persuasions are alarmed by the high proportion of widely acclaimed studies in their disciplines that fail to replicate. Some failures are due to inadequate statistical power of comparisons (cf. Button et al., 2013) or to "p-hacking" – i.e. *post hoc* selection of some significant among many non-significant comparisons within data-sets (Simmons, Nelson & Simonsohn, 2011). In addition to such errors in logic and statistics, the marked variability of age-related brain changes found within samples of healthy high-functioning individuals makes it likely that a significant proportion of comparisons that have been made between small groups of young and older people are unreliable.

During the 1990s brain images began to allow us to relate behavioural data to both gross and localized age changes in brain structure and to compare differences between old and young in relation to differences in the locations, nature and durations of their brain activity while they identify signals and chose responses to them. Advances in neuroimaging not only changed the questions that we are able to ask but also those we can imagine. An illustration is Duncan's (1984) review of research on visual search from 1950 to 1979, re-interpreting previous results and models in terms of competition and mutual suppression between concurrent processes based on activity recorded from single units in the brains of live macaques while they made perceptual discriminations. Duncan and Humphreys (1989) proposed a capacity-limited process in which a parallel processing stage of perceptual grouping and comparison is followed by competitive interaction of outputs from this stage that guide selective access to awareness and action. Duncan and Humphreys (1992) expanded these earlier suggestions into a model for control of visual search, not by top-down control involving information held in working memory but by competitive interactions between concurrently activated brain areas. If applied to age comparisons, this model would suggest that older people process information more slowly than young adults as their global information processing capacity becomes increasingly limited. This assumption fits well with the idea that global losses in capacity, by losses of connectivity or by other means, could slow all successive decision processes by the same proportion. A model and experiments by Lavie (2005), supported by parallel neuroimaging data, interprets control of visual selective attention in a similar way: the extent to which distractors are processed depends on competition for gross information-processing capacity. Though increasing perceptual load reduces the extent to which distractor items on displays are processed, increasing load on specifically "frontal" cognitive control processes increases distractor processing. Maylor and Lavie (1998) compared groups of old and younger adults on Lavie's tasks, ensuring that differences in effect sizes were not simply explained by linear scaling. Lavie's model suggests new ways to interpret the effects of age on visual search speed as consequences of progressive loss of global information-processing capacity.

Madden et al. (2007) found that increases in white matter lesion density are associated with reduced efficiency of visual search. Although, in this study, levels of white matter density were assessed only in local brain areas, changes in these probably reflect proliferation throughout the entire brain and so fit with results of experiments that assessed the effects of whole-brain changes on speed in visual search and in letter/letter coding tasks (e.g. Rabbitt, Scott, Lunn, et al. 2007). Madden et al. (2004) and Marks et al. (2007) had earlier reported results congenial to these new models for visual search by combining analyses of behavioural and diffusion-tensor imaging data (fractional anisotropy, FA) during a visual task. They found that for younger adults the best predictor of visual RT was FA in the splenium of the corpus callosum but for older adults it was FA in the anterior limb of the internal capsule. Gross brain changes, such as age-related changes in regional cerebral blood flow, also affect efficiency of visual search (Madden et al., 1996).

References

Anders, T. R., Fozard, J. L., & Lillyquist, T. D. (1972). Effects of age upon retrieval from short-term memory. *Developmental Psychology, 6*(2), 214.

Button, K. S., Ioannidis, J. P., Mokrysz, C., Nosek, B. A., Flint, J., Robinson, E. S., & Munafò, M. R. (2013). Power failure: Why small sample size undermines the reliability of neuroscience. *Nature Reviews Neuroscience, 14*(5), 365.

Duncan, J. (1984). Selective attention and the organization of visual information. *Journal of Experimental Psychology: General, 113*(4), 501.

Duncan, J., & Humphreys, G. W. (1989). Visual search and stimulus similarity. *Psychological Review, 96*(3), 433.

Duncan, J., & Humphreys, G. W. (1992). Beyond the search surface: Visual search and attentional engagement. *Journal of Experimental Psychology: Human Perception and Performance, 18*(2), 578–588.

Fisk, A. D., & Rogers, W. A. (1991). Toward an understanding of age-related memory and visual search effects. *Journal of Experimental Psychology: General, 120*(2), 131.

Fisk, A. D., Rogers, W. A., Cooper, B. P., & Gilbert, D. K. (1997). Automatic category search and its transfer: Aging, type of search, and level of learning. *The Journals of Gerontology Series B: Psychological Sciences and Social Sciences, 52*(2), P91–P102.

Lavie, N. (2005). Distracted and confused? Selective attention under load. *Trends in Cognitive Sciences, 9*(2), 75–82.

Madden, D. J., & Nebes, R. D. (1980). Aging and the development of automaticity in visual search. *Developmental Psychology, 16*(5), 377.

Madden, D. J., Spaniol, J., Whiting, W. L., Bucur, B., Provenzale, J. M., Cabeza, R., … & Huettel, S. A. (2007). Adult age differences in the functional neuroanatomy of visual attention: A combined fMRI and DTI study. *Neurobiology of Aging, 28*(3), 459–476.

Madden, D. J., Turkington, T. G., Coleman, R. E., Provenzale, J. M., DeGrado, T. R., & Hoffman, J. M. (1996). Adult age differences in regional cerebral blood flow during visual word identification: Evidence from $H_2{}^{15}O$ PET. *NeuroImage, 3*(2), 127–142.

Madden, D.J., Whiting, W.L., Huettel, S.A., White, L.E., MacFall, J.R., Provenzale, J.M. (2004). Diffusion tensor imaging of adult age differences in cerebral white matter: relation to response time. *Neuroimage, 21*(3), 1174–1181

Marks, B. L., Madden, D. J., Bucur, B., Provenzale, J. M., White, L. E., Cabeza, R., & Huettel, S. A. (2007). Role of aerobic fitness and aging on cerebral white matter integrity. *Annals of the New York Academy of Sciences, 1097*(1), 171–174.

Maylor, E. A., & Lavie, N. (1998). The influence of perceptual load on age differences in selective attention. *Psychology and Aging, 13*(4), 563.

Neisser, U. (1963). Decision-time without reaction-time: Experiments in visual scanning. *The American Journal of Psychology, 76*(3), 376–385.

Plude, D. J., Hoyer, W. J., & Lazar, J. (1982). Age, response complexity, and target consistency in visual search. *Experimental Aging Research, 8*(2), 99–102.

Rabbitt, P.M.A. (1962). Discriminations between signals and choices between responses. Unpublished Ph.D. thesis, University of Cambridge.

Rabbitt, P. (1965). An age-decrement in the ability to ignore irrelevant information. *Journal of Gerontology, 20*(2), 233–238.

Rabbitt, P. M. (1967). Learning to ignore irrelevant information. *The American Journal of Psychology, 80*(1), 1–13.

Rabbitt, P., Scott, M., Lunn, M., Thacker, N., Lowe, C., Pendleton, N.,... & Jackson, A. (2007). White matter lesions account for all age-related declines in speed but not in intelligence. *Neuropsychology, 21*(3), 363–370.

Raz, N., Ghisletta, P., Rodrigue, K. M., Kennedy, K. M., & Lindenberger, U. (2010). Trajectories of brain aging in middle-aged and older adults: Regional and individual differences. *NeuroImage, 51*(2), 501–511.

Schneider, W., & Shiffrin, R. M. (1977). Controlled and automatic human information processing: I. Detection, search, and attention. *Psychological Review, 84*(1), 1–66.

Shiffrin, R. M., & Schneider, W. (1977). Controlled and automatic human information processing: II. Perceptual learning, automatic attending and a general theory. *Psychological Review, 84*(2), 127.

Simmons, J. P., Nelson, L. D., & Simonsohn, U. (2011). False-positive psychology: Undisclosed flexibility in data collection and analysis allows presenting anything as significant. *Psychological Science, 22*(11), 1359–1366.

Sternberg, S. (1966). High-speed scanning in human memory. *Science, 153*(3736), 652–654.

New tools to study processing of signals and the failure of the information-theory account of CRTs

During my first 40 years of work in psychology, neuro images were unavailable to most of us and were often misinterpreted by most of the few who had access to them. Consequently, connections between behavioural data and neuropsychological guesswork were speculative and depended on serendipitous discovery of patients with localized brain damage in areas that, apparently, supported only particular functions but not others. The Grail for human experimental psychologists remained as it had been since Helmholtz, Wundt and Donders: to imagine and test "models" for functional processes supporting cognitive abilities that might, on some jubilant day, be related to, or, even more vaingloriously, inspire and guide future neurophysiological investigations. Meanwhile the only game in town was to make "natural history" observations of very simple behaviours, to imagine one or more hypothetical models of the functional processes that might support them and then to design experiments to choose among plausible alternatives. The behavioural observations that guided these activities frequently originated in and were funded by work in ergonomics and human factors engineering. For example, the first textbook on cognitive ageing, Alan Welford's *Aging and Human Skill* (1958), set an agenda for cognitive gerontology that was based on reports of difficulties that older adults encounter with workplace demands with discussions of how these observations might be incorporated into then current models for memory, information processing speed and decision making. The Cambridge Medical Research Council Applied Psychology Research Unit, where I was then employed, painstakingly lived up to its title. We were all tasked with ergonomic problems posed by the military, the Post Office and the Bank of England. My first years were spent working on Post Office letter sorting machines and the, then, impending conversion of a bizarrely antique UK currency of pounds, ten bob (shilling) notes, half crowns, florins, shillings, "tanners "(six penny pieces!), pennies, halfpennies and farthings (or quarter-pennies, stamped with quaint little wrens). Like all my colleagues I did my best to squeeze, out of the applied problems that justified the Unit's support, observations or insights that might be converted into academic publications (dearth of these meant termination of employment). For example, the chore of spending six hours a day teaching postmen (Higher Grade) to use the Conrad (1966) chord keyboard, then under trial for letter-sorting machines, provided me with data for an academically vendible publication as did a later study, also for the Royal Mail, of the effects on memory of crackle on telephone lines (Rabbitt, 1968a). The most remarkable of us managed this juggling act with vigour, grace and elegance. Donald Broadbent's first and most influential book, *Perception and Communication* (1958) derived his theoretical models for cognitive processes almost entirely from data on applied research, such as investigations of the efficiency of choices between simultaneously active communication channels. Similarly, his successor, Alan Baddeley, derived his influential conceptions of Working Memory from work on applied problems for the Royal Mail.

This process of observing phenomena and imagining and testing functional models for them is common to all sciences. It has usually led to proliferation of ingenious experimental paradigms that are first developed as methodological tools to ask specific questions. These often reveal further, unanticipated, phenomena that, in turn, become objects for continued investigation. In psychology, the transformation in understanding brought about by brain-imaging technologies is the most obvious and striking example. However, only those of us who were around at the time realize how trifling technological developments radically expanded the range of questions that we could ask and, more radically, of those that we could imagine. Minor applications of Ur-IT to improve equipment for presenting displays and timing and recording responses to them were conceptual fall-out from advances in computer engineering and information technology driven by purposes unwitted by psychologists whose experiments and imaginations they transformed. An example of this process is how minor technological innovations guided lines of investigations made to understand Paul Bertelson's (1961) discovery of the "repetition effect".

In 2002 Paul vehemently assured me that his discovery of the repetition effect was a "natural history" observation of a quirk in human information processing that theories current in 1962 did not predict. I completely believe him, but he was determined to emphasize this because it might have arisen as an issue in interpretation of research on CRTs. Hick (1952) and Hyman (1953) had asked whether, just as Shannon and Weaver's (1947) theory of information transmission would predict, the times that people need to detect and acknowledge signals are inversely related to their probability. Hick varied the number, and so also the conditional probability of signals to each of which his volunteer, Richard Gregory, made a different response. Hyman (1953) kept the number of signals and responses constant but varied their probabilities with respect to each other. Both investigators found that CRTs vary with signal probability in a way consistent with Shannon and Weaver's information theory. Mervyn Stone (1960) pointed out that this assumed that for the human information processing system, as for electronic devices with no memory, transitions between different events are as easy to deal with as repetitions of the same events. If, as Mervyn thought likely, humans can detect and answer repeated signals faster than altered signals, Hick and Hyman's findings could reflect a functional characteristic of the human central nervous system rather than increasing information cost of decisions.

Bertelson (1961) found that CRTs to repeated signals are, indeed, faster than to altered signals. Since he was concerned to explore a phenomenon rather than to challenge a metric, he did not mention that his result questioned Hick's and Hyman's conclusions. This point waited to be made explicit by Kornblum (1969).

Paul's next move was to ask whether the repetition effect depended on precise repetition of an identical signal or on recognition of a different signal to which the same response was made. He used a two-choice CRT task in which volunteers made the same response to either of two different signals (Bertelson, 1963). Successive events might be identical, when both signals and responses were immediately repeated, "equivalent" when a new signal required the same response, or "new" when neither a signal nor a response recurred. Paul found that CRTs were fastest for identical decisions, only slightly slower for equivalent decisions and slowest for new transitions and that, after only a little practice, CRTs to equivalent signals became almost as fast as CRTs to identical signals.

Following Neisser's (1963) proposal, I thought that the progress of this change might reflect the transition from a serial to a parallel processing mode and that we might learn some more about the nature of this transition by tracking it as volunteers were increasingly practiced. I used a four-signal/two-response task, an eight-signal/four-response task and an eight-signal/eight-response task (Rabbitt, 1968b) and found that, after 1500 trials, two of 15 volunteers responded as fast to equivalent as to identical transitions and that the others responded on equivalent transitions nearly, but not quite as fast as on identical transitions. This seemed consistent with Neisser's idea that practice can shift processing of signals from a serial to a parallel mode but also suggested that, during a transition period between these states, people can operate in a "hybrid" serial/parallel mode. Gordon Logan (1990) later proposed a more elegant, comprehensive and better articulated model for this process. My personal interest was more practical: I saw that repetition effects provide an excellent methodology to explore how people learn to discriminate between target and background items in visual search.

I became able to use this insight only when minor technological advances transformed the questions that experimenters could ask. Computers were unavailable in UK Psychological Laboratories until the early 1970s, so it took a decade before Geoff Cumming, Subhash Vyas and I gained access to a "PDP Linc8", newly acquired by the Oxford Department of Experimental Psychology, to study repetition effects in visual search (Rabbitt, Cumming and Vyas, 1977).

References

Bertelson, P. (1961). Sequential redundancy and speed in a serial two-choice responding task. *Quarterly Journal of Experimental Psychology, 13*(2), 90–102.

Bertelson, P. (1963). SR relationships and reaction times to new versus repeated signals in a serial task. *Journal of Experimental Psychology, 65*(5), 478.

Broadbent, D. E. (1958). *Perception and Communication*. Oxford: Pergamon Press.

Conrad, R. (1966). Short-term memory factor in the design of data-entry keyboards: An interface between short-term memory and SR compatibility. *Journal of Applied Psychology, 50*(5), 353.

Hick, W. E. (1952). On the rate of gain of information. *Quarterly Journal of Experimental Psychology, 4*(1), 11–26.

Hyman, R. (1953). Stimulus information as a determinant of reaction time. *Journal of Experimental Psychology, 45*(3), 188.

Kornblum, S. (1969). Sequential determinants of information processing in serial and discrete choice reaction time. *Psychological Review, 76*(2), 113.
Logan, G. D. (1990). Repetition priming and automaticity: Common underlying mechanisms? *Cognitive Psychology, 22*(1), 1–35.
Neisser, U. (1963). Decision-time without reaction-time: Experiments in visual scanning. *The American Journal of Psychology, 76*(3), 376–385.
Rabbitt, P. M. (1968a). Channel-capacity, intelligibility and immediate memory. *Quarterly Journal of Experimental Psychology, 20*(3), 241–248.
Rabbitt, P. M.A. (1968b). Repetition effects and signal classification strategies in serial choice-response tasks. *Quarterly Journal of Experimental Psychology, 20*(3), 232–240.
Rabbitt, P. M. A., Cumming, G., & Vyas, S. (1977). An analysis of visual search: Entropy and sequential effects. In S. Dornic (Ed.), *Attention and Performance VI* (pp. 363–386). Hillsdale, NJ: Erlbaum.
Shannon, C. E., & Weaver, W. (1947). *The Mathematical Theory of Communication.* Urbana, IL: University of Illinois Press.
Stone, M. (1960). Models for choice-reaction time. *Psychometrika, 25*(3), 251–260.
Welford, A. T. (1958). *Aging and Human Skill.* Oxford: Oxford University Press.

3 Modulation of selective attention by sequential effects in visual search tasks

P.M.A. Rabbitt, G. Cumming and S.M. Vyas

Introduction

The study of selective attention is concerned with our ability to process only some part of the information available from the sense organs at any particular moment.

Two main approaches to this problem may be distinguished. On the one hand workers such as Treisman (1969) have concentrated on the issue of how extraneous information is kept out. More recent researchers such as Posner and Snyder (1975) have studied the complementary problem of how relevant information is most efficiently taken in.

These two approaches have been associated with different experimental paradigms. Treisman has been mainly concerned with experiments in which subjects must shadow or monitor one continuous speech input while ignoring another, and has interpreted the data in terms of a model which assumes that unwanted information is attenuated before it is fully processed. Posner and Snyder (1975) were concerned with tasks in which pairs of stimulus displays are presented in succession and in which the speed or accuracy of a response to the second display may be considered in terms of various relationships which it has to the first. These authors have demonstrated that categorization of a stimulus display in a particular way can be facilitated by presentation of a prior stimulus display with similar physical features, which seem to "prime" the relevant analytic processes. Meyer, Schvaneveldt and Ruddy (1975) extended this approach and demonstrated that priming can also occur for pairs of complex displays (nouns) with different physical characteristics but associated meaning, such as "nurse" and "doctor".

The work reported here attempted further to investigate the nature of priming, using a different paradigm where the subject responds to a continuous series of stimuli. Rabbitt, Cumming and Vyas (1977) have shown that response facilitation, or "priming" can occur in continuous visual search tasks. In their experiments subjects were shown series of letter arrays. For each array subjects were required to make one manual response (T) if the array contained one of a set of designated target letters, and another response (N) otherwise. They found that considerable response facilitation occurred if successive displays contained identical targets in the same spatial location.

A smaller degree of facilitation was found if identical targets occurred in succession in different spatial locations. Repetition of a set of background (nontarget) items further facilitated responses, except in cases where the target had been repeated in the same spatial location. The authors concluded that in this latter case subjects did not need to process the background items so that their identity on consecutive trials could produce no further facilitation. Apparently they could recognize a match between a memory trace for the physical characteristics of one target, and perceptual input from its successor and make a T response without further perceptual analysis. They referred to this matching process as a "type A" process. This could not occur if successive identical targets fell in different spatial positions. When this happened, at least some subset of background items had to be inspected in terms of some more complex perceptual analysis based on learned discriminatory features between target and background items. These discriminatory features would vary with the particular subset of background items used (cf. Rabbitt, 1967), hence the duration of the analytic process would depend on the background items in the display. This type of process was referred to as a "type B" process. Rabbitt *et al.* (1977) argued that because responses were faster when successive identical targets occurred in different positions than when successive different targets followed each other, there could be some priming of type B analysis, i.e. repetition of a particular act of perceptual analysis might speed target detection. However, they noted an alternative interpretation of this result. Consider the possibility that the subject shifts his point of fixation between displays on a proportion of trials. Then if successive identical targets occur in different locations the subject will fixate the point at which the new target occurs by chance on a proportion of trials. Type A analysis would then occur, and mean RT will be shorter than when different targets occur successively (and type A analysis cannot occur). Thus the facilitation could be explained simply on the assumption that subjects use type A processing when they can, and it is not necessary to postulate facilitation of type B processing from these results alone.

The first experiment set out to resolve the issue of whether facilitation of type B processing can in fact occur. The rationale was as follows: type A processing depends on matching a memory trace with new perceptual input. Presumably any additional processing occurring between two presentations of identical stimuli would obliterate the stored trace making type A processing impossible. Thus if we can demonstrate facilitation when identical targets are separated by an interpolated display, this must represent priming of type B processing. Such an effect would not be explicable in terms of the eye-movement explanation outlined above.

Experiment I

Method

A Line 8 computer was programmed to present displays of five capital letters (from the normal Line 8 character set) displayed in a horizontal line across the centre of a standard Line 8 CRT display. An ancillary "generator" programme arranged that each display contained four or five letters selected at random, without replacement, from the set of 24 letters B and D through Z of the English alphabet. Half the displays, in random sequence, with equal probability might contain either the target letter C or the target letter A. These letters might occur, with random selection but equal probability, in any of the five possible left to right positions across the display. Other displays contained only background letters.

Subjects sat viewing the CRT display through a 50 cm tube in a darkened room. They rested their hands on a desk in which keys were inset beneath their left and right forefingers. They were instructed to press the key under one forefinger whenever they saw one of the two target letters (A or C) and to press the key under the other forefinger whenever they were certain that a particular display contained neither target letter.

As soon as they pressed either key the current display disappeared (the phosphor on the CRT was especially fast, with a decay time of less than 0.5 ms). The next display occurred 150 ms later. The programme also arranged that all displays presented, all responses made to them, and the elapsed time between display onset and response (RT) was recorded permanently for each event.

The program generated anew for each subject four runs of 200 successive displays. Each of 14 subjects experienced these four experimental runs during a single testing session which lasted not more than 15 mins. Seven subjects responded to target (T) displays with the left forefinger and to non-target (N) displays with the right forefinger. The others reversed these allocations. Subjects were urged to respond as fast and as accurately as possible.

Subjects

Eight girls and six men, undergraduates at the University of Oxford, aged from 18 to 20 years were each paid 50p to complete this task.

Results

The question asked was whether detection of one of the target letters facilitated recognition of the same letter if it occurred again on the next display but one.

A computer sort program examined subjects' data for errors. The overall mean error rate was 1.9%. All errors, and responses immediately following errors were ignored in the next sort, which extracted from the data all T-N-T sequences of responses. Such sequences were of two kinds. Either the targets detected on the first and third response were identical (T_1-N-T_1) or they were not (T_1-N-T_2). Mean detection RTs for the final T responses were 762 ms (S.D. = 165) for T_1-N-T_1 sequences and 819 ms (S.D. = 181) for T_1-N-T_2 sequences, these values being significantly different ($t = 5.6$, $df = 13$, $P < 0.01$).

Discussion

Targets which have been encountered during the last two trials are detected faster than targets which have not appeared so recently. In terms of the introduction it might be assumed therefore that priming of type B analysis can occur.

However, another possibility remains. It could be the case that the priming effects shown in Experiment I reflect facilitation of response selection. Subjects may be unsure, early in practice, as to which letters comprise the target set. It could be that recent experience of a given stimulus does not facilitate perceptual processing or identification of that stimulus, but rather enables the subject to decide more rapidly that the stimulus he has identified is a member of a particular target class. One way to test this notion would involve examining the effect of previous experience of background items rather than targets. Consider a sequence of two letter displays both containing the same background items, where only the second display contains a target. If repetition of background letters speeds reaction time in this case, then this improvement must be due to facilitation of perceptual analysis, since neither a response nor a particular decision is repeated. Experiment II was made to test this.

Experiment II

Method

The Line 8 was again programmed to present displays of five letters. Target symbols were A or C precisely as in Experiment I. Background symbols on each display were chosen by random sampling without replacement, from the other 24 letters of the English alphabet. The generator program was modified so that on 50% of transitions between successive displays all background symbols presented were the same, and on 50% of transitions all background symbols of successive displays were different. When background symbols were the same on two successive displays they might, with equal probability, appear in identical or in "scrambled" left to right order across the display. The operational definition of "scrambling" was that no letter should appear adjacent to any letter which had flanked it on the previous display.

When successive displays contained a target, and background items were repeated, target location might vary randomly between displays. In this case "identical" left to right order of background symbols implied only that they retained precisely the same left to right order with respect to each other, the target being randomly inserted among them. In such transitions if a T display followed an N display one background letter was replaced by a target.

Ten subjects were each given eight runs of 200 successive displays and responses. R-S intervals were constant at 150 ms. Subjects pressed one response key when either the target letter A or the target letter C occurred, and another response key when a display contained neither target. Response allocations were balanced across subjects. Subjects were asked to respond as fast and as accurately as possible. Testing took 30 min.

Subjects

Five girls and five men, undergraduates at the University of Oxford aged from 18 to 20 years were each paid 30p to do this experiment.

Results

Subjects averaged 2·4% errors. All these responses, and the responses immediately following them were discarded in computing mean RTs for transitions. All other transitions between correct responses were sorted automatically to provide the data-partitionings analysed below.

Non-target displays will again be referred to as N and target displays as T. The data-sort extracted individual subjects' mean RTs for the four kinds of response transition (i.e. T/T, N/T, T/N and N/N). For each kind of transition three relationships between background items on successive displays were possible. They might contain completely different background letters (BD); they might contain exactly the same background letters in the same left to right position (BS) or they might contain the same background letters in different left to right order (BSDO). No cases of partial overlap between sets of background letters on successive displays were allowed to occur. For purposes of data sort displays were classified as having the same background letters (collapsing BS and BSDO) or different background letters (D). Mean RTs for each of these classes were extracted for each of the response transitions (T/T, N/T, T/N and N/N). Overall means of subjects' mean RTs and associated variances are given in Table 3.1.

A 2-way analysis of variance (ANOVA) was made over individual subjects' means contributing to Table 3.1. There were significant main effects of transition classes (T/T vs. N/T vs. T/N vs. N/N, $F = 44.1$, $df = 3.37$, $P < 0.01$) and of the two classes of relationship between background letters on successive displays (i.e. (BS + BSDO) vs. D; $F = 6.33$, $df = 1.9$, $P < 0.05$). The interaction between these terms was also significant ($F = 7.30$, $df = 3.27$, $P < 0.05$).

A Scheffe's S^2 test was used to rank order significant differences between particular sub-sets of means within the ANOVA. Taking means for transitions between displays with the same background letters and rank-ordering for transition classes we get

$$\text{RT T/T}^{\star} < \text{RT N/T}^{\star\star} < \text{RT N/N}^{\star} < \text{RT T/N}$$

$^{\star}P < 0.05$; $^{\star\star}P < 0.01$.

Table 3.1

	Transition between displays			
	T/T	*N/T*	*T/N*	*N/N*
Background letters same	776 ms (σ 117)	815 ms (σ 108)	1082 ms (σ 171)	1012 ms (σ 172)
Background letters different	803 ms (σ 86)	850 ms (σ 123)	1047 ms (σ 176)	1072 ms (σ 183)

And taking means for transitions between displays with different background letters we get

$$\text{RT T/T}^{\star} < \text{RT N/T}^{\star\star} < \text{RT T/N}^{\star} < \text{RT N/N}$$

$^{\star}P < 0.05$; ** $P < 0.01$.

The finding that RT is faster to displays where targets are present is not surprising. To identify a target in a display of n items a subject need only process, on average, $(n + 1)/2$ items. In contrast, to be sure that a display does not contain a target all n items must be processed.

In general the second factor of background items influenced RTs so that RT (BS + BSDO) < RT(D). However, as can be seen from Table 3.1 the interaction between background items and transition type was significant partly because T/N transition in the "background same" case (i.e. BS + BSDO) were slower than in the background different case (i.e. D). In fact T/N (BS + BDO) transitions were the slowest of all transitions examined. Some clue as to the explanation of the phenomenon comes from the spontaneous remark of four of the 10 subjects who noted that if they had just located a target they were confused if the next display had identical background letters and did not also contain a target. They claimed that for such transitions the similarity of the displays made them pause to consider more carefully than in other cases whether a target might not again be present.

A difficulty with experimental designs employed to study transition effects is that higher-order interactions, such as the one just discussed, cloud main effects in experiments of the most natural kind, in which all types of transitions are possible, and occur in random order. In this particular experiment possible effects of the left-to-right order in which irrelevant items appeared are difficult to investigate since this factor can only be studied for cases in which background items on successive displays were the same. This implies a partial analysis of the data from the entire experiment; (data from transitions in which background items on successive displays were different must be ignored).

It is recognised that such partial analyses should be avoided whenever possible. An alternative solution is to design an experiment in which background items were always the same on successive displays, but might or might not occur in the same left to right order. This is unsatisfactory for other reasons. That is, it cannot be guaranteed that any transition effects observed in so restricted a situation will have generality over the range of all possible experiments.

Accordingly, accepting these limitations, both approaches were tried. A limited experiment (III below) was devoted to background position effects, and data from Experiment II were partially analysed to investigate these further.

The "background same" transitions were sorted to separate BS and BSDO transitions for each of the four response transition classes. Means of subjects' means for these classes of responses are given in Table 3.2.

Table 3.2

	Transition between displays			
	T/T	*N/T*	*T/N*	*N/N*
Background items in same order	762 ms (σ 84)	789 ms (σ 91)	1129 ms (σ 192)	980 ms (σ 102)
Background items in different order	790 ms (σ 113)	816 ms (σ 105)	1034 ms (σ 111)	1041 ms (σ 128)

A 2-way ANOVA gave significant main terms for differences between response classes ($F = 38.2$, $df = 3,27$, $P < 0.01$) and for BS vs. BSDO ($F = 6.2$, $df = 1,27$, $P < 0.05$). There was a significant interaction ($F = 3.4$, $df = 3,37$, $P < 0.05$).

The overall mean RT for transitions between displays on which background items were in the same left-to-right order was 916 ms (σ I40) and for displays in which they were in a different order 932.1 ms (σ 136). These means were not significantly different when tested by Scheffe's S^2. We cannot, therefore, make the general assertion that subjects usually scan faster when the order of background items on successive displays is the same. The ANOVA merely shows that there is an overall, significant, effect of order.

It is again necessary to interpret the data with respect to the significant interaction term for response class vs. background order. We see from Table 3.2 that mean RTs for BS transitions were slightly faster than mean RTs for BSDO transitions for T/T, N/T and N/N response sequences. For T/N response sequences "same order" transitions appear slightly slower than "different order" transitions.

Discussion

Experiment II shows that there is a "background repetition effect" as well as a "target repetition effect" in self-paced serial visual search. "Background" similarity or difference may be assessed in two ways, i.e. as "background item effects" and "background order effects". These were confounded in Experiment II. Experiment III was made to see whether "background order effects" and "background item effects" could be separately demonstrated in more restricted conditions, in which not all possible transitions between displays occurred.

Experiment III

Method

The same computer and programs were used. In Condition 1 background *order* effects were examined. All displays contained the same subset of background letters. On half the transitions between displays, at random, background letters appeared in the same left to right order (i.e. BS) and on all others the order of background items was scrambled as for Experiment II (i.e. BSDO). Condition 2 investigated background *item* effects. Here background letters were selected for each display by random choice, without replacement, from the entire population of 24 letters of the alphabet remaining after the target pair had been designated. An additional constraint was that on half the transitions between displays the same set of background letters recurred. In these cases, the order of background letters was always scrambled (i.e. BSDO). The display generator program was modified to allow a different pair of letters of the alphabet to be selected as targets for each of the 20 subjects. Displays were then made up by this program, as described, to provide unique runs for each subject. Subject responded with one hand to T and with the other to N displays. Response allocations were balanced across subjects. Two groups of 10 subjects each had four runs of 200 responses in each condition. Testing lasted 30 min.

Subjects

Twelve women and eight men, students at Oxford Polytechnic and the University of Oxford, aged from 17 to 24 were each paid 50p to participate.

Results

The data from Condition 1 were sorted to give means for BS and BSDO sequences broken down in terms of response transition categories. Results are shown in Table 3.3. A 2-way ANOVA gave significant main terms for effects of response transitions after the target pair had been separately designated. An additional constraint was that on half the transitions between displays the same set of background letters recurred. In these cases the left-to-right order of background letters was always scrambled.

A 2-way ANOVA gave significant main terms for effects of background items ($F = 7.41$, $df = 3{,}27$, $P < 0.01$) and for background order ($F = 7.2$, $df = 1{,}27$, $P < 0.05$). The interaction between these terms was also significant; ($F = 4.38$, $df = 3{,}27$, $P < 0.05$).

Table 3.3

	Transition between displays			
	T/T	*N/T*	*T/N*	*N/N*
Background items in same order	802 ms (σ 128)	849 ms (σ 132)	1111 ms (σ 190)	1009 ms (σ 183)
Background items in different order	856 ms (σ 124)	898 ms (σ 142)	1042 ms (σ 194)	1093 ms (σ 185)

Table 3.4

	Transition between displays			
	T/T	*N/T*	*T/N*	*N/N*
Background items identical	823 ms (σ 130)	854 ms (σ 130)	1128 ms (σ 201)	1049 ms (σ 918)
Background items different	856 ms (σ 125)	879 ms (σ 138)	1073 ms (σ 197)	1104 ms (σ 199)

The mean RTs from condition 2 sequences were similarly partitioned and are given in Table 3.4.

A 2-way ANOVA gave significant main terms for effects of response transitions; ($F = 8.2$, $df = 3{,}27$, $P < 0.01$), for effects of BSDO vs. BD ($F = 8.9$, $df = 1{,}27$, $P < 0.05$).

It seems, in general, that subjects search through displays faster when the same background items recur, even though they always recur in scrambled left to right positions. There is thus an "item" effect independent of an "order" effect. Also, given that the same background items occur on all displays, subjects seem, for target displays, to search faster when they occur in the same left-to-right serial order than when they occur in scrambled order. There is therefore an "order" effect independent of an "item" effect.

Discussion

There are now three different kinds of transient facilitation effect in the literature in visual search.

(1) Rabbitt, Cumming and Vyas (1977) found that immediate repetition of identical targets at identical display locations produces very fast detection times. They suggested that facilitation occurred because subjects were able to very rapidly compare a memory trace of the physical characteristics of one target against input from the next symbol scanned.

This facilitation disappeared if intervals between successive displays were as long as 2000 ms, or if fixations of background items intervened between successive fixations of identical targets.

(2) Experiments II and III above show that target detection is also facilitated if background items recur on successive displays. This facilitation is certainly mediated by repetition of some physical cues, since recurrence of background items in the same order (BS) facilitates detection more than recurrence of items in a different order (BSDO). On one count this facilitation appears to differ from type 1 but on another the distinction is more ambiguous. Obviously when facilitation is observed on BSDO transitions scanning of several items in succession is involved, and there is no question of refixation of the same item. Also, in the BSDO case, successive displays are

not physically identical (among other characteristics the overall shape of the nonsense-word formed by the display, and the shapes of the spaces between individual letters upon the display have changed).

A second consideration is that even in the BS condition it seems unlikely that facilitation can occur simply because repetition of background letters makes them easier to identify, or because any display matches its predecessor. The subject's task, is not to say whether successive displays are identical or different, but rather to decide whether a target letter is present or not. However the data are ambiguous. If facilitation occurred because successive displays were matched for identity, we might expect faster RTs on T/T and N/N transitions but hardly on T/N or N/T transitions. In fact on BS + BSDO transitions T/T and N/N transitions are always facilitated, T/N transitions also appear to be facilitated, but N/T transitions are slowed in both Experiments II and III. It seems that there may be a mixture of two effects: subjects notice when successive displays match, or partially match, and tend to repeat the same response when they do. This facilitates responses on T/T and N/N transitions but may confuse them on N/T transitions. Facilitation for BSDO displays in general, and facilitation on T/N transitions in particular, suggest another source of facilitation. Displays can be processed faster when a particular set of discriminating cues, necessary to distinguish a particular set of target items from a particular set of background items (Rabbitt, 1967) are repeated on successive displays. That is, facilitation is not due to identification of particular background items but to repetition of displays for which the same set of overall discriminative cues are valid.

(3) If a particular target symbol recurs during one experimental run, even if another display has intervened between its successive appearances, it is detected faster than if it has not occurred for some time (Experiment I). This facilitation is not necessarily mediated by repetition of a particular set of physical features. Rabbitt, Cumming and Vyas (1977) found that detection of a target letter printed in one case facilitated its repeated detection in another, even after a scan of several intervening items.

All these effects are transient, and depend on recurrence of items on successive displays, or on their reappearance within a brief span of displays. When we consider stable facilitation effects which may speed target detection over many hundreds of trials, we naturally cannot expect to find any direct analogue for type 1 effects involving the immediate repetition of identical displays. However type 3 and type 2 transient effects have very close parallels in type i and type ii stable effects described below.

(i) It is a neglected truism that a subject must continue to *remember* an arbitrary set of target items throughout an experimental run. All visual search tasks are thus, at least at first, "memory search tasks". All investigators who have studied visual search must, like the present authors, have noted that early in practice subjects make errors because they persistently fail to detect the presence of particular, identifiable, target set items while efficiently detecting all others. It is probable that they simply forget that particular items are target set members.

Even in very simple two-choice CRT experiments with one-to-one signal-to-response mapping Fitts and Switzer (1962) found that RT was very slow while subjects were still uncertain about the boundaries between the sub-sets of signals which they would actually receive and the total possible ensemble of signals of the same vocabulary which might conceivably occur. In visual search tasks several investigators have found advantages when target and background items come from different learned vocabularies (e.g. letters and digits) rather than when both sets are drawn from the same vocabulary. This has become known as the "category effect" in visual search (Rabbitt, 1962; Brand, 1971; Ingling, 1972). One reason for this effect may simply be that, early in pratice, it is easier for subjects to remember what targets they are looking for if they all belong to the same learned vocabulary and if all background items come from a different set. Of course, it is likely that this is not the only reason for the category effect in visual search, as experiments by Jonides and Gleitman, 1976, and Gleitman and Jonides, 1976, show).

(ii) Subjects who are practised at visual search discover, retain and use highly specific cue-systems which are optimal for discriminations between particular sub-sets of target and background items (Rabbitt, 1967). Such cue-systems may be retained to show display-specific improvements in performance up to 4 weeks later, without any intervening practice (Rabbitt, Cumming and Vyas, 1979). Thus, in their everyday lives, subjects must draw on information in long term storage about very large numbers of different, specific, cue-systems which they can deploy when, and if, particular situations demand them.

There is a direct analogy between such learned cue-systems and those which are evidently involved in type 2 transient facilitation when similarity between background items on successive displays facilitate visual search. In both cases the sub-sets of cues which subjects use discriminate between target and background sets but are not specific to any unique display.

It is interesting that after really extended practice at discriminations between the same target and background sets subjects cease to show negative transfer when they are switched to new tasks in which they search for the same target items among a new background vocabulary. The high level of skill attained with very extended practice does not seem to depend on learning and use of cue systems specific to discriminations between particular target and background items (Rabbitt, Cumming and Vyas, 1979). If, at advanced levels of practice, performance indeed becomes independent of such cue-systems, we must expect that transient facilitation effects of type 2 must also disappear.

A model for transient facilitation (priming) of recognition of one display by exposure to a preceding one has been adapted from a suggestion by Keele (1973), by Posner and Klein (1973) and Posner and Snyder (1975).

"According to this view a familiar input item such as a letter or a word automatically excites internal memory systems (logogens) which represent its physical form, name and semantic content ... The active state will be maintained for some time and will facilitate the coding of any items which share the same pathway ..." (Posner and Snyder (1975), pp. 669–70).

These authors leave us to infer the precise definition of a "pathway", but it seems that they have in mind some specificable unique route through some hypothetical coding network. On this assumption we may extend their analogy to distinguish between the more "peripheral" sections of such pathways which will incorporate structures concerned with the analysis of physical features of sensory input, and the more "central" sections which will incorporate structures concerned with such higher order classifications of input as "name and semantic content".

On this simple model, analysis of one sensory event will affect analysis of a subsequent one in so far as the first activates a particular pathway and the second may re-employ part, or all, of this activated pathway. Identical visual displays will share identical pathways, having both peripheral and central sections in common. If successive displays are not identical, but if discriminations of target from background items require use of the same sub-set of critical cues, the pathway activated by one display may partly, but not completely, overlap with the pathway required by its successor. There will thus be some facilitation. Finally, if successive, or proximate, signals are physically different but have the same names, the peripheral sections of the pathways which they require will not overlap but the central or "name analysing" sections will, and facilitation may be expected.

Posner and Snyder envisage two different ways in which such pathways may be activated. They may be activated by current input as suggested above, or alternatively they may be activated by long term memory: "Activation of a pathway in the memory system facilitates the processing of signals related to it" (Posner and Snyder, 1975; p. 670).

We can thus distinguish two different ways in which pathways may be activated and facilitation of signal processing can occur. It is convenient to think of passive activation of a pathway by appropriate sensory input as "bottom up" or "data input driven" (cf. Norman and Bobrow, 1974). In the same terminology we may consider activation by memory as "top down" or "resource driven". The critical point about "resource driven" or "memory driven" activation is that pathway activation will only be as specific as the information stored in long-term memory allows it to be. Thus, as practice is prolonged, we may expect memory driven activation to be increasingly detailed, and to increasingly involve peripheral as well as central analytic sections of the "pathways".

Conclusions

These experiments thus add to the evidence supporting the passive, "data driven" model for selective attention described by Keele (1973) and its extension to the active (in our terms "memory driven") selective attention models proposed by Posner and Klein (1973) and Posner and Snyder (1975). They suggest a taxonomy of effects which allows us to relate these models to each other, and to use them to explain the effects of practice in visual search tasks. This way of looking at selective attention allows us to comment on three different kinds of effect. First we see how attentional selectivity may be due to activation of more or less central or peripheral perceptual analytic structures. Second we see that if we follow Posner and Snyder (1975) in conceptualising these structures as pathways in a coding network, we may distinguish between activation of these pathways by "top down" (memory driven) processes or by "bottom up" (input driven) processes. While we may distinguish between these different sources of activation in terms of their origins (long term learning vs. transient passive activation) and in terms of their relative persistence (stable vs. transient) the present data emphasise that we have no reason to distinguish between their *effects*. That is, we can suppose that they are mediated through the same structures along the same pathways. In this respect this model, and the experiments which support it, allows some comment on the effects of continued practice in perceptual tasks. We have too long been content with the easy assumption that people improve with practice because they learn to carry out the same kinds of encoding operations faster and more accurately. We can now begin to discuss the striking fact that practice actually allows people to perform particular coding operations in different, and more efficient ways.

References

Bertelson, P. (1965). Serial choice reaction-time as a function of response versus signal and response-repetition. *Nature, London, 206*, 217–18.

Brand, J. (1971). Classification without identification in visual search. *Quarterly Journal of Experimental Psychology, 23*, 178–86.

Fitts, P. M. and Switzer, G. (1962). Cognitive aspects of information processing: I. The familiarity of sets and sub-sets. *Journal of Experimental Psychology, 63*, 321–9.

Gleitman, H. and Jonides, J. (1976). The cost of categorization in visual search: Incomplete processing of target and field items. *Perception and Psychophysics. 20*, 281–8.

Ingling, N. W. (1972). A mechanism for rapid information processing. *Journal of Emperimental Psychology, 94*, 239–43.

Jonides, J. and Gleitman, H. (1976). The benefit of categorisation in visual search: Target location without identification. *Perception and Psychophysics, 20*, 275–81.

Keels, S. W. (1973). *Attention and Human Performance.* Goodyear, Pacific Palisades, California, U.S.A.

Meyer, D. E., Schvaneveldt, R. W. and Ruddy, M. G. (1975). Loci of Contextual Effects on Visual Word-recognition. In Rabbitt, P. M. A. and Dornic, S. (Eds), *Attention and Performance V.* London and New York, Academic Press.

Norman, D. A. and Borrow, D. G. (1974). On data-limited and resource limited processes. CSL 74–2 May 1974, Xerox Palo Alto Research Center, California, U.S.A.

Posner, M. I. and Klein, R. M. (1973). On the functions of consciousness. In Kornblum, S. (Ed.), *Attention and Performance IV.* New York and London: Academic Press.

Posner, M. I. and Snyder, C. R. R. (1975). Facilitation and inhibition in the processing of signals. In Rabbitt, P. M. A. and Dornic, S. (Eds), *Attention and Performance V.* London and New York: Academic Press.

Rabbitt, P. M. A. (1962). Perceptual discrimination and the choice of responses. Unpublished Ph.D. Thesis, University of Cambridge.

Rabbitt, P.M. A. (1967). Ignoring irrelevant information. *American Journal of Psychology, 80,* 1–13.

Rabbitt, P. M. A. (1968). Repetition effects and signal classification strategies in serial choice-response tasks. *Quarterly Journal of Experimental Psychology, 20,* 232–40.

Rabbitt, P. M. A., Cumming, G. D. and Vyas, S. M. (1977). An analysis of visual search: entropy and sequential effects. In Dornic, S.(Ed.), *Attention and Performance VI,* p. 363–386, Potomac, Maryland; Lawrence Erlbaum Associates.

Rabbitt, P. M. A., Cumming, G. D. and Vyas, S. M. (1979). Improvement, learning and retention of skill at visual search. *Quarterly Journal of Experimental Psychology,* In Press.

Sternberg, S. (1975). Memory scanning: new findings and current controversies. *Quarterly Journal of Experimental Psychology, 27,* 1–32.

Theios, J., Smith, P. G., Haviland, S. E., Traupmann, J. and Moy, M. C. (1973). Memory scanning as a serial, self-terminating process. *Journal of Experimental Psychology, 97,* 323–36.

Treisman, A. M. (1969). Strategies and models of selective attention. *Psychological Review, 76,* 282–9.

How repeating particular discriminations, limb movements, spatial directions and coding rules affects speed and retard discriminations between signals and choices between responses

We now knew that repeating particular targets or particular background items speeds their recognition. This raised the further question of how much of this effect reflected the extent to which repeating responses might speed their choice, programming and execution. In addition to the effects of repeating identical signals and responses, CRTs also vary with the complexity of the rules by which responses are mapped on to signals. Even though neither an identical signal nor a response is repeated, does repetition of a mapping rule also speed CRTs? When Bertelson made his first experiment in 1961, experiments on repetitions of responses and mapping rules were impossible for most of us. As in all European psychological laboratories, Paul had no access to equipment that could automatically present long sequences of signals and identify time and record responses to each. He could only infer repetition advantages by measuring how the relative probabilities of repeated and alternated events affect gross mean CRTs during a card-sorting task. When, in 1963, Jim Birren took me on as a temporary research associate in his Section on Aging at NIMH Bethesda, Washington, DC, I entered a new world of possibilities where things were very different. Jim generously gave me first access to the "Psychomet", a signal presentation and response timing device that he had commissioned.

This fine, throbbing, whirring machine, as big as a pub piano, had ten signal lamps mounted in a horizontal row, each above a response touch-plate. The lamps could be programmed to light in any order and the machine recorded each signal, the plate touched to answer it and the time, in centiseconds, that volunteers took to do this. Suddenly I could test whether facilitation occurs, not just when successive signals and responses are identical but also when successive responses require use of the same hand, and movements in the same, rather than the opposite, direction. I programmed the ten signal lamps to light, one at a time, equiprobably, in random order. Volunteers answered each by tapping the response plate immediately below it, using their left hands to answer lamps one to five on the left side of the equipment console and their right hands to answer lamps six to ten on the right. Because signals were equiprobable the probability that successive responses would require different hands ($p = 0.566$) was greater than the probability that they would require the same hand ($p = 0.444$). Nevertheless, volunteers made successive responses with the same hand faster than with the other, even when successive responses required different patterns of muscle action because they involved reversal of the direction of the immediately previous movement. Continuations of directions of movement were faster than reversals. Responses were facilitated either by immediate re-use of the same limb or by attention to the area of space within which it had to be moved or by the direction of travel of a previous movement. (Rabbitt, 1965). Response repetition effects and movement repetition effects were shown to be complex, relating to limb, direction of movement, and to the area of space in which the movement is made. Response repetition effects are, also, distinct from, and additional to, signal repetition effects. The next question was to find ways to disentangle at least some of these various kinds of response-repetition effects.

Not all choices between limbs are equally easy. In his 1963 Ph.D. thesis, Ken Blyth had found that people take longer to respond to each of two digits when they must choose between responses made with either hand or either foot than when they choose between responses made with either a hand or a foot. This prompted me to ask whether choices and transitions between responses are affected not only by choices between classes of responding limbs but also by left/right laterality differences that are known to be a critical issue in programming limb movements. Returning to the Cambridge APRU, after much unseemly and annoying bragging of the advantages of US laboratories, I was generously provided with a purpose-built "Stimulus Presentation and Response Timing Apparatus" (SPARTA) that could do nearly all that the "Psychomet" could – with the slight, initial drawback that output could not be analyzed by computer and required patient transcription of logs of hundreds of responses. I asked volunteers to use their hands and feet to respond to each of four different digits presented in the centres of their visual fields. They responded fastest when they made successive responses with the same limb but were also faster when they used a contralateral limb of the same kind – left hand after right hand or vice versa – than when they used a different contralateral limb, e.g. left foot after right hand or left hand after right foot. The slowest transitions were between responses with different ipsilateral limbs, e.g. right hand following right foot or left foot following left hand. There was "limb-type facilitation" but, when choosing between different kinds of limbs, no evidence for "body-side" facilitation (Rabbitt, 1965).

In everyday life, transitions between successive responses confound different factors: partially or exactly repeating the same commands, and so also muscle movements, to shift and direct a limb and repeating or alternating attention to the left or right visual and haptic fields within which the movement must be made. The next paper reproduced describes a try at distinguishing facilitation due to repetition of movements of a given limb from the effects of repeated attention to the same areas of space defined by our preferred and non-preferred limbs. It also tested whether facilitation was affected by laterality preferences.

References

Blyth, K.W. (1963). Experiments on choice reaction time with hands and feet in combination. Ph.D. thesis, University of Cambridge.

Rabbitt, P. (1965). Response facilitation on repetition of a limb movement. *British Journal of Psychology*, *56*(2–3), 303–304.

4 Hand dominance, attention and the choice between responses

P.M.A. Rabbitt

Introduction

The etymology of the word "dexterous" emphasises the common observation that most human beings make complex movements more adeptly with one hand (usually the right) than the other. For example Wyke (1967) found that a control group of normal subjects made gross single-arm movements faster with their dominant (right) limbs than with their non-dominant (left) limbs. She also found that pursuit-tracking performance was faster and more accurate for dominant rather than non-dominant hands (Wyke, 1968). It therefore, at first, seems surprising that there is evidence that in conventional laboratory choice-reaction-time tasks (CRT tasks) responses are made equally fast with either hand (Benton and Toyut, 1959; Dimond, 1970).

This is probably because in typical CRT experiments very short and simple movements are made to simple and easily discriminable signals. When, in such tasks, marked differences in RT have been observed between hands the probable explanation lies in the fact that the signals presented require the use of coding processes which may have unique representation in one or the other cerebral hemisphere. For example words or familiar letters of the alphabet are alleged to require left-hemisphere processing, while complex patterns may have to be processed by the right hemisphere. In such cases RT differences between hands have been argued to be due to the common or separate locus of perceptual processing and of response control in the same or in different hemispheres (e.g. by Davis and Schmit, 1971, 1973).

A quite different question about the relationship between hand dominance and time for choice of responses arises if we consider how people may go about choosing which hand to use during a task in which they may use either to respond to each discrete event in turn. Although people usually have two hands they very commonly only use one of them at a time to indicate or to touch objects within their reach. On such occasions it is possible to ask whether choices between hands are resolved faster in favour of the dominant than of the non-dominant limb.

To explore the implications of this question in abstract terms it is useful to think how a machine might be programmed to use either of two effectors to reach for objects in real space. Let us only consider decisions involving a choice between effectors. Such choices would have to be made before movements with the appropriate effector were begun. A programme of instructions to guide such choices would have to operate on a series of tests and answers to tests. One such programme, which displayed a consistent "effector dominance", might run as follows:

Programme A	
Instruction number	*Content of instruction*
Step 1	Is object in range of effector L? If Yes, go to step 3 If No, go to step 2
Step 2	Is object in range of effector R? If Yes, go to step 4 If No, go to step 1
Step 3	Begin sub-routine to extend effector L towards object
Step 4	Begin sub-routines to extend effector R towards object

A machine controlled by such an hypothetical sequence of instructions would show "effector L dominance" in the limited sense that each new sequence of tests would always begin with a test for the field of effector L. Thus if all tests and programme steps took a finite time to execute, reaches with effector L would always be initiated slightly faster than reaches with effector R.

This would be quite a sensible way to programme a system, since it would solve the problem of re-entry into the test routine by a determined choice in favour of one receptor rather than another on each occasion when a decision had to be made. Over all decisions the machine would operate at least at a chance level of optimisation. That is, on 50% of trials the testing routine would be carried out as fast as it possibly could be, and effector movement would begin with minimal delay. No such programme could do better than chance unless the machine operated in a predictable universe in which more events occurred in one effector field than in the other. In this case one adaptive emendation would be to begin testing with the field in which events most commonly occurred. The "effector dominance" would reflect this circumstance.

However, even in a universe in which, over all possible trials, events were equally probable in either effector field, there might be changes in conditional probability which a better programme might use in order to optimize decision speed. For example it might be the case that an event in one effector field was usually followed by another event in the same field. One possible extension of Programme A could use this regularity in the following way:

Programme B	
Instruction number	*Content of instruction*
Step 1	Is object in range of effector L? If Yes, go to step 3 If No, go to step 2
Step 2	Is object in range of effector R? If Yes, go to step 5 If No, go to step 1
Step 3	Begin sub-routine to extend effector L and proceed to next step in sequence
Step 4	Complete reach for object Go to step 1 for test of next object
Step 5	Begin sub-routine to use effector R and proceed to next step in sequence
Step 6	Complete reach for object with effector R Go to step 2 to test for next object

A machine controlled by such a programme would show no consistent "effector dominance". Instead it would have the characteristic, adaptive under the appropriate circumstances, of initiating reaches faster when successive events required use of the same effector than when they required different effectors. Instead of showing "effector dominance" or "effector bias" it would show an "effector repetition effect".

If we consider what is known about response choices made by human beings in relation to these heuristic devices a number of empirical questions occur: First we are prompted to ask whether human beings indeed take longer to initiate a response when they have to decide which hand to use than when all responses must be made with the same hand. In the light of Programme A we may further ask whether all choices between hands are resolved faster in favour of one hand than in favour of the other. In other words whether hand dominance may be reflected in the times taken to choose between movements with the dominant and the non-dominant hands.

It is known that people respond faster when they make successive different, movements with the same hand than when they make successive movements with each hand in turn (Rabbitt, 1965). Programme B provides one possible description of a system which would have this characteristic. However Programme B uses the same device to achieve this end (order of testing of effector fields) as Programme A uses to achieve "effector dominance". Thus Programme B does not show "effector dominance", but only shows an "effector repetition effect". In terms of human performance, therefore, we may ask whether choices of successive responses are resolved always in favour of the dominant hand (Programme A scheme), whether they are resolved always in favour of the hand last used (Programme B scheme) or whether the known "response repetition effect" is weighted in favour of the dominant hand. In this case the finding would be that even when successive responses are made with the same hand, responses with the dominant hand are still made faster than responses with the non-dominant hand. This last finding could not be described by either Programme A or Programme B. It might mean that we could not explain facilitation of response choices by hand dominance and facilitation of response choices by the movement repetition effect in terms of the same mechanism.

Experiment

Apparatus and method

A Yellow Springs Instrument Company "Psychomet" testing apparatus automatically controlled the experiment. Subjects sat at the centre of a console 762 cm long and 25.4 cm high. This sloped away from them at an angle of 25° to the vertical. A line of 10 signal bulbs was inset in an horizontal line across the upper half of this console, each behind a 2.54 cm diameter circular aperture covered with translucent plastic. Apertures were 2.54 cm apart and were on each side of the console midline. A 2.54 cm square contact grid was set 10.16 cm vertically beneath each signal light. Subjects responded to the onset of any light by touching the contact grid directly beneath it with the fore-finger of one hand. When the correct contact grid was touched the signal lamp currently lit was switched off and a new lamp was switched on within 10 ms. When an incorrect contact grid was touched the signal did not change. The Psychomet identified and recorded all touches on contact grids, whether correct or incorrect, and recorded the interval between each signal onset and the next response, after timing it to within 10 ms.

Sequences of events were determined by punched-tape programmes. Six different sequences of 300 successive signals were programmed so that in each the 10 signal lamps were lit one at a time equally often in random order. All transitions between signals were equally frequent and no signal was ever immediately repeated (because such events could not be distinguished by subjects from failures of signals to change after errors had been made). Subjects responded to these sequence of signals under three conditions of experimental instruction. They answered signals, using their left hands only, using their right hands only or with either hand, choosing the left hand to answer any of the five signal lights on the left and their right hand to answer any of the five signals on the right of their body midlines and so of the midline of the console. The order of conditions was balanced across subjects to avoid systematic practice effects.

Subjects

An advertisement circulated as an "Internal Staff Memorandum" around the National Institutes of Health, Bethesda, Maryland, U.S.A., allowed recruitment of 18 left-handed female and 12 left-handed male volunteers aged from 18 to 34 years. These were a sub-set of a larger number of left-handed respondents from amongst whom they were selected on the criterion that they answered *all* questions in a questionnaire prepared by Oldfield as "left-handers". The questions asked were those later incorporated into the questionnaire, the design and validation of which are described by Oldfield (1971). These left-handed subjects were individually matched as closely as possible for age, sex and occupational status within N.I.H. (i.e, "secretary", "research worker", "technician", "nurse", "doctor", etc.) with members of a group of 30 right-handed people, 18 women and 12 men, who had answered *all* the questions as "right-handers".

Results

One class of errors was unique in the two-hand condition. These errors were contraventions of experimental instructions by subjects who, having correctly responded to a signal on one side of the console, would very occasionally respond to a sequent signal on the opposite side by touching the appropriate response grid with the same hand rather than by alternating hands as they were asked to do. Since the machine could only record touches on response grids, and could not record which hand was used to make them, the incidence of such errors could only be estimated by experimenters' observation. A count kept of such failures to obey instructions suggested a frequency of not more than 0.3%. There was no way of identifying such responses in machine output to check RTs for such events. The point to be extracted seems to be that subjects have a marked tendency to make successive responses with the same hand even when they are asked not to do so.

The errors which the machine could record (i.e. touches on inappropriate response grids) were identified by an off-line computer data sort. These amounted to 1.6% of all responses. On further examination all such errors occurred because the response grid immediately adjacent to the appropriate grid had been touched by mistake. Incidence did not differ between groups or between conditions. All errors, and the first correct response following each error, were excluded from further analysis. The remaining correct responses were sorted to obtain each subject's mean RTs for each of the 90 possible transitions between successive responses in each task. (N.B. repetitions of the same signal never occurred so that for each response, N, there were 10 possible previous positions, N - 1 x 9 possible current positions, N.)

This partitioning of data was necessary because the one-hand tasks involved some long hand movements across the console, while in the two-hand task the same transitions between signals on opposite sides of the console were answered by movements of alternate hands. Thus comparisons between overall mean RTs for each of the three conditions were not informative since these long, and relatively slow, reaches affected mean RTs in two conditions but not in the third. The only possible direct comparison was between identical sub-sets of response transitions within each task. That is, the only sub-sets of responses which could be validly compared were cases of repeated hand movements in the two-hand task and identical movements between the five left hand and the five right hand keys made respectively in the left-hand and in the right-hand tasks. Means of individual subjects' mean RTs computed for three sub-sets of transitions are given in Table 4.1.

A three-way mixed design Between-Within-Within subjects Analysis of Variance (ANOVA) was made across individual subjects mean RTs contributing to Table 4.1. The main term for differences between groups was not significant ($F = 2.30$, $df = 1{,}58$, $P > 0.05$) nor was the overall term for Right hand vs. Left hand ($F = 3.79$, $df = 1{,}58$, $P > 0.05$). However the third main term for differences between one-hand and two-hand tasks was significant ($F = 12.46$, $df = 1{,}58$, $P < 0.01$). None of the interaction terms was significant (in all cases $F < 1$, $p > 0.05$).

We see from Table 4.1 that this means that RTs for these particular transitions between responses were slower when subjects had to choose which hand to use on each trial than in either of the two conditions in which the same hand was used throughout. There was no overall RT difference between left-handed and right-handed subjects when this sub-set of response transitions was examined. Nor was there any apparent effect of hand-dominance on the magnitude of the RT difference between one-handed and two-handed tasks. The apparent interaction between hand dominance and hand choice in the two-hand task was not significant on this gross analysis.

This partial sampling of data deliberately excluded transitions between successive responses which required long reaches between small contact switches. It is precisely these long reaches, however, which might show differences in fine control of responses with dominant and non-dominant bands such as were found by Wyke (1968). To check for possible differences in dexterity, overall mean RTs were computed for all responses in the one-hand tasks. These are given in Table 4.2.

A two-way Between-Within ANOVA gave no significant main effect of hand employed ($F = 3.41$, $df = 1{,}58$, $P > 0.05$) or of hand dominance ($F = 2.44$, $df = 1{,}58$, $P > 0.05$). There was no significant interaction ($F = 1.42$, $df = 1{,}58$, $P > 0.05$). Thus when only one hand was used to make all responses both groups of subjects were equally fast with either hand, and both left and

Table 4.1 Times for precisely comparable reaches made with either hand in a single hand task, and for repeated movements with the same limb in a two-hand task. Means of individual mean RTs for groups of 30 left-handed and right-handed subjects

	Left hand in one-hand tasks	*Right hand in one-hand tasks*	*Left hand in two-hand task*	*Right hand in two-hand task*
Left-handed subjects	437 ms ($\sigma = 43$)	434 ms ($\sigma = 41$)	474 ms ($\sigma = 48$)	496 ms ($\sigma = 52$)
Right-handed subjects	441 ms ($\sigma = 38$)	449 ms ($\sigma = 36$)	486 ms ($\sigma = 51$)	466 ms ($\sigma = 61$)

Table 4.2 Times for all reaches made using the left and right hands alone in turn, single limb tasks. Means of individual mean RTs for 30 left-handed and 30 right-handed subjects

	Left-hand task	*Right-hand task*
Left-handed subjects	493 ms (σ = 64)	489 ms (σ = 71)
Right-handed subjects	502 ms (σ = 74)	497 ms (σ = 81)

Table 4.3 Comparison between times for successive movements with the same hand and for successive movements with different hands made in the two-hand task. Means of individual mean RTs for 30 left-handed and 30 right-handed subjects

		Successive movements with same hand	*Difference between dominant and non-dominant hands*	*Successive movements with different hands*	*Difference between dominant and non-dominant hands*
Left-handed subjects	Left hand (dominant)	474 ms (σ = 48)	22 ms	548 ms (σ = 67)	23 ms
	Right hand (non-dominant)	496 ms (σ = 52)		571 ms (σ = 72)	
Right-handed subjects	Left hand (non-dominant)	486 ms (σ = 51)	20 ms	555 ms (σ = 64)	23 ms
	Right hand (dominant)	466 ms (σ = 61)		532 ms (σ = 67)	

right handers were as fast as each other. Some reasons for this apparent failure to replicate Wyke's (1968) findings are discussed below.

There remained the question whether hand dominance might show an effect when, in the two-hand task, subjects had to decide on every trial which hand to use to answer the signal presented to them.

Data for the two-hand task were sorted out to separate mean RTs for successive movements with the same hand (mean RTs as given in Table 4.1) or with alternate hands. These mean RTs were further broken down to separate RTs with left and with right hands (i.e. dominant and non-dominant hands in each group). Means of individual subject's mean RTs are given in Table 4.3.

A three-way Between-Within-Within subjects ANOVA gave a significant main term for differences between movements with repeated and with alternate hands (F = 10.41, df = 1,58, $P < 0.01$). The main term for differences between dominant and non-dominant hands was also significant (F = 6.62, df = 1,58, $P < 0.05$).

The main term for differences between right-handed and left-handed groups was not significant (F = 3.04, df = 1,58, $P > 0.05$). No interaction term was significant ($F < 1.5$ in all cases).

As we see from Table 4.3, when subjects had to choose between hands they responded faster with their dominant than with their non-dominant hands. As Rabbitt (1965) earlier found subjects responded faster when they made successive responses with the same hands. A critical point is that, in the present experiment, this "response repetition effect" did not interact with the "hand dominance effect". That is, the difference in RTs between dominant and non-dominant hands remained the same whether successive responses were made with the same hand or with different hands. As far as this analysis allows us to comment, these two effects were independent of each other rather than interactive. There was, again, no overall difference in the mean RTs of left-handed and right-handed subjects, nor did subject handedness affect the magnitude of any of the other effects observed.

Discussion

When subjects used the same hand to make all responses throughout a task they responded equally fast with either hand. In this respect, Wyke's (1967, 1968) results were not replicated. Probable explanations are that the contact switches used in this experiment were larger than the response plates she employed (Wyke, 1967), that most of the reaches necessary were shorter than those her subjects made, and that subjects in this experiment received more practice than those she tested. It is also possible that hand dominance effects appear in tasks demanding precise continuous control of fine movements, but not in tasks, such as the present one, in which most reaches required coarse, rapidly executed ballistic movements.

When subjects had to choose which hand to use on each trial they all took longer than when no such choice was necessary. Thus the first new finding in this experiment was that a choice between hands requires a finite time. When choices had to be made between hands, both left- and right-handed subjects responded faster with their dominant than with their non-dominant hands. There was therefore an effect of hand-dominance on time for motor choice under conditions in which no effects of hand dominance on speed or accuracy of motor control were apparent. This suggests that the effects of hand dominance on processes governing motor control need not necessarily be discussed in terms of the same mechanisms as those postulated to govern choices between responding limbs.

As Rabbitt (1965) found, subjects who had to use both hands during a task responded faster when they used the same hand to make successive, different responses than when they made successive responses with different hands. However the effects of hand dominance upon time for response did not disappear when successive responses were repeated. The RT difference between dominant and non-dominant hands remained approximately the same whether limb repetitions or limb alternations were considered. This suggests that factors which lead to RT reduction for dominant hand movements in response choice may be different from factors which lead to RT reduction when the same limb is immediately re-employed.

As an heuristic device to discover what kinds of models may be useful in interpreting these data, we may consider again hypothetical sequences of instructions which might simulate these effects in machines.

Programme A would simulate the dominant hand advantage in RT on choices between hands. However, as it stands, it is a rigid programme and would produce a dominant hand advantage even when a single hand was used on all trials. This was not found. It would fail to simulate the limb repetition effect.

Programme B would not simulate a dominant hand advantage on response choice. However it would simulate the finding that both hands were equally fast when used alone. It was constructed to simulate the limb repetition effect.

Note that neither programme sequence has anything to say about factors which might affect the efficiency of *control* of one effector relative to the other. Such differences might be inherent in the structure of particular machines, or in the structure of the programmes used to govern them. These differences would operate at some stage after selection of an appropriate effector had been made. This logical distinction emphasizes the empirical distinction in the present data between effects of hand dominance upon time for hand choice (which appear to be present) and effects of hand dominance upon times for movement control (which were absent in this experiment, but which were found by Wyke, 1967, 1968).

Both these programmes use the same device to simulate the particular effects with which they are concerned. This device lies in the assumption that before a choice between limbs is made the fields of deployment of the two effectors are interrogated, *one at a time and successively* to determine which is appropriate. The exercise in simulation is useful because it focuses attention on a particular difficulty in description: we may use this assumption to explain either a permanent advantage for one effector of a pair, or a transient advantage for the effector most recently deployed. But the mechanism of independent serial interrogation of effector fields carries within it a rigidity that prevents any system which employs it from simulating both advantages at once.

In terms of human performance models for the present data we also cannot have things both ways. We cannot explain both the effects of hand dominance on response choice, and the limb repetition effect in terms of the single assumption that attentional bias is permanently, or transiently, directed towards the field of operation of one limb or the other.

A let-out, either for machine simulation programmes or for human performance models, is that these two kinds of facilitation may be related to separate stages in response selection and execution. That is, we may assume that effector dominance affects response choice, and that effector repetition affects response execution, but not *vice versa*. In this case Programme A would simulate the data with the additional postulate that the execution of any particular response proceeds faster if the same response execution sub-routine has been used on the last trial. Definition of entry to response execution routines may be programmed in terms similar to those used to describe entry to response *choice* routines in Programme B. It is important to note that the converse modification of Programme B would not achieve the same end. If we postulate a permanent advantage in response *execution* for one effector over the other, Programme B can simulate both the effector repetition effect and a "dominant effector" advantage when choices are made between effectors. However responses would still be *executed* faster with one effector than with the other even when no choices had to be made between responding effectors, and the same effector was used on all trials. In other words, this modification of Programme B would simulate a "dominant limb advantage" of a kind which did not appear in this experiment.

Scrutiny of our data in terms of machine simulation models therefore raises some useful points for analysis. It is necessary to suppose that reductions in RT due to permanent or transitory biases in order of entry to effector execution sub-routines are independent of, and additive to, reductions in RT due to permanent or transitory biases in order of entry to *response selection* sub-routines. Our conclusions for future human performance models may, consequently, be stated as follows.

When simple reaches are made to large contact plates, hand dominance does not seem to affect the speed of response execution, since when only one hand was used throughout the task there was no effect of "handedness" in either group. It seems that hand dominance only affects limb or effector selection, because the effects of that hand dominance only appear when choices have to be made between effectors. The further conclusion that effector repetition facilitates response execution rather than response selection is also justified by data. In the two-hand task hand repetition reduced RT by the same amount for both dominant and non-dominant hands. If hand repetition had affected the time taken for response selection this could not be the case.

The data thus raise the possibility that hand-dominance can, at least in some circumstances, be described in terms of the operation of an attentional bias to one effector field rather than another. In appropriate tasks the effects of such attentional bias can be shown to be distinct from other effects (such as the hand repetition effect described by Rabbitt, 1965) which appear to concern the *execution* rather than the selection of responses.

References

Benton, A. L. and Toyut, R. J. (1959), Reaction time in unilateral cerebral disease. *Contemporary Neurology, 19*, 247–56.

Davis, R. and Schmit, V. (1971). Timing the transfer of information between hemipheres in man. *Acta Psychologica, 35*, 335–46.

Davis, R. and Schmit, V. (1973). Visual and verbal coding in the interhemispheric transfer of information. *Acta Psychologica, 37*, 219–40.

Dimond, S. J. (1970). Hemisphere refractoriness and the control of reaction time. *Quarterly Journal of Experimental Psychology, 24*, 610–17.

Oldfield, R. C. (1971). The assessment and analysis of handedness: The Edinburgh Inventory. *Neuropsychologia, 9*, 97–113.

Rabbitt, P. M. A. (1965). Response facilitation on repetition of a limb movement. British *Journal of Psychology*, *56*, 303–04.

Wyke, M. (1967). Effect of brain lesion on the rapidity of arm movement. *Neurology*, *17*, 1113–20.

Wyke, M. (1968) The effects of brain lesion in the performance of an arm-hand precision task. *Neuropsychologia*, *6*, 125–34.

Choosing between dominant and non-dominant limbs

Rabbitt's (1978) findings suggest that we can distinguish between two hypothetical programmes of instructions that the brain might follow when selecting, programming and executing movements. They also, incidentally, confirm that repetition effects are excellent tools to identify and study facilitation associated with attention to signals and to responses. The opportunities that this methodology offers have not yet been sufficiently exploited. For example, we do not yet know whether facilitation due to signal repetition and to response production are separate and additive or interact in some more complicated way. For example, if signal repetition facilitation is independent of response repetition facilitation, the functional processes involved in anticipating and recognizing signals and of choosing and making responses to them may be separate, and sequential. If signal and response repetition effects interact, the processes of identifying signals and choosing responses to them must have elements in common and overlap in time.

Another question was whether, besides repetitions of individual signals and the responses made to them, RTs on any trial are affected by immediate repetitions or changes of the rules by which signals are mapped on to responses. In other words, whether RTs may be facilitated if the same learned, arbitrary associations, or rules by which signals are mapped on to responses, are immediately re-used. One way to test this is to vary the left-to-right spatial compatibility of signals to responses. Duncan (1977) explored this with a task in which volunteers answered members of a horizontal row of ten signal lamps by pressing a different one of ten keys set under the thumbs and fingers of both hands. Half of the lamps were answered by keys directly beneath them (spatially compatible left-to-right mapping) and the others by keys that did not spatially correspond (incompatible mapping). RTs were faster when successive signals required the same mapping rule, even though neither an individual signal or response was repeated. Rabbitt, Vyas and Fearnley (1975) found similar facilitation with repetition of mapping rules in a more complex task in which volunteers answered letters and digits by simultaneously depressing keys with different patterns of fingers of one or both hands.

It was also becoming clear that "immediate repetition effects" are only a subset of "recency effects". Investigators began to analyze the time taken to identify an item not only in relation to an immediately preceding event but to others that had occurred much earlier during a long series and found facilitation by remote as well as immediate context (e.g. Falmagne, 1965; Kornblum, 1973; Falmagne, Cohen & Dwivedi, 1975; Smith, Chase & Smith, 1973; Kirby, 1976). Perhaps the most interesting exploration was by Monsell (1978), who showed that the CRT to a signal on any trial of a continuous series varies inversely with the number of intervening trials X, since it last appeared. Speed of signal identification is affected by persisting traces of their previous occurrences but these apparently become less accessible with X, lapse of time and accumulation of intervening events. This raised a further question: whether the speed of a response to a signal on any trial is not only affected by memory for earlier occurrences of the same signal but is also affected by memories of patterns of sequences of previous signals and responses. Remington (1969) and Kirby (1976) showed that this is indeed the case and that differences in patterns of five previous signal and response repetitions and alternations significantly affect trial-to-trial variations in RTs.

To explore the effects of repetitions and disjunctions of signals, responses and rules relating responses to signals, Subhash Vyas and I used a continuous serial task during which our volunteers made Posner and Mitchell's (1967) "Same/Different" classification decisions. This allowed us to track the effects of signal repetitions, response decision rule repetitions and alternation effects over sequences of up to two successive decisions.

References

Duncan, J. (1977). Response selection rules in spatial choice reaction tasks. In S. Dornic (Ed.), *Attention and Performance VI* (pp. 49–71). Hillsdale, NJ: Lawrence Erlbaum Associates.

Falmagne, J. C. (1965). Stochastic models for choice reaction time with applications to experimental results. *Journal of Mathematical Psychology*, *2*(1), 77–124.

Falmagne, J. C., Cohen, S. P., & Dwivedi, A. (1975). Two-choice reactions as an ordered memory scanning process. In P.M.A. Rabbitt & S. Dornic (Eds), *Attention and Performance V* (pp. 296–344). London: Academic Press.

Kirby, N. H. (1976). Sequential effects in two-choice reaction time: Automatic facilitation or subjective expectancy? *Journal of Experimental Psychology: Human perception and performance*, *2*(4), 567.

Kornblum, S. (1973). Sequential effects in choice reaction time: A tutorial review. In S. Kornblum (Ed.), *Attention and Performance IV* (pp. 259–288). London: Academic Press.

Monsell, S. (1978). Recency, immediate recognition memory, and reaction time. *Cognitive Psychology*, *10*(4), 465–501.

Posner, M. I., & Mitchell, R. F. (1967). Chronometric analysis of classification. *Psychological Review*, *74*(5), 392.

Rabbitt, P.M.A (1978). Hand dominance, attention and the choice between responses. *Quarterly Journal of Experimental Psychology*, *30*(3), 407–416.

Rabbitt, P.M.A., Vyas, S. M., & Fearnley, S. (1975). Programming sequences of complex responses. In P.M.A. Rabbitt & S. Dornic (Eds), *Attention and Performance V* (pp. 395–417). London: Academic Press.

Remington, R. J. (1969). Analysis of sequential effects on choice reaction times. *Journal of Experimental Psychology*, *82*(2), 250.

Smith, E. E., Chase, W. G., & Smith, P. G. (1973). Stimulus and response repetition effects in retrieval from short-term memory: Trace decay and memory search. *Journal of Experimental Psychology*, *98*(2), 413.

5 Interference between binary classification judgments and some repetition effects in a serial choice reaction time task

P.M.A. Rabbitt and S.M. Vyas

A very common finding in choice reaction time (CRT) experiments with human *S*s is that *S*s respond faster when a particular signal is repeated on immediately successive trials than when a new signal occurs. This is known as the repetition effect. The relative magnitudes of repetition effects obtained under different experimental conditions are usually compared by obtaining the difference scores of reaction time (RT) to new signals and RT to repeated signals (Bertelson, 1961, 1963; Kornblum, 1969; Rabbitt, 1968).

Bertelson (1963) was the first to suggest that *S*s in a self-paced serial CRT task compare the percept of each signal presented with their memory traces of the preceding signal. Bertelson assumed that if a match occurred, that is, if the current signal *n* was the same as the previous signal *n* - 1, S could make a relatively fast response because he did not have to further process signal *n* to determine which of a possible set of signals it might be. However if signal n and the memory trace of signal *n* − 1 were found to be different, more extended perceptual analysis would be necessary and identification of the new signal would take longer.

Bindra, Williams, and Wise (1965) do not quote Bertelson but arrive at the same hypothesis from different arguments. Williams (1966) described a series of experiments which were unusual because RTs to repeated signals were found to be considerably longer than RTs to new signals. Bindra et al. (1965) explain this by the assumption that serial CRT tasks are special cases of binary classification tasks in which *S*s have to make one response if successive signals are the same and another if they are different. They found that in such binary classification tasks if pairs of signals are easy to discriminate, RT *same* < RT *different*. However, if signals are difficult to discriminate, RT *different* < RT *same*. On this premise they explain Williams' results by the hypothesis that if the interval between the response to one signal in a series and the moment of onset of the next signal is very long (RS interval), *S's* memory trace of signal *n* - 1 has decayed at the moment when he compares it to signal *n*. Because the comparison between a decayed trace and a new signal might constitute a relatively difficult discrimination, Bindra et al. (1965) supposed that in this case RT *different*< RT *same*, so that RTs to new signals might be expected to be shorter than RTs to repeated signals.

This line of argument was pursued in a subsequent paper (Bindra, Donderi, & Nishisato, 1968). While the experiments described are ingenious and suggest that the magnitude of the repetition effect in CRT tasks does vary inversely with the duration of the RS interval, they do not replicate Williams' (1966) results nor provide adequate support for the Bindra et al. (1965) argument. A further difficulty is raised by a study by Smith (1968). Using RS intervals as long as 15 sec., that is, equal to the longest intervals used by Williams, she found that the repetition effect was reduced, but still present.

The hypothesis that the repetition effect is a special case of a binary classification effect is therefore only weakly supported by indirect evidence. The most direct test would appear to be a serial CRT task in which *S* is required to respond to each signal in succession, making one response if it is the same as its predecessor and another response if it is not. Williams (1966, Experiment IV) describes such a task, presenting her data so that mean RTs for the second of all possible pairs of successive responses can be compared. Four kinds of transition between successive responses were possible. The response *same* can follow the response *same* (SS) the response *same* can follow the response *different* (DS); the response *different* can follow the response *same* (SD) and the response *different* can follow the response *different* (DD). Williams obtained the rank-order: SD (562 msec.) = SS (576 msec.) < DS (686 msec.) < DD (773 msec.).

This obviously does not fit the Bindra et al. (1965) hypothesis in any possible variation. Williams (1966) used relatively long RS intervals. Thus on the assumption that poor memory traces made discriminations difficult, we might expect RT DD or RT SD< RT SS or RT DS. On the alternative possibility that Williams used highly discriminable signals and that her RS intervals were not long enough to produce substantial trace decay, we might predict that RT DS < RT SD or RT DD.

Since this is an unexpected and somewhat cryptic result, it may be questioned whether it was due to some idiosyncracy in Williams' (1966) experimental procedure. In particular, she used a discrete task with relatively long RS intervals, the display/control arrangements of her apparatus were unusual, RS intervals were interrupted by warning signals, and the signals she used were complex and perhaps difficult for her relatively unpracticed *Ss* to code. Accordingly, her experiment was repeated using a self-paced task with very short RS intervals, very simple display/control assignments, very simple, familiar, and easily discriminable signals, and highly practiced *Ss*.

Experiment I

Method

An automatic stimulus-presenting and reaction timing apparatus (Medical Research Council Sparta) was programmed to present random sequences of 501 signals, 1 at a time, in a self-paced mode. Signals were equiprobable and each was the onset of the digit 4 or the digit 6 on a "Digitron" S-10 numerical in-line display. After automatic presentation of the first signal *S* pressed a switch that changed the display to the next signal and so began the experimental sequences. From this moment *S* was required to respond by pressing a key with one forefinger if the displayed digit was the same as its predecessor and a key beneath his other forefinger if it was different. The *RS* interval was constant at 50 msec. throughout a run. Sparta automatically recorded on punched tape each signal presented, the response made to it, and the elapsed time between signal presentation and response (RT). *S*s experienced four runs of 500 successive responses each; that is, they each made a total of 2,000 responses during two experimental sessions on successive days.

Subjects. Six students, ages 18–20 yr., were recruited from Oxford Polytechnic. None had any knowledge of the purpose of the experiment and all were paid for their time.

Results

Only the last 1,000 responses made by each *S* were analyzed. Errors averaged 4.8%. There were no reliable differences in error incidence between response classes. All errors and the responses immediately following errors were discarded in computing mean CRTs.

The four possible classes of transition between successive responses, i.e., SS, DS, SD, and DD transitions, were partialled out by post hoc computer data sort. Mean RTs were obtained across *S*s and were rounded off to three significant figures, although Sparta's time resolution was only .01 sec. These data are set out in Table 5.1.

An analysis of variance (ANOVA) was made on the mean RTs for each group. The terms for=difference between transition classes ($p < .01$) and for difference between *S*s ($P < 0.5$) were significant. The interaction term was not. The error term from the ANOVA was used to calculate the range statistic S^2 to further examine differences between transition classes. The following rank - order emerged:

$$\text{RT SS} \overset{**}{<} \text{RT SD} \overset{*}{<} \text{RT DS} \overset{**}{<} \text{RT DD}$$

$^{**}p <. 01$.
$^{*}p <.05$.

Table 5.1 Mean reaction times (RTs) on a serial binary classification task pooled over six *S*s

Response transition type	*Mean RT (in msec.)*	Σ
SS	348	49
DS	457	56
SD	403	53
DD	582	71

Note: Abbreviations: SS = *same/same*. DS = *different/same*, SD = *same/different*, DD = *different/different*.

Discussion

William's (1966) results were mainly replicated. Her rank-ordering for transitions was:

$$SD = 562 \text{ msec.} = SS = 576 \text{ msec.} < DS = 686 \text{ msec.} < DD = 773 \text{ msec.}$$

The rank order obtained in the present experiment was:

$$SS < SD < DS < DD.$$

The difference to be explained, therefore, 'is that Williams found no significant difference between RT SS and RT SD, while we found RT SS < RT SD ($p < .01$).

It is likely that this discrepancy can be related to a particular feature of Williams' (1966) experiments. In all of her experiments Williams found that RT for repeated events was greater than RT for alternated events (i.e., for new signals). She used very long intertrial intervals (ITIs) of approximately 6 sec., which were presumably irregular because she employed them to record RTs and to reset her apparatus. This is not a sufficient explanation in itself, since Smith (1968) used even longer, though regular, ITTs, obtaining a repetition effect even with ITI lags of 15 sec. However, Williams employed a warning signal before each trial. A minor pilot experiment by the present authors replicated Williams' experiments with and without a warning signal. With a warning signal Alternative RT < Repetitive RT. Without a warning signal Repetitive RT < Alternative RT. It thus appears that although no information is conveyed by the warning signal, it serves to break *S*'s set in some way, such that he begins to behave in a way consistent with a demonstration of the "gambler's fallacy" in prediction of random binary events.

The discrepancy between the results of Williams' (1966) Experiment IV and those of Experiment I in the present study is, in any case, minor and not important to the general conclusion. If it is the case that *S*s in serial CRT tasks proceed by comparing on each trial each signal against its immediate predecessor, we would expect that the results of Williams' Experiment IV and of our Experiment I should be predictable from the literature on repetition effects. As we have seen it is clear that they are not.

Any explanation for Williams' (1966) Experiment IV and for Experiment I above must, therefore, take into consideration the fact that the two experiments compare RTs for the second of two successive responses made to the third of three successive signals, and that these responses are based on relationships between these signals. Thus, three different kinds of sequential effects are involved in this task. First, successive signals may be the same or different: second, successive judgments may be the same or different, and finally, successive motor responses implementing these judgments may also be the same or different. In the experiments we have discussed, the nature of the successive judgments made is confounded by the fact that the motor responses which implement them may also be "the same," or "different," irrespective of the nature of the particular judgment on a given trial. Williams (1966) offers this as a possible explanation for her results. She assumes that her *S*s made mediating responses *same* or *different* to signals as they occurred. Thus confusion might occur when an *S* had to make the judgment different but implement it by pressing the key he pressed on the previous trial (e.g., in the DD response sequence). Similarly, *S* might be confused if he had to make the judgment *same* but implement it by pressing a different key from that pressed on the previous trial (e.g., DS sequences). If such confusions occurred we might expect RT DD and RT DS to be slower than RT SS and RT SD, since in the latter cases no confusion would occur between the nature of the judgment made and the choice of a response to implement it. Williams' explanation has two faults. First, it is post hoc and not tested by her experiment or by the present replication. Second, it does not explain why RT DD> RT DS. We should expect confusion between judgment and response to operate in both cases. Further, since in DD sequences both judgment and motor responses are repeated, we would expect these judgments to be faster. Some additional assumptions are therefore necessary.

To test Williams' (1966) hypothesis a necessary condition is to design an experiment in which the nature of the competition between successive judgments and the responses made to implement them is altered. This is possible by adapting Experiment I so that *S* responds on four keys rather than on two, not only classifying each signal as being the same or different from its predecessor but also indicating which signal it was. The response keys may, therefore, be designated 4 *same*, 4 *different*, 6 *same*, and 6 *different*, When the Signal 4 occurs *S* must press the key "4 *same*" if the previous signal was also a 4, and the key "4 *different*" if the previous signal was a 6. Occurrences of the Signal 6 are dealt with in the same way. We thus see that DD response sequences always require selection of two successive different responses so that conflict between judgment and response cannot occur. Only with SS judgment sequences are successive motor responses identical. With all other judgment sequences, whatever the nature of the second judgment, *S* has to select a new (that is, a *different*) response to implement it. Under these circumstances DS judgment sequences might be expected to be especially hard to implement, since *S* has to make the judgment *same* but choose a new (*different*) response to convey his decision.

If Williams' (1966) hypothesis is correct, we might therefore predict that RT DD and RT SD should both be faster than RT DS. Experiment II was carried out to test this.

Experiment II

Method

Sparta was again used with the identical programs of signals prepared for Experiment I. It was only necessary to change the experimental instructions so that *Ss* used four rather than two keys, following the allocations described above. All *Ss* were again given four experimental runs of 500 responses each during two experimental sessions.

Subjects. The *Ss* were 16 students from Oxford Polytechnic, ages 17–25. They were paid for their time but had no other interest in the purpose of the experiment.

Results

The last 1,000 responses made by each *S* were analyzed as before, omitting errors and responses following them. Error scores averaged 3.8% and errors appeared to be randomly distributed across transition classes.

A computer data sort, as for Experiment I, divided responses into the four transition classes: SS, DS, SD, and DD. Overall means and sigmas are set out in Figure 5. An ANOVA was carried out across the means obtained for individual *Ss*. As before terms for differences between transition classes ($p < .001$) and between *Ss* ($p < .01$) were significant but the interaction term was not. The S^2 test was used to rank order the obtained RTs with the following results:

$$\text{RT SS} \overset{**}{<} \text{RT DD} = \text{RT SD} \overset{*}{<} \text{RT DS}$$

$^{*}p$ <.0.5
$^{**}p$ <.01

Discussion

This new rank-ordering is clearly consistent with predictions from Williams' (1966) hypothesis. In tasks of this kind we must therefore take into account the fact that the nature of successive judgments made by *Ss* may interfere with the choice of responses which they make to implement them. It seems that *Ss* do not simply follow instructions and compare each successive signal against its predecessor, but that they unnecessarily and involuntarily compare each successive response with the preceding response. It is possible, though we have no proof for this, that *Ss* make mediating verbal responses *same* or *different* while carrying out this task, and that the selection of overt motor acts, for which the identical mediators are *also* used, is thereby hindered.

This is a plausible explanation, and *Ss* did indeed often say aloud *same* and *different* while-carrying out this task. However, it is a post hoc hypothesis and the results available do not allow comment on it.

The main point established is that there are several component processes intervening between the onset of a signal and choice of a response to it, Any one of these processes may or may not be repeated. Earlier work (Rabbitt & Vyas, 1973) has shown that repetition of coding rules may reduce RT even when neither a given signal nor a particular response is repeated. It is a tempting inference that the overall observed magnitude of a given repetition effect

Table 5.2 Mean reaction times (RTs) on a serial binary classification task pooled over 16 *Ss*

Response Transition type	*Mean RT (in msec.)*	Σ
SS	423	56
DS	651	72
SD	586	67
DD	546	57

Note: Abbreviations: SS = *same/same*, DS = *different/same*, SD = *same/different*, DD = *different/different*. The *Ss* identified the signal currently displayed and also indicated its relationship (*same or different*) to its predecessor.

may be predicted as the sum, or some other simple function, of component repetition effects. The present experiments show that this is not the case. The component processes intervening between perception of a signal and choice of a response may interfere with each other in complex ways, so that the resultant effects are only predictable if we can claim to know precisely what *S* is doing when he identifies signals and selects responses to them.

It seems that this finding does not exhaust the list of questions requiring further investigation. We have shown that the nature of judgments which *Ss* make may conflict with their selection of appropriate responses to implement them. We do not yet know whether successive judgments may be made easier or more difficult by the particular sequences of .signals on which they must be based.

In other words, we have so far shown that interference, probably between. verbal mediating responses, brings about complex interactions. This is not a sufficient basis to launch criticisms of models for the repetition effect, since it is obtained in a special situation shown to be different to that operating in serial CRT tasks (though Bindra et al., 1965, and Bindra et al., 1968, imply, if taken seriously, that the two types of task should give similar results). It remains to be seen whether there are other similar interactions that may occur as a result of *signal* recency, or *judgment* type, irrespective of whether or not verbal or other mediating responses are used.

We may consider another version of Experiment I in which *Ss* see, one at a time, any one of eight equiprobable signals presented in a random sequence. Suppose that these signals are arbitrarily divided by experimental instructions into four classes of two signals each. For convenience we may label these A1, A2, B1, B2, C1, C2, D1, and D2. The *S* responds on two keys. If a signal from any one of these classes is followed by another signal from the same class, he presses the key designated *same*. If a signal from one class follows a signal from any other class, he presses a key designated *different*.

Experiment II was carried out to test how far the nature of *S*'s judgments was affected by the physical identity or dissimilarity of sequences of successive signals. Two points are of interest, one obvious and the other rather less so. First, we should expect from the literature on binary classification tasks that *same* judgments made on the basis of physical identity of successive signals are must faster than *same* judgments made on the basis of categorical equivalence (Posner, 1969). A second point arises out of comments made by *Ss* carrying out Experiment I above. They complained that it was often the case that they remembered signals two back in a sequence, and were confused because they did not know which one was the relevant signal for comparison against that currently on the display. For example, with DD response sequences they would be confronted with signal sequences of the type 4, 6, 4, or 6, 4, 6. When responding to the last signal they complained that they remembered both of its predecessors. Thus *Ss* said that they were sometimes confused because a comparison of signal n against signal $n - 2$ would require the judgment same while a (correct) comparison of signal n against signal $n - 1$ would require the response *different*. A similar difficulty was held to occur with response sequences of the type DS. These were made to signal sequences of the type 6, 4, 4 or 4, 6, 6. Here comparison of signal n against signal $n - 2$ would require the (incorrect) response *different*, while comparison of signal n against signal $n - 1$ would require the response *same*.

The point of the procedure in Experiment III is, therefore, that DD response sequences might be made either to signal sequences of the type A_1 B_N A_1 or to sequences of the type A_1 B_N A_2 the first signal might be physically identical to the third or might simply be physically dissimilar but categorically equivalent. We thus have two possibilities: We might predict that because the first and the third signals were identical confusion would be more likely alternatively, we might consider that S would in this case be repeating an identical judgment. He would first have compared signal B_N against the first signal A_1 and would then be immediately required to make the same comparison, matching A_1 again against the remembered signal B_N. In this case we would predict some facilitation, since we might expect repetition of a particular *comparison*, irrespective of the order of presentation of signals to be compared, to reduce CRT. (See, for example, Rabbitt & Vyas, 1973.)

Experiment III

Method

Sparta was programmed with four random sequences of the signals 1, 2, 3, 4, 5, 6, 7, and 8. Each sequence was 801 signals long and all signals were equiprobable. The *Ss* were instructed to treat these signals as being divided into the four equivalent sets 1 and 2, 3 and 4, 5 and 6, and 7 and 8. They responded, classifying successive signals as being the same or different from their predecessors as described above. They experienced two runs in experimental sessions on consecutive days, the 1,600 responses from the last session being used to derive the results discussed below.

Subjects. The *Ss* were 12 students from Oxford Polytechnic, ages 19–22 yr. They were paid for their time.

Results

The overall percentage of errors committed was 6.2%. Incidence of errors did not reliably discriminate between response transition classes. All errors and responses following them were omitted from the data sort.

The data sort was necessarily more complex than that undertaken for Experiment I. The response transition SS was subdivided into three classes. The first class contained signal sequences in which three successive signals were identical, e.g., 1, 1, 1; 2, 2, 2; etc. The second class contained sequences in which the last two signals were identical, but categorically equivalent to the first, e.g., 2, 1, 1; 1, 3 3; etc. The final class contained sequences in which the last two signals were categorically equivalent but physically dissimilar, e.g., 2, 2, 1; 8, 8, 7; etc.

The response transition class DS was similarly broken down into classes in which the third signal was physically identical to the second (8, 2, 2; 4, 5, 5; etc.) and in which the third signal was physically dissimilar to the second but categorically equivalent to it (8, 1, 2; 4, 5, 6; etc.)

The response transition class SD was not broken down. However, three subclasses of the response transition sequence DD were derived, as discussed above. First, there were signal sequences in which the first and third signal were not physically identical, but were categorically equivalent (1, 8, 2; 3, 7, 4; etc) Second, there were cases in which the first and third signal were identical (1, 8, 1; 3, 7, 3; etc.). Finally, there were cases in which the signals were all physically dissimilar and from different classes (1, 3, 5; 8, 6, 4; etc.)

Overall mean RTs and sigmas were calculated across all *Ss* for these transition classes and are presented in Table 5.3.

As in Experiments I and II, an ANOVA was carried out on individual *Ss*' mean RTs across all transition classes. Terms for differences between transition classes ($p < .001$) and for differences between *Ss* ($p < .01$) were significant, but did not appear to interact. The S^2 was again used to evaluate differences between transition classes.

In broad outline it can be seen that the rank-order of transition classes in Table 5.3 corresponds quite closely to that which we might predict from Experiment I. The comparisons of interest here concern differences within response transition classes.

Within the SS response transition classes we see that the RTs are fastest when all three successive signals are physically identical. Cases where the first signal was physically identical to the third are somewhat slower ($p < .01$) than cases where the second and third signals were identical. Both of these cases, however, are slower than the case where all three signals were identical ($p < .01$).

Within the DS transition class, cases in which the second and third signals were physically identical were, as expected, faster than cases in which the second and third signals were simply categorically equivalent ($p < .05$).

Finally, we consider the three possible types of DD response sequences. The fastest of these occurred when the first signal of a triad was physically

Table 5.3 Mean reaction times (RTs) in a serial binary classification task pooled over 12 *S*s

Response transition type	*Mean RT (in msec.)*	Σ
Same/same		
All signals identical	273	29
Second and third signals identical	342	33
First and third signals identical	374	31
Different/same		
Second and third signals identical	479	56
Second and third signals equivalent	543	61
Same/different		
Pooled data for all cases	423	38
Different/different		
First and third signals identical	524	45
First and third signals equivalent	599	61
All three signals from different categories	557	65

Note: Eight signals were arbitrarily divided into four equivalent categories of two signals each. The *S*s classified successive signals as being from the same or different categories. Results are broken down in terms of all possible transitions between the responses *same* and *different*, and are further subdivided in terms of the categorical equivalence or physical identity of sequences of signals to which these responses were made.

identical to the third ($p < .05$). This is interesting because it suggests that when *S*s have to immediately repeat a comparison which they have just made, their RTs are reduced. The next fastest DD sequences occurred when all three successive signals were neither physically nor categorically identical. The slowest DD response sequences occurred when the first and third signals were categorically equivalent ($p < .05$). This suggests that the introspections of *S*s in Experiment I were reliable. That is to say, it is possible that they occasionally became confused as to whether to compare a signal n correctly against its predecessor $n - 1$ or incorrectly against a previous, still remembered signal $n - 2$. In the case in which all three successive signals came from different classes no confusion could occur, since either comparison (correct or incorrect) would lead to the judgment *different*. However, when the first and third signals were categorically equivalent, a comparison of signal n against signal $n - 2$ would lead to the judgment same, while the correct comparison of signal n against signal $n - 1$ would lead to the contrary judgment *different*.

Discussion

There are no grounds for the assumption that in serial CRT *S*s must *necessarily* behave in the same way as when they are obliged by experimental instructions, as in Williams' (1966) study and in the present study, to compare each successive signal against its predecessor. However, the present experiments do add to our information about the range of possible sequential effects in continuous tasks. They suggest that sequential effects are extraordinarily pervasive, and may have several quite *different*, and, as far as we can tell, quite *independent* effects, which may potentiate with each other, interact, or even, oppose each other. The main contribution of these data is to show once again (see Rabbitt & Vyas, 1973) that "repetition effects" are of many different kinds and are not to be explained in terms of any simple, unitary model.

Our specific findings, and some of their implications, may be summarized as follows.

1. The hypothesis put forward by Williams (1966) to account for the results of her Experiment IV appears to be correct. That is to say, the nature of successive judgments which *S*s make in serially comparing successive signals may interfere with the selection of the responses by means of which they are required to convey their judgments. In particular it seems that the production of covert (sometimes !) verbal mediating responses *same* and *different* may interfere with the selection of overt motor responses on a keyboard where experimental instructions have obliged *S* to attach verbal labels to the keys he uses. For example, an *S* is slowed when he has to repeat a response on the *different key* or select a new key in order to implement the judgment *same*.

   It must be stressed that though Williams' (1966) hypothesis appears to be correct, it is precisely *because* of this that we may decide that neither her data, nor those in subsequent experiments (Bindra et al., 1968; Bundra et al., 1965) can be taken seriously as a demonstration that *S*s in serial CRT tasks of the conventional kind proceed by comparing each signal against the trace of its predecessor before carrying on any more extended analysis to determine which signal it may be. If *S*s indeed did this, we should expect to find, if only early in practice, the same pattern of interference between verbal mediating responses and overt categorical responses as we have found in these experiments. Since this has not been reported in the literature we must conclude that this type of task, which *should* (if the Bindra et al., 1965 hypothesis were true) give the same results as might be predicted from the literature on repetition effects, is in fact a quite different experimental situation as far as *S*s are concerned.

   This may seem an uncomfortable intrusion of "cognitive" factors into tasks in which it has been supposed that CRT can give an index of the durations of each of a number of independent and additive processes that can be isolated for study by appropriate experimental manipulations. It may seriously be questioned whether elegant and elaborate methods that employ the CRT subtraction technique as a theoretical premise have the generality which has been hoped from them (see Briggs & Blaha, 1969; Sternberg, 1969). Evidently such models may be successful where experiments are rigid, limited in scope, and very carefully controlled. However, the present data suggest that there are more things to be controlled than previous investigators have taken into account. We can only recommend a modest caution for the future.

2. It is clear that the conflict between judgments expressed as intervening verbal responses and judgments expressed as key presses is only one source of systematic variance in tasks of this type. At least two kinds of *recency* effect, as distinct from repetition effects, are apparent here. (*a*) CRT is reduced by immediate repetition of a particular *judgment*, whether or not this judgment involves recurrence of the same signals or successive implementations of the same response. Thus, "judgment repetition effects" or "judgment recency effects" join the long list of different kinds of repetition effects set out by Rabbitt and Vyas, 1973, in discussing other data. (*b*) There are, nevertheless, repetition effects that relate to the identity of signals successively displayed. (*c*) There are, further, recency or repetition effects that relate to the recurrence of particular *pairs* of signals about which a given judgment must be made. For example, CRT is less when the first signal is identical to the third in an SS judgment sequence, or when the first signal is identical to the third in a DD judgment sequence.
3. The identity or dissimilarity of signals is only one effect that causes variance in CRT. Quite another matter is the identity or dissimilarity of signal *classes* about which judgments are made. In Experiment III it was clear that DD judgment sequences were made faster when the three signals were nonidentical and from different classes (A-B-C *class* sequences) than when the three successive signals were nonidentical, but the first and third signals were from the same class (A-B-A *class* sequences) It is, therefore, not merely the physical properties of the signals used, but the nature of the logic by which they are separated into classes of equivalent signals which controls the behavior of *S*s in tasks such as this one.
4. These results bear on the question of whether signals remembered for comparison against others are "stored" in only one or in more than one symbolic or other "representation" in memory (see, for example, a review by Posner, 1969). It is clear that signals *are* remembered as particular signals (since identity of the first and third of three successive signals speeds RT in SS judgment sequences, in contrast to the case where all three successive signals are not identical but come from the same category). It is also clear that signals are *also* remembered in terms of the classes to which they belong. The other critical point is that it is not only particular signals or categories of signals which are remembered, but also judgments and no doubt mediating verbal responses made to implement these judgments, mediating verbal responses made to implement overt key-pressing responses, and perhaps the overt key-pressing responses also. Thus recency effects must be interpreted in terms of the recency of storage of any one of a large number of quite separate and

perhaps mutually interfering memory traces for various sensory events, mediating responses, types of categorization, and overt motor acts. Thus it is as naive to speak of recency effects depending on "trace strength" when we must necessarily consider the strengths of a number of distinct kinds of memory trace, subject to types of interference quite other than those traditionally discussed in the literature (and also, perhaps, to decay at quite independent rates).

5. A somewhat unexpected finding is that *S*s seem to be sometimes unable to *forget* signals in a sequence, even when it is clearly to their advantage to do so. A human *S*, apparently, is not like an efficient computer which can clear its memory store of information once used but no longer relevant. The *S*s appear to have been confused because they matched a current signal not merely to its predecessor but also to another signal two back in the sequence to which they were responding. The memory search carried out by *S*s thus appears to have been, in this respect, rather inefficient. It also seems to be the case that there is no distinction between the type or location of the memory "store" in which an immediately previous signal and a signal received two responses back are held.

   It is, perhaps, more relevant to the further progress of work on human performance to try to understand the reason for this inefficiency than to persistently devise tasks in which human beings behave in as controlled and predictable a manner as possible. It is usually held that it is necessary to understand performance in constrained situations so that our data may be as tightly quantifiable as possible, and so that we may derive reliable comparisons between the durations, capacities, and efficiencies of the various functional processes we postulate. It seems that this is not a feasible strategy. In tasks which are still relatively simple, such as those in the present experiments, it is clear that *S*s behave in quite different ways than our conventional CRT models can take into account. In particular, the use of language as mediation in CRT tasks is seen to change performance in ways that quite override the possibility of deriving indices for the complexities of component functions in CRT tasks.

6. It cannot be too strongly stressed that the effects observed here relate to a particular, and somewhat early, level of *practice*. It is certainly true, also, that *S*s in these experiments were practiced far longer than is conventional in memory search experiments (see Sternberg, 1969) and longer than is usual in most laboratory CRT studies. Nevertheless, in the nature of things, we might well regard intermediary verbal responses as a temporary device used by *S*s to facilitate performance on a task which eventually would become "automatic" without their help.

The effects of practice represent the single question consistently avoided by all *E*s in this line of research. We know that *S*s get faster and more accurate with practice. We even make statements about the difference between practiced "automatic" performance at skilled tasks and the more fumbling and variable performance usually studied in laboratories. We are not prepared to say *how* or *why* people improve with practice. The tacit assumption is that *S*s, when practiced, go through the same sequences of functional operations but go through them faster and more accurately.

It is not useful to think in this way. If, for example, *S*s first use and later discard verbal mediating responses, it cannot be claimed that when they are practiced they are doing the task *in the same way* as when they are not. In comparing practiced and unpracticed performance we may well be comparing quite different functional processes leading to the same end—satisfaction of *E*. Clearly *E* cannot be satisfied unless he knows how these processes differ or can give plausible reasons why one way of doing a task may be gradually abandoned so that a better way can be employed. In this respect the nature of practiced and unpracticed performance may prove to be less interesting than the nature of performance during the period of transition between them.

The problems raised by undertaking a cognitive approach to the investigation of human skills are certainly formidable. However, the alternative is no longer viable. If life is more difficult for investigators in the future, it may also prove to be more rewarding and interesting than the pursuit of the barren simplicity to which our laboratory techniques have so far constrained us.

References

Bertelson, P. Sequential redundancy and speed in a serial two-choice responding task. *Quarterly Journal of Experimental Psychology*, 1961, 13, 90–102.

Bertelson, P. S-R relationships and reaction times for new versus repeated signals in a serial task. *Journal of Experimental Psychology*, 1963, 65, 478–484.

Bindra, D., Donderi, D. C., & Nishisato, S. Decision latencies of "same" and, "different" judgments. *Perceptions & Psychophysics*, 1968, 3, 121–130.

Bindra, D., Williams, J. A., & Wise, J. S. Judgments of sameness and difference: Experiments on decision time. *Science*, 1965, 150, 1625–1627.

Briggs, G., & Blaha, J. Memory retrieval and central comparison time in information processing. *Journal of Emperimental Psychology*, 1969, 79, 365–402.

Kornblum, S. Sequential determinants of information processing in serial and discrete choice reaction time. *Psychological Review*, 1969, 76, 113–131.

Posner, M.L. Abstraction and the process of recognition. In G. H. Bower and J. T. Spence (Eds.), *The Psychology of learning and motivation: Vol. III*. New York: Academic Press, 1969.

Rabbitt, P.M.A. Repetition effects and signal classification strategies in serial choice-response tasks. *Quarterly Journal of Experimental Psychology*, 1968, 20, 232–240.

Rabbitt, P.M.A., & Vyas, S. What is repeated in the "repetition effect"? In S. Kornblum (Ed.), *Attention and Performance IV.* New York: Academic Press 1973.

Smith, M. C. Repetition effects and short-term memory. *Journal of Experimental Psychology*, 1968, 77, 435–439.

Sternberg, S. The discovery of processing stages: Extensions of Dander's method. *Acta Psychologica*, 1969, 71, 665–672.

Williams, J. A. Sequential effects in disjunctive reaction time: Implications for decision models. *Journal of Experimental Psychology*, 1966, 71, 665–672.

New technology drives unexpected discoveries and provokes new questions

Over the last 30 years neuropsychology has been transformed by technologies that allow us to record events in our living brains while we perform simple tasks and even go about our everyday lives. As a result, experiments are now considered uninformative unless they explore links between behavioural measures and brain events. In this new world the behavioural tasks that we developed between 1950 and the mid 1990s and the conclusions that we derived from them still seem ingenious, but in a pitiful way. The dwindling remnants of my generation of human experimental psychologists (the job description I still cherish) are amused to recall a previous conceptual transformation that occurred when far simpler, cheaper and so immediately and widely accessible advances in technology of presenting complex displays and recording the nature and speed of responses to them abruptly transformed the behavioural tasks we could use, the precision with which we could record and time reactions to them and so, most importantly, the questions we could imagine. In retrospect the most striking aspect of this revolution was how very fast it happened. In 1962 when I needed to measure the times that people need to scan displays of letters, the only equipment that the MRC Applied Psychology Research Unit in Cambridge had for this purpose was a stop-watch and a card sorting box, which had been battered by being Sherpered up and down Everest to test the effects of high altitude and anoxia on decision speed. My colleagues in the Cambridge Department of Experimental Psychology fared no better. The cutting edge of their Reaction Timing technology was a single "Dekatron" that measured durations of events to an accuracy of 100 msec. – but only one at a time, and with long intervals for re-sets between trials. The single departmental electronic calculator was jealously monopolized by a pack of rat people and by undergraduate practical classes. A year after completing my Ph.D. thesis on card sorting experiments I had the transformative privilege of using the "Psychomet", whose mind-transforming effects I have already described, and a primitive computer donated to NIMH as surplus to the needs of a local bank. I still puzzle how credit for discoveries ought to be shared between those who make them and inventors of very simple devices that allow privileged first observations. In one narrative the moons of Jupiter had been around throughout human history and, once Lippershey's telescope became available, all that Galileo needed to do was to improve its resolution from 3 to 33 diameters and point it at them.

The Psychomet inspired a far less scientifically and theologically momentous intellectual epiphany than Galileo's observations. It forced on me evidence for something that human beings had been aware of for millennia but had not previously been able to measure: we do not passively respond to events one at a time but recognize and answer each in relation to what has just happened and what we expect to happen next. A different equipment, the "Donders" apparatus, a monstrous, huge room-filling machine built by Philips at Eindhoven to simultaneously record the reaction times of all of several people performing the same task, also confirmed, a little later, what humans had always known: when we try to respond too fast, errors become increasingly likely. Schouten and Bekker (1967) found that their volunteers' errors were consistently faster than their correct responses and realized that superimposition of distributions of CRTs for faster errors on those for slower correct responses showed that people control their performance by trading off speed against accuracy within a narrow time band within which even tiny increases in speed increase the probability of errors. This implied that humans actively optimize speed and accuracy by discovering and avoiding a narrow, optimal speed-error trade-off band. More radically, this also meant that even in the simplest RT tasks with which Wundt had launched Human Experimental Psychology in Leipzig in 1879, RTs are not passive learned reflexes with speeds determined by the physical lengths and conduction latencies of the neural pathways along which information must travel (as Helmholtz's classic experiments had assumed). In any task, we actively control our performance by monitoring the speeds of our responses and deliberately adjusting them to discover and observe our personal speed-error trade-off limits. A critical detail is that, to do this, we must be able to recognize our errors.

The "Donders" was capable of this additional discovery and may even have provided evidence for it, but Schouten and Bekker (1967) did not follow through. In 1963 the "Psychomet" forced me to realize that this is what happens. Slightly later a different, less convenient and flexible piece of equipment taught Burns (1965) the same lesson. Both of us confirmed that errors are faster than correct responses but we were also surprised that, on at least 70% of occasions, our volunteers involuntarily and very rapidly "corrected" these fast errors by making the responses that they should have made (Burns 1965; Rabbitt, 1966a; 1966b). These "Error Correcting Responses" (ECRs) are much faster than other correct responses, often following the completion of errors within 40 or 50 msec. This means that the processes that produce an ECR must already be in train before the error that they acknowledge has been completed. One way this could happen is if recognitions of signals and productions of responses to them are made by different members of a set of parallel processes, some of which terminate slightly sooner than others. On this "parallel processing" or "committee" model a risky fast process is more likely to result in an error but this can be recognized and "corrected" when a slightly slower and more accurate process terminates in the specification of a correct response. We do not need to assume parallel processing to explain error correction because the same outcome would be predicted by a single process model, such as Audley and Pyke's (1965) "accumulator model", that assumes that information may continue to be collected even after a premature response has been made. In either case, the responses that Burns and I termed "error corrections" would be outcomes of extended, and so more accurate, computations.

Volunteers find it hard to suppress their fast ECRs even when they are vehemently instructed to do so. Whenever they manage to do this the correct response that they make to the next signal (Error + 1 response) is unusually slow (Rabbitt, 1968). If they are asked not to "correct" their errors but to signal awareness of them by pressing a special key that they use for no other purpose, they often fail and, when they succeed, their error-signalling responses are also very slow (Rabbitt, 1968). The discovery that we very rapidly recognize our errors completed Schouten and Bekker's (1967) insight by showing that we can monitor and control our performance without external feedback and explains how we can locate and observe our personal "speed-error trade-off" zones. Responses in continuous tasks are attempts to find and observe a "target zone" of reaction times within which speed and accuracy are maximized. To seek this zone the speed of each response must be compared with that of its predecessors. Because means of correct CRTs merely reflect the outcome, but not the process, of this control, they are uninformative indices of how precision of control varies between tasks and individuals.

Incidentally, evidence that we gradually discover and select the minimum times that we need to respond correctly is a warning that when we conclude that slowing of mean CRTs is an index of "general slowing" of all mental processes in old age (e.g. Salthouse, 1996) we have not explained nearly enough. Age may slow mean CRTs because it slows neurophysiological processing in the brain and so also shifts the speed-error trade-off limit so that we need to take longer in order to make correct responses. Age may also slow mean CRTs because it brings about changes in our brains that degrade our ability to sensitively control our CRTs to maximize our speed and accuracy. Rabbitt (1979) found that although age markedly slows performance on CRT tasks, it has little or no effect on the reliability and speed of ECRs. Declining control of performance in old age does not, necessarily, reflect loss of sensitivity to errors. Further, recognition of errors does not, on its own, give us enough information to control our performance. To maintain maximum speed and accuracy we must be able to judge how fast we are responding and so adjust our speed appropriately from trial to trial. There is evidence that as we grow older we become less competent at this.

To find direct evidence that we can judge our response speeds and appropriately alter them, and discover what factors might affect our competence to do this, Maylor et al. (1992) tested whether ingestion of alcohol and improvement with practice affect the reliability and sensitivity with which young adults judge the speed of their responses during a continuous four-choice CRT task. We asked them, whenever they became aware that they had made an unusually fast *correct* response, to press an additional, fifth, key not used for any other purpose. They could do this, and the correct responses that they signalled as "fast" were, on average, 122 msec. faster than the average of all their other, un-acknowledged correct responses. This was direct evidence that people are sensitively aware of their response speeds even when their fastest responses are not identified because they are errors. Maylor, Rabbitt and Connolly (1989) had also found that ingesting alcohol increased volunteers' response times by approximately 40 msec. but did not affect their ability to judge their response speeds. In contrast, practice improved both response speed and the ability to detect and signal fast responses.

The precision with which we monitor the speed of our responses from trial to trial during a task sets a limit to our ability to control our performance to maximize both speed and accuracy. This means that the variance in our CRTs during a task is at least as informative an index of our ability to control our responses as are simple means of correct responses on which nearly all models for CRT have been based. The next paper describes a study of individual differences in variability during CRT tasks. In this study all individuals were relatively elderly, so we investigated the effects of another individual difference variable: fluid intelligence (*gf*).

References

Audley, R. J., & Pike, A. R. (1965). Some alternative stochastic models of choice 1. *British Journal of Mathematical and Statistical Psychology, 18*(2), 207–225.

Burns, J. T. (1965). The effect of errors on reaction time in a serial reaction task. Unpublished Ph.D. thesis, University of Michigan.

Maylor, E. A., Rabbitt, P.M.A., & Connolly, S.A.V. (1989). Rate of processing and judgment of response speed: Comparing the effects of alcohol and practice. *Perception and Psychophysics, 45*(5), 431–438.

Maylor, E. A., Rabbitt, P.M.A., James, G. H., & Kerr, S. A. (1992). Effects of alcohol, practice, and task complexity on reaction time distributions. *Quarterly Journal of Experimental Psychology Section A, 44*(1), 119–139.

Rabbitt, P. M. (1966a). Errors and error correction in choice-response tasks. *Journal of Experimental Psychology, 71*(2), 264–272.

Rabbitt, P.M.A. (1966b). Error correction time without external error signals. *Nature, 212*(5060), 438.

Rabbitt, P. M. (1968). Three kinds of error-signalling responses in a serial choice task. *Quarterly Journal of Experimental Psychology, 20*(2), 179–188.

Rabbitt, P. (1979). How old and young subjects monitor and control responses for accuracy and speed. *British Journal of Psychology, 70*(2), 305–311.

Salthouse, T. A. (1996). The processing-speed theory of adult age differences in cognition. *Psychological Review, 103*(3), 403–428.

Schouten, J. F., & Bekker, J.A.M. (1967). Reaction time and accuracy. *Acta Psychologica, 27*, 143–153.

6 There are stable individual differences in performance variability, both from moment to moment and from day to day

P.M.A. Rabbitt, P. Osman, B. Moore and B. Stollery

People's unadjusted scores on intelligence tests modestly, but consistently, predict their performance on most laboratory tasks including tests of working memory (Carpenter, Just, & Shell, 1990), learning of word lists (Rabbitt & Yang, 1996), efficiency of selective attention (Horn, 1982) and initial performance on simple tasks (Rabbitt, 1993b), and, much more strongly, rate of improvement at complex video games (Rabbitt, Banerji, & Szymanski, 1989).

It is therefore surprising that models to explain these diverse relationships have been based solely on correlations between intelligence test scores and simple measures of perceptual and motor speed, such as the times taken to discriminate between briefly presented stimuli (inspection times, or tachistoscopic recognition thresholds, TRTs; Brand & Deary, 1982; Deary, 1995) or to select appropriate responses to each of two or more signals (choice reaction time tasks, CRTs; Eysenck, 1986; Jensen, 1980; Jensen & Whang, 1993; Vernon, 1983, 1985).

Perhaps this quite extreme assumption has seemed plausible because, at first sight, and in contrast to tasks involving memory, learning, and complex decisions, TRT and CRT tasks seem so irreducibly simple that performance on them must be limited only by a single functional performance characteristic of the cognitive system, which may plausibly reflect a "primitive" neurophysiological property of the central nervous system such as a synaptic transmission latency, the maximum conduction speed of neural pathways, or "level of neural random noise" (Caryl, 1994; Eysenck, 1986; Reed, 1993; Reed & Jensen, 1992). A logically unentailed and even more radical speculation has been that information-processing speed, and hence "neurological speed", is not just one of many, but actually the sole functional determinant of individual differences in efficiency at all cognitive tasks, including intelligence tests, and so must be the "biological basis of intelligence" (Eysenck, 1986). A logically identical hypothesis is that age-related decline observed in all cognitive skills, including the solution of intelligence test problems, is entrained by slowing of elementary neuropsychological processes in old age (Hertzog, 1989; Salthouse, 1985, 1991, 1996, 1999, in press).

One problem with these speculations is that mean TRTs and CRTs are relatively uninformative task performance indices because they only coarsely summarize markedly skewed distributions of observations on individual trials. People's fastest correct CRTs are relatively little affected by differences in their ages or levels of intelligence (Rabbitt, 1988; Rabbitt & Goward, 1994; Rabbitt & Vyas, 1969; Smith & Brewer, 1995). Substantial individual differences in mean CRTs often reflect differences in the numbers of unnecessarily slow responses that people make rather than limits to their fastest correct decisions. To illustrate this we compared the entire distributions of 1,000 successive CRTs cumulated over 10 runs of 100 signals and responses made on a four-choice CRT task by each of two male undergraduates aged 19 years, one of whom (A) scored 36 and the other (B) 22 points on the Cattell and Cattell (1960) Culture Fair intelligence test. Both responded equally accurately (A made 0.72% and B 0.69% errors). A, who had the higher Cattell score, had a significantly faster mean CRT than B (difference = 69 ms; $t(a) = 5.2$; $p < .01$). This was not because A's fastest responses (mean of first decile = 218 ms) were significantly different from B's (mean of first decile = 222 ms) but only because B made many more slow responses than A. It is as reasonable to conclude that A and B differ in terms of the *trial-to-trial variability* of their performance as to conclude that they differ in the *maximum speed* with which they can correctly process information. It is also as reasonable to speculate that individual differences in the variability, rather than the speed, of neurological processes may also be a biological "primitive" underlying individual differences in intelligence.

A comparison between two specially selected individuals is merely illustrative. In another experiment 60 undergraduates aged from 17 to 21 years, 30 with Cattell scores between 20 and 31 points (M = 26.2, SD = 4.5) and 30 with Cattell scores between 32 and 40 points (M = 35.2, SD = 5.4) each made 200 correct responses in each of four different CRT tasks. As usual, on all tasks, the group with lower Cattell Scores had significantly slower mean CRTs and significantly larger standard deviations. Models to describe fast decisions must account not only for the effects of task demands on mean CRTs but also for the properties of entire CRT distributions and not just on means alone (Luce, 1986). This makes it useful to ask whether differences in the distributions of CRTs produced by high and low Cattell scorers are disproportionately greater than we would expect from differences in their mean CRTs. To test this we computed coefficients of variation (CVs, i.e., SD/M, Howell, 1992) for each volunteer in each experiment. Group averages for CVs are shown in Table 6.1. Low Cattell scorers had significantly larger CVs in all four tasks.

This suggests that individuals' degrees of trial-by-trial variability during an easy CRT task may be stable characteristics that consistently rank order their performance with respect to each other over long periods of time and across different tasks. If this is so, it would follow that if we test individuals on a particular task over many separate experimental sessions and days of practice the summed distribution of all of the CRTs that each of them makes over all these sessions will be characteristic of his or her performance. Let us call

Table 6.1 Individuals' mean CRTs, *SD*s and CVs

Culture Fair score	*N*	*CRT task*	*CRT*[a] *M*	*CRT*[a] *SD*	*CV*
High	30	2	346	41	.13
		4	419	55	.14
		6	481	68	.14
		8	530	81	.15
Low	30	2	411	67	.16
		4	507	91	.18
		6	596	111	.18
		8	625	115	.18

CRT = choice reaction time; CV = coefficient of variation.
[a]In ms.

these empirically derived distributions "characteristic distributions". If the assumption that each individual's degree of variability remains stable over long periods of time is correct, we can then estimate each individual's trial-to-trial variability on any single, future experimental session by taking a random sample from his or her empirically derived characteristic distribution.

The standard errors of people's characteristic distributions directly mirror the standard errors of the distributions of responses that they make during individual experimental sessions. It follows that as the standard errors of individuals' characteristic CRT distributions increase, so must the standard errors of the distributions of the means of the samples of CRTs, which they, in effect "sample" from these distributions on each of many different, future experimental sessions. This would mean that individuals who show greater variance in CRTs from trial to trial within each of many different experimental sessions must also show greater variance in mean CRTs between many different experimental sessions. It would also follow that if individual differences in age or in level of general intellectual ability systematically affect the trial-by-trial variability of CRTs recorded during any single experimental session they must, for that reason, also affect session to session and day-to-day variability in mean CRTs between different experimental sessions and over long periods of time. We designed an experiment to test this prediction.

To do this it is necessary to bear in mind that people's variability from session to session (between-session variability, BSV) on any task is certainly affected by many factors other than their variability within each experimental session (within-session variability, WSV). An obvious example is that early in practice individuals' mean CRTs fall more rapidly, and so vary more, from session to session (Rabbitt, 1993b). The effects of practice on easy CRT tasks are known to interact with those of age and general intellectual ability because older and less able people initially improve faster than younger and more able people (Rabbitt, 1993a). To avoid possible confounds with practice effects, participants' levels of within- and between-session variability were compared only on sessions on which no further improvements due to practice could be detected.

A different potential confound is that, for any individual, performance varies systematically during a 24-hour cycle. Unless individuals are compared at the same times of day, circadian changes may mask other sources of variability between sessions. Time-of-day effects may be further confounded by systematic individual differences in ability because both the time courses and amplitudes of circadian fluctuations also systematically vary between individuals (Colquhoun & Corcoran, 1964). Thus unless the times of day at which tasks are carried out are taken into consideration performance differences between more and less able individuals may be confounded with their idiosyncratic patterns of circadian variability. For this reason each individual was always tested at the same time of day, and testing times were balanced across participants.

Even after the effects of practice and of circadian changes have been excluded and balanced it still remains likely that BSV is affected by other factors that may also vary systematically with age or general intellectual ability. For example, it might be that mild variations in health cause participants to experience relatively "good" and "bad" days, and it is plausible that the effects of these fluctuations may be greater in more frail and less able individuals. To check this all participants were given six different tasks on every one of 36 successive testing sessions. This allowed us to determine whether individuals' levels of performance on all the different tasks they carried out co-varied from day to day independently of practice effects and circadian effects, and, if so, whether the extent of this day-to-day co-variance differed systematically with age or level of general ability.

Experiment

Methods

Participants

A total of 98 people, 68 women and 30 men aged from 52 to 79 years (M = 69.1, SD = 7.1) were selected from a panel of well-documented volunteers enrolled for the Manchester longitudinal study of cognitive ageing (Rabbitt, Donlan, McInnes, Bent, & Watson, 1993) to equally represent three age groups, 50 to 61 years, 61 to 70 years, and 71 to 79 years. These age groups were matched in terms of total scores summed over all four parts of the Cattell and Cattell (1960) Culture Fair intelligence test (CF) because the aim was to investigate differences in variability associated with age as well as those associated with general intellectual ability. The overall range of scores was 14 to 40 points (M = 28.75, SD = 5.92).

Of these individuals, 80 completed all of 36 weekly sessions. These were divided into two groups of high and low Culture Fair test scorers. Table 6.2 shows that matching of age groups for CF test scores remained satisfactory. Balance of testing times for high and low test scorers was also maintained.

Table 6.2 Demographics of high- and low-ability groups

		Age[a]		*Cattell Culture Fair scores*		
Ability	N	M	SD	M	SD	*Range*
Lower	36	65.72	7.07	23.74	4.62	14–31
Higher	44	66.27	7.079	32.81	3.014	32–40

[a]In years.

Tasks and procedure

The six tasks were constant and variable mapping conditions of each of three letter categorization tasks in which volunteers responded by pressing either the Z or the / key on a standard computer keyboard with one hand to appearances of each member of one, and with the other hand to appearances of each member of another set of 2, 4, or 6 different capital letters. These appeared, one at a time, 20 mm high, in the centre of a monitor screen. Allocations of response keys to target and background sets were balanced across volunteers. At each level of signal uncertainly (i.e., 4, 8, or 12 letters) there were two experimental conditions. In the constant mapping condition (CM) targets in all set-size conditions and throughout the experiment were always "nested"; that is, they were selected from the same two pools of six items (target letters from the set BZERFT and background letters from the set DYPUSJ). In the variable mapping (VM) condition target and distractor sets were both changed from session to session, being selected anew by random sampling from the letters CWQCMHKNVALX.

In all conditions of all tasks as soon as either response key was pressed the letter currently visible immediately disappeared and was followed, 150 ms later, by the next in a random equiprobable series, which was generated afresh for each block of trials by the program controlling the experiment. All responses were timed to within 0.01 s and were recorded. All errors were identified and listed. Because errors are known to be faster and the three responses immediately following each error are known to be atypically slower than all other correct responses (Rabbitt, 1969) these were excluded from computations of means and distributions of correct CRTs. The data were not trimmed in any other way except that very rare responses slower than 3 s were discarded because they invariably represented momentary lapses of memory for the target and background sets, and their incidence did not vary with age or CCF score.

Each volunteer was given an initial familiarization session on each of the six tasks. Volunteers came to the laboratory in groups of 4 to 6 and were tested in separate, quiet, experimental cubicles. Testing sessions took place at four times of day, and each volunteer was always tested at the same one of these times: 10.00, 12.00, 14.00, and 16.00 hours. The times were balanced across older and younger and across higher and lower Cattell test score groups. With rest pauses each session lasted between 60 and 90 min. During each session each volunteer completed two runs of 100 trials on each of the six tasks. Before each run on each task the program identified and presented the two sets of letters to be used and generated random sequences of target and background letters to test recall until 100% accuracy had been reached on each of three successive runs. Scored trials then began. Feedback on accuracy was given after each run. At the end of each testing session further feedback was given on mean CRTs and accuracy for all tasks experienced. Volunteers were constantly urged to try to improve their speed and accuracy as much as possible throughout the year during which the experiment was run.

Preliminary inspection of the data revealed a subtle methodological problem. The program that verified participants' knowledge of the letter categories at the beginning of each run identified on as a "target" and the other as a "background" set. This training evidently influenced the strategy that participants used to identify symbols, as CRTs to "target" letters were significantly faster than those to "non-target" letters in all conditions of all tasks on all sessions. This is consistent with previous findings with Sternberg's (1969) memory-search paradigm that people discriminating between symbol sets initially carry out a serial, self-terminating memory search of the target set, respond as soon a match is identified, and, if no match is found, make a slower non-target response by default (see Sternberg, 1969). If this strategy is used it is likely that low CF participants will carry out self terminating memory searches more slowly than high CF participants so that differences between mean target (T) and no-target (NT) CRTs will be proportionately greater for the LCF than for the HCF group. Thus if these T and NT responses are pooled, slower individuals will, necessarily, show greater differences between these response categories and therefore also greater trial-to-trial variability. To eliminate this confound data were sorted to obtain means and standard deviations for T and NT CRTs for each condition of each task, and independent analyses were made on each of these 12 sub-categories of responses from the six experimental tasks. Variability of the T responses may still be affected by differences in speed between groups but variability of the NT responses would not be affected because these are made by default after all comparisons against members of the target set have been made. Analyses of NT responses are, therefore, especially critical for the relationships to be investigated. Analyses of T responses were also carried out to make supplementary points such as the distinction between those proportions of BSV that are and those that are not associated with individual differences in WSV. It is important to note that, although this detailed analysis was also carried out to test for unexpected interactions, differences between means and standard deviations of T and NT responses do not affect the main point of this comparison, which is that, in all CRT tasks, consistently greater within-session variability, whatever its cause, is necessarily reflected in greater between-session variability.

In the variable target conditions the decision to allocate different randomized sets of target and background letters to each volunteer on each session also has methodological implications. This must increase between-session variability and so tend to mask the full effects of within-session variability on between-session variability. However, this makes randomization of signal sets a conservative procedure for the question asked by the present experiment because, by increasing variance from another source it can only reduce the probability of finding the effect for which we test. Moreover the present experiment allows a check on this because the problem does not apply to the constant target set condition in which each participant always responded to the same target and background letters so that variance from session to session was minimized. Note, however, that the decision whether or not to randomize displays across participants becomes important if the aim of an experiment is to estimate the contribution of within-, and hence of between-session variability to variability between individuals tested on a single occasion. People who vary more with respect to themselves from session to session will also, necessarily, vary more with respect to each other when they are compared on any single occasion. In this case randomization of stimuli from session to session, or between individuals, would be inappropriate because it would add an unknown amount to the inter-individual variability that can be accounted for by intrinsic within-session variability and, consequently, by between-session variability.

Results and analyses

Both high and low CF scorers improved markedly with practice on all sub-sets of responses in both the variable and the constant mapping conditions. To examine practice effects, two-way analyses of variance (ANOVAs) were carried out on mean CRTs from each session on each of the 12 sub-conditions to check for differences between Culture Fair groups and successive practice sessions. There were highly significant main effects for differences between CF groups and between days of practice but in no case was there any significant interaction between CF group effects and practice effects. In all conditions of all tasks between-session variability markedly reduced with practice but the amount of this reduction was very similar in high and low CF groups. Nevertheless, as an additional safeguard, further analyses were made only on data from sessions in which practice effects were no longer present. To do this, scores for Sessions 31 to 35 were averaged to provide a baseline mean CRT for each sub-set of data from each task. Then, to smooth the data, 10 blocks of three consecutive sessions were averaged. Each block was then compared with the baseline using a 5% (one-tailed) t test. Table 6.3 gives differences between the means of each block and the baseline for each test condition and associated t values.

For each task the last block of 10 successive sessions that produced a significant t statistic was identified, and only those sessions that followed it were used in the analysis. A constraint was imposed such that the number of sessions sampled was held equivalent across the target and no-target CRT samples for each (Mapping × Stimuli) condition. To do this the minimum of the pair of numbers computed earlier was adopted.

Table 6.3 Differences between combined sessions and baseline for each test condition

	Constant						*Varied*					
	2 stimuli		*4 stimuli*		*6 stimuli*		*2 stimuli*		*4 stimuli*		*6 stimuli*	
Sessions	*T*	*N*	*T*	*N*	*T*	*N*	*T*	*N*	*T*	*N*	*T*	*N*
01 – 03	193.7	225.6	248.6	293.7	369.3	365.3	221.2	230.0	318.1	298.6	282.6	286.9
	14.14	13.34	14.68	17.38	15.27	18.10	14.43	13.45	18.10	15.38	10.28	12.04
04 – 06	132.2	145.5	146.1	167.8	263.0	238.5	142.9	151.5	222.4	201.6	211.8	203.8
	11.99	11.90	11.55	12.63	14.81	15.90	11.50	11.76	13.28	12.04	9.72	9.12
07 – 09	98.65	98.99	119.5	152.0	185.4	183.4	92.89	95.36	153.3	160.0	146.2	133.7
	10.52	11.38	10.45	14.16	12.80	14.52	9.27	9.92	11.91	12.98	6.64	6.53
10 – 12	78.01	83.63	95.74	101.2	177.7	143.3	71.63	82.78	100.3	97.53	131.3	137.6
	9.21	8.35	9.69	10.92	13.49	11.20	8.38	6.99	8.11	8.79	7.19	7.27
13 – 15	40.24	56.06	62.94	67.68	126.7	100.3	44.46	44.17	69.40	51.15	96.8	83.51
	6.92	7.79	7.05	7.72	9.49	9.29	5.19	4.82	7.16	5.23	6.40	4.71
16 – 18	32.77	33.84	52.87	51.40	106.7	85.81	21.96	18.17	61.90	48.96	67.08	53.43
	6.61	5.18	5.63	7.67	9.74	8.02	3.53	2.83	5.56	4.32	4.29	3.31
19 – 21	21.80	24.40	24.21	43.43	60.95	57.66	25.82	32.19	31.76	56.27	44.63	35.11
	4.15	4.27	3.35	6.04	6.25	5.74	3.36	4.13	3.70	5.32	2.35	2.21
22 – 24	7.85	8.74	10.67	23.57	32.56	16.16	**5.19**	**8.17**	24.09	34.48	**10.28**	**11.10**
	1.56	1.76	1.46	4.01	3.92	1.92	**0.86**	**1.45**	3.16	4.12	**0.80**	**0.73**
25 – 27	**1.83**	**0.61**	7.58	10.00	25.06	12.56	**2.24**	**8.09**	12.98	23.89	**9.47**	**11.31**
	0.43	**0.10**	1.29	1.74	3.29	1.57	**0.33**	**1.12**	1.65	2.88	**0.83**	**0.76**
28 – 30	**1.82**	**– 0.76**	**0.66**	**0.32**	20.12	4.87	**– 11.94**	**– 5.73**	14.29	3.00	**–0.29**	**–0.85**
	0.47	**– 0.14**	**0.11**	**0.06**	2.65	0.69	**– 2.24**	**– 0.99**	1.83	0.34	**–0.03**	**–0.06**
31 – 35	**0.00**	**0.00**	**0.00**	**0.00**	**0.00**	**0.00**	**0.00**	**0.00**	**0.00**	**0.00**	**0.00**	**0.00**
	–	–	–	–	–	–	–	–	–	–	–	–

Note: The first figure in each cell is the average difference between the combined sessions and the baseline (sessions 31–35). The second entry is the associated *t* value from a paired-comparisons *t* test; *t* values greater than 1.66 denote significance at the (one-tail) 5% level. Bold represents the sessions deemed to exhibit negligible practice effect, and are the sessions to be sampled. T = target; N = no target.

Relationships of within- and between-session variance to age and to Cattell scores

Table 6.4 shows correlations of BSV with age, CF score, and WSV for each of the 12 sub conditions in this experiment (i.e., for T and NT in three conditions of signal uncertainty in constant and in variable mapping conditions). BSV is defined as the weighted standard deviation of weighted means, using the "Proc Means" procedure described in the SPSS-X users guide (1988). WSV is defined as the weighted pooled standard deviation where the weights are the numbers of stimuli correctly answered during each session, from which are calculated the mean and standard deviation of CRTs on each session.

Table 6.4 shows that in all conditions of all tasks BSVs correlated significantly and negatively with CF scores and positively with WSVs. In this sample, in which age groups were matched in terms of CF scores, correlations between BSV and WSV scores and age were not significant. It seems that no age differences are observed when variance associated with CF scores is partialled out by matching of groups. To put this another way all individual differences in CRT variability associated with individual differences in age seem to be picked up by individual differences in CF scores. As age did not appear as a significant independent factor in determining CRT variability it was ignored in all subsequent comparisons.

This analysis confirms that between-session variability is significantly correlated with within-session variability and that individual differences in both between- and within-session variability are predicted by CF scores. A further question is whether within-session variability entirely, or only partially, accounts for between-session variability. In the latter case we would also wish to know whether peoples' ages or Cattell scores predict the amount of

Table 6.4 Correlations of BSV with age, CF score, and WSV

Condition	*No. of stimuli*		*Age (N = 80)*		*CF score (N = 76)*		*WSV (N = 80)*	
			Corr.	*Prob.*[a]	*Corr.*	*Prob.*[a]	*Corr.*	*Prob.*[a]
Constant	2	target	.223	.047	−.486	.000	.849	.000
		no target	.136	.229	−.611	.000	.899	.000
	4	target	.062	.583	−.480	.000	.792	.000
		no target	.191	.090	−.601	.000	.742	.000
	6	target	.205	.068	−.562	.000	.811	.000
		no target	.170	.131	−.535	.000	.721	.000
Varied	2	target	.202	.072	−.527	.000	.804	.000
		no target	.161	.154	−.460	.000	.853	.000
	4	target	.183	.104	−.458	.000	.626	.000
		no target	.113	.320	−.491	.000	.745	.000
	6	target	.082	.472	−.456	.000	.780	.000
		no target	.195	.083	−.524	.000	.826	.000

Note: BSV = between-session variability; WSV = within-session variability; CF = Culture Fair.
[a]prob > |rho| under H_0: rho = 0.

this additional between-session variability which is due to factors other than within-session variability.

Testing whether within-session variability entirely, or only partly, accounts for between-session variability

The analysis was based on the assumption made in the introduction to this experiment that, by summing the distributions of responses that individual volunteers make during separate experimental sessions, it may be possible to derive for each a characteristic CRT distribution from which it is possible to derive good estimates of the distributions of CRTs that they will produce during any further experimental sessions that they experience. On the assumption that within-session variability remains stable across all of the different experimental sessions from which these data are collected, this can be done by repeatedly sampling each person's empirically derived characteristic CRT distribution to simulate the distributions of CRTs that would be obtained during further, independent, experimental runs. Note that the properties of these simulated distributions must be identical to those of the empirically derived characteristic distribution from which they have been drawn. In particular the standard error of the distribution of the means of these simulated distributions will vary directly with the standard error of the particular characteristic distribution from which they have been drawn. Comparison of empirically observed against simulated distributions of mean CRTs across sessions now distinguishes two possibilities. One is that, in empirically observed trials, the session-to-session variability of mean CRTs is entirely and solely caused by the trial to-trial variability in individual CRTs within experimental sessions. The other is that within-session variability contributes to, but does not entirely account for, between-session variability because other factors also intervene. For example, minor variations in health from day to day might also affect between-session variability independently of within-session variability. In this case we would expect that the actual, empirically observed, variability in mean CRTs between the sessions from which data has been summed in order to derive the characteristic CRT distributions would be greater than the between-session variability simulated by repeated random sampling of characteristic CRT distributions.

More formally, by proposing that there exists, for each person, a single underlying distribution that is deemed to represent all of the y distributions under consideration one is assuming the answer to the question asked—that is, that a single distribution is sufficiently representative of the y distributions (i.e., that day-to-day variability in mean CRTs is no greater than might be expected by sampling this distribution on successive occasions). It is possible to simulate such a process by randomly sampling from this distribution, computing means, and so on, and then comparing these simulated variances of means with the real, observed variances in means. If there is evidence for a contradiction—for example, if the observed variance ranks greater than 95% of the simulated variances—it is possible to conclude that there is no evidence for the assumption made: That is, that the BSV is greater than can reasonably be explained by the WSV. In functional terms this would imply that state changes between testing sessions increase BSV beyond the limits that can be accounted for by WSV.

Estimates of characteristic CRT distributions were derived for each volunteer from subsets of T and NT CRTs in each of the six tasks. Then n data points were sampled from each individual's estimated characteristic CRT distribution, where n is the number of successive responses made during a given test session (i.e., 100 less number of errors, post error responses, and atypically slow responses). It was then possible to compute the mean of this sample, to repeat this procedure y times, where y is the number of sessions being modelled, and to compute for each individual the variance of these y simulated means. For each individual 999 such variances were simulated, and the actual, empirically observed variance was added to this set of variances to make a total of 1,000 observations. To give a $p = .05$ level of confidence for the comparison the results were checked to discover whether or not the experimentally observed variance fell within the subset of the 50 largest variances of the combined set of 1,000 variances. This process was repeated 12 times for each volunteer using the T and NT distributions of CRTs on each of the six tasks.

Hence for the ith person, sample N_{ij} variates from this distribution were obtained where N_{ij} is the number of stimuli correctly responded to by the ith person on the jth testing session: $i = 1, \ldots, 80; j = c, \ldots, 35$ where $(36-c)$ is the number of sessions being modelled. Rounding errors that occurred to set CRTs to the nearest 0.01 s, the limits of resolution of the apparatus, were incorporated. For each session, j, X_{ij}, the mean of the N_{ij} simulated CRTs, was calculated. The weighted standard deviation Si of the simulated means X_{ij} $(j = c, \ldots, 35)$ was computed, using the N_{ij} as weights $(i = 1, \ldots, 80)$; this process was repeated 999 times to obtain 999 simulated (weighted) standard deviations: The weighted standard deviation of observed means was added, all 1,000 values were rank ordered, and the rank order of the real (weighted) standard deviation was observed for that volunteer and that session. This process was repeated for all volunteers.

For convenience the characteristic CRT distributions for each individual were assumed to be normal. It is empirically known that this is not the case, but the approximation is permissible because the index of interest is the standard deviation that was assigned to the distribution (in fact, means of distributions are also irrelevant as we are only concerned with the variations of, and about, the simulated means). Nevertheless to test the assumption of normalcy 1,000 variances of 10 means were computed from blocks of 25 variates of the normal distribution and paired with 1,000 similarly derived variances from the uniform distribution, the standard deviation of each distribution being arbitrarily set to 150. It was found that in 511 cases the variance was larger in the normal case, giving a decision well within the approximate 95% confidence level (469,531) for the null hypothesis that there was no difference between the variance of means from the two distributions. To determine the standard deviation it was decided to adopt the pooled estimate based on relevant sessions—that is, the WSV as defined earlier.

Table 6.5 presents the ranked BSV for each volunteer for each condition.

Table 6.6 presents (non-parametric) inter-correlations between test conditions of the BSV variable. Significant positive correlations suggest consistency of findings across conditions.

Table 6.7 gives the number of significant rankings for each test (extreme variable) and a standard Z score for each test condition.

Table 6.5 Ranked BSV for each subject

Subject	*Age*	*CF*	*Combined ranked BSV*	*Number of significant correlations*
41	58	40	10712	28
42	56	29	8645	8
43	66	17	8505	6
44	68	25	6568	5
45	68	28	9360	4
46	52	40	11224	31
47	59	34	9042	5
48	57	30	8236	1
49	56	28	9575	6
50	72	21	7839	4
51	72	30	8179	4
52	61	36	9652	15
53	64	32	9568	5
54	63	19	8103	2
55	70	14	8521	3
56	58	31	9994	4
57	74	22	6715	6
58	60	32	9029	7
59	63	–	9406	8
60	73	19	8909	6
61	54	33	9168	3
62	55	33	10655	9
63	64	33	8200	7
64	79	34	8252	12
65	71	33	9727	7
66	72	30	10767	9
67	58	38	7907	10
68	74	26	9052	10
69	65	34	4361	6
70	73	32	11142	18
71	59	23	7237	6
72	76	23	8807	7
73	71	35	9629	3
74	77	28	8161	3
75	64	36	9169	6
76	54	–	8094	7
77	58	34	9322	4
78	58	27	11158	10
79	73	31	8971	6
80	57	27	11230	7

CF = Culture Fair score; BSV = between-session variability.

Table 6.6 Correlations or ranked BSV across test conditions

	c_t_2	*c_n_2*	*c_t_4*	*c_n_4*	*c_t_6*	*c_n_6*	*v_t_2*	*v_n_2*	*v_t_4*	*v_n_4*	*v_t_6*	*v_n_6*
c_t_2	–											
c_n_2	.222	–										
	(.048)											
c_t_4	.345	.221	–									
	(.002)	(.049)										
c_n_4	.202	.306	.194	–								
	(.073)	(.006)	(.085)									
c_t_6	.201	.230	.184	.384	–							
	(.073)	(.040)	(.103)	(.000)								
c_n_6	−.050	.081	.169	.171	.255	–						
	(.658)	(.476)	(.134)	(.129)	(.023)							
v_t_2	.251	.224	.254	.332	.197	.144	–					
	(.025)	(.046)	(.023)	(.003)	(.080)	(.202)						
v_n_2	.302	.237	.163	.258	.114	.069	.214	–				
	(.007)	(.035)	(.149)	(.021)	(.313)	(.544)	(.056)					
v_t_4	.139	−.065	.203	.179	.049	.326	.133	.264	–			
	(.220)	(.566)	(.070)	(.112)	(.665)	(.003)	(.241)	(.018)				
v_n_4	.302	.148	.151	.319	.181	−.080	.067	.317	.238	–		
	(.007)	(.191)	(.180)	(.004)	(.109)	(.482)	(.553)	(.004)	(.034)			
v_t_6	.376	.119	.130	.062	.208	.196	.180	.178	.215	.005	–	
	(.001)	(.293)	(.250)	(.585)	(.065)	(.082)	(.110)	(.114)	(.056)	(.967)		
v_n_6	.008	.083	−.037	.342	.184	.170	.172	.041	.124	.167	.150	–
	(.944)	(.463)	(.745)	(.002)	(.102)	(.131)	(.127)	(.718)	(.273)	(.140)	(.184)	

Note: $N = 80$. Figures in parentheses denote Prob>|rho|under H_0: rho = 0.

Table 6.7 Significance of subjects' ranked BSV for each test condition

Condition	*No. of stimuli*		*Mean*	*z*	*Prob >z*	*Extreme*	*Prob > extreme*
Constant	2	target	746.50	7.638	.000	28	.000
		no target	827.49	10.147	.000	38	.000
	4	target	666.33	5.153	.000	29	.000
		no target	792.31	9.057	.000	32	.000
	6	target	668.11	5.209	.000	17	.000
		no target	697.65	6.124	.000	19	.000
Varied	2	target	854.49	10.983	.000	51	.000
		no target	779.40	8.657	.000	25	.000
	4	target	647.40	4.576	.000	19	.000
		no target	774.04	8.491	.000	26	.000
	6	target	725.39	6.983	.000	29	.000
		no target	854.30	10.975	.000	46	.000

Let us denote the ranked BSV of each volunteer in a particular test condition by X_{ij} ($i = 1, \ldots, 80; j = 1, \ldots, 12$). On H_0, $X_{ij} = U[0, 1000]$—that is, the uniform distribution over the range 1 to 1,000. Then $\Sigma\left(X_{ij}\right) = 500$, and $var\,(X_{ij}) = 1{,}000{,}000/(12 \times 80)$: that is, 1,041.67. Let $\bar{X}_{ij}$ denote the mean of X_{ij} over i. Then, by the central limit theorem, $\bar{X}_{ij}$ is approximately normally distributed with mean 500 and variance 1,000,000/ (12 × 80): that is, 1,041.67. This implies that $Z_{ij} = (\bar{X}_j - 500)\sqrt{1,\,041.67}$ is an approximately standard normal variable (see $\mathcal{Z}$ scores in Table 6.7). In this case a one-tailed 5% critical region is $\bar{Z}_j > 553.1$. All sub-sets of responses in all conditions of all tasks produce highly significant results for this comparison.

An alternative method of assessing significance, and the one that motivated the design of the simulation exercise, is to count the number of X_{ij} ($i = 1 \ldots 80$) that are greater than 950. This is represented by the variable extreme given in Table 6.7 the number expected by chance is 4. One-tailed significance may be addressed from the cumulative probabilities of the binomial (80, .05) distribution: $P(X \geq 8) = .04659$, $P(X \geq 10) = .00653$, and $P(X \geq 12) = .00061$. For a test of size no greater than .05 the critical region would be $X \geq 8$, for a test no greater than .01 a critical region would be $X \geq 10$, and for a test no greater than .01 the critical region would be $X \geq 12$. On these alternative criteria, all entries are, again, highly significant. Thus there is strong evidence that there is significant residual between-session variability, even after the effects of within-session variability have been taken into consideration. The next question is whether individual differences in Culture Fair scores also predict the amounts of this additional variability, which cannot be accounted for in terms of within-session variability.

Testing whether individuals' CF scores or ages predict the amount of the "residual" variability in their mean CRTs between sessions, which cannot be accounted for in terms of their trial-to-trial variability within sessions

To assess whether the extent of this residual BSV differs systematically between high and low CF scorers we obtained correlations between the BSV for each subject and his or her age and CF score. These are given in Table 6.8. Note that although only one of these comparisons is statistically reliable, 11 of the 12 possible correlations with CF score are positive. Further, if the ranking is summed across conditions there is an overall, significant positive association. Thus, although it is not possible to claim any systematic effects of CF scores for any particular sub-set of responses in any of the six tasks, when all conditions are considered together higher CF scorers show greater BSV than lower CF scorers. That is to say, although low CF scorers show greater BSVs as a consequence of their greater WSVs, after this has been taken into consideration the *residual* BSV is greater for higher than for lower CF scorers.

Checking whether individuals experience state changes from session to session that may affect their performance on all tests independently of their WSVs or BSVs

The experiment allowed a check on the results of this simulation study by a different method that has some intuitive appeal, but is perhaps statistically less rigorous: that is, to examine whether levels of performance on the six different experimental tasks co-varied between sessions. There are two difficulties

Table 6.8 Correlations of ranked BSV with age and CF score

			Age		*CF score*	
Condition	*No. of stimuli*		*Spearman's rho* (N = *80*)	p-*value for* H$_0$: *rho* = *0*	*Spearman's rho* (N = *76*)	p-*value for* H$_0$: *rho* = *0*
Constant	2	target	−.069	.542	.126	.279
		no target	−.048	.673	.176	.129
	4	target	−.076	.504	.242	.036
		no target	−.004	.971	.178	.124
	6	target	−.036	.755	.083	.474
		no target	−.181	.108	.092	.429
Varied	2	target	−.056	.625	.192	.097
		no target	−.126	.264	.167	.150
	4	target	−.016	.885	.034	.771
		no target	−.028	.808	.148	.201
	6	target	−.158	.161	.172	.137
		no target	−.089	.434	.068	.559
Sum of all conditions			−.137	.226	.263	.022

CF = Culture Fair.

with this comparison: (1) Unless each test is correlated with and external standard of performance the analysis suffers from interdependence of correlations; and (2) the correlation analysis, but not the simulation analysis, assumes that no state changes occur within the period of time during which all tests are given—that is, during an experimental session. Evidently the correlational analysis must fail to detect state changes that occur during particular experimental sessions and not merely between different experimental sessions. Setting aside these problems, if volunteers experience state changes from session to session that affect their performance on all tasks that they experience during any single experimental session, we would expect performance on all tasks to co-vary across sessions, being worse during "bad sessions" and better during "good sessions". If volunteers do not experience such state changes we may suppose that their mean CRTs on each of the experimental tasks will randomly fluctuate around an average performance level. In this case we would not expect that, during individual test sessions, relatively better or worse performance on one task will be accompanied by relatively better or worse performance on all others.

For each volunteer data from the last 10 sessions were chosen to exclude practice effects. All 66 inter-correlations between test conditions were computed, and the number of correlations that were significantly positive at the 5% level (one-tailed) were recorded. These are given in Table 6.9, which also includes the sum, across test conditions, of the ranked BSV variables. Significance of each total may be assessed using the binomial theorem. However this assumes independence of correlations. This, of course, is not strictly the case, because if scores on Test A are positively correlated with those on Test B and Test C then it is likely that scores on Tests B and C are also positively correlated. The cumulative probabilities of the binomial (66, .05) distribution are given in Table 6.9.

Table 6.10 shows correlations with age and with CF score and the number of significant correlations obtained to assess whether the extent of fluctuation between sessions is affected by these individual difference variables.

Again when groups are matched in terms of CF scores there is no evidence for any residual effects of age. Consistently with the simulation study this analysis once again suggests that individuals with higher CF scores experience more marked relative state changes than do individuals with lower CF scores or, alternatively, that the greater intrinsic variability of low CF scorers masks the effects of other, systematic, state changes that they experience.

General discussion

For both T and NT responses in all six tasks the variability of individuals' CRTs during individual sessions predicted the variability of their mean CRTs from session to session and from day to day. One way to model this is to suppose that the distributions of CRTs that individuals produce during particular experimental runs can be regarded as independent samples from

Table 6.9 Correlations of ranked BSV with the number of significant correlations

Condition	*No of stimuli*		*Number of significant correlations*	
			Spearman's rho	p-*value for* H_0*: rho* = *0*
Constant	2	target	.382	.001
		no target	.211	.060
	4	target	.427	.000
		no target	.233	.037
	6	target	.259	.020
		no target	.002	.985
Varied	2	target	.219	.051
		no target	.163	.148
	4	target	.126	.266
		no target	.183	.104
	6	target	.203	.070
		no target	.150	.183
Sum of all conditions			.382	.001

Note: N = 80. BSV = between-session variability.

Table 6.10 Correlation of the number of significant correlations with age and CF score

	Age		*CF score*	
	Spearman's rho (N = *80*)	p-*value for* H_0*: rho* = *0*	*Spearman's rho* (N = *80*)	p-*value for* H_0*: rho* = *0*
Number of significant correlations	−.021	.855	.249	.030

CF = Culture Fair.

their characteristic "latent" distributions of CRTs and that the variability of these latent CRT distributions is consistent within and characteristic of individuals. Because the variability of the means of the "session samples" must reflect the standard error of the latent CRT distributions from which they are drawn it follows that variability in mean CRT from session to session will be affected by variability within individual sessions, so that extent of variability from session to session and from day to day will also be a stable individual difference characteristic. This was found to be the case. These stable individual differences in between-session variability are not explained by individual differences in rates of improvement with practice or by circadian effects. Individual differences in both within-session variability and between-session variability correlate modestly, but consistently and negatively, with scores on the Cattell and Cattell (1960) Culture Fair intelligence test but, after variance associated with Cattell scores has been taken into consideration, not with age between 50 and 79 years. In this experiment, in which age groups were selected to be balanced for Cattell scores, no effects of age were found. We must conclude that Cattell scores pick up all individual differences in variability that are associated with increasing age.

In most studies reported in the literature younger and older groups have been matched in terms of vocabulary test scores. This is accepted as good practice because vocabulary scores change little or not at all with age and, in young adults, correlate strongly with scores on tests of fluid ability. It follows that if older participants currently have similar vocabulary scores to younger participants they must, when they were young, have also had similar scores on tests of general fluid ability. However, because scores on tests of fluid ability markedly decline with age, the practice of matching groups on vocabulary test scores guarantees that older groups have significantly lower current scores on tests of fluid intelligence. We now know that individuals with lower intelligence test scores also have high BSVs. Consequently in studies in which groups of young and older adults are matched in terms of vocabulary test scores, or are selected at random, both within-session (WSV) and day-to-day variability (BSV) will increase with sample age.

Individual differences in WSV do not completely account for all differences in BSV. A simulation study showed that individuals' BSVs were significantly greater than could be accounted for by their WSVs alone. This was confirmed by a correlational analysis, which found significant co-variation across experimental sessions in mean CRTs from six different tasks. Evidently people experience systematic state changes between sessions that are independent of the effects of differences in their trial-to-trial variability during individual experimental runs and are also independent of circadian variability or of improvements due to practice.

Both simulation analyses and correlational analyses found stronger evidence for these systematic state changes in a high than in a low CF group. Two explanations seem possible: The first is that magnitudes of state changes are similar in both groups but are only detectable in the high CF group because, in the low CF group, their effects are masked by greater intrinsic BSV. The alternative explanation is that, independently of their lower WSVs, high CF individuals experience more marked state changes from session to session. The present results cannot decide this issue.

Methodological consequences of associations of between to within-session variability

Implications for comparisons of inter-individual variability between older and younger population samples

The extent to which individuals' mean CRTs vary from day to day must also determine the extent to which their mean CRTs will vary from each other when they are all tested on a single occasion. Useful meta-analyses of results from published experiments in which the younger and older groups compared have been matched for vocabulary test scores show that, on a variety of different tasks, inter-individual variability increases with the age of the samples tested (e.g., Morse, 1993). A new point from the present experiment is that, irrespective of their ages, members of groups of individuals with lower general intellectual ability will also vary more with respect to each other than will members of groups with higher general ability. As intelligence test performance markedly declines with age if groups of older and younger people are selected at random or, as we have seen, are matched on vocabulary test scores, the present results mean that inter-individual variability in CRTs will necessarily be greater in the older group.

Until now a sufficient explanation for the increase in inter-individual variability with age has been that because individuals age at different rates so differences between the most and least able individuals must increase with the age of the group sampled (Rabbitt, 1981). Although divergence in trajectories of ageing must indeed increase variability between individuals as sample age increases it now seems that increased BSV, driven by increased WSV, and consequent on declining general mental ability, must also play a part. This has general implications for the methodology of many kinds of study in cognitive gerontology. For example, studies to assess the effects of fluctuations in health on day-to-day variability in performance of older people must take into account the point that much of this variability is associated with declining general intellectual ability.

Age differences in variability and task difficulty

A voluminous literature shows that increases in task demands such as signal discriminability, signal response compatibility, or numbers of signal and response alternatives not only cause increases in mean CRTs but also in CRT variability (Luce, 1986). We now see that these increases in within-session variability must necessarily also bring about corresponding increases in between-session variability. That is, the more difficult that CRT tasks are made the more widely individuals' performance on them will vary from trial to trial and day to day. One of the most robust findings in cognitive gerontology is a pervasive Age × Task Difficulty interaction, such that differences in both the means and variances of CRT distributions obtained from older and younger adults markedly increase as tasks become more difficult (Cerella, 1985; Salthouse, 1985, 1991). It follows that increases in task difficulty must also exaggerate differences in day-to-day variability between old and young people, and it also follows that increases in task difficulty must also exaggerate differences in inter-individual variability within older and younger cohorts.

Implications of these findings for studies of circadian and other cyclical changes in performance

These findings raise hitherto unrecognized methodological problems for an extensive literature on circadian variations in performance. Humans experience regular patterns of change in efficiency during the course of the 24-hour cycle (e.g., Blake, 1967a, b; Colquhoun & Corcoran, 1964). Recent studies have asked whether circadian variations are affected by old age (e.g., Li, Hasher, Jonas, Rahhal, & May, 1998). In our own laboratory we have also compared patterns of circadian variations in mean CRTs between younger (60–65-year-old) and older (>70-year-old) individuals. Time-of-day effects could only rarely be detected in either of these age groups and, when they were statistically reliable, were much smaller than those reported for younger adults. Even when they were detectable, variations with time of day were also smaller in the older (>70 years) than in the younger (<65 years) groups. In our experiments as, perhaps, in Li et al.'s (1998) recent work, age groups were matched on vocabulary test scores. This is accepted as good practice because vocabulary scores change little or not at all with age and, in young adults, correlate strongly with scores on tests of fluid ability. However, because scores on tests of fluid ability markedly decline with age the practice of matching groups on vocabulary test scores guarantees that older groups have significantly lower current scores on tests of fluid intelligence. We now know that individuals with lower intelligence test scores also have higher BSVs. Consequently, as our unpublished studies suggest, unless intrinsic age differences in WSV and BSV are measured and taken into consideration, circadian variability will appear to be undetectable, or greatly reduced, in older samples.

The issue is of wider interest because of findings of differences in both the absolute extent and the patterns of circadian variability in performance shown by individuals who are classified as "introverts" and as "extroverts" in terms of their scores on the Maudesley personality inventory (MPI: see review by Broadbent, 1971). MPI scores are known to be modestly correlated with intelligence test scores, though the direction of this correlation is uncertain. Broadbent concludes that there are advantages for introverts, whereas a meta-analysis by Ackerman and Heggestad (1997) concludes advantages for extroverts. In either case the literature on individual differences in circadian rhythms must be re-evaluated before we know how far differences in observed amplitudes of circadian variability between introverts and extroverts can be accounted for by consistent differences in their characteristic WSVs and so in their BSVs, which are associated with differences in their levels of general intellectual ability.

Theoretical implications of associations between mean CRTs and performance variability

The basic theoretical question is how variability on simple tasks can be incorporated into functional models for individual differences in fluid intellectual ability and in age. All current functional models for fast decisions have been developed to account for changes in CRT distributions rather than in mean CRTs brought about by various task demands (Luce, 1986). Thus, in terms of these models CRT variability and mean CRTs are merely more or less informative indices of the same functional processes, and there seems no difficulty in principal in adapting most such models to account for individual differences in CRT variability. A further step would be to use them to derive more detailed functional specifications of the nature of differences between older and younger individuals (Salthouse, 1985, 1991) or between individuals of higher and lower general intellectual ability (Caryl, 1994; Eysenck, 1986; Reed, 1993; Reed & Jensen, 1992). This is problematic because available models account for CRT variability in terms of very different functional assumptions. Thus it does not yet seem sensible to select any one of them as the most plausible specification of a unique "primitive" performance characteristic of the central nervous system that determines individual differences in all cognitive skills associated with general intelligence or with cognitive ageing. To illustrate this it is helpful to compare some attempts to model age differences in CRTs.

Perhaps the simplest possible model for age-related slowing in CRTs assumes that each signal that occurs during a CRT task activates the same chain of N successive information processing units which, acting in series, identify it and then select and execute an appropriate response to it. If each successive unit has an operating time, t, observed CRTs will be a function of t (i.e., $N \times t$). That is, CRTs will be slower for difficult decisions that require chains of many units than for easier decisions that require fewer units. These simple assumptions can account for the robust findings that across tasks with very different levels of difficulty and qualitative demands, mean CRTs for groups of older or less able people can be closely estimated by multiplying mean CRTs for groups of younger or more able people by a single, empirically derived age or ability constant (Cerella, 1985). If we suppose that greater age or reduced ability lags the operating time for each unit by a constant, L ms, changes in mean CRT with age and ability will be a simple linear function of L (i.e., $\mathrm{L}t \times N$). In terms of this simplistic description the fact that distributions of CRTs always vary widely about their means can most easily be explained by supposing that the operating time, t, of each unit is not constant, but also varies from trial to trial. In this case observed distributions of CRTs, which are the summed operating times of all units, will precisely reflect the unobservable distributions of the termination times for individual units (see Rabbitt, 1992). On the assumption that the lag for each unit, L, is constant, additive, and independent of unit operating time t, the effect of greater age or lower ability will be to move the entire CRT distribution along the RT axis without altering its shape. In this case mean CRTs will increase, but with no change in the shapes of the CRT distributions from which they are derived. In fact this is not the case, and greater age, lower ability, and the ingestion of alcohol multiplicatively scale entire CRT distributions, with markedly greater effect on slow than on fast CRTs (see Maylor & Rabbitt, 1987; Rabbitt & Maylor, 1991). This makes it necessary to assume that the age scaling of distributions of unit operating times, t, is multiplicative, rather than additive and so increases slower operating times relatively more than faster operating times. Given this assumption, even this simple adaptation of the unit lag model, which would be congenial for explanations of individual differences in terms of delayed synaptic transmission or slower neural conduction pathways, can generate the prediction that a change in a single hypothetical neurophysiological system performance parameter, unit lag, will markedly affect the variances, as the prediction that a change in a single hypothetical neurophysiological system performance parameter, unit lag, will markedly affect the variances, as well as the means, of distributions of observed CRTs.

However, we suggest that the available data can be equally well explained in terms of any of the wide variety of quite different assumptions about the nature of functional processes underlying fast decisions. For example, to account for the logarithmic or power functions that characterize improvements with practice in decision speeds on all tasks Crossman (1958) assumed that, early in practice, decisions may be made by any one of a number of different pathways.

Some of these pathways are optimally direct, involve few units, and so complete identification of a signal and selection of a response faster than others that are longer and involve more units. Early in practice pathways are selected more or less at random with the result that average decision times are slow, and variability from trial to trial is large. As practice continues more optimal pathways are progressively selected, and less efficient pathways are discarded with a consequent logarithmic or power-function reduction in mean decision times and a directly correlated reduction in trial-to-trial variance. This model can also account for individual differences in means and variances of decision times without any assumption of changes in the transmission lags of neurophysiological units. Instead we may suggest that older or less able individuals have impoverished decision networks with a smaller likelihood of maximally efficient pathways, or that they are less able to optimize pathway selection. Note that in this case we appear to lose parsimony because we must invoke not one but several distinct functional system performance characteristics to explain joint and correlated changes in the forms of CRT distributions. However in return for this we obtain a model that is capable of explaining not only individual differences in mean CRTs and CRT variance but also differences in the rates at which people of different ages and levels of ability improve the means and standard deviations of their CRTs during practice at simple tasks.

Much more elegant and plausible parallel process models are discussed by Luce (1986) and Townsend and Ashby (1983), who focus on the fact that CRT distributions can be modeled by Poisson distributions or gamma functions. Such descriptions closely fit the output characteristics predicted for "distributed parallel self-terminating" systems, which assume that to make any decision a number of pathways are simultaneously activated and proceed to termination. A response is chosen by selecting the first pathway to terminate ("first-past-the-post horse-race model") or by averaging of a sample of the outcomes of a sub-set of these processes. In these cases time-proportionate lagging of all pathways by a multiplicative constant would produce the linear scaling of CRT distributions just as in the model by Crossman (1958) discussed earlier. Thus, alternative explanations of individual differences can be based on the assumptions that decision criteria, or the number of available parallel pathways, vary between older and younger and between more and less able people.

Predictions similar to those made by distributed parallel process models can be derived from quite different functional assumptions suggested by Rabbitt and Vyas (1969) and Smith and Brewer (1995). These are that people actively control the distributions of their CRTs by varying their response speed from trial to trial so as to locate a region where they maximize both speed and accuracy. Individuals are known to make the most of their errors because they transgress this optimal trade-off region, but to be able to recognize most of the errors that they make and to use this feedback to slow down in order to improve accuracy. In contrast they can detect unnecessarily slow responses only by reference to an internal "clock" or "timekeeper". This was considered necessary to explain the fact that whereas older and younger people differ hardly at all in terms of the fastest correct responses that they can make, or in their speed–error trade-off limits, they do differ substantially in their mean CRTs. As we have noted, these differences in mean CRTs reflect the fact that older people make many more unnecessarily slow responses—that is, to the greater within-session variability of the aged. Rabbitt and Vyas (1969) suggested that this may be due to failures of speed monitoring, or to imprecision of the internal clock that is used to calibrate response speed. Recently Wearden, Wearden, and Rabbitt (1997) have shown that whereas older and younger individuals may be equally accurate in their *mean* judgements of time-interval duration, or in their mean accuracy of interval generation, older and less able participants show markedly greater variability in both these tasks. Thus individual differences in accuracy of time estimation could directly account for the effects of age and ability on CRT variability.

Note that these models have not been selected as the best articulated or most plausible available. They are only described as an illustration that in our present state of understanding any number of CRT models derived from very different functional assumptions can all account for all existing data on consistent individual differences in mean and median decision times and trial-to-trial variance. Unfortunately it cannot be guaranteed that further behavioural data from CRT experiments alone will resolve this problem. Townsend and Ashby (1983) have formally shown that even when such data become available it is most likely that they will still be well fitted by a variety of very different functional models. We may have to face the fact that, in principle, data on the means and distributions of CRTs may not uniquely support any single functional model that maps on to a uniquely plausible description of decision-making processes in the human central nervous system. At present the best way forward seems not to search for a single factor that explains individual differences in performance even in all CRT tasks, but rather to hope advances in techniques, such as evoked potential recording, scanning and imaging, or multiple cell recording, make new kinds of data available.

Where do we go from here?

These findings suggest that in all tasks for which the performance index measured is in units of speed or time less able and older people will be found to vary more from moment to moment and, for that reason alone, also from day to day. Wearden et al. (1997) found that less able individuals also show greater variability from trial to trial in time interval estimation, interval bisection, and interval production tasks. Models for time estimation assume that individuals generate or judge intervals by reference to a standard that varies more or less from trial to trial during an experiment. Thus, like consistent individual differences in trial-to-trial variability of CRTs, individual differences in variability can also be modelled as samplings of more or less variable characteristic distributions of variability of internal standards held in memory. This would mean that individual differences in moment-to-moment variability would directly translate into equivalent differences in average variability from day to day and also differences in variability between individuals compared on a single occasion.

An obvious next question for research is whether individuals who consistently show greater variability in CRTs also show greater variability in other tasks. It seems that, at least for time judgements, this must be the case because individuals' Cattell Culture Fair scores predict their trial-by-trial variability in both CRT and time estimation tasks. However comparisons of the same individuals on both CRT tasks and time estimation tasks would provide necessary, more conclusive evidence. A more general question is whether variability in CRT tasks or in time estimation tasks is also associated with variability in the accuracy of psychophysical judgements such as of brightness, colour, line-length, the frequence or loudness of tones, or weight. Further questions are whether individual differences in variability of thresholds can also be modelled in terms of characteristic distributions of threshold variability, with the result that variability within any individual experimental session also reflects variability from day to day and variability between individuals.

References

Ackerman, P.L., & Heggestad, E.D. (1997). Intelligence. Personality and interests: Evidence for overlapping traits. *Psychological Bulletin, 121*, 219–245.

Anderson, M. (1995). Evidence for a single global factor of developmental change—too good to be true? *Australian Journal of Psychology, 47*, 18–24.

Blake, M.J.F. (1967a). Relationship between circadian rhythm of body-temperature and introversion–extroversion. *Nature, London, 199*, 1312.

Blake, M.J.F. (1967b). Time of day effects on performance in a range of tasks. *Psychonomic Science, 9*, 349–350.

Brand, C.R., & Deary, I.Z. (1982). Intelligence and inspection time. In H.J. Eysenck (Ed.), *A model for intelligence*. New York: Springer-Verlag.

Broadbent, D.E. (1971). *Decision & stress*. New York: Academic Press.

Carpenter, P.A., Just, M.A., & Shell, P. (1990). What one intelligence test measures: A theoretical account of the processing in the Raven's progressive matrices test. *Psychological Review, 97*, 404–431.

Caryl, P.G. (1994). Early event-related potential correlate with inspection times and intelligence. *Intelligence, 18*, 15–45.

Cattell, R.B., & Cattell, A.K.S. (1960). *Handbook for the individual or group Culture Fair intelligence test.* Champaign, IL: IPAT.

Cerella, J. (1985). Information processing rate in the elderly. *Psychological Bulletin, 98*, 67–83.

Colquhoun, W.P., & Corcoran, D.W.J. (1964). The effects of time of day and social isolation on the relationship between temperament and performance. *British Journal of Social and Clinical Psychology, 3*, 226–231.

Crossman, E.R.F.W. (1958). A theory of the acquisition of speed-skill. *Ergonomics, 2*, 153–166.

Deary, I.J. (1995). Auditory inspection time and intelligence: What is the direction of causation? *Developmental Psychology, 31*, 237–250.

Eysenck, H.J. (1986). The theory of intelligence and the psychophysiology of cognition. In R.J. Sternberg (Ed.), *Advances in the psychology of human intelligence* (Vol. 3). Hillsdale, NJ: Lawrence Erlbaum Associates, Inc.

Hertzog, C. (1989). Influences of cognitive slowing on age differences in intelligence. *Developmental Psychology, 25*, 636–651.

Horn, J.L. (1982). The theory of fluid and crystallised intelligence in relation to concepts of cognitive psychology and aging in adulthood. In F.I.M. Craik & S. Trehub (Eds.), *Aging and cognitive processes.* Boston: Plenum.

Howell, C.L. (1992). *Statistical methods for psychology* (3rd ed., p. 42). London: Duxbury Press.

Jensen, A.R. (1980). Chronometric analysis of mental ability. *Journal of Social and Biological Structures, 3*, 181–224.

Jensen, A.R., & Whang, P.A. (1993). Reaction times and intelligence: A comparison of Chinese–American and Anglo–American children. *Journal of Biosocial Science, 25*, 397–410.

Li, K.Z.H., Hasher, L., Jonas, D., Rahhal, T.A., & May, C.P. (1998). Distractability, circadian arousal and aging: A boundary condition? *Psychology and Aging, 13*, 574–583.

Luce, R.D. (1986). *Response times: Their role in inferring elementary mental organisation.* Oxford, UK: Oxford University Press.

Maylor, E.A., & Rabbitt, P.M.A. (1987). Effects of alcohol and practice on choice reaction time. *Perception and Psychophysics, 42*, 465–475.

Morse, C.K. (1993). Does variability increase with age? An archival study of cognitive measures. *Psychology and Aging, 8*, 156–164.

Rabbitt, P.M.A. (1969). Psychology refractory delay and response–stimulus interval duration in serial, choice-response tasks. In W. Koster (Ed.), *Attention and performance II* (pp. 195–219). Amsterdam: North Holland Publishing Company. Also in *Acta Psychologica, 30*, 195–219.

Rabbitt, P.M.A. (1981). Cognitive psychology needs models for changes in performance with old age. In A.D. Baddeley & J. Long (Eds.), *Attention and performance IX*. Hillsdale, NJ: Lawrence Erlbaum Associates, Inc.

Rabbitt, P.M.A. (1988). The faster the better? Some comments on the use of information processing rate as index of change in individual differences in performance.

In I. Hindmarch & B. Aufdembrinke (Eds.), *Psycho-pharmacology and reaction time*. London: John Wiley.

Rabbitt, P.M.A. (1992). Many happy repetitions: A celebration of the "Bertelson Repetition Effect", 1961 to 1991. In J. Allegria, D. Hollander, J. Junca de Morais, & M. Radeau (Eds.), *Analytic approaches to human cognition*. Amsterdam: Elsevier.

Rabbitt, P.M.A. (1993a). Crystal Quest: An examination of the concepts of "fluid" and "crystallised" intelligence as explanation for cognitive changes in old age. In A.D. Baddeley & L. Weiskrantz (Eds.), *Attention, selection, awareness and control*. Oxford, UK: Oxford University Press.

Rabbitt, P.M.A. (1993b). Does it all go together when it goes? *Quarterly Journal of Experimental Psychology, 46A*, 285–434.

Rabbitt, P.M.A., Banerji, N., & Szymanski, A. (1989). Space Fortress as an IQ test? Predictions of learning and of practised performance in a complex interactive video-game. *Acta Psychologica, 71*, 243–257.

Rabbitt, P.M.A., Donlan, C., McInnes, L., Bent, N., & Watson, P. (1993). The University of Manchester longitudinal study of cognitive change in normal old age. *Zeitschrift fur Gerontologie, 26*, 176–183.

Rabbitt, P.M.A., & Goward, L. (1994). Age, information processing speed and intelligence. *Quarterly Journal of Experimental Psychology, 47A*, 741–760.

Rabbitt, P.M.A., & Maylor, E.A. (1991). Investigating models of human performance. *British Journal of Psychology, 82*, 259–290.

Rabbitt, P.M.A., & Vyas, S.M. (1969). An elementary preliminary taxonomy for some errors in laboratory choice RT tasks. *Acta Psychologica, 33*, 56–76. Also in A. Sanders (Ed.), *Attention and performance III*. Amsterdam: North Holland Publishing Company.

Rabbitt, P.M.A., & Yang, Q. (1996). What are the functional bases of individual differences in memory ability? In D. Herrmann, C. McEvoy, C. Hertzog, P. Hertel, & M.K. Johnson (Eds.), *Basic and applied memory research. Theory in context* (Vol. 1., pp. 127–159). Mahwah, NJ: Lawrence Erlbaum Associates, Inc.

Reed, T.E. (1993). Effects of enriched (complex) environment on nerve conduction velocity: New data and implications for the speed of information processing. *Intelligence, 17*, 461–474.

Reed, T.E., & Jensen, A.R. (1992). Conduction velocity in a brain-nerve pathway of normal adults correlates with intelligence level. *Intelligence, 16*, 259–272.

Salthouse, T.A. (1985). *A cognitive theory of aging*. Berlin: Springer-Verlag.

Salthouse, T.A. (1991). *Theoretical perspectives on cognitive aging*. Hillsdale, NJ: Lawrence Erlbaum Associates, Inc.

Salthouse, T.J. (1996). The processing-speed theory of adult age differences in cognition. *Psychological Review*, 103, 403–428.

Smith, G.A., & Brewer, N. (1995). Slowness and age: Speed–accuracy mechanisms. *Psychology and Aging*, 11, 326–347.

SPSS-X Users guide (3rd ed.). (1988). Chicago, IL: SPSS, Inc.

Sternberg, S. (1969). Memory scanning: Mental processes revealed by reaction time experiments. *American Scientist, 57*, 421–457.

Townsend, J.T., & Ashby, F.G. (1983). *Stochastic modelling of elementary psychological processes*. Cambridge, UK: Cambridge University Press.

Vernon, P.A. (1983). Speed of information processing and intelligence. *Intelligence*, 7, 53–70.

Vernon, P.A. (1985). Individual differences in general cognitive ability. In L.C. Hartledge & C.F. Telzner (Eds.), *The neuropsychology of individual differences: A developmental perspective*. New York: Plenum.

Wearden, J.A., Wearden, A.J., & Rabbitt, P.M.A. (1997). Age and IQ effects on stimulus and response timing. *Journal of Experimental Psychology: Human Perception and Performance*, *23*, 239–251.

Variability and how we control our performance

It is statistically inevitable that moment-to-moment and day-to-day variability should be strongly related. This is because the distribution of a person's CRTs during a single testing session can be considered as a sample drawn from a much larger distribution of all the CRTs that he or she may produce over many different sessions experienced during many weeks or months. It follows that the variance of CRTs in each individual session-sample must mirror the variance of the distribution of CRTs cumulated over all sessions over these longer periods. In this respect trial-to-trial variance in CRTs reflects a stable individual performance characteristic of any person we study. Rabbitt et al. (2001) compared individuals with higher and lower scores on the Cattell "Culture Fair" Intelligence Test and found that those with higher *gf* scores were less variable both in terms of the CRTs they produced during single testing sessions and in terms of their average scores for sessions experienced on different days. Thus trial-to-trial and day-to-day variability are directly linked and reflect performance characteristic that is associated with fluid intelligence. Slower mean CRTs of lower *gf* individuals reflects their poorer ability to control their response speeds from trial to trial as much as it reflects the maximum speed with which they can make individual correct responses. So *gf* affects precision of control as much as, or more than, it affects maximum information processing rate.

Many convincing studies have shown that trial-to-trial variability during CRT tasks increases in old age (Hultsch et al., 2002; Hultsch, Strauss et al., 2008) and with the onset of dementias (Hultsch et al., 2000). We may speculate that weakening of control over variability of performance with increasing age largely, or perhaps even entirely, accounts for age-related slowing of CRT means.

When volunteers' mean CRTs and calendar ages are used in regression equations as joint predictors of scores on tests of other cognitive abilities, such as memory, a usual finding is that once CRT has been taken into consideration age makes no independent prediction (Salthouse, 1996). This has encouraged the hypothesis that "global slowing" is a unique system performance characteristic that can be measured in simple CRT tasks and accounts for all age-related variance in a variety of different cognitive abilities (cf. Salthouse 1996; 2000). I suggest that it is premature to conclude that "speed" is a basic functional characteristic of the central nervous system.

In other contexts, other investigators have directly identified response speed as measured by CRTs with neurophysiological characteristics such as neural conduction speed, synaptic transmission time and the latency of cortical evoked responses (Eysenck, 1987; Jensen, 1982; Hendrickson & Hendrickson, 1980) and identified these as the biological basis of fluid intelligence (*gf*). The results by Rabbitt et al. (2001) suggest that these speculations are premature and incomplete. Individual differences in mean CRTs do not simply reflect lags of excitation in neural networks but also the efficiency of more complex higher-order processes of self-monitoring and control of responses.

References

Eysenck, H. J. (1987). Speed of information processing, reaction time, and the theory of intelligence. In P. A. Vernon (Ed.), *Speed of Information-processing and Intelligence* (pp. 21–67). Westport, CT: Ablex.

Hendrickson, D. E., & Hendrickson, A. E. (1980). The biological basis of individual differences in intelligence. *Personality and Individual Differences, 1*(1), 3–33.

Hultsch, D. F., MacDonald, S. W., & Dixon, R. A. (2002). Variability in reaction time performance of younger and older adults. *The Journals of Gerontology Series B: Psychological Sciences and Social Sciences, 57*(2), P101–P115.

Hultsch, D. F., MacDonald, S. W., Hunter, M. A., Levy-Bencheton, J., & Strauss, E. (2000). Intraindividual variability in cognitive performance in older adults: Comparison of adults with mild dementia, adults with arthritis, and healthy adults. *Neuropsychology, 14*(4), 588–598.

Hultsch, D. F., Strauss, E., Hunter, M. A., & MacDonald, S.W.S. (2008). Intraindividual variability, cognition, and aging. In F.I.M. Craik & T. A. Salthouse (Eds), *The Handbook of Aging and Cognition* (3rd edn) (pp. 491–556). New York, Hove: Psychology Press.

Jensen, A. R. (1982). Reaction time and psychometric *g*. In H. J. Eysenck (Ed.), *A Model for Intelligence* (pp. 93–132). Berlin, Heidelberg: Springer.

Rabbitt, P., Osman, P., Moore, B., & Stollery, B. (2001). There are stable individual differences in performance variability, both from moment to moment and from day to day. *Quarterly Journal of Experimental Psychology Section A, 54*(4), 981–1003.

Salthouse, T. A. (1996). The processing-speed theory of adult age differences in cognition. *Psychological Review, 103*(3), 403–428.

Salthouse, T. (2000). *A Theory of Cognitive Aging* (Vol. 28). Amsterdam: North-Holland.

Detecting our errors to control what we do

It is a plausible guess that the processes of identifying signals and choosing correct responses to them involve stages that occur successively in time: that is to say we must first recognize a signal, then choose an appropriate response to it from among a set of learned alternatives and then programme some part of our body to make this response. If we do not take enough time to reliably complete any one of these processes, errors become likely. We may mistake one signal for another; we may select the wrong response or, having chosen a correct response, we may for some unknown reason helplessly make another. This prompts the question whether we can equally efficiently and rapidly detect failures in each and any of these separate and putatively successive processes. This, in turn, begs the question whether the factors that make choices between responses more difficult, and so increase the numbers of errors that we make, may also affect the accuracy and speed with which we can recognize and correct the resulting response-confusion errors.

Early recognition of what later was formally discussed as the "Simon effect" (e.g. Simon, Sly & Vilapakkam, 1981) showed us that even in easy CRT tasks in which people respond to signals by making responses involving "natural" or "compatible" (C) left to right spatial mappings of signal lights on to keys, they respond faster and more accurately than when they must choose between responses involving arbitrary, spatially "incompatible" (I) mappings of unfamiliar signal/response-key allocations that they must learn to use.

Shirley Phillips and I wondered whether people can recognize errors due to misremembering a spatially incompatible signal/response mapping because, in this case, they would, in fact, have made the (incorrect) response that they intended. We asked whether such errors could be recognized and, if they could, whether they were detected more slowly, and perhaps less frequently than errors made with spatially compatible mappings (Rabbitt & Phillips, 1967).

Burns (1965) had found that, even in tasks with incompatible mappings, errors are faster than other correct responses and that volunteers can correct errors in both compatible and incompatible mapping conditions. He suggested that this is because such errors are, in effect, second attempts following near misses that have provided partial information of what the appropriate response should have been. Shirley and I had used a similar task to ask a different question: in Spatially Incompatible (IM) mapping tasks many errors are caused by forgetting, or by confusions between, arbitrary signal/response mappings but in Spatially Compatible (CM) tasks forgetting or confusion of signal/response allocations rarely occurs. We argued that in IM tasks errors may happen either because insufficient time has been taken or because a mapping rule has been forgotten or confused. We asked whether these additional, probably slow, errors due to confusions of mapping rules can be corrected and, if so, whether volunteers take longer to do this.

We practiced volunteers for four runs of 500 signals and responses in both CM and IM conditions. In both cases, and at all levels of practice, Error

Correcting Responses were faster than immediate repetitions of correct responses. This is not what we would have found if Burns' (1965) hypothesis were correct. In the C condition ECRs became slightly, but not significantly faster with practice. In contrast, in the I condition ECRs were, at first, some 300 msec. slower than in the C condition but, as practice continued, they approached the same speed.

In this study the incidence of errors in the C condition varied between subjects from 1.1 to 6.8% (mean 3.2) and in the I condition from 2.6 to 9.2% (mean 4.8). This replicated Burns' (1965) finding that errors made in either mapping condition can be detected and corrected. We also found that, early in practice, average RTs for errors were slower in the I than in the C condition. This suggested that errors in different mapping conditions occur for different reasons. In the C condition, as in all of the simpler tasks we earlier discussed, errors are premature fast responses. In the I condition, although some errors may also be premature fast responses, many others are slower, unsuccessful attempts to remember the correct mapping assignments.

In the C condition Error-Correction Reaction Times (ECRTs) were faster than Correct RTs during all four practice runs. Practice reduced mean ECRTs slightly, but not significantly, from 447 msec. to 399 msec. In the I condition CRTs reduced with practice from 643 msec. (i.e. much slower than in the C condition), to 415 msec. – statistically indistinguishable from the C condition. This suggested that early in practice volunteers often took enough time to recognize that they had confused the mapping rule and, having done so, needed additional time to organize a new, appropriate response from scratch.

We concluded that errors in the I condition were a mixture of slow failures to recall mapping rules and much faster premature responses. After 1500 practice trials, mapping rules had been successfully learned so that the few rule-confusion errors that occurred were impulsive fast responses – as was the case at all levels of practice in the C condition. We could, of course, have directly checked this by comparing not only the means but the distributions of RTs for errors and ECRs in both compatibility conditions across successive levels of practice. I have, for the last 50 years, been painfully embarrassed that I did not think to do this and that, as far as I know, it still remains an open question. Our summary lessons were: (1) people can very rapidly correct fast, impulsive errors; (2) the times taken to correct fast impulsive errors do not change with practice; (3) people can also, but much more slowly, correct failures to recall mapping rules that occur early in practice.

These findings showed that both fast impulsive errors and slow mapping confusions can be corrected but the marked difference in the speeds of corrections for these two classes of errors suggested that different processes are involved in each case. An obvious question was whether people can also correct errors due to incorrect identifications of signals. The next paper reproduced describes a study that Geoff Cumming, Subhash Vyas and I made to test this.

References

Burns, J. T. (1965). The effect of errors on reaction time in a serial reaction task. Unpublished Ph.D. thesis, University of Michigan.

Rabbitt, P.M.A., & Phillips, S. (1967). Error-detection and correction latencies as a function of S-R compatibility. *Quarterly Journal of Experimental Psychology, 19*(1), 37–42.

Simon, J. R., Sly, P. E., & Vilapakkam, S. (1981). Effect of compatibility of S-R mapping on reactions toward the stimulus source. *Acta Psychologica, 47*(1), 63–81.

7 Some errors of perceptual analysis in visual search can be detected and corrected

P.M.A. Rabbitt, G. Cumming and S.M. Vyas

Introduction

We know that people can detect and correct most of the errors which they make when they carry out laboratory keyboard tasks (Rabbitt, 1966*a*, *b*; 1967, 1968; Rabbitt and Vyas, 1970). One way in which they manage to do this arises from the fact that they can see, feel or hear when they have made a response which was different from the one they intended. If we formalise this statement by analogy with servo-mechanisms we may say that errors in response execution can be detected if feedback from each response is monitored, and checked against some "program" which specifies the response actually required. When a discrepancy between this program and the response feedback is noted, an error is detected. If there is no discrepancy the response has been correctly executed.

Megaw (1972) studied errors made by subjects carrying out gross hand-movements in response to discrete signals. He found that E.M.G. recordings showed anticipatory changes in muscle tension up to 100 ms before any overt limb movement could be observed. Thus feedback from responding muscles might be available to a subject even before the beginning of an incorrect response could be recorded by experimental equipment. The finding that error correction responses (ECRs) can be made very rapidly indeed after errors may partly reflect this fact (Rabbitt, 1966*a*, *b*; 1968).

There is little doubt that people correct many, or even most, of their errors by monitoring kinaesthetic feedback in the way Megaw (1972) has suggested. It is also clear that visual feedback can be used to detect errors. For example skilled typists deprived of sight of their copy miss many errors which they otherwise can notice (Long, 1976). The question is whether *all* errors are detected and corrected in this way.

There are several reasons to doubt this. One is that during simple keyboard tasks an ECR may follow an error within intervals as short as 14–40 ms, or even less (Rabbitt, 1966*a*). In all other experiments discussed by Rabbitt (e.g. 1966*b*; 1967, 1968) only mean ECRTs have been presented. Re-analyses of these data, however, show that in fact in all experiments every individual subject made at least one ECR within 10 ms of completing a preceeding error. In all these experiments subjects had to answer each of two or more signals by depressing the appropriate one of the same number of response keys. Each key had to be depressed with a different finger. Errors were "corrected" by making the response which should have been made. Thus these experiments all strongly suggest that subjects sometimes initiated *two* separate responses, one with each of two fingers. These responses occurred either in very rapid succession, or simultaneously within the resolution of the experimental equipment used (i.e. 10 ms). To call one of such a pair of responses an "error correction" seems to miss an important distinction. How can we be certain that, at the moment in time when the responses were initiated, the subject knew *which* of them was correct? Our current models for response programming and execution evidently need to be adapted to explain how *two* responses, one correct and one incorrect, may be simultaneously initiated.

A different reason for doubting that errors can only be corrected by feedback checking, comes from considering the *kinds* of errors which subjects apparently can correct. On a feedback-checking model there would be no way in which a man could possibly detect or correct an error of perceptual identification. If he mistook one signal, A, for another, B, and made a response appropriate to B, feedback checking could only reassure him that he had made the response he intended. Thus any demonstration that people can correct errors of perceptual discrimination must imply that feedback monitoring is not the only means by which errors can be detected.

In practice it is very difficult to show that errors of perceptual discrimination can be corrected. Rabbitt and Vyas (1978, in press) report three experiments in which subjects discriminated between pairs of signals. Some discriminations were trivially easy, and others were more difficult. More errors were made to difficult discriminations. Since the choice between responses was the same in all cases, we may assume that these "extra" errors represent failures of perceptual discrimination rather than of response choice or execution.

In two of these experiments, when subjects responded to pairs of tones, the same *absolute* number of errors was corrected at both levels of discrimination difficulty. That is, a much smaller *proportion* of errors was corrected when the discrimination was difficult. There was thus no evidence that subjects could correct any of the "extra" errors due to discrimination failure. The hypothesis that *only* response errors could be corrected, and that these could be corrected by checking kinaesthetic feedback, completely accounts for these results.

However in the third experiment, where subjects made relative line length judgments, this was not the case. As before, many more errors were made to difficult than to easy discriminations, and a much smaller *proportion* of these "extra" errors were corrected. However the absolute number of errors corrected did increase slightly, but significantly, as discrimination became more difficult. In this case we cannot say that *no* errors of perceptual discrimination were ever corrected.

The general difficulty is that analyses of errors, and of ECRs, must always be carried out *post hoc* after data have been collected. For this reason it is usually impossible to be certain whether any particular error was due to a failure of perceptual discrimination, to a failure in response execution, or to a failure in some other transaction between signal onset and response completion.

One way of getting around this problem is to find a task in which all responses are equally easy to make, but in which all errors can be, *post hoc*, taken to represent one of two different *kinds* of perceptual mistake. In this case the same numbers of response errors will be classified as "type 1" or "type 2" mistakes, and the same numbers of response errors, so classified, will be corrected in each case. A finding that type 1 errors are more frequent than type 2 errors, (or *vice versa*) must then mean that one kind of perceptual mistake is more common than the other. A further finding that more errors of one kind than the other are corrected must further mean that at least some kinds of perceptual mistake can be detected by subjects who make them.

Consider a visual search task in which subjects inspect one display of letters at a time. If any member of a designated set of target letters is present they make one response. If no target letter is present they make another. On *post hoc* analysis all their errors can be divided into two classes. Either they will indicate that no target letter was present when one was there (Omission Error, OE) or they will indicate that a target letter was present when it was not (False Identification Error, FI). If both responses are equally easy, the same number of response errors will be subsequently counted into each of these classes. Thus if *N* OEs > *N* FIs or *N* FIs > *N* OEs we may deduce that one sort of perceptual mistake is more common than the other. Further, since both kinds of response errors should be corrected equally often, if we find that a larger absolute number of OEs than FIs are corrected (or *vice versa*), we must deduce that this difference represents an advantage in correctability for that particular kind of perceptual error.

Experiment

Method and apparatus

A Linc 8 computer was programmed to present horizontal lines of capital letters of the English alphabet across the middle of a Cathode Ray Tube display. These letters were drawn up in points in the conventional Linc 8 format, and were 6 mm high, averaged 4 mm wide and 2 mm apart. A generator program was used to set up, afresh for each subject, 10 different sequences of 100 successive displays. In five of these sequences each display contained five letters and in the remainder each display contained nine letters. For each subject a different four letters of the alphabet was randomly selected and designated his "targets". Subjects peered through a viewing tube, with a head rest to keep their eyes 40 cm from the display and to reduce head movements.

They scanned displays one at a time, pressing a response key under one fore-finger if they saw any of their four targets on a display, (T response) and pressing another key under the other fore-finger if they decided that no target was present (NT response).

The generator program automatically constructed sequences so that half the displays each contained one target letter while the others contained background letters only. All target letters occurred equally often and might appear with equal probability in any left-to-right display position. Background letters were also selected at random from the 22 non-target letters of the alphabet. They also occurred equally often in all display positions. The only constraint was that all letters on each display were always different.

Subjects experienced these 10 runs of displays, in counter-balanced order for display size, during a single $1\frac{1}{2}$ th experimental session. Each run took about 3 min, and there were rest pauses during which data were analysed and summary feedback on average errors and RT was given. Each run began with the signal "READY" on the Cathode Ray Tube followed, 2 s later, by the first display of the sequence. The subject then responded, and the display disappeared within 2 ms and was followed, 50 ms later, by the next in the sequence. The subject continued responding as quickly and accurately as possible until the sequence ended.

Subjects were told to try and detect all the errors they might make, and to immediately signal them by making an ECR—that is, by immediately pressing the key they should have pressed (always, obviously, the alternate key). They then had to pause for 5 s, counting aloud to 10 before responding to the new display confronting them. This was done so that intentional ECRs could be discriminated in computer output from other cases in which the subject failed to detect an error, and simply responded to the next display in sequence. No response following any error was counted as a valid ECR unless it was followed by such a pause.

The computer recorded every display presented, recorded the response made to it, (and labelled it correct or wrong) and recorded the elapsed time between the onset of each display and the sequent key press to within 1 ms Error Correction Reaction Time (ECRT) was thus timed from the onset of the display immediately following the incorrect response. This was taken into account by adding a constant of 50 ms (response-display interval) to the ECRTs recorded by the computer.

The procedure of organising events so that each display was immediately followed by another, entailing ECRs made in the presence of a new display, has obvious drawbacks but was deliberately chosen for the following reasons.

First it was important to give the subjects no external indication when an error had occurred. Delay of the Error + 1 display would have constituted such a cue.

Second, it would have been possible to have response-display intervals long enough for the subject to make an ECR if necessary, before the next display occurred. Pilot experiments with R-D intervals of 1500 ms or longer showed no deviations in the relative *proportions* of different kinds of error detected, so that it is unlikely that the main conclusions of this study would be affected by this change. With such long R-D intervals performance was slow, and RTs were much more variable.

A deciding factor in favour of very short R-D intervals was that each new display provided a very effective mask, such as might be assumed to terminate at least iconic persistence of the preceeding event (Sperling 1960; Ericksen and Steffy, 1964; Neisser, 1967). Thus error correction cannot be assumed to occur because subjects were able to continue to analyse the persisting trace of a display after it had faded from the Cathode Ray Tube. Other pilot experiments coupling long R-D intervals with random dot masks superimposed on the Cathode Ray Tube as each response was made were not encouraging. Subjects responded slowly and erratically, with unusually high variance in RTs.

The decision was made to leave these methodological curiosities for further investigation and to accept the present technique, with its limitations, as the best for the current purpose.

Subjects and procedure

Subjects were 20 male laboratory assistants and research students aged between 18 and 27 years. None had any knowledge of the purpose of the experiment or of the hypotheses motivating it. All subjects served for a single $1\frac{1}{2}$ session during which they each experienced 10 runs of 200 successive displays. These runs were with the five letter and nine-letter display conditions alternately, half starting with five-letter displays and half with nine-letter displays.

Results

The data from all 10 runs experienced by each subject with each display size were printed out and errors were located and classified either as "Omissions" (O) (when a subject signalled that a target was not present when, in fact, it was) or "False Identifications" (FI) (when a subject signalled that a target was present when, in fact, it was not).

The overall mean error rate was 3.908% for the five-letter displays and 5.85% for the nine-letter displays. This difference was significant by Wilcoxon's matched pairs signed ranks test across individual subjects' data ($T = 2$; $P < 0.01$ two tailed).

The numbers of O and FI errors committed and corrected in each condition are set out in Table 7.1

Table 7.1 Analysis of errors committed and corrected

Five-letter displays		*Number of Errors*	
Omission errors:	Total	258	(74.8% of all errors)
Corrected O errors		95	(36.8% of total Os)
Uncorrected O errors		163	(63.2% of total Os)
False identification errors:	Total	87	(25.2% of all errors)
Corrected FII errors		72	(82.76% of all FIs)
Uncorrected FI errors		15	(17.24% of all FIs)
	Total errors	345	(3.508% of all recorded responses)*
Nine-letter displays			
Omission errors	Total	430	(75% of all errors)
Corrected O errors		130	(30.2% of total Os)
Uncorrected O errors		300	(69.8% of total Os)
False identification errors:	Total	143	(25% of all Errors)
Corrected FI errors		77	(53.8% of total FIs)
Uncorrected FI errors		66	(46.2% of total FIs)
	Total errors	573	(5.85% of all responses)*

* Responses made to displays following corrected and uncorrected errors not recorded.

A two-way Analysis of Variance (ANOVA) showed that more O errors than FI errors occurred ($F = 14.2$, $df = 1.9$, $P < 0.01$) and that more errors were made with the nine-letter displays than with the five-letter displays (F = 12.8, df = 9, $P < 0.01$). There was a significant interaction between these terms; ($F = 6.5$, $df = 1,9$, $P < 0.05$). Table 7.1 shows that the interaction occurs because, as display size increased, the number of Omissions increased more sharply than the number of False Identifications.

A second ANOVA showed that more O errors than FI errors were corrected ($F = 13.1$; $df = 1,9$, $P < 0.01$) and that more errors were corrected in the nine-letter display condition than in the five-letter display condition ($F = 16.2$, $df = 1,9$, $P < 0.05$). The interaction between these terms was significant ($F = 7.3$, $df = 1,9$, $P < 0.05$).

Table 7.1 shows that the interaction occurs because more O errors were corrected in the nine-letter display condition than in the five-letter display condition, while about the same number of FI errors were corrected in both conditions.

It may be misleading to consider only the total *numbers* of errors which were corrected. Table 7.1 shows that while fewer FI than O errors were made, a higher *percentage* of FI than of O errors were subsequently corrected.

This was checked by obtaining the percentages of FI and of O errors corrected by each individual subject in each condition, and by comparing these percentages, within conditions, by Wilcoxon's tests. In both the five-letter display condition ($T = 3$; $P < 0.01$ two-tailed) and in the nine-letter display condition ($T = 2$; $P < 0.01$ two-tailed) higher *percentages* of FI than of O errors were corrected.

Errors of response selection and execution should appear equally often as "O" or as "FI" errors. It follows that not all errors made were response errors, since many more O errors than FI errors occurred.

By a similar argument we would expect increases in the complexity of displays to lead to more errors of perceptual analysis but not to more response errors. Since the number of both kinds of errors increase with display complexity, we must again suppose that both classes of errors represent-failures of perceptual analysis. Some errors in both classes will be "response errors". But the number of response errors should be the same in both classes, and should not increase with display complexity.

Previous work has suggested that while most response errors are correctable, most perceptual errors are not (Rabbitt and Vyas, 1970, 1977). If equal numbers of response errors are classified as O and FI errors, and if *only* response errors can be corrected, the same number of errors should be corrected in both cases. Since many more O errors than FI errors are corrected, we must assume that some of these *corrected* O errors are perceptual rather than response errors.

It follows that at least some perceptual errors can be detected and corrected. Differences in the times taken to commit and to correct O and FI errors may suggest how this is done. RTs for all classes of responses made in this experiment are given in Table 7.2.

Table 7.2 Mean RTs for all classes of responses analysed

	RT (ms)	*Sigma*
Five-letter displays		
Correct target detections (T RTs)	969	189
Correct "No target responses" (NT RTs)	1208	323
All omission errors (O RTs)	1189	364
Corrected omissions	1141	302
Uncorrected omissions	1217	323
Error correction RTs after omissions	880	312
All false identification errors (FI RTs)	1009	382
Corrected false identifications	996	371
Uncorrected false identifications	1069	238
Error correction RTs after false identifications	908	198
Nine-letter displays		
Correct target detections (T RTs)	1162	293
Correct "No target" detections (NT RTs)	1591	285
All omission errors (O RTs)	1614	435
Corrected omission errors	1521	430
Uncorrected omission errors	1654	383
Error correction RTs after omissions	836	195
All false identification errors	1212	358
Corrected false identification errors (FI RTs)	1289	342
Uncorrected false identification errors (FI RTs)	1338	281
Error correction RTs after false identifications	1693	293

Correct responses

A two-way ANOVA showed that T responses were faster than N responses ($F = 18.6$, $df = 1{,}9$, $P < 0.01$) and that RTs to five-letter displays were faster than RTs to nine-letter displays ($F = 20.1$, $df = 1{,}9$, $P < 0.01$). The interaction between these terms was significant ($F = 11.1$, $df = 1{,}9$, $P < 0.01$).

To explain the difference between T RTs and N RTs we may test Neisser's (1963) suggestion that subjects carrying out visual search conduct a serial scan of a display which they terminate when a target is located, or when all symbols have been examined. This would imply that when no target was present subjects would have to scan all the letters on a display (X). This allows an estimate of scanning time per letter. From the present data N RT nine-letter displays (1591 ms) minus N RT five letter displays (1208 ms) = 383 ms as an estimate for the additional time required to scan four extra letters = 95.75 ms/letter.

Neisser's (1963) suggestion would also imply that when targets were present on displays subjects would scan, on average over all T displays, (X + 1)/2 letters. That is, they would scan, on average, three letters on the five-letter displays and five letters on the nine-letter displays. The difference in T RTs for nine-letter and for five-letter displays is 193 ms, giving us an estimated scanning rate of 193/2 ms = 96.5 ms/letter.

Estimates for scanning times per letter can also be derived by comparing N RTs and T RTs within each condition of display size. For five-letter displays this gives an estimate of 1208 − 969 = 239/2 = 119.5 ms/letter, and for nine-letter displays an estimate of 1591 − 1162 = 429/4 = 107.25 ms/letter.

These four independent estimates are in reasonable agreement, so that Neisser's (1963) hypothesis of serial, self-terminating scanning for visual search tasks is tenable for these results. The finding that N RT > T RT follows as a natural consequence of this.

Errors

A two-way ANOVA showed that FI errors were faster than O errors ($F = 12.8$, $df = 1{,}0$, $P < 0.01$) and that error RTs for five-letter displays were faster than error RTs for nine-letter displays ($F = 11.2$, $df = 1{,}9$, $P < 0.01$). The inter action between these terms was significant ($F = 13.6$; $df = 1{,}9$, $P < 0.01$).

This pattern of results can also be interpreted in terms of Neisser's (1963) hypothesis if we assume that, when making most of their errors, subjects did not merely make impulsive motor errors with no reference to the display but rather acted in "good faith". That is, when they made O errors subjects had nevertheless scanned all, or most, of the letters on the display, and when they made Fl errors they mistook a *particular* background letter on a display for a member of the target set.

It is a reasonable assumption that when errors occurred subjects had nevertheless inspected the displays confronting them, since we cannot otherwise account for the fact that all errors made to nine-letter displays were slower than all errors made to five-letter displays, and for the fact that O errors were typically slower than FI errors.

On the hypothesis of "good faith" estimates for scanning times per letter can be obtained in a way analogous to that used for correct responses. So for O errors we can assume that scanning times were proportional to the total number of letters on a display, X, while for FI errors we can assume that scanning times were proportional to $(X + 1)/2$, as for correct target identifications.

Comparing O RTs between five-letter and nine-letter displays we get an estimate for scanning time per letter of 1614 − 1189 ms = 425/4 = 106.25 ms/letter.

Comparing FI RTs across display sizes we get an estimate of 1212 − 1009 ms = 203/2 = 101.5 ms/letter.

Comparing O RT with FI RT within each display size condition we get an estimate of 90 ms/letter for five letter displays and 100.5 ms/letter for nine-letter displays.

These four estimates agree quite closely, and our assumptions about the scanning processes underlying O and FI errors remain tenable. Thus on these assumptions RTs for FI errors are most appropriately compared with correct T RTs, and RTs for O errors with correct N RTs.

A two-way ANOVA showed no differences between FI RTs and T RTs ($F = 2.3$, $df = 1{,}9$). The effects of display size were significant for both classes of responses ($F = 10.8$, $df = 1{,}9$, $P < 0.01$). The interaction between these terms was not significant ($F = 1.7$, $df = 1{,}9$).

A similar ANOVA showed no difference between O RTs and N RTs ($F = 2.5$, $df = 1{,}9$). The effects of display size were significant ($F = 14.3$, $df = 1{,}9$, $P < 0.01$) but there was no interaction between these effects ($F = 2.7$; $df = 1{,}9$).

Hence scanning times for displays when both classes of errors occurred were about the same as RTs for the equivalent classes of correct responses.

A remaining question was whether RTs for corrected errors differed from RT for uncorrected errors, as was found in other experiments by Rabbitt and Vyas (1979, 1977).

A two-way ANOVA found no difference between RTs for corrected and uncorrected O errors ($F = 1.8$, $df = 1{,}9$). The term for display size was significant ($F = 16.4$, $df = 1{,}9$, $P < 0.01$). There was no significant interaction ($F = 1.2$, $df = 1{,}9$).

Similarly there was no significant difference between RTs for corrected and uncorrected FI errors ($F = 1.7$, $df = 1{,}9$). The term for display size was significant, ($F = 21.4$, $df = 1{,}9$, $P < 0.01$) but there was no significant interaction ($F = 2.8$, $df = 1{,}9$).

Thus although Table 7.3 shows that overall mean RTs for corrected errors were somewhat faster than overall mean RTs for uncorrected errors this trend is not significant. Earlier findings with CRT tasks in which subjects responded to simple auditory or visual displays (Rabbitt and Vyas, 1970, 1977) are not replicated here.

Error correcting responses

A two-way ANOVA showed that ECRTs made after FI errors were slower than ECRTs made after O errors ($F = 18.7$, $df = 1{,}9$, $P < 0.01$). ECRT varied significantly with display size ($F = 13.6$, $df = 1{,}9$, $P < 0.01$). The interaction between these terms was significant ($F = 14.2$, $df = 1{,}9$, $P < 0.01$).

We see from Table 7.3 that this significant interaction means that FI ECRTs increased sharply with display size, but that ECRTs following O errors were the same for both display sizes.

Discussion

The main question asked was whether some perceptual errors can be corrected. To decide this we must first decide whether *any* of the errors corrected in this experiment can be confidently considered, on *post hoc* analysis, to be perceptual errors.

It is a reasonable assumption that two kinds of errors can occur in CRT tasks: Errors representing failures of perceptual discrimination and errors representing failures of response selection or execution. Since both responses used in this task were equally easy, and occurred equally often, and since the allocation of responding hands to T and N response keys was balanced across subjects, we may safely assume that roughly the same *numbers* of response errors would have been included in each of the two *post hoc* categories of O and FI errors. Since many more O errors than FI errors were committed at each display size, it must follow that the number of "response errors" included in the O category cannot possibly be greater than the *total number* of all errors included in the FI category. On this argument we have to assume that most O errors represented failures of perceptual analysis of displays.

A second fact also shows that both O and FI classes include errors of perceptual analysis. There is no reason why the number of response errors which are made should be greater when displays contain nine letters than when they contain five. Nevertheless more O and more FI errors are made to the nine-letter than to the five-letter displays.

Similar arguments allow us to be sure that at least some perceptual errors were detected and corrected.

If we suppose that *only* response errors can be corrected, then the number of response errors corrected should not differ, whichever hand is used to make them. In other words the number of corrected errors should be the same for both O and FI events. In fact, over both conditions of display load, significantly more O errors than FI errors were detected.

As we argued above, there is no reason to assume that as display discriminability varies more or fewer response errors are made, or corrected. While the number of corrected FI errors is the same for both types of displays, significantly more O errors are corrected in the nine-letter than in the five-letter condition.

It follows that some failures in perceptual analysis which resulted in O errors must have been subsequently detected and corrected.

While it is clear that some "perceptual" O errors are correctable the situation for FI errors is not so plain. We must assume that subjects made *both* "response errors" and "perceptual errors". It is a reasonable assumption that equal numbers of response errors were lumped, by *post hoc* analysis, into the categories of "O" and "FI" errors. It is also a reasonable assumption that the total number of perceptual errors in both classes increased with display size, though the total number of response errors did not.

Since there were only half as many FI errors as O errors, and since we have assumed that both sets must contain roughtly the same number of response errors, we must also assume that response errors formed a much larger *proportion* of the FI set than of the O set.

Previous work has shown that response errors tend to be fast responses and that subjects can generally correct them (Rabbitt, 1966*a, b*, 1967, 1968; Rabbitt and Vyas, 1970; 1978). On the extreme assumption that all *corrected* FI errors were, in fact, response errors we have a plausible account of these results; i.e. since FI errors contain a higher *proportion* of response errors, and since response errors are known to be fast, this would provide a reason why FI RT < O RT. Further, since most response errors can be corrected we can assume this is why a higher *proportion* of FI errors than of O errors was corrected.

Finally if, in the FI category, only response errors are correctable, this would provide an explanation why, though more FI errors are made to the nine-letter displays than to the five-letter displays, the number of Fl errors *corrected* remains the same in the two cases.

There are three facts discrepant with these assumptions:

First, Error Correction responses following FI errors are actually *slower* than error correction responses following O errors. Since we know from earlier work that error correcting responses following response errors are typically very fast indeed, this fact is not easy to explain (see Rabbitt and Vyas, 1970; Rabbitt and Vyas, 1978)

Second, if *only* response errors are corrected, whatever the display size may be, it is surprising that error correcting responses following FI errors should be signifiantly slower in the nine-letter display than in the five-letter display condition.

Third, if most FI errors are, in fact, response errors which have little reference to perceptual analysis of the display, it is surprising that the data fit the "good faith" model of error commission so well. That is to say it is surprising that the differences between O and FI RTs can be so well explained on the assumption that when making O errors subjects scan all, or most, of the letters on a display, but when making FI errors they stop their scan because they have mistaken a particular background letter for one of the targets.

We can therefore conclude that subjects made errors of perceptual analysis which resulted in both O and FI errors. They also made response errors, and a similar number of such response errors were included in both categories by *post hoc* data sort. We can be certain that some of the perceptual failures, leading to O errors, were subsequently detected and corrected. We can at least leave open the possibility that "perceptual" FI errors could also be detected, and discuss the results on these premises. Using these assumptions we may consider how either sort of error might then be detected.

A subject who made an O error could only realise this fact if he located a target letter which he had missed on his first inspection. In order to locate this target letter at all he would have to extend his original analysis of the display, or to re analyse the entire display as best he could in the time available to him to do so.

The ability to detect O errors would therefore depend on the time for which a particular display (which had been wrongly classified) remained available for "extended analysis" or "re-analysis". Displays could remain available either physically on the Cathode Ray Tube used to present them, or perhaps in the form of "iconic memory traces" (Sperling, 1960; Neisser, 1966) which persist for a short time after a display has been switched off.

In the present experiment displays terminated within 2 ms of any overt response. They were also followed, within 50 ms, by another display which effectively masked its predecessor and might be expected to terminate any lingering "iconic trace" (Ericksen and Steffy, 1964; Sperling, 1960; Averbach and Sperling, 1961). The time available for "extended processing" or "re-analysis" must therefore have been very brief. It would follow that O errors would have been correspondingly difficult to detect. In this case if an O error could not be detected very quickly indeed, it would not be possible to detect it at all. We would thus predict that only some O errors could be detected, and that those which were detected would be corrected rather rapidly—as was in fact the case.

The argument for FI errors is rather different. We have assumed that FI errors occurred when a subject mistook some particular background letter for a target letter. In this case it would also be logical to assume that even very brief "extended analysis" or "reprocessing" of the display would include *this particular letter*, and would rapidly disabuse the subject of this particular mistake. It would follow that subjects should have more frequently been able to detect that they had made FI errors than that they had made O errors. A higher *percentage* of FI errors than of O errors was, in fact, detected.

However, though a subject could discover that he had made a response *to the wrong letter* it does not follow from this that he could also be certain that this *response* was wrong. There might still be a target letter elsewhere on the display. In this case a subject could not make a confident error correction response until he had inspected the display further. His detection of his misapprehension could only motivate him to continue his perceptual analysis of the display, so far as he was able, in order to check whether there might not be a target present after all.

Specifically, we may suggest that with either display size, the same time was available for extended analysis of a display after a response had been made, and that this time was only sufficient for further inspection of some constant set of N letters. The probability of detection of an O error would vary with the probability that this sample of N might include a target which had previously been missed. We know that N must have been less than five, otherwise all O errors would have been detected in the five letter display condition. Therefore it follows that the probability of detection of a missing target must reduce as display size increased from five to nine letters.

It also follows that the time taken to detect O errors should have been independent of display size. This is because we have assumed that N would be the same in the five as in the nine letter display condition, because in both cases it is limited by the time available for extended processing. If a missed target were not detected in the sample N, there would be nothing further a subject could do about it. If it were detected in the sample N, it would be detected as fast in the nine letter as in the five letter condition.

When a subject mistook a background letter for a target and made an FI error, he would usually, and very quickly, realise that he had made this *particular* mistake. However this would not be enough to tell him that he had responded incorrectly. He would have to continue to analyse the display, as best he could, to discover whether a target letter might not be present after all. If this extended analysis detected a target letter which he had previously missed, he would not need to make an "error correction response". If extended analysis still did not detect a target, a correction response might, or might not, be appropriate, and he would have to make up his mind what to do. It is likely, under these circumstances that ECRs made after FI errors would be slow and unconfident. This would particularly be the case with nine-letter displays as against five-letter displays, leading to the observed increase in FI ECRT with display size.

A final point arises because in previous experiments (Rabbitt, 1966*a*, *b*, 1967, 1968) "false ECRs" were very rare indeed, while in this experiment they were quite common. That is, having made a correct response, a subject would sometimes make the opposite response, and then pause to indicate that he believed that he believed that he had made an error and corrected it. These "false ECRs" were of two kinds. A subject might "correct" a valid T response (indicating his belief that he had signalled that a target was present when it was absent) or he might "correct" a valid N response (indicating that he believed that he had signalled that a target was absent when one was present). These responses are given, for both display sizes, with their associated reaction times, in Table 7.3.

With five-letter displays no subject ever made a "false error correction" following a valid N response but six subjects each made two false corrections and one subject made one false correction after a valid T response.

With nine-letter displays, one subject made one false correction following a valid N response. In contrast four subjects each made three corrections, five subjects each made two corrections and two subjects each made one correction after valid T responses.

Table 7.3 Summary of "False Error Correction"

	No. of cases observed	*RT of valid responses preceeding false ECR*	*RT for "false ECRS"*
Five-letter displays			
T response "correcting" valid N responses	0	—	—
N responses "correcting" valid T responses	13	1008 ms	1096 ms
Nine-letter displays			
T responses "correcting" valid N responses	1	1492 ms	1763 ms
N responses "correcting" valid T responses	23	1194 ms	1873 ms

The mean "false correction RTs" derived in Table 7.3 are based on very few responses. However they suggest that false correction RTs, when they occur, are relatively slow responses, and fall into the range of correct ECRTs following FI errors rather than of ECRTs following O errors.

Such sparse data are only suggestive, but they are consistent with the assumptions we have made. I.E. subjects make FI errors because they sometimes mistake a particular background letter for a target. They can rapidly discover this has happened, but then cannot be certain that a target is not, after all, present elsewhere on the display. They may continue to analyse the display as best as they can, but the opportunity to do this is so brief that even if they fail to find a target they cannot be certain that one was not present. They then have to decide whether to make an ECR or not. If they do make an ECR there will be occasions when they are wrong. Such occasions would appear in our data as "false corrections" following valid T responses.

The same argument suggests that false corrections following N responses should be rare. If, on an initial scan, a subject does not find a target on a display and responds accordingly, an extended analysis can have three outcomes. On most occasions an extended scan will fail to reveal a target, and there is no reason why the subject should doubt his previous judgement. On some occasions an extended scan will detect that a target was, after all, present. In this case he can make a confident, and correct, ECR. It is possible that in a very few cases his extended scan may lead him to mistake some background letter on the display as a target. In other words, having made a correct N response his extended scan may lead him to make a FI error, and a consequent "false" ECR.

We have seen that Fl errors are relatively rare, so that what is, in effect, the commission of an FI error during extended processing of a display, following production of a correct N response, will be a very rare event indeed. If such events occur at all subjects will be seen to make false error corrections following valid N responses One subject may have done this on one occasion during this experiment.

Conclusions

This experiment suggests that, besides being able to correct errors of response selection and execution by monitoring proprioceptive or visual feedback, people can also correct some of the errors of perceptual discrimination which they make in visual search tasks.

We must now assume that perceptual analysis of a display can continue for some period of time while, or shortly after, an incorrect response is made to it. This allows us to explain differences in the probabilities of correction of "Omission" and "False Identification" errors, differences in the latencies of these errors, and differences in the times taken to correct them. The occurrence, and nature, of a few "False Error Correction" responses, following valid responses to displays, can also be explained on the same assumptions.

References

Averbach, E. and Sperling, G. (1961). Short-term storage of information in vision. In CHERRY, C. (Ed.), *Information Theory; Proceedings of the Fourth London Symposium*. London: Butterworths.

Ericksen, C. W. and Steffy, R. A. (1964). Short-term memory and retroactive interference in visual perception. *Journal of Experimental Psychology, 68*, 423–34.

Long, J. (1976). Visual feedback and skilled keying: differential effects of masking the printed copy and the keyboard. *Ergonomics, 19*, 93–110.

Megaw, E. (1972). Directional errors and their correction in a discrete tracking task. *Ergonomics, 15*, 633–43.

Neisser, U. (1963). Decision time without reaction time: experiments in visual scanning. *American Journal of Psychology, 76*, 376–85.

Neisser, U. (1966). *Cognitive Psychology*. New York: Appleton Century Crofts.

Rabbiti, P. M. A. (1966*a*). Error correction time without external error signals. *Nature (London), 212*, 438.

Rabbiti, P. M. A. (1966*b*). Errors and error correction in choice-response tasks. *Journal of Experimental Psychology, 71*, 264–72.

Rabbiti, P. M. A. (1967). Time to detect errors as a function of factors affecting choice response time. *Acta Psychologica, 27*, 131–42.

Rabbitt, P. M.A. (1968). Three kinds of error-signalling responses in a serial choice task. *Quarterly Journal of Experimental Psychology, 20*, 179–88.

Rabbiti, P. M. A. and Vyas, S. M. (1970). An elementary preliminary taxonomy for some errors in laboratory choice RT tasks. *Acta Psychologica, 33*, 56–76.

Rabbiti, P. M. A. and Vyas, S. M. (1977). Can perceptual errors be detected? *Journal of Experimental Psychology, Human Perception and Performance* (in press).

Sperling, G. (1960). The information available in brief visual presentations. 74, No. 11. *Psychological Monographs*.

Correcting perceptual errors

Rabbitt, Cumming and Vyas' (1978) results suggest that humans can correct at least some of both kinds of the "perceptual" errors they make: Omissions, when they miss a target that was present, and False Positives, when they mistake a non-target for a target. A likely explanation for both these achievements is that people can, very briefly, continue to process information from a display even after they have responded to it. In Rabbitt, Cumming and Vyas' experiment each response, whether correct or incorrect, was followed 50 msec. later, by a new display. Arguably during this time further processing can occur and can amend an incorrect identification. The interval between each response and the next signal, the Response Signal Interval (RSI), is, in effect, a signal/mask interval as used in the Averbach and Sperling (1961) studies and so effectively sets a limit to the time available for post-error processing of each signal before its' perceptual trace is obliterated by the next.

One way to test this idea would have been to repeat Rabbitt, Cumming and Vyas' (1976) experiment, varying the duration of RSIs to discover whether longer RSIs increase the probability of error detection and correction. Belated recognition of missed opportunities is one of the multiple distresses of re-reading work that, after 40 years, has been charitably edited by failing memory. Instead of this simple and sensible experiment Geoff Cumming, Subhash Vyas and I made a much more tedious study, asking volunteers to respond to displays of increasing levels of difficulty in a situation in which we varied the interval between their onset and subsequent termination by a masking field. The next paper reproduced describes this.

References

Averbach, E., & Sperling, G. (1961). Short-term storage of information in vision. In C. Cherry (Ed.), *Information Theory* (pp. 196–211). London: Butterworth.

Rabbitt, P., Cumming, G., & Vyas, S. (1978). Some errors of perceptual analysis in visual search can be detected and corrected. *Quarterly Journal of experimental Psychology, 30*(2), 319–332.

8 Processing a display even after you make a response to it. How perceptual errors can be corrected

P.M.A. Rabbitt and S.M. Vyas

Introduction

People make errors even in very simple tasks in which they only have to decide which one of a set of signals has occurred, and to make an appropriate response to it as soon as they can. Indeed it seems that unless people make errors, and recognise them when they do so, they cannot control and improve their performance (Rabbitt, 1979b, 1980; Rabbitt and Vyas, 1970). Many experiments have shown that people do detect most of the errors which they make in simple keyboard tasks (e.g. Rabbitt, 1966a, b; 1967, 1968). But we do not know whether they can detect all the possible kinds of errors which they make, and we only have explanations as to how they can detect some of them.

At least three different kinds of error can occur. A man may mistake one signal for another (a perceptual error). He may correctly identify a signal, but nevertheless choose the wrong response to it—possibly because he has forgotten what he was asked to do (a response selection error). Finally, he may correctly identify a signal, choose the correct response but fail to execute the response correctly (a motor error).

We know that motor errors may be rapidly detected by comparing visual or kinaesthetic feedback from a response which was actually made against a plan, or motor program, which specified the response which was intended (e.g. Megaw, 1972). We do not yet know whether people can detect any of their errors of response selection, and so we have no model to explain how they may do this. Rabbitt, Cumming and Vyas (1978) found that people can correct at least some perceptual errors which they make during visual search tasks. They proposed a "parallel process committee decision" model to explain how this might be done.

This model, also described by Rabbitt and Rodgers (1977), is illustrated in Figure 8.1.

The model proposes that as soon as any signal appears, each of a number of independent, parallel decision processes (committee members) begins to accumulate evidence in order to decide which event has occurred. But all these processes take different times to reach a decision so that some terminate

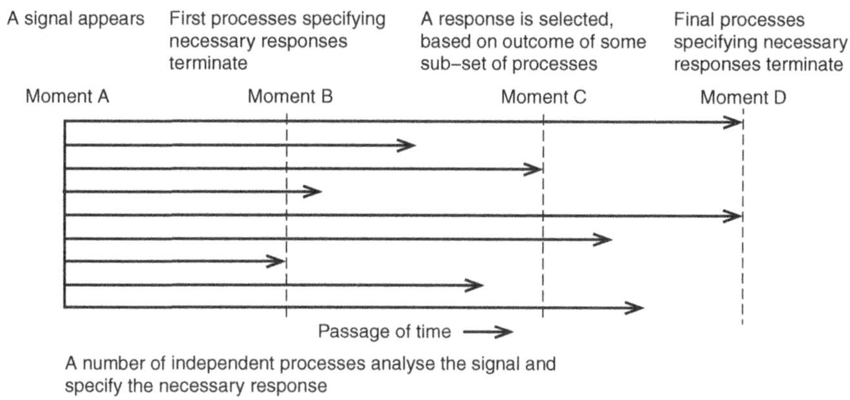

Figure 8.1 Committee decision model illustrated. A number of independent parallel processes analyse the signal and specify the necessary response. They terminate at various moments, the first at B and the last at D. At something intervening moment C a subject can use the outcomes of all processes which have so far terminated (the Vote) to select a response. However, other processes continue to terminate and their outcomes are added to the vote. If the total committee Vote, when the last processes terminate at D, agrees with the outcomes at C, the response is validated. If they disagree, then the response is questioned and an error is assumed.

before others (some committee members vote earlier than others). The model further proposes that a man makes his decision about the nature of a signal by considering the outcomes (votes) of one or more of these processes. He can either make this decision very rapidly, basing it only on the outcomes of the first one or few processes which terminate, or he can wait until all votes are in.

We may consider various assumptions about the relative reliability of these independent decisions. For instance we might suppose that the longer a committee member takes to make his decision the less reliable his vote will be. In this case it would follow that the longer a subject waits to decide which signal has occurred the more slow, unreliable decisions he will poll and the more likely he will be to make an error. The present authors have evidence that, in particular tasks in which visual discriminations are extremely difficult, slow decisions are indeed likely to be incorrect. But a very large number of studies have shown that in easy choice response tasks (CRT) there is a trade-off between speed and accuracy such that the faster a man responds the more likely he is to make a mistake (Pacella and Fisher, 1969; Pacella, Fisher and Karsh, 1968; Pacella and Pew, 1968; Pew, 1969; Rabbitt, Rabbitt, 1979; Rabbitt and Vyas, 1970; Schouten and Bekker, 1967).

This means that when we consider simple tasks we may either suppose that all committee members have the same, limited probability of accuracy independent of their voting speed or that the faster any committee member votes the more likely he is to be wrong. In either case this would mean that the committee model would predict that the longer a man waits to make a response, and the more independent votes he polls, the more likely he is to be correct.

On these assumptions the committee model can explain how a man may know when he has made a perceptual error. If he has made a fast error because he has impulsively based a response on the earliest votes which came in then, as subsequent votes come in, a more accurate consensus will accumulate and the earlier mistake will become apparent (Rabbitt *et al.*, 1978). Note that similar predictions can also be derived from a number of other, single process models all of which can be adapted in ways which make them interchangeable with the committee model, and with each other so far as all arguments in this paper are concerned (e.g. Audley, 1960, 1973; Laming, 1968; Vickers, 1979). The committee model is discussed here because it seems necessary to account for other data on error detection and correction (Rabbitt and Rodgers, 1977) which are beyond the scope of this paper.

Following this general account of the way in which perceptual errors may be detected all these models make the same predictions about relationships between the time taken to make an error, the probability that the error will be detected and the time which will be taken to detect it. These are graphically illustrated in Figure 8.2.

All these models assume that if a man bases a decision on a very brief sample of evidence his discrimination will only be correct by chance. As the duration of the sample he takes increases so does the probability that his decision will be correct. There is, however, a limiting sample duration, N ms, at which the limits of resolution of his perceptual information processing system are reached, and at which the probability of an error asymptotes at a very low, but finite, value. It is important to bear in mind that we cannot assume that the perceptual information processing system is perfect and that even with optimal samples, as long as N ms, errors may sometimes occur.

Let us suppose that a man makes decisions on samples of D ms and that $D < N$. If D is very brief a decision based on the sample D and a subsequent decision based on the optimal sample size, N will have the same outcome only with chance probability. As D increases so will the probability that decisions based on D will have the same outcome as decisions based on N—until, of course, when $D = N$ decisions based on D and N will always have the same outcome. In other words the longer a man takes to make a decision the less likely it will be that further sampling will allow him to amend it. Thus the probability that a perceptual error will be corrected will reduce as the time taken to make the error increases.

It also follows from all this that the time which a man takes to make an error should affect the time he takes to recognise it. If a man makes a very fast error, based on a very brief sample of D ms, he will have a relatively ample subsequent period of N—D ms within which he can accumulate further

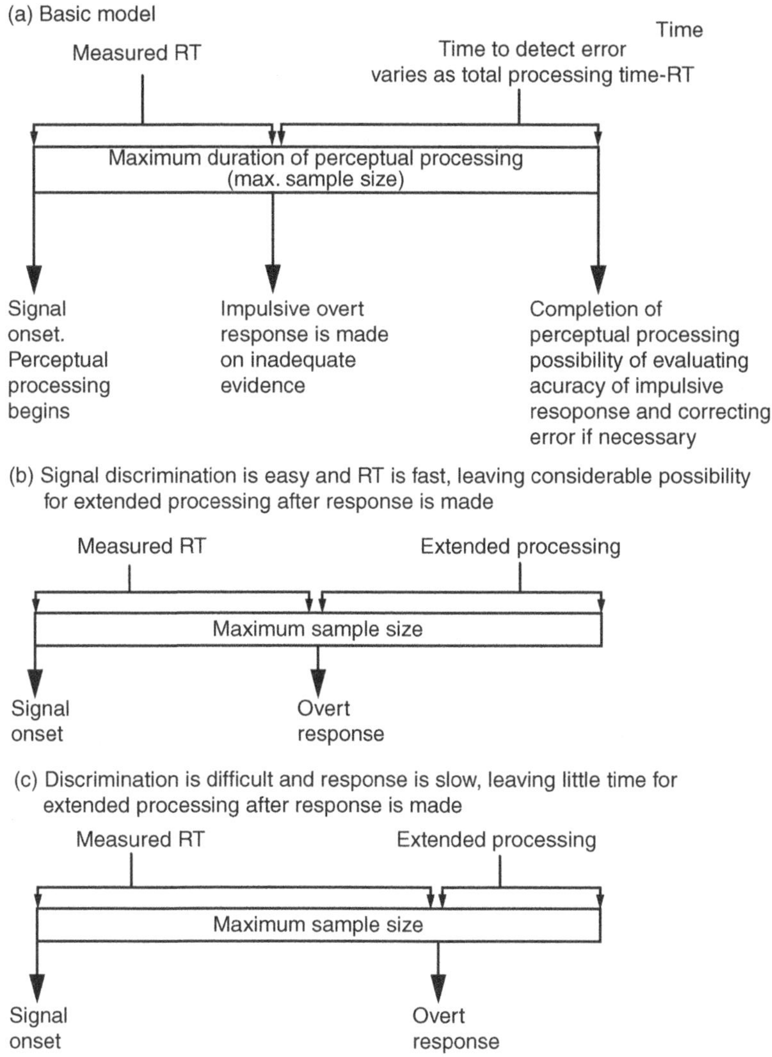

Figure 8.2. Hypothetical relationships between the time taken to make an error, the probability that it will be detected, and the time taken to detect it on the Extended Sampling Time (EST) model for correction of perceptual errors.

evidence which may allow him to correct it. As *D* increases so *N*—*D* will reduce. Thus evidence that a fast error has occurred may accumulate over a relatively long time but evidence that a slow error has occurred will either be available very rapidly or not at all. We might expect that, on average, the times taken to correct fast errors will be longer than the times taken to correct slow errors.

During the last 15 years the present authors have carried out many experiments to investigate how people correct errors during serial, self-paced CRT tasks (e.g. Rabbitt, 1966*a*, *b*, 1967, 1968; Rabbitt and Phillips, 1967; Rabbitt and Vyas, 1970). We have routinely examined data from each of 154 subjects tested during these experiments to see if we could discover any associations between the times taken to make individual errors, the probability of their correction and the times taken to correct them. No such relationship have been found. However in all these experiments, subjects responded to very simple, easily discriminable signals by selecting easy and compatible responses to them. Thus it is likely that very few of their errors were due to failures of perceptual discrimination or response selection. If nearly all their errors were failures of response execution (motor errors) which they recognised by evaluating motor or visual feedback, there would be no reason to expect any relationship between error latency and correctibility or correction speed.

Experiment I was made to see whether such relationships might be observed when subjects had to make relatively difficult discriminations between signals.

Experiment I

Method

Subjects discriminated between two tones which were presented one at a time, pressing one key to the onset of one and another key to the other. Tones were generated by an Advance Electronics Frequency Generator (type 2A/AX C8) and were delivered binaurally at 75 db sound pressure through Sony G18 B headphones. Closure of a switch by the experimenter produced a warning click (50 db, and *z* ms duration) through the headphones. A lagged relay then introduced a constant delay of 1 s before a tone switched on. Tone onset started two Venner millisecond timers. Very slight pressure (50 g and a throw of 2.5 mm) on either response lever terminated the tone and stopped one timer. The other timer continued to run unless it also was stopped by pressure on the other lever. Signal lamps told the experimenter which lever had been pressed first so that he knew whether the first response which the subject made had been an error. This arrangement allowed the subject to be told to correct any error he noticed by making the response which he should have made. In this case the first timer recorded his error RT and the second recorded the elapsed time between signal onset and error-correction. The elapsed time between the commission of an error and its correction (E.CRT) was then the difference in the readings of the two timers.

Subjects each experienced 150 trials under each of two conditions. They made "Easy" discriminations between pairs of tones 200 Hz apart, or "Difficult" discriminations between pairs of tones 25 Hz apart. In each condition the two tones occurred equally often in random order. Because the apparatus had to be manually re-set, and data-logging took some time, intertrial intervals were long ($\bar{x}$ 10 s) and quite variable ($\pm$ 3 s). Half the subjects first experienced the "Easy" condition and then the "Difficult" condition. The rest reversed this order of practice.

Subjects completed two 25-min runs in a single (I h) experimental session. Knowledge of results (RT in ms and accuracy) was given after each trial. Subjects were urged to respond as quickly and accurately as possible. Each subject discriminated between two different pairs of tones selected from the frequency range 500–2000 Hz.

Subjects

These were 18 women and 6 men, aged between 17 and 20 years. They were students at Oxford Polytechnic with no knowledge of Psychology, or any interest in the experiment beyond a £I payment for their time.

Results

In the "Easy" condition 108 of the 3600 responses recorded were incorrect (3% errors). All subjects made at least one error, and corrected at least one error. Of the 108 errors made 92 (i.e. 85.2%) were corrected.

In the "Difficult" condition, 407 (11.38%) of the 3600 responses recorded were incorrect. All subjects made at least six errors and corrected at least one of them. They corrected 98 (24.1%) of these 407 errors. Thus subjects made more errors in the Difficult than in the Easy condition (Wilcoxon's test, T=70, $P < 0.01$ two- tailed) but they corrected almost exactly the same number of errors in both cases (Wilcoxon's test, T=6, $P > 0.05$ one-tailed).

Since many subjects contributed only one observation to each of these sub-sets of responses, comparisons of the characteristics of corrected and uncorrected errors can only be tentative. Nevertheless mean Correct RTs, mean error RTs and E.CRTs for each condition are given in Table 8.1. These means do not include RTs for uncorrected errors in the Easy condition, since these were so rare that comparisons were meaningless.

A one-way analysis of variance (ANOVA) was used to compare means of individual subjects' mean RTs for correct responses, for corrected and uncorrected errors and for error correction in the Easy and the difficult conditions. This gave F (7,161) = 56.4, P < 0.01, and the error term was used to calculate Turkey's "*a*" statistic (Linton and Gallo, 1975, p. 319). This gave differences between means of 60.48 ms for significance at $P < 0.01$ and of 50.00 ms at $P < 0.05$.

Checking this analysis against Table 8.1 we see that correct RTs for Difficult discriminations were slower than correct RTs for Easy discriminations (P <0.01). In the Difficult condition errors which were subsequently corrected were significantly faster than errors which were not corrected ($P < 0.01$). Corrected errors were also significantly faster than correct responses, while RTs for uncorrected errors were as slow as correct responses. In the Easy condition corrected errors (most errors) were significantly faster than correct responses. Not enough errors went uncorrected to allow comparisons.

Table 8.1 Mean RTs and SDs for correct responses, for all errors, for sub-sets of corrected and for uncorrected errors and for all error correcting responses in "Easy" and "Difficult" conditions of Experiment I. Data were insufficient to present RTs for "uncorrected errors" in the "Easy" condition

	Conditions	
	"Easy"	*"Difficult"*
Overall mean correct RTs	342 ms σ = 38	431 ms σ = 59
Overall mean errors RTs	306 ms σ = 24	389 ms σ = 38
Mean RTs for corrected errors	294 ms σ = 21	312 ms σ = 30
Mean RTs for uncorrected errors	—	413 ms σ = 41
Overall mean RTs error correcting responses	262 ms σ = 38	276 ms σ = 49

RTs for corrected errors in the Easy condition were also significantly faster than RTs for corrected errors in the Difficult condition ($P < 0.01$). No subject ever made a "false" error correction response after making a correct response.

Discussion

Subjects made more errors in the D than in the E conditions. Since they made similar, simple motor responses to all signals these "extra" errors in the D conditions must have been due to failures of perceptual discrimination between signals. Since subjects corrected the same *absolute number* of errors in the E and D conditions we have no evidence that any of the "extra" errors in the D conditions could be detected and corrected. That is, we have no evidence that subjects could correct any of the additional errors caused by more difficult perceptual discriminations.

In the D condition, errors which were subsequently corrected were faster than those which remained uncorrected. Errors which were not detected were as slow as correct responses. All the "extra" errors made in the D conditions seem to have been both slow and undetected. A simple hypothesis to explain these data is that in both E and D conditions subjects made the same numbers of fast motor errors and subsequently detected most of them by monitoring feedback. In the D condition they also made many slower errors due to perceptual or memory failures, but they could not detect any of these. Experiment I obviously cannot prove this since it simply shows that, on *post hoc* analysis, correctable and uncorrectable errors had different RTs and fails to find any evidence that any identifiable perceptual errors could subsequently be corrected.

The model illustrated in Figure 8.2 suggests an alternative explanation. The faster a premature response, the less will be the evidence on which it is based and the less likely it is to be accurate. However the faster a response the more time a subject can spend gaining additional information by extending processing up to his maximum sample duration. When all signals can be readily identified at maximum sample durations the earlier during a sample a subject completes an impulsive, correct response the more likely he is to be able to amend it as he extends his analysis up to sample maximum. In contrast, if discriminations are so difficult that errors occur even when subjects extend their samples to maximum duration before they initiate a response, they will have little opportunity to improve their information and to detect errors by extended processing. Since, by elementary sampling theory, the probability of a correct judgement will increase as the square root of sample size, extension of long samples will give sharply diminished returns in terms of increased probabilities of correct discriminations. On this model, too, fast errors should be more easily detected than slow errors and slow errors should become more common as discriminations become more difficult.

To circumvent the logical ambiguities introduced by our dependance on *post hoc* analysis we may use another prediction from the model illustrated in Figure 8.2. Evidently if we can *externally* reduce the durations of the samples of information which people take from displays they will make more errors (since the accuracy of their discriminations will be reduced). But if they can only correct motor errors the numbers of errors which they can *correct* will not alter (since motor errors are corrected only by monitoring feedback). In contrast, on the extended processing model, if we externally reduce the durations of informational samples which people take we should not only increase the numbers of errors which people *commit*, but we should also reduce the absolute number of errors which they can *correct* since, by definition, an externally curtailed sample cannot be extended to allow a change of judgement after an incorrect response.

In short, according to the extended processing model, reduced display discriminability when subjects are free to extend their samples beyond the moments at which they initiate responses should have different effects from reduced discriminability due to externally controlled reductions of sampling time (display duration). To test this we used a relative line length discrimination task with five different levels of display difficulty. Displays were tachistoscopically presented for fixed durations and were immediately followed by a random noise masking field to curtail further processing. The shortest display duration (100 ms) was known to be briefer than the fastest errors made by any subject in a pilot experiment so that we might assume that subjects would be forced to terminate their perceptual sampling of displays before they could respond to them. A second display duration (200 ms) fell within the lower bounds of RTs recorded during a pilot experiment. A third display duration of 500 ms was slower than most correct responses which subjects made in the pilot experiment. In this case the display would usually remain visible for some time after a response had been made, giving subjects a chance to extend their samples or even to "double take" by making a second, independent judgement after an initial response had been completed.

Experiment II

Apparatus and method

An Electronic Developments "Oxford" C18 three-field tachistoscope presented pairs of parallel vertical lines of different lengths. Half the subjects pressed a response key on the side on which the shorter line appeared and half pressed a key on the side of the longer line. The longer (standard) line was 50 mm on all displays. The shorter line was 40, 44, 46, 48 or 49 mm. Displays were duplicated so that no individual display could be identified by adventitious cues such as smudges or marks. Displays were presented in random order, and were rotated at random so that the standard line appeared, with equal probability, on the left or on the right. The ends of the lines varied by ±3 mm with respect to each other and to the edges of the framed display so that subjects could not use the distances between line-ends and display-card edges as reliable cues. Displays were presented for 100, 200 or 500 ms and immediately followed by a random chequer board high contrast masking field with a cell size of I mm square. This field remained visible for 2 s.

Six pairs of subjects each experienced all of the three display duration conditions in one of the 6 possible orders. Each subject experienced each level of display difficulty 100 times at each display duration (i.e. 1500 responses). The experiment required six 1-hour sessions with each subject.

The response levers and timing equipment were the same as those used in Experiment I. Subjects were continually urged to respond as fast and as accurately as they could and to correct any errors as rapidly as possible. They were told whether each response they made had been correct or wrong, given their RTs in ms and, if they made ECRs, they were told whether these were correct or not, and given their ECRTs.

Subjects

These were eight women and four men, students at Oxford Polytechnic aged from 17 to 22 years, who were paid £1 a session to complete the experiment.

Results

The total numbers of errors which were made and corrected at each level of discrimination difficulty (difference in line length) at each level of exposure duration are set out in Table 8.2. In this experiment, unlike any other reported in the literature, (except for similar findings by Rabbitt *et al.*, 1978) at the most difficult discriminations subjects sometimes made "false" ECRs by pressing an incorrect lever immediately after pressing a correct lever under the impression that they had made an error and were correcting it as instructed. These "false ECRs" are separately entered in Table 8.2.

A two-way within/within ANOVA was carried out over individual subjects' error scores. Errors increased as display durations became shorter F (2, 22) = 12.8, $P < 0.01$ and as line lengths became more similar F (4, 44) = 14.2, $P < 0.01$. There was a significant interaction F (8, 88) = 11.8, $P < 0.01$. It seems that reduced exposure duration and reduced display discriminability increase errors, independently and in combination.

A further two-way ANOVA was made to compare the number of errors which were *corrected* over the 15 conditions. A larger *absolute number*

Table 8.2

Display duration (ms)		*Display difficulty*				
		1 *"Easiest"*	*2*	*3*	*4*	*5* *"Hardest"*
	Uncorrected errors	8	25	53	90	212
	Percentage of total errors	12.12%	30.12%	40.76%	51.72%	74.39%
100	Corrected errors	58	58	77	84	73
	Percentage of total errors	87.88%	69.88%	59.24%	48.29%	25.61%
	False ECRs	–	–			
	Total errors	66	83	130	174	285
	Total errors as percentage of all responses	5.5%	6.92%	10.83%	14.5%	23.9%
	Uncorrected errors	1	5	19	51	173
	Percentage of total errors	1.82%	6.58%	18.10%	36.69%	70.04%
200	Corrected errors	54	71	86	88	74
	Percentage of total errors	98.42%	93.42%	81.90%	63.31%	29.96%
	False ECRs					6
	Total errors	55	76	105	139	247
	Total errors as percentage of all responses	4.58%	6.33%	8.75%	11.58%	20.58%
	Uncorrected errors	1	4	8	24	165
	Percentage of total errors	1.96%	7.41%	8.70%	19.35%	66.80%
500	Corrected errors	50	50	84	100	82
	Percentage of total errors	98.04%	92.59%	91.30%	80.65%	33.20%
	False ECRs			1	5	29
	Total errors	51	54	92	124	247
	Total errors as percentage of all responses	4.25%	4.5%	7.67%	10.33%	20.58%

of errors were corrected as displays became more difficult F (4, 44) = 9.2, $P < 0.01$ though as we see from Table 8.3 *the percentage* of errors corrected sharply declined as discriminability reduced. More errors were corrected as display durations became longer F (2, 22) = 12.4, $P < 0.01$. The interaction was significant F (8, 88) = 4.4, $P < 0.01$.

In contrast to the results of Experiment I, except for the least discriminable displays (see Table 8.2 level 5), it seemed that subjects might have been able to detect and correct at least some of the "extra" errors which they made as discriminations became harder. The significant interaction term seems to mean that when discriminations were very easy subjects corrected about as many errors at short exposure durations as at long durations, but that when discriminations were difficult errors were only corrected at longer exposure durations.

Means of individual subjects' mean RTs for correct responses, for corrected and uncorrected errors, for error correcting responses (ECRs) and for false error correcting responses (FECRs) are given in Table 8.3.

A two-way ANOVA across data for correct responses showed significant effects of discrimination difficulty F (4, 44) = 12.4, $P < 0.01$ and of display duration F (2, 22) = 7.0, $P < 0.01$. The interaction term was not significant; F = 1.4. Table 8.3 shows that this is a very intriguing effect. As we might expect RTs become slower as line lengths become more similar and discriminations become more difficult. In contrast, although short exposure durations also reduce discriminability and increase errors, RTs become *faster* as displays become briefer. This is direct evidence that RT not only depends on display discriminability *per se*, but also on the time for which subjects are allowed to sample displays in order to make judgments about them. If displays remain visible until after responses are made subjects seem to be able to adjust to difficult displays by taking longer to consider them and so somewhat maintain their accuracy. However, if their sampling times are externally limited by onset of a masking field they cannot improve their judgments by extending their sampling times and their accuracy is thereby reduced. Thus in these cases they respond faster because they can gain nothing by delay. Apart from its theoretical interest this finding reassures us that curtailment of display duration by a masking field actually did reduce the time which subjects could spend extracting information from displays.

A three-way ANOVA was made across means of individual subjects' mean RTs for errors. Corrected errors were faster than uncorrected errors F (1, 11) = 20.8, $P < 0.01$. Overall error RT increased with display difficulty F (4, 44) = 6.2, $P < 0.01$ and reduced with display duration F (2, 22) = 9.74, $P < 0.01$. The only significant interaction term was for Corrected vs. Uncorrected errors × Display discrimination difficulty F (4, 44) = 9.26, $P < 0.01$. This interaction apparently means that RTs for corrected errors increased less than RTs for uncorrected errors as line lengths became more similar (see Table 8.3). The interaction was examined by Tukey's "*a*" test, which

Table 8.3 Level of discrimination difficulty

Display duration (ms)		*1 ("Easiest")*	*2*	*3*	*4*	*5 ("Hardest)*
100	Overall correct RT	347.2★, σ=43.6	355.7★, σ=51.4	377.8★, σ=59.7	367.5★, σ=63.9	401.0★, σ=74.8
	Overall error RT	254.2★, σ=60.5	307.3★, σ=78.0	364.7★, σ=131.0	342.7★, σ=102.5	362.9★, σ=92.3
	RT for corrected errors	247.6★, σ=45.4	278.0★, σ=42.6	310.2★, σ=61.0	315.5★, σ=51.3	330.2★, σ=75.8
	RT for uncorrected errors	302.1★, σ=111.3	375.2★, σ=44	443.87★, σ=68.0	368.1★, σ=62.1	374.2★, σ=81.7
	Overall factor correction RT	277.6★, σ=182.6	293.4★, σ=161.2	280.1★, σ=89.3	333.7★, σ=149.2	372.2★, σ=111.1
	RT for false ECRs	—	—	301.0★, σ = 0	255.7★, σ = 42.1	378.5★, σ=58.4
	RT for correct response followed by false ECRs	—	—	299.0★, σ=0	302.7★, σ=56.1	397.7★, σ=42.4
200	Overall correct RT	350.5★, σ=43.5	361.8★, σ=43.4	372.6★, σ=45.9	381.2★, σ=56.1	421.6★, σ=95.9
	Overall error RT	273.9★, σ=64.2	308.6★, σ=63.6	344.4★, σ=119.5	380.9★, σ=150.8	367.7★, σ=98.5
	RT for corrected errors	260.1★, σ=61.3	295.3★, σ=58.2	296.3★, σ=55.3	324.5★, σ=55.8	319.5★, σ=58.5
	RT for uncorrected errors	1019.0★, σ=0	475.5★, σ=58.1	562.1★, σ=65.4	478.21★, σ=59.2	388.3★, σ=80.9
	Overall error correction RT	204.0★ σ=72	269.1★, σ=94	279.3★, σ=145.9	288.0★, σ=74.9	327.6★, σ=104.2
	RT for false ECRs	—	—	—	661.0★, σ= 0	3379.9★, σ=71.4
	RT for correct responses followed by false ECRs	—	—	—	396.0★, σ=0	355.5★, σ=48
500	Overall Correct RT	351.6★, σ=40.9	362.0★, σ=43.0	392.6★, σ=43.0	398.0★, σ=52.5	429.1★, σ=84.3
	Overall error RT	259.1★, σ=68.9	291.2★, σ=59.6	293.0★, σ=64.8	348.7★, σ=99.9	425.0★, σ=126.8
	RT for corrected errors	261.6★, σ=74.1	295.6, σ=54.1	301.9★, σ=49.0	321.4★, σ =45.6	360.6★, σ=79.4
	RT for uncorrected errors	134.0★, σ= 0	236.2★, σ= 72.0	199.55★, σ=49.0	462.5★, σ =56.2	457.0★, σ=80.2
	Overall error correction RT	298.5★, σ=133.9	250.1★, σ=86.1	319.8★, σ=148.3	310.8★, σ=98.4	381.6★, σ=168.1
	RT for false ECRs	—	—	122.★, σ=0	468.5★, σ= 16.4	372.6★, σ= 41.4
	RT for correct responses followed by false ECRs	—	—	231.0★, σ x 0	280.5★, σ= 14.1	363.5★, σ = 72.6

showed that while RTs for uncorrected errors (like RTs for correct responses) increased significantly with every increase in display difficulty ($P < 0.05$ in all cases) this was not so for corrected errors where the only significant difference was between RTs in the two most difficult conditions (4 and 5) and in the two easiest conditions (1 and 2).

A two-way ANOVA compared ECRTs with correct RTs across all five levels of discrimination difficulty. ECRTs were, indeed, faster than correct RTs $F\ (1, 4) = 18.4$, $P < 0.01$ and both ECRT and correct RT increased as displays became more difficult $F\ (4, 4) = 12.6$; $P < 0.01$. The interaction term was not significant $F = 1.3$. It seems that as displays became more difficult error correction latencies increased by about the same amount as did latencies of correct responses (see Table 8.3). It is difficult to see how this could happen if the *only* errors which could be corrected were motor confusions detected by monitoring kinaesthetic feedback. Since the same simple responses were made at all conditions of display difficulty we have no reason to suppose that feedback monitoring should take longer for difficult than for easy displays.

ECRTs alone were further investigated by a two-way ANOVA and found to increase with display difficulty $F\ (4, 4) = 12.2$, $P < 0.01$ but not to change with display duration $F\ (2.22) = 2.6$, $P > 0.05$. The interaction term was not significant.

Discussion

The model illustrated in Figure 8.2 predicts that people can extend their sampling of information from a display beyond the moment at which they initiate a response to it. They may thus acquire additional information which allows them to validate, or to amend, a premature response. This may, perhaps, seem plausible in the case of Experiment II in which displays remained visible after responses had been made to them, but less plausible in Experiment I where a signal automatically terminated as soon as a response was made. Two pieces of evidence from earlier studies should be borne in mind.

Megaw (1972) showed that changes in muscle tension signalling the initiation of a simple response may occur up to 100 ms before any overt movement can be recorded. Thus even when a signal was physically terminated by an overt response it may have been available for extended processing for up to 100 ms from the moment when the response was *initiated*. Further, people can continue to extract information from signals or displays for at least 200 ms after the moment they are switched off unless they are followed, sooner than this, by a masking field or signal (Averbach and Coriell, 1961; Averbach and Sperling, 1961; Ericksen and Spencer, 1969; Ericksen and Steffy, 1964; Sperling, 1960).

Thus in Experiment I and in similar tasks, perceptual processing might have continued for as long as 100 ms between initiation and completion of a response, and possibly even for a further 200 ms after the response had been made and the signal terminated. In contrast in Experiment II, where masking fields were used, we may assume that the effective duration of perceptual processing could be no longer than 100, 200 or 500 ms as display duration permitted. Since RTs ranged from 180 to 600 ms we can infer that subjects had correspondingly more or less opportunity for extended sampling or re-sampling, between the moment of response initiation and the moment of mask onset. Eight features of the results suggest that subjects did, indeed, correct some of their perceptual errors and further suggest that the extended sampling time (EST) hypothesis can explain how they did this.

(1) As line lengths became more similar subjects made more errors. These extra errors must have been due to perceptual rather than to motor confusions. Most extra errors were slow responses and most were not corrected. But although the *percentage* of corrected errors sharply reduced the *absolute number* of corrected errors became greater as discriminations became more difficult. Thus at least some extra errors, caused by discrimination failures, must have been detected and corrected.

(2) There is no reason to suppose that the time taken to correct motor errors should vary with the difficulty of the perceptual discriminations which subjects have to make. But error correction times increased as line lengths became more similar and reduced as exposure durations became shorter. We cannot explain this on the hypothesis that only motor errors were corrected by monitoring feedback. We shall see, below, how the model illustrated in Figure 8.2 predicts that increased discrimination difficulty and reduced exposure duration will affect error correction times in opposite ways.

(3) Uncorrected errors were as slow as correct responses. This agrees with the idea that when a man processes as large a sample of perceptual evidence as he can the accuracy of his decision will be the best his perceptual system can attain. Since, by definition, he cannot further extend his perceptual sample, an error made after a long sample will not be detected. Fast errors, based on sub-maximal samples,' may be detected by extending processing to sample maximum. In Experiment II corrected errors were always faster than uncorrected errors, as this model would predict.

It is not possible to argue that this was because *all* corrected errors were fast motor confusions detected by checking feedback. Like all other responses corrected errors became slower as lines became more similar and faster as exposure durations became shorter. If *all* errors were fast motor confusions there is no reason why this should have happened. We must conclude that at least some corrected errors were not motor confusions, and were detected by other means than feedback monitoring.

From Table 8.2 we see that across all exposure durations errors increased from 172 (4.8%) at the easiest (level 1) line lengths to 437 (12.13%) at level 4 displays and to 779 (21.64%) at level 5 displays. Overall line length conditions errors increased from 568 (9.46%) at 500-ms exposures to 622 (10.37%) at 200 ms and to 738 (12.3%) at 100 ms. Display difficulty and exposure duration acted both independently and jointly to produce more errors.

A critical finding is that display difficulty and exposure duration nevertheless had very different effects on the probability of error correction, We must assume that some of the extra errors produced by line length similarity were corrected. But as exposure duration became shorter the number of corrected errors fell from 366 (6.1%) in the 500-ms condition and 373 (6.22%) in the 200-ms condition to 274 (4.57%) in the 100-ms condition. This reduction was significant. Now it can- not be argued that reductions in display difficulty were more marked as exposure duration fell from 200 ms to 100 ms (increase of 3% errors) than as line length similarity increased from level I to level 4 (increase of 7% errors). Thus it seems that while subjects could correct *some* of the extra errors which they made when display discriminability was reduced by line length similarity, they could not correct *any* of the extra errors which they made when a *lesser* reduction in display discriminability was achieved by reducing exposure duration.

The extended sampling time (EST) model would predict this finding on the assumption that onset of a high-contrast masking field effectively terminates processing of a preceding display (Averbach and Coriell, 1961; Averbach and Sperling, 1961; Ericksen and Spencer, 1969; Ericksen and Steffy, 1964; Sperling, 1960; Turvey, 1973). At brief exposure durations subjects' perceptual samples are externally terminated and thus cannot be extended to amend their judgments. In contrast, provided that exposure durations are long enough, as line lengths become more similar, subjects can revise premature judgments by extending sample duration. This would explain the finding that for the most difficult displays significantly more errors are corrected at long than at short exposure durations (i.e. there is a significant positive interaction between increased display difficulty and extended exposure duration to produce larger numbers of corrected errors).

(5) RTs for correct responses increased with line length similarity and reduced with exposure duration. The interaction is significant. By the same arguments outlined in (4) above this is consistent with the idea that perceptual sample durations increased with line length similarity but were externally curtailed by masking field onset.

(6) In all previous studies of error correction known to the authors when signals were easy to discriminate false error corrections were extremely rare occurring with a probability of less than 0.0001 (Burns, 1965; Rabbitt, 1966*a, b*, 1967, 1968; Rabbitt and Phillips, 1967; Rabbitt and Vyas, 1970). In contrast, for the most difficult displays in Experiment II, false error corrections became relatively frequent, but only when exposure durations were 200 ms or longer. This can be explained by the assumption that when discriminations are very difficult processing may be extended beyond the moments of initiation of *all* responses, whether these are correct or not. In Experiment II discriminations were sometimes so difficult that subjects made errors even when they sampled at maximum duration (i.e. even when error RTs were as long as correct RTs). Thus if subjects made fast responses they might, with chance probability (i.e. 50%) be correct as well as wrong. As processing was extended,

on most (but not on all) occasions, correct responses would be validated. On some occasions (as with slow, long-sample errors) extended processing after an impulsive *correct* response might lead to the wrong conclusion and a man might decide that he had made an error although he had not. If we had a much larger sample of observations we could test precise predictions relating incidence of false ECRs to error rates at various RT bands.

The present results can only offer general support for this model on three points of detail:

(i) As predicted, false ECRs occurred only to the most difficult discriminations here error rate was fairly high even at maximum RTs.
(ii) False ECRs only followed fast correct responses. The RTs for the (correct) responses which they followed were closely comparable to RTs for fast, corrected errors.
(iii) For even the most difficult displays false error correcting responses never occurred at 100-ms exposure duration, were very rare at 200-ms exposure duration and were only relatively common at 500-ms exposure duration. Thus incidence of false error correcting responses, as of valid error correcting responses, sharply reduced at brief exposure durations. This is consistent with the idea that both correct and false Error Correcting Responses were triggered by extended processing, and that extended processing becomes impossible when exposure duration externally limits sampling time. False ECRs occur when extended processing leads to an incorrect second opinion about a display.

(7) In previous experiments, in which signals were very discriminable so that most errors were probably motor confusions, the time taken to make an error has been found to be independent of the time taken to correct it (Rabbitt, 1966*a*, *b*, 1967, 1968, etc.). In the most difficult conditions of Experiment 11, where many failures of perceptual discrimination occurred and some of them were corrected, the EST model would predict a negative correlation between error RT and error correction RT. If an impulsive response has been based on a very short perceptual sample we might expect the subject to be able to revise his judgement as he prolongs his processing to sample maximum. The faster the error RT the longer the interval between the moment of commission of the error and the moment when sample maximum is reached. In contrast the slower the error response the less time will elapse between error commission and sample maximum. Similarly, when samples are externally curtailed by brief exposure durations, if perceptual errors can be corrected at all they should be corrected relatively quickly, since processing time is limited by exposure duration. But in Experiment II although Error Correction RT did reduce at brief exposure durations it actually increased as line lengths became more similar.

We must recognise that subjects certainly make two different kinds of errors which they correct in different ways, and that our *post hoc* analyses do not allow us to identify them so as to study them separately. It is safe to assume that subjects made about the same numbers of motor confusions at all levels of line length similarity. As lines became more similar they also made increasing numbers of perceptual errors. We can safely assume that at the easiest discriminations most corrected errors were motor confusions while at the difficult discriminations some corrected errors were due to perceptual failures. In all earlier experiments in which correction latencies for errors (which were probably mostly motor confusions) have been found to be very fast indeed-on occasions as fast as 14ms (Rabbitt, 1966*a*). If, in Experiment II, perceptual errors took longer to detect than motor errors, as line lengths became more similar and more perceptual errors occurred and more were corrected, the *overall mean* RTs for all error correcting responses was increasingly weighted by slower, corrected perceptual errors and so gradually increased. The prediction of an inverse relationship between error RT and error correction RT would apply only to the subset of perceptual error corrections which we have assumed to be relatively slow responses. Unfortunately *post hoc* data analysis gives us no reliable way to identify this interesting subset of responses.

Obviously a much more ambitious experiment is needed in which each of many individual subjects makes, and corrects, several hundreds of errors at each of many levels of discrimination difficulty, This would allow us to test, at least, a first simple prediction that error correction latencies are bimodal, with one distribution of fast motor error corrections whose mean is invariant with discrimination difficulty and a second distribution of slower, putatively perceptual, error corrections, the *number* of which increases with discrimination difficulty, but whose *mean RT reduces* with discrimination difficulty.

As far as this investigation goes our experiments support the hypothesis that subjects can detect and correct most of their motor confusions and some of their failures of perceptual discrimination and that they do these things in different ways. Further, the extended sampling time model is a very useful guide to our further understanding of how people may detect and correct some failures of perceptual discrimination.

References

Audley, R. J. (1960). A stochastic model for individual choice behaviour. *Psychological Review*, 67, 1–15.

Audley, R. J. (1973). Some observations on theories of choice reaction time: tutorial review. In Kornblum, S. (Ed.), *Attention and Performance IV.* New York: Academic Press.

Audley, R. J. and Pike, A. R. (1965). Some alternative stochastic models of choice. *British Journal of Mathematical and Statistical Psychology,* 18, 207–25.

Averbach, E. and Coriell, A. S. (1961). Short-term memory in vision. *Bell System Technical Journal*, 40, 309–28.

Averbach, E. and Sperling, G. (1961). Short-term storage of information in vision. In Cherry, C. (Ed.), *Symposium on Information Theory.* London: Butterworths.

Burns, J. T. (1965). Unpublished PhD thesis, University of Michigan, Ann Arbor, Michigan.

Ericksen, C. W. and Spencer, T. (1969). Rate of information processing in visual perception: some results and methodological considerations. *Journal of Experimental Psychology Monographs*, 79, (No. 2) Part 2.

Ericksen, C. W. and Steffy, R. A. (1964). Short-term memory and retroactive interference in visual perception. *Journal of Experimental Psychology*, 68, 423–34.

Laming, D. R. J. (1968). *Information Theory of Choice Reaction Times*. New York: Academic Press.

Linton, M. and Gallo, P. Jr. (1975). *The Practical Statistician*. Monterey, California: Brooks Cole Publishing Co.

Megaw, E. D. (1972). Directional errors and their correction in a discrete training task. *Ergonomics*, 15, 633–44.

Olsen, R. (1977). Three kinds of speed-error trade-off. In DORNIC, S. (Ed.), *Attention and Performance IV.* Hillsdale, New Jersey: Lawrence Erlbaum Associates.

Pacella, R. G. and Fisher, D. F. (1969). Effect of stimulus degradation and similarity on the trade-off between speed and accuracy in absolute judgments. *Journal of Experimental Psychology*, 81, 7–9.

Pacella, R. G., Fisher, D. F. and Karsh, R. (1968). Absolute judgement in speeded tasks: quantification of the trade-off between speed and accuracy. *Psychonomic Science*, 12, 225–6.

Pacella, R. G. and Pew, R. (1968). Speed-accuracy trade-off in reaction times: Effect of discrete criterion times. *Journal of Experimental Psychology*, 76, 19–24.

Pew, R. (1969). The speed-accuracy operation characteristic. *Acta Psychologica*, 30, 16–26.

Rabbitt, P. M. A. (1966*a*). Errors and error correction in choice response tasks. *Journal of Experimental Psychology*, 71, 264–72.

Rabbitt, P. M. A. (1966*b*). Error correction time without external error signals. *Nature (London)*, 212, 438.

Rabbitt, P. M. A. (1967). Time to detect errors as a function of factors affecting choice response time. In Sanders, A. F. (Ed.), *Symposium on Attention and Performance*, pp. 131–142; and *Acta Psychologica*, 27, 131–42.

Rabbitt, P. M. A. (1968). Three kinds of error-signalling responses in a serial choice task. *Quarterly Journal of Experimental Psychology*, 20, 179–188.

Rabbitt, P. M. A. (1979*a*). Current paradigms and models in human information processing. In Hamilton, V. and Warburton, M. (Eds), *Stress and Human Performance*, Ch. 4. London, New York: John Wiley.

Rabbitt, P. M. A. (1979*b*). How old and young subjects monitor and control responses for accuracy and speed. *British Journal of Psychology*, 70, 305–11.

Rabbitt, P. M. A., Cumming, G. and Vyas, S. (1978). Some errors of perceptual analysis in visual search can be detected and corrected. *Quarterly Journal of Experimental Psychology*, 30, 319–32.

Rabbitt, P. M. A. and Phillips, S. (1967). Error detection and correction latencies as a function of S-R compatibility. *Quarterly Journal of Experimental Psychology*, 19, 37–42.

Rabbitt, P. M. A. and Rodgers, B. (1977). What does a man do after he makes an error? An analysis of response programming. *Quarterly Journal of Experimental Psychology*, 29, 727–43.

Rabbitt, P. M. A. and Vyas, S. M. (1970). An elementary preliminary taxonomy of errors in choice reaction time tasks. *Acta Psychologica*, 33, 56–76.

Schouten, J. F. and Bekker, J. A. M. (1967). Reaction time and accuracy. *Acta Psychologica*, 27, 143–53.

Sperling, G. (1960). The information available in brief presentations. *Psychological Monographs*, 74, Whole No. I I.

Taylor, M. M. (1967). Detectability theory and the interpretation of vigilance data. *Acta Psychologica*, 27, 271–85.

Turvey, M. T. (1973). On peripheral and central processes in vision. Interference from an information-processing analysis of masking with patterned stimuli. *Psychological Review*, 8o,1–52.

Vickers, D. (1979). *Decision Processes in Visual Perception*. London: Academic Press.

What awareness of our errors tells us about consciousness

At this point in our exploration of error detection and correction we knew that impulsive response errors, S-R mapping confusions and errors of perceptual discrimination can be detected and corrected and that the processes underlying perceptual analyses of signals and the selection and execution of responses to them can continue even after the moment when a wrong response has been physically completed. Other investigators have found that people find it very difficult to prevent themselves correcting errors by making the responses that they should have made, even if they are explicitly asked not to do this. Nevertheless, even when we have successfully inhibited an error correction response, we can clearly become aware of an error at some level because correct responses immediately following errors are atypically slow (Rabbitt, 1968). We are less accurate at acknowledging our errors if we are asked not to correct them by making the response that we should have made but, instead, to signal them by pressing a response key that is used only for this purpose. Nevertheless, even when we do not signal our errors we must be aware of them at some level because we respond unusually slowly to the next signal (Rabbitt, 1968). Finally, if we are asked whether we remember errors two or three responses after we have made them, we can identify few of them, and are more likely to recall those that we have signalled than those that we have ignored, or have automatically corrected, by making the responses that we should have made.

When taken together these various pieces of evidence suggested that while doing very simple things such as pressing keys in response to signal lamps, our level of awareness of what we have done at any moment increases with the time that the task allows us. Thus if events, such as our identifications of signals and our acknowledgements of them, are very brief, we do not become consciously aware of what we are doing until after we have done it. In other terms we sometimes may not be consciously aware of things that we have done unless we have extra, uninterrupted time to become so. Further, we can only remember events of which we have become consciously aware. For me these were uncomfortable ideas because, during the late 1950s, I had been overawed as an undergraduate by lectures by formidable Oliver Zangwill, who made it clear that my most important credential of respectability as a "human experimental psychologist" would be to disdain ever to discuss conscious awareness. (Scientists, like all other human beings, too easily assimilate beliefs whose lack of substance they fail to recognize.) The next paper is an account of my first and, in my old age I now know, my only breach of the dogma of my early education.

Reference

Rabbitt, P. M. (1968). Three kinds of error-signalling responses in a serial choice task. *Quarterly Journal of Experimental Psychology*, *20*(2), 179–188.

9 Consciousness is slower than you think

P.M.A. Rabbitt

If people are asked to "correct" all of the errors that they make in very easy serial, self-paced choice reaction time (CRT) tasks by immediately making the responses that they should have made, they can successfully do so on 86.5 to 96.2% of occasions (Rabbitt, 1968, 1990). These "Error-correcting responses" are sometimes completed within 40 ms after the errors that they follow (Rabbitt, 1966a, b). This is not long enough for humans to recognize what they have done wrong, work out what response they should have made, and then programme, choose, and complete an appropriate error-correcting response. So, these "correction responses" must sometimes be, in effect, "delayed correct responses" that have been initiated before the errors that they answer have been completed. That is, production of an incorrect and a correct response must overlap in time. When people are asked not to make error correction responses they can suppress most, but not all, of them. Consistent with the idea that error correction responses are delayed correct responses that are completed after impulsive errors, they are, at least sometimes, involuntary and cannot be consciously withheld (Maylor & Rabbitt, 1987, 1989; Rabbitt, 1990).

If we assume that any response that a person makes during a simple task may be the outcome of the first of two or more parallel processes to reach completion (see theoretical review by Townsend & Ashby, 1983) we might expect that if fast errors are rapidly followed by fast valid error-correcting responses, fast correct responses must also occasionally be followed by equally rapid invalid error correction responses. When the only data available are records of responses and CRT tasks it is not possible to show that this does not occasionally happen because there is no clear basis for deciding whether or not any given error is an "invalid correction" for the immediately preceding correct response. However, in the data so far examined errors as fast as the fastest error-correcting responses (i.e., 40 ms or less) have not been observed, and mean reaction time (RTs) for error-correcting responses are significantly faster than mean RTs for errors (Rabbitt, 1966a, b).

These observations suggest that error correction responses are very much more likely to be valid than invalid. This conclusion would follow from the general assumptions that all functional models for the ways in which people make fast decisions have to make in order to explain empirical findings that as response speed increases accuracy sharply declines. That is, response speed trades off against accuracy (Rabbitt & Vyas, 1969; Schouten & Bekker, 1967). Models for fast decisions explain speed–accuracy trade-off by assuming that errors represent premature decisions, which have been initiated before processes of signal identification and response selection have continued for long enough to attain reliability (Luce, 1986; Rabbitt & Vyas, 1969; Townsend & Ashby, 1983). If we further assume that error correction responses are actually delayed correct responses that occur when processing is extended to a more accurate conclusion beyond the moment of completion of a fast impulsive error, we might expect them to be correspondingly likely to be accurate. We must assume that processing also continues after fast correct responses but we must also assume that the longer that processing continues the more likely it is that a decision will be accurate. It follows that we must suppose that extended processing will always, or nearly always, confirm correct responses, even if these have been based on insufficient evidence and so have been incautiously fast.

The speed and accuracy with which people make error correction responses contrast with their relative slowness and inaccuracy when they are asked deliberately to acknowledge all of their errors by making the same "error-signalling response" to each of them (Rabbitt, 1968, 1990). In easy four-choice CRT tasks the latencies of young adults' error-signalling responses range from 584 to 748 ms with hit rates of only 65.1 to 66.0% (Rabbitt, 1990). Young adults' ability consciously to recall errors that they have neither corrected nor signalled is also unreliable (Rabbitt, 1990).

When people are asked to ignore all of their errors in order to respond as fast as possible to the signals that immediately follow them they nevertheless register them at some level. We know this because their correct responses to the new signals immediately following unacknowledged errors are significantly slower than their other correct responses (Rabbitt, 1968, 1990). When error-signalling instructions are given, errors that have not been overtly signalled nor subsequently recalled are nevertheless immediately followed by slow responses (Rabbitt, 1990). Even those errors that are not overtly signalled nor consciously recalled are, apparently, automatically and involuntarily registered.

All these comparisons have been made in continuous serial self-paced CRT experiments in which each response triggered a new signal within 150 ms (the response–signal interval, RSI). This has meant that if the processes necessary deliberately to select an error-signalling response or to develop a memory trace of an error require longer than 150 ms they will be liable to interruption by onset of a new, attentionally salient, signal. Rabbitt, Cumming, and Vyas (1977) and Rabbitt and Vyas (1981) found that some errors of perceptual discrimination can be detected and corrected provided that participants are allowed sufficient uninterrupted "dead time" after the display to which they incorrectly responded has been terminated. They concluded that perceptual processing of a display can continue even after it has been terminated, and even after an incorrect response has been made to it. By analogy we might expect that as RSIs are increased beyond 150 ms successful extended processing will become increasingly possible, and the likelihood that errors will be accurately signalled and subsequently remembered will correspondingly increase.

Old age markedly slows all responses, even in very simple tasks (Birren, 1979; Birren, Woods, & Williams, 1980). It also impairs the accuracy with which people can deliberately signal and consciously recall their errors but does not affect the reliability of their fast automatic error corrections or the incidence of slow responses following unacknowledged errors (Rabbitt, 1990). On the model suggested this might occur because old age markedly slows information processing so that older people need longer uninterrupted periods of time to consciously recognize that they have made errors, to select and make error-signalling responses to them, and to develop consciously accessible memory traces of them. Older people will be correspondingly more often distracted by the onsets of new signals that occur after brief RSIs and, as RSI durations are increased, will show correspondingly greater improvements in error signalling and recall.

To test this hypothesis the accuracy of error correction, error signalling, recall of errors, and the frequency with which unacknowledged errors are immediately followed by slow responses were compared between two groups of young and older adults as response–signal interval durations were increased from 150 ms through 500 and 800 ms, to 1000 ms.

Method

Groups of 40 older people (16 men and 24 women) aged from 66.2 to 78.4 years (mean 71.2 years, *SD* 5.1) and 40 young adults aged from 18 to 21 years (mean 20.1 years, *SD* 1.1) were matched on scores on the Raven (1965) Mill Hill "A" vocabulary test (old = 46.4, *SD* 6.2; young = 41.9, *SD* 7.1).

A Macintosh LS II microcomputer presented random runs of 200 signals and recorded and timed responses made to each of them whether these were correct or errors. Signals were 2.0-cm diameter black, filled-in circles that appeared one at a time in one of four 4 × 4-cm outline boxes, which were constantly present in a horizontal line across the centre of a 28-cm monitor screen. Participants responded by pressing the appropriate one of a corresponding row of four 2.0-cm diameter circular buttons that were comfortably located beneath the first and second fingers of each of their hands, inset flush with the surface of a 26 × 16-cm desk. The computer program switched on each new signal at a constant interval (RSI) after the previous response, whether this was correct or wrong. RSI durations and elapsed times between the onsets of signals and completions of responses to them (CRTs) were timed to within 1 ms. In an error correction condition participants were asked to respond to their errors by immediately making the responses that they should have made. In an error-signalling condition they acknowledged errors by pressing an additional 2.0-cm diameter error-signalling response button on the same response box. In a No Response condition they were instructed to ignore all of their errors in order to respond as fast as possible to the signals that immediately followed them. In this No Response condition the program also stopped the run of signals at pseudo-random intervals to ask participants whether or not they recalled making an error during the last three responses. Five of these interrogations were made three responses after an error had occurred, and five after runs of nine successive correct responses. In this condition all participants made at least five errors during each run of 200 successive signals and responses. Within each of the error correction, error-signalling, and no response conditions, three runs of 200 signals and responses were given at each of four RSI durations of 150, 500, 800, and 1000 ms. Participants experienced the three conditions at each of the four RSI interval durations in pseudo-random order during two 1-hour experimental sessions.

Results

To check that the pattern of differences in mean CRTs for all correct responses, errors, error correcting responses, and responses immediately following unacknowledged errors was the same as that found in earlier studies, mean CRTs for correct responses, errors, and error correcting responses in the error correction condition, and for correct responses, error signalling responses, and responses immediately following errors (E + 1) responses following signals in the error-signalling condition were compared at each RSI condition.

Analysis of response time

For each age group in each RSI condition separate one-way analyses of variance (ANOVAs) examined differences between mean CRTs for correct responses, error, and error correction responses in the error correction condition, and between correct responses, error signalling responses, and responses following failures of error signalling in the error-signalling condition. Tukey's q tests were used to make paired comparisons between mean CRTs for individual categories of response within each task condition.

In the 150-ms RSI condition of the error correction task the ANOVA for the young group found overall significant differences between CRTs for correct responses, errors, and error correcting response, $F(2, 173) = 54.188$, $P < .001$. Paired comparisons found that errors were faster than correct responses ($q = 5.31$, $p < .001$), error-correcting responses were faster than correct responses ($q = 14.56$, $p < .001$), and error correction responses were also faster than errors ($q = 9.23$, $p < .001$). The ANOVA for the old group also found overall differences between correct responses, errors, and error correction responses, $F(2, 173) = 139$, $p < .001$, with errors ($q = 9.52$, $p < .001$) and error-correcting responses ($q = 22.5$, $p < .001$) faster than correct responses, and error-correcting responses faster than errors ($q = 13.9$, $p < .001$) for all comparisons.

In the 150-ms RSI condition of the error-signalling responses task the ANOVA for the young group found an overall significant difference between correct responses, error-signalling responses, and responses to the next signals immediately following unsignalled errors, $F(2, 173) = 25.94$, $p < .001$. Paired comparisons found that error-signalling responses ($q = 9.2$, $p < .001$) and responses immediately following unsignalled errors responses ($q = 8.5$, $p < .001$) were significantly slower than correct responses. Mean CRTs for error signalling responses and for responses following unsignalled errors did not differ ($q = 0.7$, $p > .05$). The ANOVA for the old group also found overall differences between these three response categories, $F(2, 173) = 28.96$, $p < .001$. Paired comparisons found that error-signalling responses ($q = 10.73$) and responses immediately following unsignalled errors ($q = 4.61$) were significantly slower than correct responses ($p < .01$ for both comparisons) and that error-signalling responses were slower than responses following unsignalled errors ($q = 4.61$, $p < .01$).

In the 500-ms RSI condition of the error correction task the ANOVA for the young group found overall significant differences between mean CRTs for correct responses, errors, and error-correcting responses, $F(2, 173) = 101.52$, $p < .001$. Paired comparisons found that correct responses were slower than error responses ($q = 10.87$, $p < .001$) or error-correcting responses ($q = 20.13$, $p < .001$) and that error-correcting responses were faster than error responses ($q = 9.6$, $p < .001$). The ANOVA for the old group also found overall significant differences between these three response categories, $F(2, 173) = 84.131$, $p < .001$. Paired comparisons found that correct responses were slower than error responses ($q = 6.03$, $p < .001$) and slower than error-correcting responses ($q = 18.02$, $p <.001$) and that error-correcting responses were faster than error responses ($q = 11.9$, $p < .001$).

In the 500-ms RSI condition of the error-signalling task the ANOVA for the young group found overall significant differences between correct responses, error-signalling responses, and responses immediately following unsignalled errors, $F(2, 173) = 38.66$, $p < .001$. Paired comparisons found that correct responses were faster than error-signalling responses, ($q = 11.93$, $p < .01$) or responses immediately following unsignalled errors ($q = 8.9$, $p < .001$), but found no significant difference between error-signalling responses and responses immediately following unsignalled errors ($q = 2.97$, $p > .05$). The ANOVA for the old group also found overall significant differences between these three response categories, $F(2, 173) = 47.04$, $p < .001$. Paired comparisons found that correct responses were faster than error-signalling responses ($q = 11.9$, $p < .001$) and also faster than responses immediately following unsignalled errors ($q = 11.7$, $p < .001$) but found no significant difference between error-signalling responses and responses immediately following unsignalled errors ($q = 0$, *ns*).

In the 800-ms RSI condition of the error correction task the ANOVA for the young group found overall significant differences between mean CRTs for correct responses, error responses, and error-correcting responses, $F(2, 173) = 99.31$, $p < .001$. Paired comparisons found that correct responses were slower than error responses ($q = 12.8$, $p < .001$) and error-correcting responses ($q = 19.62$, $p < .001$) and that error-correcting responses were faster than error responses ($q = 6.79$, $p < .001$). The ANOVA for the old group also found overall significant differences between these three response categories, $F(2, 173) = 110.22$, $p < .001$. Paired comparisons found that correct responses were slower than error responses ($q = 14.74$, $p < .001$) and slower than error-correcting responses ($q = 20.32$, $p < .001$) and that error-correcting responses were faster than error responses ($q = 5.58$, $p < .001$).

In the 800-ms condition of the error-signalling task the ANOVA for the young group found overall significant differences between the correct responses, error-signalling responses, and responses immediately following unsignalled error responses, $F(2, 173) = 28.39$. Paired comparisons found that correct responses were faster than error-signalling responses ($q = 10.04$, $p < .001$) and responses immediately following unsignalled errors ($q = 8.18$, $p < .001$), but found no significant difference between error-signalling responses and responses immediately following unsignalled errors ($q = 1.85$, $p > .05$). The ANOVA for the old group also found overall significant differences between these three response categories, $F(2, 173) = 21.01$, $p < .01$. Paired comparisons found that correct responses were faster than error-signalling responses ($q = 8.28$, $p < .001$) and faster than responses immediately following unsignalled errors ($q = 7.5$, $p < .001$) but found no significant difference between error-signalling response and responses immediately following unsignalled Errors ($q = 0.73$, *ns*).

In the 1000-ms RSI condition of the error correction task the ANOVA for the young group found overall significant differences between mean CRTs for correct, error, and error correcting responses, $F(2, 173) = 106.52$, $p < .001$. Paired comparisons found that correct responses were slower than error responses ($q = 12.15$, $p < .001$) and slower than error-correcting responses ($q = 20.53$, $p < .001$) and that error-correcting responses were faster than error responses ($q = 8.32$, $p < .001$). The ANOVA for the old group also found overall significant differences between these three response categories, $F(2, 173) = 62.17$, $p < .001$. Paired comparisons found that correct responses were slower than error responses ($q = 14.74$, $p < .001$) and slower than error-correcting responses ($q = 20.32$, $p < .001$) and that error-correcting responses were faster than error responses ($q = 5.58$, $p < .001$).

In the 1000-ms RSI condition of the error-signalling task the ANOVA for the young group found overall significant differences between correct responses, error-signalling responses, and responses immediately following errors, $F(2, 173) = 10.2$, $p < .001$. Paired comparisons found significant differences between correct responses and both error-signalling responses ($q = 4.9$, $p < .001$) and responses immediately following unsignalled errors

($q = 5.9$, $p < .01$) but no significant differences between error-signalling responses and responses immediately following unsignalled errors ($q = 1.06$, $p > .05$). The ANOVA for the old group also found significant overall differences between these three response categories, $F(2, 117) = 8.76$, $p < .01$. Paired comparisons found that correct responses were faster than error-signalling responses ($q = 5.03$, $p < .01$) and faster than responses immediately following unsignalled errors ($q = 5.22$, $p < .01$) but found no differences between error-signalling responses and responses immediately following unsignalled errors ($q = 1.19$, $p < .05$).

To aid interpretation of these comparisons, Figures 9.1a, 9.1b, 9.1c, and 9.1d show mean CRTs for response categories in the error correction and error-signalling tasks for younger and older adults separately in the 150-, 500-, 800-ms, and 1000-ms conditions. As times for correct responses were almost identical in the error correction and the error-signalling conditions, to simplify comparisons only CRTs for correct responses are plotted. Means for the old and young groups are separately presented at each RSI condition.

The pattern of differences in mean CRTs for response categories replicates that found in earlier studies. For both age groups, in both the error correction and error-signalling conditions and at all RSI durations errors were faster than correct responses, and error-correcting responses were faster than errors. When RSIs were 500 ms or shorter, both error-signalling responses and responses immediately following unsignalled errors were significantly slower than correct responses. When RSIs were increased to 800 ms and then to 1000 ms, error-signalling responses and responses immediately following unsignalled errors remained slower than correct responses but no longer differed from each other.

The finding that patterns of mean CRTs for response categories were consistent with those earlier reported in the literature meant that the explanation suggested for these earlier results might also be tested on these new data. That is, they could be used to test the hypothesis that increases in RSI durations between 150 and 1000 ms did not affect the incidence of error correction responses or of slow responses following unsignalled error responses, but did increase the number of successful error-signalling responses and the number of occasions on which errors were correctly recalled.

Analysis of errors

Percentages of errors ranged from 2.8% to 6.9%, with an average of 5.2% over all participants. A three-way between-within-within ANOVA found no differences in the mean numbers of errors made by the two age groups, $F(1, 78) = 0.09$, between the three conditions, $F(2, 78) = 0.14$, or between the four RSI durations, $F(3, 78) = 0.62$. There were no significant interactions, $F(3, 78) < 1$ in all cases. The absence of any systematic effects of age, conditions, or RSI durations on the numbers of errors made allowed percentages of valid error correction responses and error-signalling responses and of

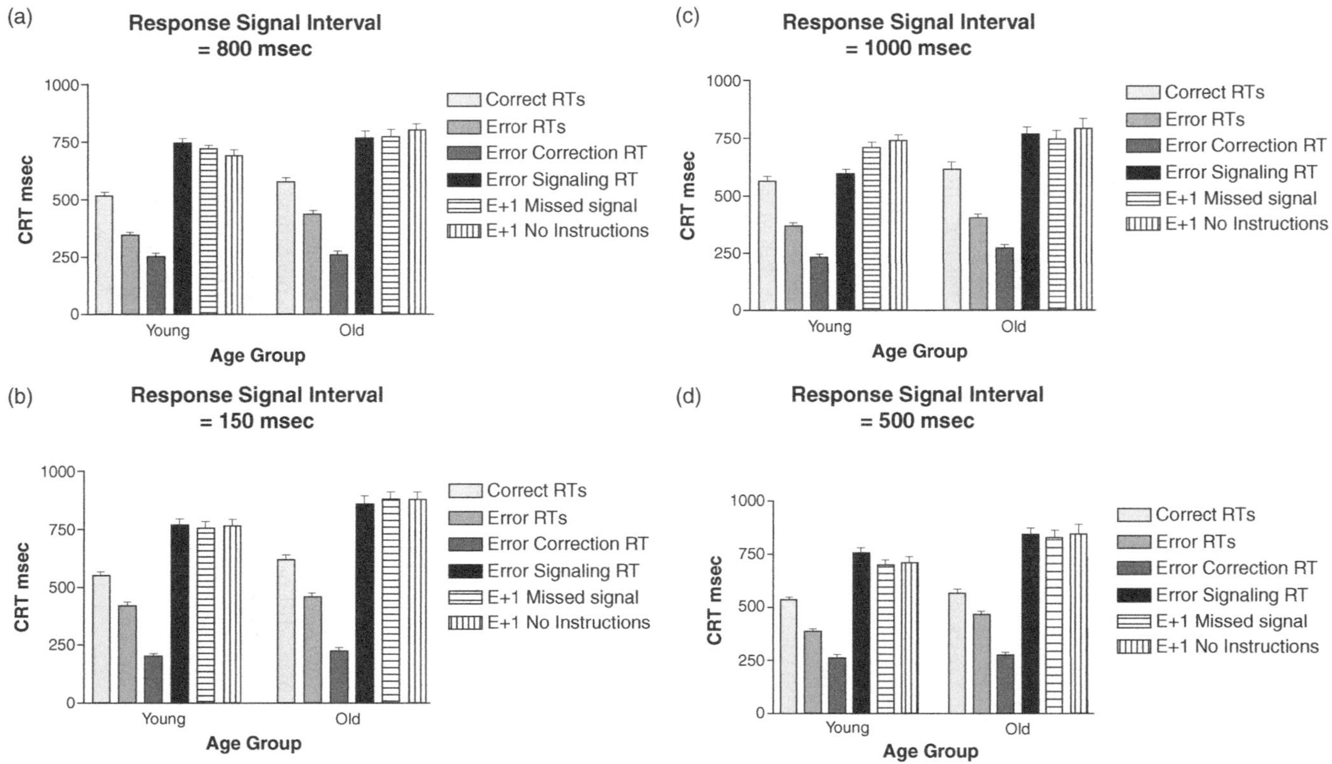

Figure 9.1 CRTs for correct responses, errors, error-correcting responses, error-signalling responses, and responses immediately following errors (E + 1 responses) in a continuous serial CRT task. Means for E + 1 responses that occurred in the error-signalling condition and in the no instruction condition are separately plotted. Panels a, b, c, and d plot data from conditions in which response–signal intervals (RSI) were 150, 500, 800, and 1000 ms, respectively. Error bars indicate standard errors about the mean.

numbers of correct recalls of errors in the no response condition to be pooled for each age group and condition. Group means are shown in Table 9.1.

In the error correction condition a two-way between-within ANOVA found that percentages of appropriate error correction responses were unaffected by age, $F(1, 78) = 0.67$, or by RSI duration, $F(3, 234) = 0.485$, and that there was no interaction between the effects of age and RSI duration, $F(3, 234) = 0.727$.

In the error-signalling condition the number of errors that were acknowledged by error-signalling responses reduced with age, $F(1, 78) = 32.6$, $p = 0.000$, and increased with RSI duration, $F(3, 234) = 36.54$, $p = 0.000$. There was a significant interaction between the effects of age and RSI duration, $F(3, 234) = 7.02$; $p < .00001$.

In the no response condition the number of errors that were immediately followed by responses that were more than 1.5 *SD* slower than the mean RT for all other correct responses made during that run was not affected by age, $F(1, 78) = 0.63$, *ns*, but significantly reduced as RSIs increased, $F(3, 234) = 6.2$, $p < .001$. There was no significant interaction between the effects of age and RSI duration, $F(3, 234) = 0.09$, *ns*.

In the no response condition a further ANOVA found that the probability of recall of errors fell with increasing age, $F(1, 78) = 5.2$, $p < .01$, and increased with increasing RSI duration, $F(3, 234) = 7.0$, $p = .000$. There was no significant interaction between the effects of age and RSI duration, $F(3, 234) = 0.76$.

These comparisons can be interpreted by reference to Table 9.1. When RSIs were 150 ms the young group appropriately signalled 56% of their errors but the old group signalled only 29% of their errors. For both age groups percentages of correctly signalled errors increased with RSI duration. The young group reached their ceiling accuracy (79.9%) at RSIs of 800 ms but the old group reached comparable accuracy (75.8%) only at RSIs of 1000 ms. At these longer RSIs accuracy of error signalling in the error-signalling condition approached accuracies of error correction in the error correction condition.

Table 9.1 also illustrates the form of the interaction between the effects of age and RSI on correct recall of errors in the no response condition. For both age groups probability of correct recall that an error had occurred during the last three responses did not differ from chance expectancy of 50% when RSIs were 150 ms but improved as RSI durations increased, reaching ceiling accuracy of 74.3% at 800 ms for the young group, and of 69.8% at 1000 ms for the old group.

During the error correction and error-signalling conditions the computer counted occasions on which an uncorrected or unsignalled error was immediately followed by a correct response, which was >1.5 *SD* slower than the mean for all other correct responses that had been made during the same experimental run. Because participants corrected most of their errors in the error condition there were not enough data on responses following

Table 9.1 Percentages of error corrections, correct error-signalling responses, recalls of errors, and unusually slow responses following unacknowledged errors in the no response to errors condition at four response–signal intervals

Condition	*RSI*[a]															
	Young adults								*Old adults*							
	150		*500*		*800*		*1000*		*150*		*500*		*800*		*1000*	
	M	*SD*	*M*	*SD*	*M*	*SD*	*M*	*SD*	*M*	*SD*	*M*	*SD*	*M*	*SD*	*M*	*SD*
Error Correction	81.2	5.4	82.3	7.4	85.1	8.2	81.5	8.2	78.6	7.4	77.2	6.9	80.4	9.3	81.2	10.4
Error signaling	56.0	18.8	61.2	12.1	79.9	14.9	78.9	11.0	29.0	13.11	32.0	10.9	58.1	16.24	75.8	11.1
Recall of errors	44.6	9.2	46.8	11.5	61.4	16.2	68.4	15.4	40.3	11.2	45.9	12.2	56.2	8.5	62.6	9.7
No response to errors	77.5	11.4	70.2	9.6	71.6	16.15	70.5	16.0	73.1	11.1	71.3	12.5	70.9	12.1	70.6	14.75

[a]In ms.

uncorrected errors to compare age groups or RSI durations. In the error-signalling condition there were no differences between age groups or RSI durations in the incidence of unusually slow responses immediately following unsignalled errors.

Discussion

In the 150-ms RSI condition differences between mean CRTs for categories of responses resemble those earlier reported by Rabbitt (1990). Both young and old adults rapidly and accurately corrected most of the errors that they made but all, especially the old, were much slower and less accurate when they were required to signal their errors by making the same response to all of them, and they poorly recalled errors that they had not signalled or corrected. Nevertheless even errors that were not overtly signalled, nor subsequently recalled, were apparently registered at some level because they were followed by slow responses.

As RSIs were increased through 500, 800, and 1000 ms, error correction remained fast and accurate, and the accuracy of error signalling and error recall steadily improved. Error-signalling reached comparable levels of accuracy to error correction for the young adults at RSIs of 800 ms and for older adults at RSIs of 1000 ms.

These findings are consistent with the hypothesis that, for both young and elderly adults, the processes resulting in automatic correction of an error can be completed before they are interrupted by a new signal within 150 ms or less. However, the deliberate selection of a particular response to signal an error and the formation of a memory trace that will allow it to be later recalled require further processing that takes much longer and so may be interrupted if a new signal occurs. Young adults need up to 800 ms and older adults need up to 1000 ms to complete this further processing.

Taken together with previous data by Rabbitt (1966a, b, 1968, 1990) the present results confirm that both elderly and young adults can very rapidly and accurately "correct" most of the errors that they make in simple perceptual-motor tasks. Because error correction responses are so fast it seems likely that they are actually "delayed correct responses" that proceed in parallel with the impulsive, fast errors that they follow. This would explain why they are often involuntarily made even when error correction has been prohibited by experimental instruction (Maylor & Rabbitt, 1987).

The other side of this coin is that we must assume that even when a correct response is made, further information about it continues to be processed and accumulated. However, because we must also assume that the longer processing is extended the more likely it is to terminate in a correct decision, we must conclude that extended processing following fast correct responses will invariably validate rather than disconfirm them. A detailed inspection of the data from the present experiments found no events that could be classified in this way so that, as far as we can tell, "false error corrections" are not observed.

An ingenious experiment by Coles, Gratton, Bashore, Eriksen, and Donchin (1985) provides direct evidence that people may initiate both an incorrect and a correct response to a display in parallel. Participants squeezed dynamometers with their left and right hands to signal recognition of the capital letter S or the capital letter H on displays in which the target S or H was centrally embedded in strings of four distractors, which were also either S or H and either the same as (compatible condition) or different from (incompatible condition) the central target letter. Especially in the incompatible condition participants sometimes squeezed both dynamometers so that an initial, partially completed, incorrect response was often followed by a slower than average correct responses.

The results from Coles et al. (1985) suggest that apparent "error corrections" can occur because correct and incorrect responses may sometimes be made in parallel, but they do not provide evidence that errors can also be corrected because processing can continue after an incorrect response has been made. However, there is some direct evidence that this can happen. Rabbitt and Vyas (1981) found that, as might be expected, young adults make more errors as perceptual discriminations of relative line lengths are made more difficult. Lines were presented tachistoscopically and followed by masking fields. When display durations were very brief participants could detect and correct few of the "additional" perceptual errors made as line discrimination difficulty increased. However, as display durations were prolonged participants could detect and correct more of these perceptual errors. Rabbitt and Vyas (1981) concluded that perceptual processing of a display can continue to reach a more reliable conclusion even after an incorrect response to it has been completed. However, onset of masking fields immediately after brief displays interrupts extended processing and so prevents revision of incorrect decisions.

Like these earlier results, the present data suggest that if people are allowed enough uninterrupted time they can extend their processing of events beyond the moment when they respond to them. This allows them not only to improve the reliability of their identifications of signals and choices of responses but also to increase the amount of information that they gain from them. In the present experiment, as RSI durations increased, both young and older participants were more often able to recognize their errors and to acknowledge them by making deliberate error-signalling responses, and they were also more often able to recall errors to which they had not responded. Recognition that an error has occurred, and the selection of an appropriate response to it, require further processing, which can only be completed if it is not interrupted by a new event. Unless time for further processing is available participants also cannot reliably recall that they have made an error. The memory literature provides a context for this findings. As Craik and Lockhart (1972) first showed, the longer that people have to process information about an event the more "deeply" or "elaborately" they can encode it, and the more likely they are subsequently to remember it.

On these assumptions we may regard the acquisition of information about simple events as processes that may be extended in time beyond initial responses to them, not only allowing increasingly reliable decisions about them but also allowing increasingly elaborate and detailed categorizations of them and the formation of more robust and accessible memory traces of them. These results suggest that what previous studies have regarded as "error-correcting responses" (Rabbitt, 1966a, b, 1968, 1979) may more accurately be described as "delayed correct responses" that are initiated in parallel with fast impulsive errors and terminate only slightly after them. On this model, when a person "corrects" an error it does not follow that she or he has, at that moment, yet consciously recognized that an error has occurred, or had time to select an appropriate response to it, or processed the event sufficiently deeply to lay down a durable memory trace of it. These processes cannot be completed unless further time for extended processing is available. It is sad to conclude that the slowing of information processing with increasing age makes older people increasingly unable consciously to recognize or remember many of the errors that they make during fast, continuous tasks, and so deprives them of feedback that might allow them to adjust their performance within safe limits.

References

Birren, J.E. (1979). Tutorial review of changes in choice reaction time with advancing age. In H. Baumeister (Ed.), *Bayer Symposium No.* 6 (pp. 232–247). Bonn: Springer-Verlag.

Birren, J.E., Woods, A.M., & Williams, M.V. (1980). Behavioural slowing with age. In L.W. Poon (Ed.), *Aging in the 1980s: Psychological issues* (pp. 293–308). Washington, DC: American Psychological Association.

Coles, M.G.H., Gratton, G., Bashore, T.R., Eriksen, C., & Donchin, E. (1985). A psychophysiological investigation of the continuous flow model of human information processing. *Journal of Experimental Psychology, 11*, 529–553.

Craik, F.I.M., & Lockhart, R.S. (1972). Levels of processing: A framework for memory research. *Journal of Verbal Learning and Verbal Behavior, 11*, 671–684.

Luce, R.D. (1986). *Response times: Their role in inferring elementary mental organisation.* Oxford: Oxford University Press.

Maylor, E.A., & Rabbitt, P.M.A. (1987). Effect of alcohol and practice on choice reaction times. *Perception and Psychophysics, 42*, 465–475.

Maylor, E.A., & Rabbitt, P.M.A. (1989). Relation between rate of preparation for and processing of an event requiring a choice response. *Quarterly Journal of Experimental Psychology, 41A*, 47–62.

Rabbitt, P.M.A. (1966a). Error-correction without external error signals. *Nature, 212*, 438.

Rabbit, P.M.A. (1966b). Errors and error-correction in choice response tasks. *Journal of Experimental Psychology, 71*, 264–272.

Rabbitt, P.M.A. (1968). Three kinds of error-signalling responses in a serial choice task. *Quarterly Journal of Experimental Psychology, 20*, 179–188.

Rabbitt, P.M.A. (1979). How old and young subjects monitor and control responses for accuracy and speed. *British Journal of Psychology, 70*, 305–311.

Rabbitt, P.M.A. (1990). Age, IQ and awareness of errors. *Ergonomics, 33*, 1291–1305.

Rabbitt, P.M.A., Cumming, G., & Vyas, S.M. (1977). Some errors of perceptual analysis in visual search can be detected and corrected. *Quarterly Journal of Experimental Psychology, 30*, 319–332.

Rabbitt, P.M.A., & Vyas, S.M. (1969). An elementary preliminary taxonomy for some errors in laboratory choice reaction time tasks. *Acta Psychologica, 33*, 56–76.

Rabbitt, P.M.A., & Vyas, S.M. (1981). Processing a display even after you make a response to it. *Quarterly Journal of Experimental Psychology, 33A*, 223–239.

Raven, J.C. (1965). *The Mill Hill Vocabulary Scale*. London: Lewis.

Schouten, J.F., & Bekker, J.A.M. (1967). Reaction time and accuracy. *Acta Psychologica, 27*, 143–153.

Townsend, J.T., & Ashby, F.G. (1983). *Stochastic modelling of elementary psychological processes*. Cambridge, UK: Cambridge University Press.

Longitudinal studies of ageing

The first attempts to understand how mental abilities change with age used tasks designed to test models to explain the effects of differences between experimental conditions on young adults. This inevitable, but lazy, appropriation of a "mainstream" methodology to examine individual differences, including those due to ageing, overlooked two issues: the models had not been designed to explain individual differences and most of the tasks used to test them only measured how fast and how accurately people can do things. Consequently, models for how ageing affects the functional processes supporting discriminations between signals and choices between responses were derived from comparisons of decision speed. As we have seen, possible differences in efficiency of control of variance in response speed to optimize speed-error trade off were overlooked. Because age slows all decisions, and because, in old age, individual differences in speed account for most of individual variance on memory tasks, it seemed possible that all age-related changes in cognitive abilities can be attributed to "general slowing" of information processing in the brain (Salthouse 1996; 2000). This view was respected by most investigators but resisted by an obstinate subset who still hoped to develop experimental paradigms and models to collect and interpret behavioural data to identify specific and local rather than global changes in function. For me "General slowing theory" seemed to negate the usefulness of trying to fractionate overall mean decision times to yield estimates of the relative durations of sub-processes. (In the event, attempts at RT fractionation were discounted by the Brinley effect, (cf. Verhaegen, 2015) but this, as we have seen, is another story). During the early 1980s, especially in memory studies, it still seemed possible to believe that one could design tasks that would be more sensitive to age-related changes in some functional sub-processes than in others.

A different, and much more promising approach to understanding cognitive changes in old age is to consider how they are related to the marked biological changes and increased incidence of pathologies evident in later life. Because the incidence and rate of progress of changes markedly differ between individuals, we can study them only by assessing very large numbers of people as they age over as many years, and on as many different cognitive tasks, as we can cajole them to perform. The first studies of large groups during the early twentieth century were "cross-sectional" comparisons of data obtained from groups of people of different ages on a single occasion. At that time a dominant interest in human psychology was to explore what intelligence tests can tell us about individual differences in rates of age-related mental changes by asking, for example, whether a single index can assess developmental gains and involutional declines in general competence across all mental abilities (general fluid intelligence, *gf*) or whether we can identify and assess different and functionally independent cognitive skills that develop and decline independently of each other during successive periods of the lifespan. The first cognitive/gerontological studies used intelligence and memory tests to assess the amounts and rates of change in intelligence test scores (e.g. Jones and Conrad, reprinted 1998) from groups of people in successive decades. Studies compared the amounts of these changes between men and women (Conrad, Jones and Hsiao,1933) and asked whether different mental abilities, such as *gf* and memory, improved and declined at the same or at different rates during our lives.

A more useful project is to collect longitudinal data to explore what was then termed the "Medical Model" of cognitive ageing, which relates cognitive changes to the incidence and accumulation of physiological changes and pathologies that affect our neurobiological efficiency and, consequently, our cognitive competence. The earliest, most systematic and insightful proposer of this agenda was Nathan Shock, whose Baltimore Longitudinal Study (Shock, 1984) collected, analyzed and archived data on health, physiological and sensory changes and biometric variables in parallel with measures of performance on tests of memory information processing speed and general intelligence from a large group of volunteers over four decades. This remarkable project became a template for many subsequent and more tightly focussed studies that have collected information on relationships between particular aspects of health such as cardiovascular function (Kannel and Feinleib, 1972) on physical performance (Seeman et al., 1994) and on relationships between socio-economic advantage on changes in life expectancy and rates of cognitive change (e.g. as in the much later classical study by Marmot, 2005).

By 1980 I was becoming dispirited by my unsuccessful efforts to find particular behavioural tasks that are uniquely sensitive to age-related functional changes in the cognitive system. At this point I had the extraordinary luck to obtain funding to recruit a large population of older people and collect information on their health, socio-economic and cognitive status and scores on depression inventories and other indices of mental health at regular intervals over a period of five years. Because longitudinal data accumulate slowly we did not entirely abandon attempts to decompose results from single laboratory tasks to test models for age-related changes in perception, decision and memory, and we also taxed the patience, good will and remarkable generosity of our 6506 volunteers to make smaller cross-sectional studies on a variety of tests of memory and speed of processing. Of necessity our first analyses of data examined the validity and reliability of the tests we were using, such as self-report questionnaires on competence in everyday life (Abson and Rabbitt, 1988; Rabbitt and Abson, 1990; 1991). As data accumulated, we were also able to examine cross-sectional relationships between biological, demographical and cognitive measures. For example, how mental abilities are affected by depression (Rabbitt et al., 1995) or by pathologies that become increasingly prevalent in later life and by approach to death. We were unsurprised to find that diabetes (Bent, Rabbitt & Metcalf, 2000), and other pathologies that accompany the approach to death, impair cognitive efficiency (Rabbitt et al., 2002). A cross-sectional analysis of how cognitive abilities of older people vary with their ages and individual levels of depression assessed on the Beck et al. (1961) depression scale gave new information that guided our later work. A familiar finding is that decline in cognitive abilities is associated with increases in depression, assessed by scores on the Beck depression scale. Rabbitt et al. (1995) added the new point that the negative relationship between levels of depression and cognitive ability are not only found within ranges of higher Beck scorers, indicating levels of depression of clinical interest, but also within ranges of scores so far below the average for a normal population that they must reflect differences in above-average contentment rather than in dysphoria. Depression scale scores within these below-average ranges are mainly influenced by socio-economic factors and experience of pathologies. An analysis of our longitudinal data on the Yesavage Geriatric Depression Scale (Yesavage, 1988) by Mary Lunn and Kate Hunter (unpublished) found that in lower ranges of Yesavage scores, reflecting differences in contentment rather than in depression, differences in levels of depression-inventory scores are almost entirely determined by health issues such as the presence or absence of diabetes and cardiovascular problems and, more weakly, by socio-economic issues. Within ranges of above-average levels of depression scores, the effects of pathologies and of socio-economic factors are overwhelmed by other, endogenous factors that, apparently, have more severe effects on mental abilities. In the lower ranges of Yesavage scores, levels of depression are driven solely by pathologies and socio-economic factors, and the link between depression and mental ability occurs because pathology drives depression and lowers intelligence. In the higher ranges of depression scores, effects of pathologies and socio-economic factors on intelligence are no longer significant. Aichele, Rabbitt and Ghisletta (2017) have since made a similar point using different statistics on the same data-set. This is a crucial lesson for all analyses of the effects of external factors, such as education, housing, nutrition, income and other socio-economic advantages on maintenance of cognitive abilities in old age. For all such factors the question arises whether there may be threshold ranges of influence. For example, we may expect that cognitive abilities continuously improve with levels of socioeconomic advantage and general health until a point where further prosperity and well-being have little or no effect on maintenance of ability.

While we made such cross-sectional analyses of our data as were possible, I speculated how we could frame and ask questions of our longitudinal data. The next paper reproduced describes my conclusions.

References

Abson, V., & Rabbitt, P. (1988). What do self rating questionnaires tell us about changes in competence in old age? In M. M. Gruneberg, P. E. Morris & R. N. Sykes (Eds), *Practical Aspects of Memory: Current Research and Issues* (Vol. 2, pp. 186–191). New York: Wiley.

Aichele, S., Rabbitt, P., & Ghisletta, P. (2017). Illness and intelligence are comparatively strong predictors of individual differences in depressive symptoms following middle age. *Aging and Mental Health*, 1–10.

Beck, A. T., Ward, C. H., Mendelson, M., Mock, J., & Erbaugh, J. (1961). An inventory for measuring depression. *Archives of General Psychiatry, 4*(6), 561–571.

Bent, N., Rabbitt, P., & Metcalfe, D. (2000). Diabetes mellitus and the rate of cognitive ageing. *British Journal of Clinical Psychology, 39*(4), 349–362.

Conrad, H. S., Jones, H. E., & Hsiao, H. H. (1933). Sex differences in mental growth and decline. *Journal of Educational Psychology, 24*(3), 161–169.

Jones, H. E., & Conrad, H. S. (1998). The growth and decline of intelligence. In M. Powell, Lawton & T. A. Salthouse (Eds), *Essential Papers on the Psychology of Aging* (p. 149). New York: New York University Press.

Kannel, W. B., & Feinleib, M. (1972). Natural history of angina pectoris in the Framingham study: Prognosis and survival. *American Journal of Cardiology, 29*(2), 154–163.

Marmot, M. (2005). Social determinants of health inequalities. *The Lancet, 365*(9464), 1099–1104.

Rabbitt, P., & Abson, V. (1990). "Lost and Found": Some logical and methodological limitations of self-report questionnaires as tools to study cognitive ageing. *British Journal of Psychology, 81*(1), 1–16.

Rabbitt, P., & Abson, V. (1991). Do older people know how good they are? *British Journal of Psychology, 82*(2), 137–151.

Rabbitt, P., Donlan, C., Watson, P., McInnes, L., & Bent, N. (1995). Unique and interactive effects of depression, age, socioeconomic advantage, and gender on cognitive performance of normal healthy older people. *Psychology and Aging, 10*(3), 307–313.

Rabbitt, P., Watson, P., Donlan, C., McInnes, L., Horan, M., Pendleton, N., & Clague, J. (2002). Effects of death within 11 years on cognitive performance in old age. *Psychology and Aging, 17*(3), 468–481.

Salthouse, T. A. (1996). The processing-speed theory of adult age differences in cognition. *Psychological Review, 103*(3), 403–428.

Salthouse, T. (2000). *A Theory of Cognitive Aging* (Vol. 28). Amsterdam: North-Holland.

Seeman, T. E., Charpentier, P. A., Berkman, L. F., Tinetti, M. E., Guralnik, J. M., Albert, M., ... & Rowe, J. W. (1994). Predicting changes in physical performance in a high-functioning elderly cohort: MacArthur studies of successful aging. *Journal of Gerontology, 49*(3), M97–M108.

Shock, N. W. (1984). *Normal Human Aging: The Baltimore Longitudinal Study of Aging.* Bethesda, MD, Washington, DC: US Government Printing Office.

Verhaegen, P. (2015). *The Elements of Cognitive Ageing.* Oxford: Oxford University Press

Yesavage, J. A. (1988). Geriatric depression scale. *Psychopharmacology Bulletin, 24*(4), 709–711.

10 Does it all go together when it goes? The Nineteenth Bartlett Memorial Lecture

P.M.A. Rabbitt

It is of intense economic, social, and personal interest to all of us to know how cognitive performance changes with age. The study of cognitive gerontology also redresses a theoretical parochialism of models in cognitive psychology, which describe only "steady-state" systems that neither exist in nature nor help us to understand the functional bases of individual differences or of cognitive change. Brilliant derivations of cognitive psycho-logical models from single neuropsychological case studies do not rectify this weakness because they concern the effects of localized lesions, which cause abrupt changes in very specific aspects of cognitive performance. The ageing of the brain brings about slight, slow, diffuse, and global rather than dramatic, sudden, specific, and localized cognitive changes. More-over, these changes are confounded with the accumulation of a lifetime store of information, procedures, and skills, with changes in motivation and in physiological and mental well-being and with individual differences in the complex ways in which diverse genetic legacies play themselves out over very different life experiences.

Paradigms in cognitive psychology have been developed to compare average scores between different experimental conditions. Most studies in cognitive gerontology have borrowed these paradigms to compare average scores of "older" and "younger" groups and have invariably found that the old perform less efficiently. Because this is unenlightening, investigators usually also examine interactions between age groups and experimental conditions. Cognitive psychological paradigms encourage this type of analysis because differences between experimental and control conditions have been developed as ostensive definitions of particular hypo-thetical constructs such as "spread of activation or inhibition", "trace decay", "attentional efficiency", "trace strength", "working memory capacity", "psychological refractoriness", or "information processing speed". To import this methodology to describe age differences is to assume that hypothetical constructs that have been ostensively defined by paradigms painstakingly designed to mitigate the effects of between-subject variability will, nevertheless, precisely identify the diffuse, global, and interactive changes that occur with age. We can no longer postpone analysis of this predicament with the modest disclaimer that until neurophysiologists develop better models for age changes in the brain, exploration with sub-optimal tools is an honourable alternative to inertia. When we examine actual data, we find that changes in the *variability* of performance are much more pervasive, and potentially more informative, than the shifts in *average* scores, which these paradigms and models have been designed to detect and explain. For example Figure 10.1 presents data collected by Rabbitt and Phillips (unpublished), who compared 564 individuals aged between 20 and 79 years on a serial, self-paced 10-choice reaction time (CRT) task. Though changes in CRT between the age-decades of 20 and 30 are small, they are nevertheless statistically significant, and the rate of change progressively accelerates in all subsequent decades.

To conclude from this either that each *individual's* performance continuously declines between the ages of 20 and 90, or that age is a *main* determinant of CRT, would miss a crucial point. Over the entire sample, the correlation between chronological age and CRT was r = 0.3, so that age only accounted for about 9% of the overall variation between individuals. Figure 10.2 plots average CRTs against corresponding standard deviations for successive age decades. We see that between-individual variance in CRTs increases regularly with the age of the group sampled.

It is interesting to plot the precise form of this increase in between-individual variance with age-related decline in average performance. Figure 10.3 shows distributions of scores on the AH 4 (1) IQ test (Heim, 1968) for 3 cohorts of 312 individuals aged from SO to S9,60 to 69, and

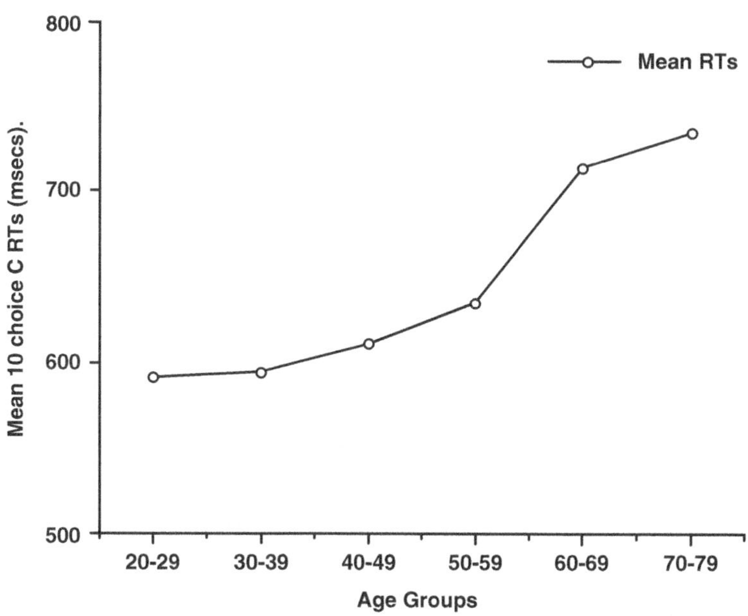

Figure 10.1 Mean CRTs for successive decade samples from 564 individuals aged between 18 and 93 years.

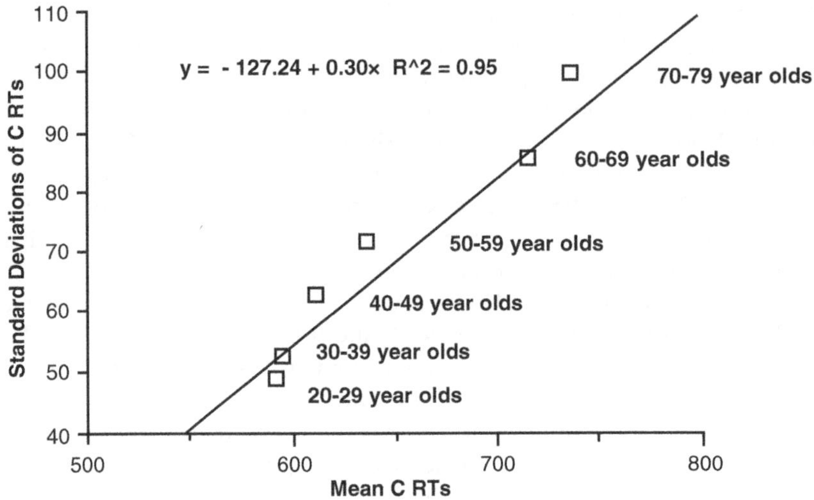

Figure 10.2 Mean CRTs plotted against corresponding SDs for successive decade samples of 564 individuals aged between 18 and 93 years.

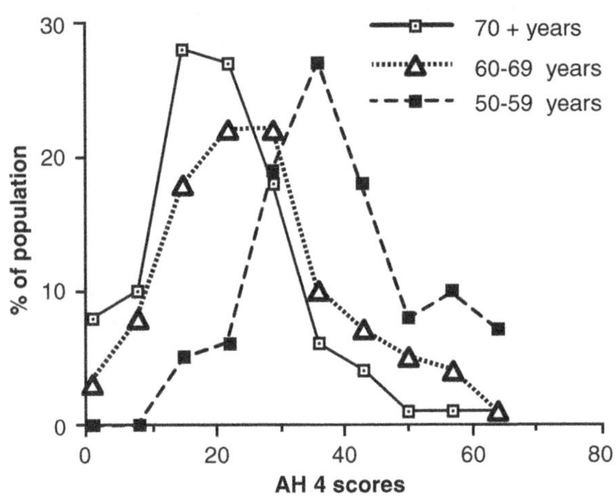

Figure 10.3 Distributions of AH 4 test scores for 3 groups of about 340 individuals aged 50–59, 60–49. and 70–79 years.

70 to 79 years, and Figure 10.4 gives distributions of the numbers of words out of a list of 30 that these same individuals could immediately recall.

On both tasks, increases in average scores with group age largely reflect corresponding declines in the numbers of the more-with proportional increases in the numbers of less—able performers. The most interesting effect of age is not that it depresses average scores, but, rather, that differences in

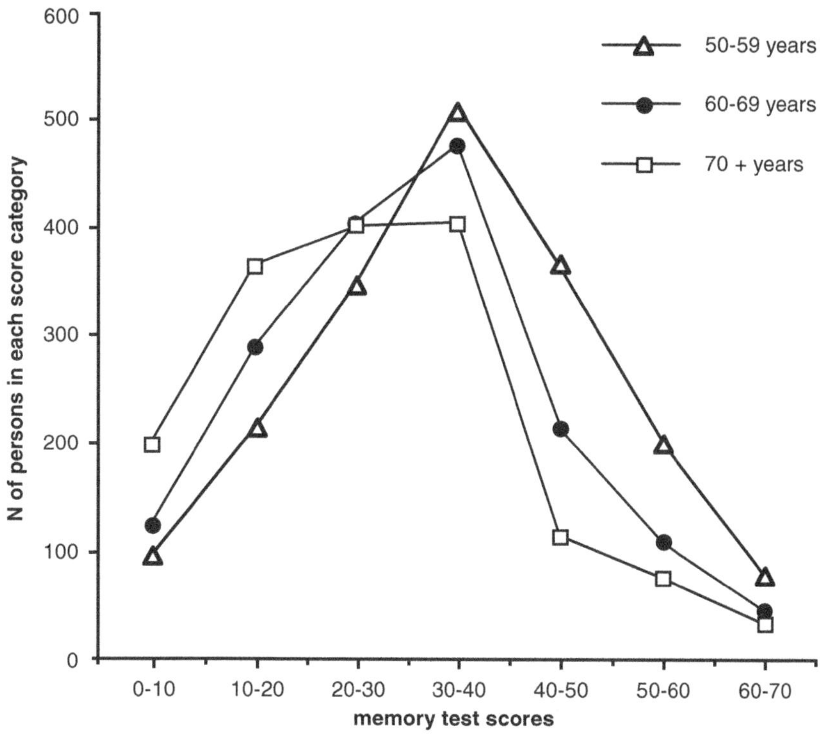

Figure 10.4 Distributions of correct items recalled out of a list of 30 words by 3 cohorts of 340 individuals aged 50–59, 60–69, and 70–79 years.

ability between the most and least able individuals steadily increase with the ages of the groups sampled. Figure 10.5 illustrates this with scores from a digit span task in which volunteers were tested at all list lengths from 4 to 9 items. This simple task has the crucial advantage that it allows all volunteers to obtain non-zero cumulative scores of correctly reported lists, so that variance within the least able groups is not curtailed by floor effects. Only when tasks are designed to prevent floor and ceiling effects can we see that, as average scores fall, within-individual variance steadily increases with group age.

Demonstrations that variability between individuals increases with the ages of the groups sampled are consistent with actuarial statistics, which show that people have very different life spans and provide formal endorsement for folk wisdom that people "age" at very different rates. Gerontologists acknowledge this by distinguishing "chronological ageing", time measured by external standards such as calendars or clocks, which passes at the same rate for all organisms, from "biological" or "functional" ageing, which occurs at very different rates in diverse species and individuals. Marked individual variations in rates of cognitive ageing immediately raise the question whether,

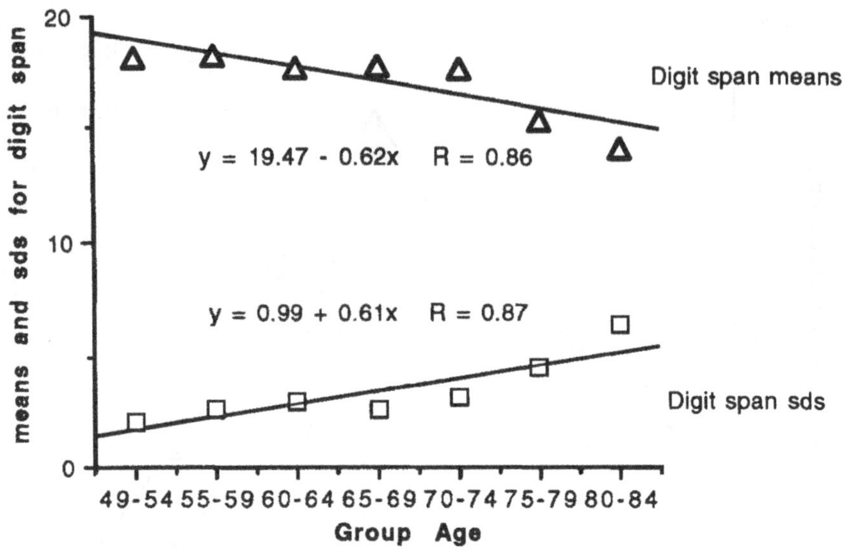

Figure 10.5 Mean number of groups of digits recalled, and corresponding SDs, for individuals aged from 50 to 86 years.

and how, cognitive changes with age are related to particular concomitant physiological changes. Further questions are whether all cognitive abilities change at the same or at different rates, and whether people may not only experience different rates of cognitive ageing but also show characteristically different "patterns", "syndromes", or "careers" of cognitive change. These questions provide the title and the main theme of this paper.

Longitudinal twin studies and differences in longevity between men and women suggest that much of the variance in biological and behavioural ageing is genetically determined (Plomin & McClearn, 1990). Genetics cannot be the sole determinant, because more individuals live longer as the societies to which they belong experience improvements in nutrition, health habits, availability of medical treatment, and reduced occupational and environmental health hazards. The most direct evidence that individual differences in health also contribute to increased variability between individuals comes from findings that a variety of pathologies cause cognitive decrements, so that healthy individuals not only live longer but also maintain cognitive integrity later in life (see review by Holland & Rabbitt, 1991; Siegler & Costa, 1985). Figure 10.6 compares distributions of scores on the AH 4 (1) IQ test (Heim, 1968) obtained from groups of diabetics and controls who had been individually and precisely matched on age between 50 and 80 years, on scores on the Mill Hill Vocabulary test, on gender and on socio-economic status (Rabbitt & Bent, in preparation). It seems that non-insulin-dependent diabetes (but not insulin-dependent diabetes) can depress cognitive ability

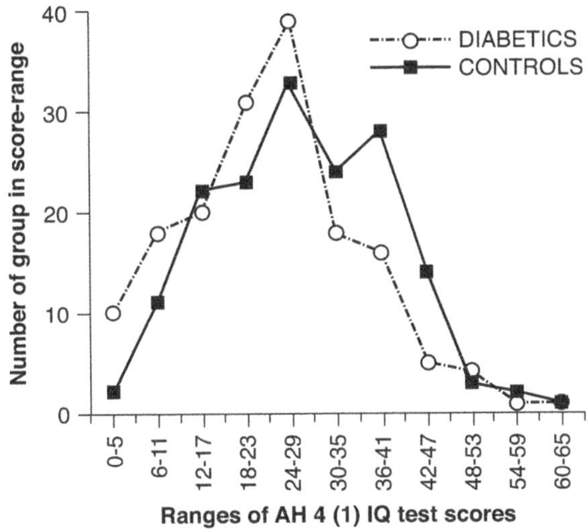

Figure 10.6 Distributions of AH 4 (1) test scores for 64 diabetics and controls matched in age, gender, and Mill Hill (A) test score.

in middle age. Diabetes and other conditions, such as cardiovascular insufficiency, become increasingly common as age advances and must contribute to the increase and progressive skew of between-individual variance in performance on most cognitive tasks. The most important questions remain unanswered: for example, whether illness interact with age so as, in effect, to accelerate cognitive ageing in those who suffer them; whether illnesses increase within-individual variance as well as between-individual variance because they have local effects of some cognitive skills rather than global effects on all of them; whether different illnesses bring about different patterns, as well as different amounts, of cognitive change; how far age-related changes in the central nervous system and their expression in performance and behaviour are accounted for by a lifetime's history of pathologies and to what extent people who remain completely free of all pathologies may indefinitely retain all their faculties.

While cognitive psychologists have deliberately invented subtle paradigms and statistical techniques for partialling out between-subject variance, psychometricians have been entirely concerned with individual differences. Psychometric tests might therefore seem the best-evolved instruments with which to determine whether the average gap between people's strongest and weakest cognitive skills increases as they grow old and whether or not different cognitive skills change at different rates.

If cognitive skills age at different rates, the accuracy with which a person's performance on one skill predicts his/her performance on all others

Table 10.1 Correlations Between Scores on 13 Tests, Age between 50 to 86 Years, and Unadjusted Scores on the Cattell "Culture Fair" IQ Test

	Age	*CFIQ*
Cattell Culture Fair IQ Test	−0.447	—
WAIS Vocabulary	−0.149	0.497
Baddeley "Silly Sentences" (Sp)	−0.314	0.484
Visual Search Speed	−0.325	0.593
Letter/Letter Coding (Sp)	−0.367	0.331
Memory for Code (from above)	−0.200	0.012
Rate of improvemental in L/LC	−0.018	0.302
Immediate free recall of words	−0.336	0.362
Delaryed free recall of words	−0.359	0.362
Memory for people	−0.251	0.349
Memory for object names	−0.411	0.407
Memory for locations of objects	−0.211	0.183
Memory for symbol location	−0.364	0.549

Note: $N = 386$.

must steadily decline as he/she grows older. Table 10.1 shows that unadjusted scores on either of two IQ tests, the AH 4 and the Cattell "Culture Fair", modestly predict performance on many different laboratory indices of memory and information-processing speed. In fact, predictions from these IQ test scores are much better than those from individuals' chronological ages in the range from 50 to 96 years, which, in our test batteries, never account for more than 25% of all variance. Indeed, when individual variance in scores on either of these two simple pencil-and-paper tests has been partialled out, predictions from chronological age are no better than chance.

Our longitudinal screenings of large groups of people aged between 50 and 96 years continue to confirm that scores on most laboratory tasks decline with age and that unadjusted IQ test scores are the best predictors of performance on all other performance measures. In contrast, scores on vocabulary tests such as the Mill Hill, or the WAIS, show little or no change with age. Figure 10.7 shows distributions of Mill Hill vocabulary test scores for the same three decade samples whose distributions of AH 4 (1) scores and free recall scores were shown in Figures 10.3 and 10.4. The identity of both means and distributions of vocabulary test scores between 50 and 80 years contrasts with progressive age-related decline and increase in variance and skew of AH 4 and free-recall scores.

This demonstration that *cognitive skills age at different rates* entails the further question whether *different cognitive skills may change at different rates in different individuals.* One approach is to examine changes in the levels of correlation between vocabulary test scores and other measures within successive age groups. Figure 10.8 shows that correlations between vocabulary and other performance measure steadily decline as age increase from 50 to 86 years.

We can examine a different aspect of these changing relationships by standardizing scores on all tests and tasks and plotting average differences between

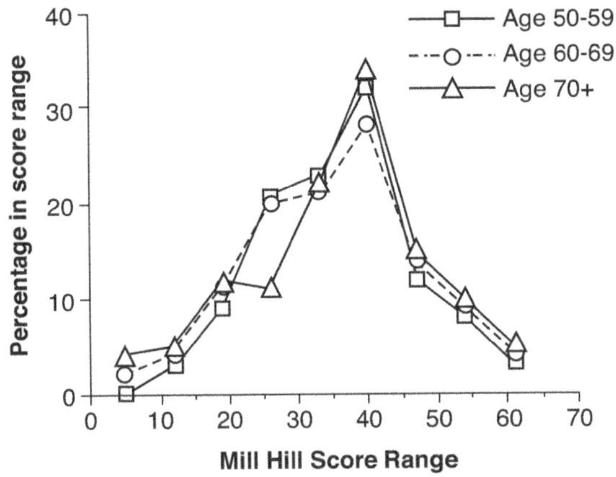

Figure 10.7 Distribution of Mill Hill (A) vocabulary test scores for three cohorts of about 340 individual aged 50–59, 60–69, and 70–79 years.

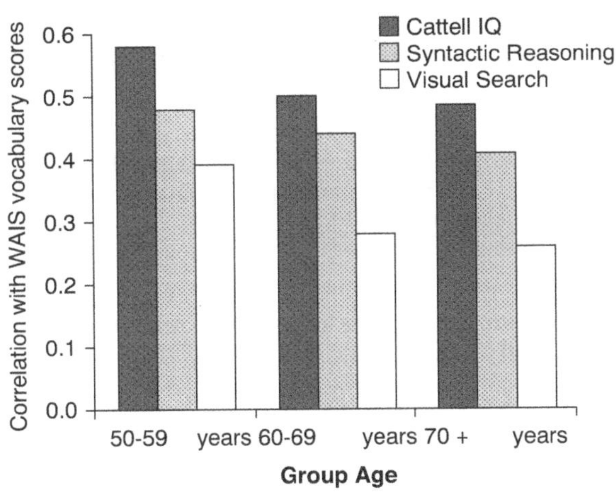

Figure 10.8 Age and correlations between Mill Hill (A) vocabulary test scores and other performance measure within a group of 340 individuals aged 50–79 years.

them as a function of age. This is done in Figure 10.9. As we would expect from a comparison between Figures 10.3 and 10.4 on the one hand, and 10.7 on the other, absolute differences between scores on vocabulary tests and on other tasks increase with age.

Note that Figures 10.8 and 10.9 give us quite distinct pieces of information; Figure 10.9 shows that vocabulary scores remain relatively stable, whereas scores on other tasks decline. This growing gap has no necessary consequence for *correlations* between measures. The weakening of correlations with increasing age shown in Figure 10.8 suggests something

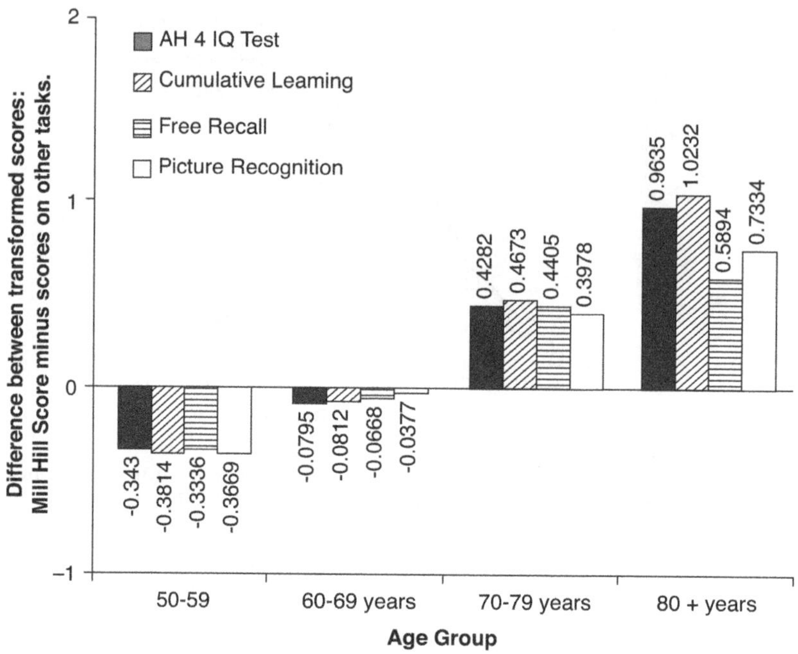

Figure 10.9 Age and absolute differences between standardized scores on Mill Hill (A) vocabulary test and on other performance measure for a group of 340 individuals aged from 50 to 86 years.

different: *individual variations* in the relative amounts of decline of scores on other tasks compared to scores on vocabulary tests increase with age. In other words, cognitive ageing, as measured by the increasing disparity between performance on vocabulary tests and other tasks, proceeds at different rates in different individuals.

On average, age increases discrepancies between Mill Hill and AH 4 test performance, but it is logically possible that, within any age group, individuals vary widely in terms of the sizes of the discrepancies they show. In practical terms this suggests that *for any older individual the current discrepancy between his or her attainments on vocabulary tests and on other measures of performance may be a convenient index of the age-related decrement which he or she has experienced up to the date of assessment.* This would provide a useful index that we can use to test whether some categories of individuals change faster than others. For example, we can ask whether women, who live longer on average, also show slower cognitive ageing than men or whether people with different levels of ability change at the same rate. Figure 10.10 illustrates one way in which we can ask whether the performance of groups of different levels of initial ability changes at different rates as they age. A total of 1,456 volunteers

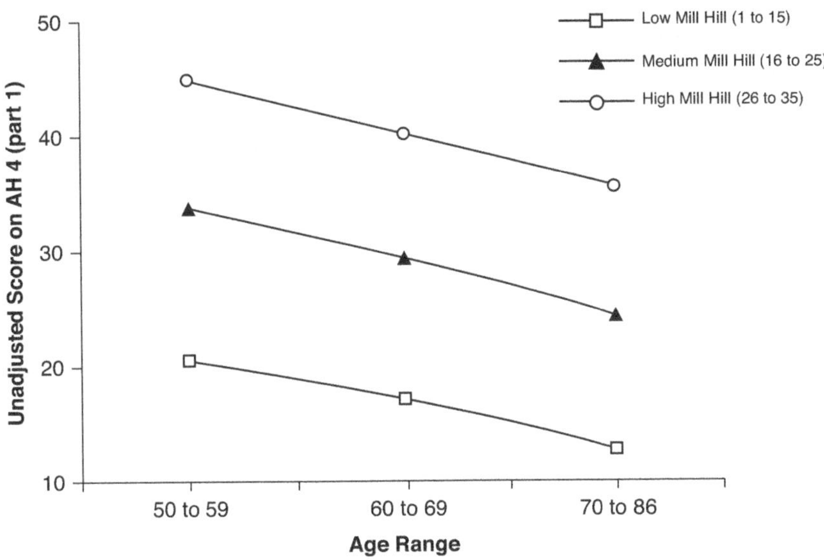

Figure 10.10 Changes in average AH 4 (1) IQ test scores between decade samples aged 50–59, 60–69, and 70–86 years, stratified by Mill Hill (A) vocabulary score bands.

were divided into bands according to their current Mill Hill vocabulary test scores. Within each band, average AH 4 test scores are plotted for successive decade samples. We know that within each Mill Hill band people who are now in their 60s or 70s had, when they were in their 50s, very similar AH 4 test scores to current 50-year-olds. Thus the rates at which AH 4 test scores decline across successive decades in three sub-populations vary between groups with very different levels of youthful attainment. A two way between/between ANOVA confirms that AH 4 test scores vary between Mill Hill bands and age groups but shows no interaction. Further analyses showed that the straight lines in Figure 10.10 provide the best fits that could be made to the data for each of the different groups. It seems that high, medium, and low ability samples lose the same absolute number (but, it is important to note, very different *proportions!*) of AH 4 (part 1) test score points as they grow older.

Why Should Skills Decline at Different Rates?

Why should vocabulary survive while other aspects of cognitive performance decline? Horn and Cattell (1967) pointed out that vocabulary is one of many cognitive skills that depend on the acquisition and continued use of large bodies of information. They termed this acquired conceptual tool kit "crystallized intelligence" (g_c), in contrast to "fluid intelligence" (g_f), which is essential for the rapid solution of novel, and so by this definition necessarily unpractised, problems such as those in IQ tests. Horn and Cattell (1967) suggested that as age increases, g_c, remains relatively unaffected, but g_f, markedly declines. It is, of course, the case that individuals who have high levels of fluid ability when they are young will consequently be able to learn and understand more, and more elaborate, data and procedures, and so will also build up proportionately richer bodies of crystallized skills to carry into later life. The complex relationships between levels of early fluid and later crystallized intelligence do not end there. If we suppose, with Eysenck (1986) or Salthouse (1982; 1985; 1991), that the functional basis of individual differences in g_f, are differences in the rates at which people process information throughout their lifetimes, we must conclude that higher youthful g_f, will not only buy additional information processing capacity and so, in effect, extra time with which to acquire more skills and knowledge about the world, but will also allow information and skills that are employed repeatedly to be over-learned to a much greater degree. As we know that the more a skill is over-learned, the more resistant it becomes to loss over time, we may also expect that the investment of high g_f, in youth brings proportionate returns not merely in terms of the quantity and quality, but also in the durability, of g_c, in old age.

In addition to these empirical problems, there are many important epistemological difficulties in making sharp distinctions between "fluid" and "crystallized" "intelligence". The most obvious is that they are completely confounded in all descriptions of "intelligent behaviour" given by laymen, ethologists, and expert psychometricians, who all agree on definitions based on competence in dealing with the demands of everyday life. These demands differ very widely between animal species, human societies, and individual persons, and certainly also change systematically as increasing age alters both our life roles and the resources we can bring to meet them (Berg & Sternberg, 1992; Jerison, 1982; Sternberg & Powell, 1982). Another epistemological problem is the elusiveness of any boundary of definition between "fluid" and "crystallized" abilities when we try to categorize the intellectual achievement of discovering that a novel and complicated new problem can be solved by adapting a familiar class of solution or that the essence of a difficult new idea can be conveyed to a novice by a particularly subtle and apt metaphor, or when we reflect on the implications of Bartlett's (1932) famous demonstration that new material is learned faster and recalled better when it can be incorporated without distortion into previously acquired "schemata". These must remain important issues for a quite different paper. For the present we may consider the quite restricted ways in which the dichotomy between the rates with which simple information can be processed, learned, re-called, and forgotten and the reliability with which acquired information and procedures can continue to be accessed has been used to account for changes in patterns of performance in old age.

Functional Models for "Crystallized" and "Fluid" Skills

To develop functional models to explain why g_f, abilities are more and g_c, abilities are less affected by age, we must clarify distinctions between them This paper considers only three of the many ways in which this task can be approached. The first is to ask whether the difference between these two kinds of "intelligence" is that between semantic and procedural information—that is, whether age-robust g_c, is, in effect, our total data base of semantic knowledge about the world (such as words and their meanings, and connected bodies of factual information), the internal representations of which do not incorporate any particular systems of procedural rules (ways of doing things). Whereas, in contrast, age-labile g_f, skills are, in effect, abstract systems of procedural rules for solving problems and detecting relationships, which can be applied equally efficiently across many quite different semantic data bases, but which are not represented in terms of any particular body of knowledge.

A second approach is to ask whether the differences in functional representation that make g_c skills robust and g_f, skills age-labile are the result of changes that practice produces in the brain areas or in the neural networks in which they are represented.

A third approach is to consider whether it is in fact the case that all the abilities that we categorize as examples of g_f are, in fact, homogeneous in their representation and so are all affected by the ageing of the brain by the same amount and in the same way. For example, it has been assumed that all g_f abilities may decline with age at about the same rate because they all ultimately depend on a single, common performance parameter that is common to the entire central nervous system (CNS) such as the maximum speed at which it can process information (Salthouse, 1982; 1985). Contrariwise, we may ask whether g_f skills are actually hetero-geneous in their representation and so change at different rates, either because they are supported by different performance parameters of the CNS or because they are localized in anatomically distinct brain modules, which may be affected by age to different extents.

Does "g_c" Only Comprise Large Acquired Databases, or Does It Also Include Procedural Skills?

Though Horn and Cattell (1967) and Horn (1982; 1986) clearly regard g_c, as embodying an acquired tool-kit of effective problem-solving strategies as well as data-bases of information about the world, they do not actually demonstrate the survival of procedural, rather than of merely semantic, information into old age. However, studies by Belinda Winder in our laboratory amusingly show that older people can not only retain remark-able vocabularies but also preserve, well into old age, the complex procedures necessary to "do clever things with words" by solving difficult cryptic crossword puzzles.

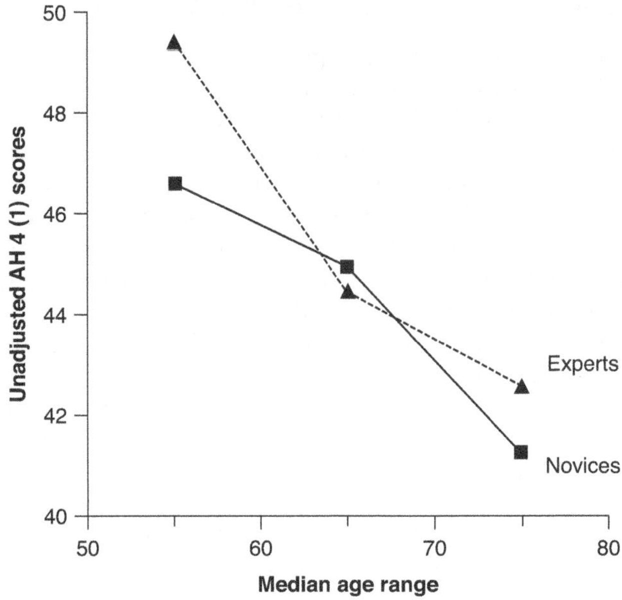

Figure 10.11 Matching of expert and novice cryptic crossword solvers by age and AH 4 (1) test score.

She matched each of 52 expert crytic crossword puzzle solvers with a novice of the same gender, age, and unadjusted AH 4 (1) IQ test score. Figure 10.11 plots AH 4 (1) scores of experts and novices as a function of their ages and shows that matches were very exact and that, in consequence, AH 4 test scores declined with age at the same rate in both groups.

Winder then tested her experts and controls on the same open-ended set of cryptic crossword clues. Figure 10.12a shows scores for novices and experts as a function of their ages and Figure 10.12b as a function of their IQ test scores. Unsurprisingly, all experts scored higher than any novice. More interestingly, whereas novices' scores fell with their ages and rose with their AH 4 scores, experts' scores were unaffected either by age or by general ability. Main effects and interactions were statistically significant.

Although these crossword puzzle experts had the same AH 4 (1) scores as their controls, they had much higher Mill Hill vocabulary test scores. It seems that maintained skill at cryptic crosswords partly depends on a lifetime's acquisition of a rich vocabulary but also on learning, and retention into old age, of the restricted and arbitrary, but non-trivial, procedural rules necessary to decode cryptic clues. "Crystallized intelligence" for crossword puzzle solving involves retention of particular, specialized problem-solving procedures as well as a relatively rich body of semantic information.

Horn (1982; 1986) based his distinction between "fluid" and "crystallized" abilities on factor analyses of scores on tests of vocabulary and acquired

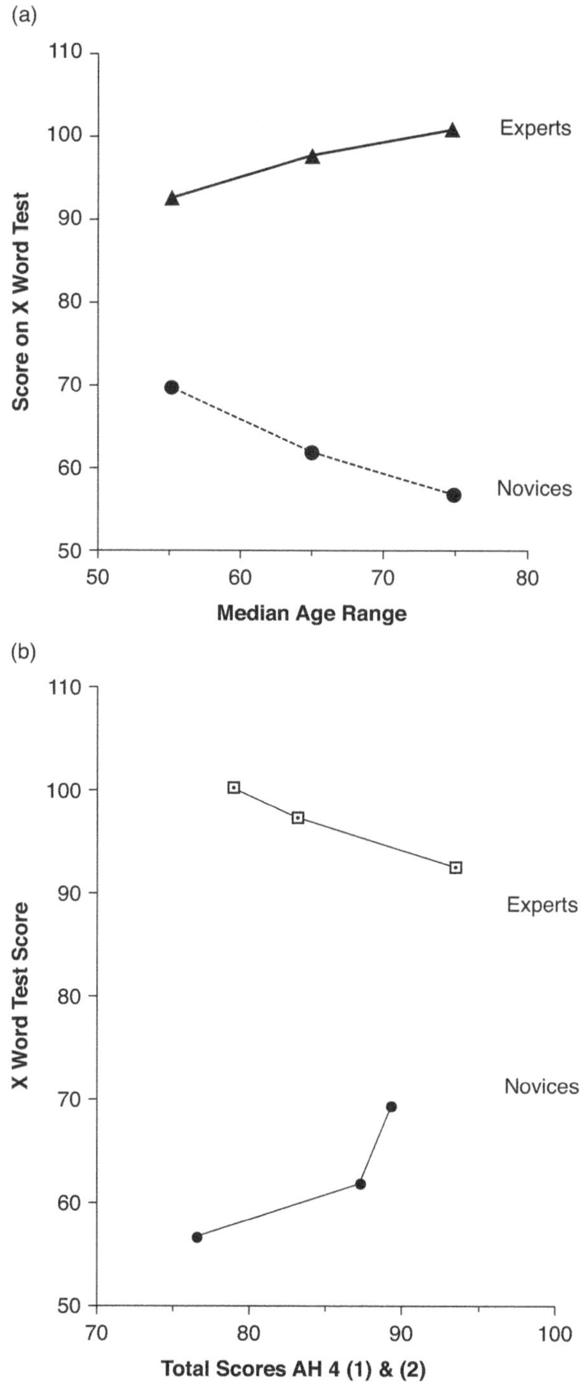

Figure 10.12 (a) Crossword puzzle solving scores for experts and novices as a function of their ages. (b) Crossword puzzle solving scores for experts and novices as a function of their mean AH 4 (1) IQ test scores.

information, on performance IQ tests, and on scores on simple laboratory tasks involving learning, memory, and information processing, which had been obtained from groups of young and elderly adults. Scores on tests of acquired information were found to be weakly associated with chronological age. In contrast, scores on performance IQ tests and on memory and information-processing tasks were strongly associated with each other and with chronological age. This main dichotomy is more convincing than Horn's attempts to decompose fluid abilities further into independent components such as "inspection speediness", "attention division", "persistence", "carefulness", and "working memory" (Horn, 1986). It is interesting that in spite of the fact that Horn (1986) now offers some of the most effective arguments against a single-factor theory of fluid intelligence, his early demonstrations of associations between IQ test scores and simple indices of information processing rate and learning rate in laboratory tasks anticipated, and indeed were much more sophisticated than, those in a more recent literature, which have received far more attention. Brand and Deary (1982), Eysenck (1986), Jensen (1982a, b; 1985), Nettelbeck and Brewer (1981), Nettelbeck and Lally (1976), Vernon (1985), Vernon and Jensen (1984), and many others have, since, adopted Spearman's (1904; 1927) suggestion that most, if not all, "valid" performance IQ tests load on a single common factor, "g". They take modest associations (e.g. of $r = 0.2$ to 0.4) between scores on performance IQ tests and scores on laboratory measure of information processing rate such as tachistoscopic recognition thresholds ("Inspection Times", or ITs) or Choice Reaction Times (CRTs) to be evidence that a single common factor, "g_f" is directly reflected by a corresponding "basic" performance index, "information processing rate". This has been proposed as an unique behavioural index of biological (Blinkhorn & Henderson, 1982; Eysenck, 1986) and hence inheritable global neurophysiological efficiency. Following a similar line of reasoning Salthouse (1985; 1991) bases the only coherent theory of cognitive ageing that we yet have on the working hypothesis that slowing of information-processing rate is the most sensitive and direct reflection of the global ageing of the brain, and that it functionally entrains age-changes in all other performance indices, including IQ test scores.

Horn's work has defined both of the central themes for current discussions of cognitive ageing that form the basis of this paper. The first is to find ways to replace the purely descriptive taxonomy of differences between age-robust and age-labile cognitive skills with a testable, functional model that can eventually be used to relate relative preservation and loss to changes in the human cognitive system and so perhaps eventually to biological ageing of the CNS. The second is to find ways of testing whether or not age-related changes in all age-labile skills are, indeed, secondary reflections of changes in a single "master" performance parameter identified by psychometric tests as "g_f' and in laboratory tasks as "information processing rate". In practice, the two problems turn out to be closely related. To clarify this, it is necessary to examine carefully the terminology that has grown up to discuss them.

How Does Practice "Crystallize" a Cognitive Skill?

It is usually assumed that complex problem-solving skills can be developed and maintained by continued practice, but that their efficient execution may depend on the integrity of "lower-order" fluid abilities such as information-processing rate, working memory capacity, or attentional selectivity. It is further assumed that decline in these lower-order abilities cannot be checked by continued use, so that, as they deteriorate, the higher-order procedures that they support can no longer be sustained (Horn, 1986). This speculation is captured in a genial metaphor by Salthouse (1988) as the distinction between a reference library and an increasingly frail librarian who runs it. The passage of time has little effect on the integrity of the books or their contents, but the librarian becomes increasingly slow and inaccurate at retrieving information from them. Like many pleasant analogies used by psychologists, this is a Trojan Mouse for a very specific, untested hypothesis: that "data storage" and "data retrieval" are managed by functionally separate systems and that the latter deteriorates with age, whereas the former does not. A slightly altered hypothesis is that sustained practice may perhaps preserve learned data or procedures, but the "performance characteristics" of the ageing brain such as "information-processing speed" or "working memory capacity" decline to point at which these stored procedures can no longer be run. An equally tendentious metaphor that captures this particular nuance might be a decaying computer, which gradually loses memory and processing power and so progressively becomes unable to run more and more of a set of programs, still perfectly preserved on floppy discs, which it could previously use with no trouble.

As so often in psychology, attractive metaphors raise more obscurities than they resolve. The metaphor of intact libraries or floppy discs and failing librarians or computers implies that processes of "storage" and "retrieval" are functionally distinct and, possibly, even supported by different neurophysiological sub-systems that "age" at different rates. It is, in fact, very dubious whether there is any theoretical rationale for making hierarchical distinctions between complex "higher-order" cognitive skills or "data-bases" that may indefinitely remain intact in memory and "lower-order" "performance indices" that gradually atrophy. We know that practice can maintain specific complex higher-order performances such as cryptic crossword puzzle solving, but we do not know to what extent it can also maintain the lower-level performance measures such as choice reaction times, inspection times, or measures of working memory capacity, which were classified by Horn as indices of age-labile fluid intelligence. Concretely, can older people also retain fast reaction times if they practice them continuously? Further, if practice can also preserve indices of "fluid" ability into old age, does it do so "across the board", or only in very domain-specific situations? Concretely, do fast reaction times maintained by practice within such skills as typing or piano-playing generalize to give an advantage even in other, relatively novel situations? These are necessary questions, because if we find that, like vocabulary and procedures, CRTs and ITs can also be maintained by practice within the contexts of highly practised domain-specific situations, we must conclude that retention of a higher-order skill implies the maintenance of all of its lower-order "component" sub-skills, and the crystallized fluid distinction reduces to a dichotomy between "more" and "less" practice. This can be tested empirically.

The most frequently cited evidence for g_c has been the preservation of recognition vocabulary into old age, and, as we have seen, distributions of scores on such instruments as the Mill Hill Part "A" or the WAIS vocabulary tests remain identical for individuals in their 50s, 60s, and 70s. A computerized version of the Mill Hill test allows us to measure not only the accuracy, but also the latency, with which words are matched against their synonyms. Figure 10.13a plots latencies obtained from two groups of 40 individuals, aged 18 to 35 and 63 to 79 years, all of whom scored at the same level of accuracy for word definitions (i.e. all would have attained the same unadjusted scores on the pencil-and-paper version of the Mill Hill). It is unsurprising that older volunteers responded more slowly than young and that all volunteers recognized synonyms for common words (easier Mill Hill items) faster than those for rare words (more difficult Mill Hill items). Frequency of use directly reflects lifetime practice Figure 10.13a shows that age differences in latency are much larger for rare than for common items. We might be tempted to take this significant interaction as evidence that practice does "crystallize" information-processing rate in particular contexts, so that highly practised decisions show less age-related slowing than do less practised decisions. However, Figure 10.13b uses the technique invented by Brindley (1965) and brilliantly developed by Cerella (1985) to examine such age/ask difficulty interactions by plotting latencies at ascending levels of item difficulty (word frequency) for the older against those for the younger group. As for all studies examined in Cerella's (1985) classic analysis, the data points plotted in Figure 10.13a are well fitted by a straight line. At all levels of word frequency (and so familiarity, or, in other terms, greater lifetime practice with particular words) decision latencies for older individuals can be obtained by multiplying decision latencies for younger individuals by the same simple constant (in this case 1.6).

Perfect (1989) reports precisely analogous results in a different context in which older and younger individuals were timed at selecting answers to "Trivial Pursuit" questions on topics on which they were more or less familiar. Decision latencies decreased with item familiarity (lifetime practice) and increased with age. The increase in latency with item familiarity was steeper for older than for younger subjects, and a Brindley/Cerella plot again showed that, across all levels of item familiarity, retrieval times for older individuals could be obtained by multiplying those of younger individuals by simple constants.

We have asked two related questions: (1) whether, albeit in very restricted and specific domains, extended practice may not only maintain the availability of information but also the speed with which decisions are made;

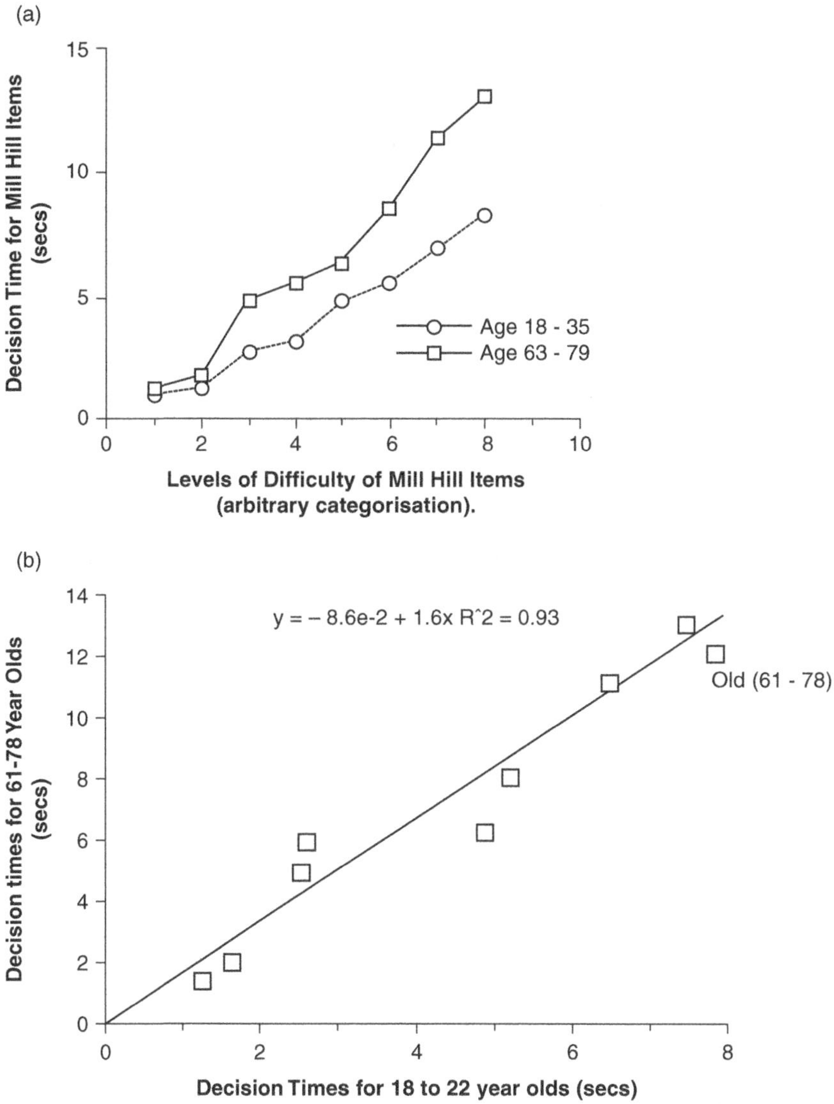

Figure 10.13 (a) Latencies for matching Mill Hill (A) items to synonyms as a function of age and item difficulty. (b) Latencies for matching Mill Hill (A) items to synonyms as a function of item difficulty. Latencies for older plotted against latencies for younger subjects.

(2) whether practice directly counters the slowing associated with increasing age. These results confirm, as we have long known, that selective practice (relative familiarity) does increase the speed with which simple tasks can be carried out. In these particular tasks of retrieving more and less over-learned semantic information the effects of practice are markedly greater in older

than in younger groups (though, as we shall see, this is by no means always the case). To this extent, in these particular tasks the data seem to suggest that selective practice preserves information- processing speed into old age. However, the Brindley/Cerella plots modify this picture because they suggest that the slowing associated with ageing is, effectively, the same at all levels of familiarity (i.e. of practice with particular words). Though familiarity reduces retrieval times, *it does not seem to affect the size of the multiplicative constant that reflects age-related slowing*—that is, practice merely shifts data points up and down an unaltered function that describes the effects of age on information-processing rate across different levels of difficulty in a particular task. Thus, in these particular situations (though, as we shall see, they represent a particular sub-set from which we cannot generalize), practice and age appear to have orthogonal effects on information processing rate. That is, older people do not behave exactly like unpractised young people.

We shall again take up this question when we discuss some experiments that examine the relative benefits gained by extended practice on simple tasks by younger and older and more and less able individuals. For the present we would make the point that it can be misleading to use metaphors that imply the existence of distinct functional systems or processes, such as librarians and books, or storage discs and computers, which are affected by different degrees by age or by other conditions. It is also misleading to think in terms of a distinction between some processes that have the special quality that they can be "crystallized" by experience and become age-robust, and so become qualitatively distinct from others that remain "fluid" and vulnerable, no matter how much they are practised. The possibility still remains that practice and age may affect processes at all "levels", but in different ways. The easiest way to examine this hypothesis is to compare the effects of individual difference factors such as age and IQ test attainment with those of practice across a series of different tasks. In all of the experiments described, age groups were precisely matched in terms of their unadjusted scores on the AH 4 intelligence test. In all these paradigms, with one exception (Rabbitt, Banerji, & Szemanski, 1989), we found no residual effect on performance indices of chronological age, *per se*, once effects of individual differences in IQ test attainment had been partialled out. The point was to compare the relative sizes of individual difference effects and practice effects. Consequently, as age groups were usually closely matched in terms of unadjusted IQ test scores, the data have been plotted to contrast high and low test score groups rather than older and younger people.

Comparisons of Individual Difference Effects and Practice Effects on Simple Performance Indices

It has been suggested that Choice Reaction Time (CRT) tasks provide exceptionally clear and direct indices of individual differences in information processing rate, and that these differences are manifestations, in cognitive performance, of the biological basis of individual differences in fluid intelligence, g_f (Eysenck, 1986; Jensen, 1985; Salthouse, 1982; 1985). It is therefore interesting to compare the sizes and nature of the effects of individual differences in IQ test attainment and of practice on easy CRT tasks.

Rabbitt and Goward (in press) did this by dividing 90 individuals aged between 53 and 76 years into 9 equal groups, balanced in terms of age decade (50 to 59; 60 to 69; 70 to 76 years) and in terms of IQ test score (low, 14 to 17; medium, 27 to 28; high, 41 to 43 points on the AH 4 test). All were given 10 blocks of trials each on an easy 4-choice CRT task. Figure 10.14 gives practice curves for the three IQ test score groups.

We see that the high-test-score groups responded most quickly, the medium groups more slowly, and the low groups more slowly still. These individual differences in speed were significant, and much larger than those brought about by practice. Moreover, the practice effects are paradoxical: the low-test-score group improves most, the medium-test-score group slightly less, and the high-test-score group hardly at all. From these results alone we might reach the surprising conclusion that IQ test scores positively predict overall speed but *negatively* predict learning rates. The same paradox appears in many different studies when data from successive age groups, who are not matched for IQ test scores, are plotted to show inter-actions between age and practice. Younger subjects are faster but show less improvement, and the elderly are slower but show more improvement.

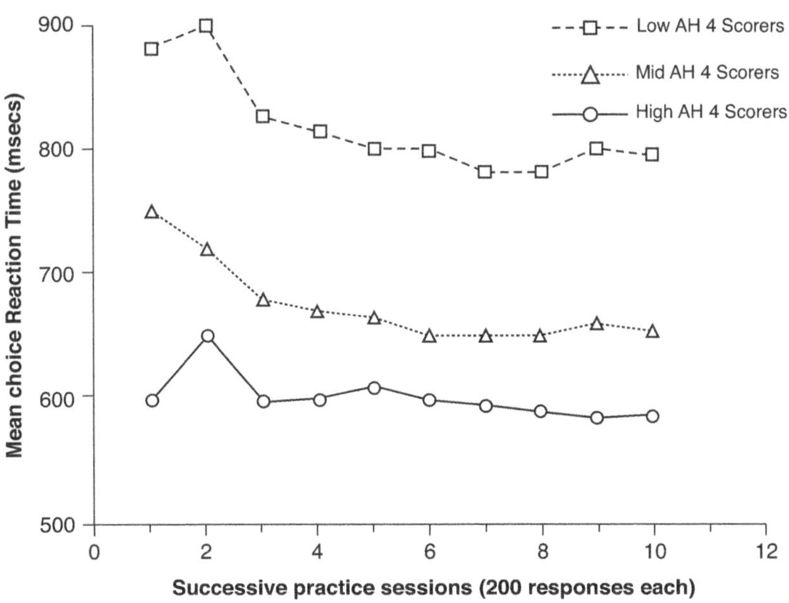

Figure 10.14 Effects of practice on mean 4-choice CRTs of groups of 30 individuals aged 50–76 years, with high, medium, and low scores on the AH 4 (1) IQ test.

Can it really be that the older or less "intelligent" people are, the faster they learn? This is not a trivial point, because it has been seriously suggested that individual differences in information processing rate reflect the neurological basis of individual differences in intelligence, and so have "knock on" effects on all other tests of cognitive performance (e.g. Brand & Deary, 1982; Eysenck, 1986; Jensen, 1982a; 1985). It has also been suggested that slowing of information processing with age is the primary change in neuropsychological efficiency that entrains secondary changes in all or most other cognitive abilities, including learning and memory (Salthouse, 1985; 1991). A finding that in very simple tasks information- processing rates may be *negatively* correlated with learning rates presents obvious difficulties for such hypotheses.

Figure 10.15a plots data from an exact replication of this experiment and Figure 10.15b data from a variant in which the same subjects responded on each trial to the immediately previous signal rather than to the one currently present (data by Stollery, Moore, & Rabbitt, unpublished). In the simpler version of the task, the effects of individual differences are again much larger than those of practice, but in the more difficult version the reverse is the case.

An extreme example of this latter trend is learning curves for high and low AH 4 test scorers on a complicated video game, "Space Fortress" (Rabbitt, Banerji, & Szemanski, 1989). Here, early in practice IQ test scores correlated only modestly with video-game performance ($r = 0.3$), and so accounted for only about 9% of variance between individuals. However, in this extremely complex task individual differences in IQ test ability interacted positively with practice effects. As training continued, high test scorers rapidly pulled ahead, so that late in practice the correlation between test score and game performance improved to over $r = 0.6$ and accounted for over 36% of total variance.

It seems that individuals' IQ test scores are weakly correlated with their information-processing rates and, partly for this reason, only weakly predict initial performance in most tasks, including complex video games. In very simple tasks, individuals with high IQ test scores reach their performance asymptotes very rapidly and so gain little from extended practice. Lower test scorers begin further from their asymptotes and so have more to gain. Thus in simple tasks IQ test scores are either negatively or not at all correlated with the amount of improvement with practice. In complex tasks both high and low test scorers start very far from their eventual asymptotes. These asymptotes are, indeed, much higher for more able individuals. IQ test scores are, as usual, weakly correlated with information-processing speeds, but their much stronger correlations with rates of acquisition gradually become evident as more complicated tasks are examined. Hence, in complex tasks IQ test scores better predict performance late than early in practice; moreover, for all groups the magnitudes of the changes brought about by practice are typically much greater than the magnitudes of initial differences associated with IQ test scores.

Figures 10.14 and 10.15 show that when we compare individual differences in age and individual differences in experience, we are not dealing

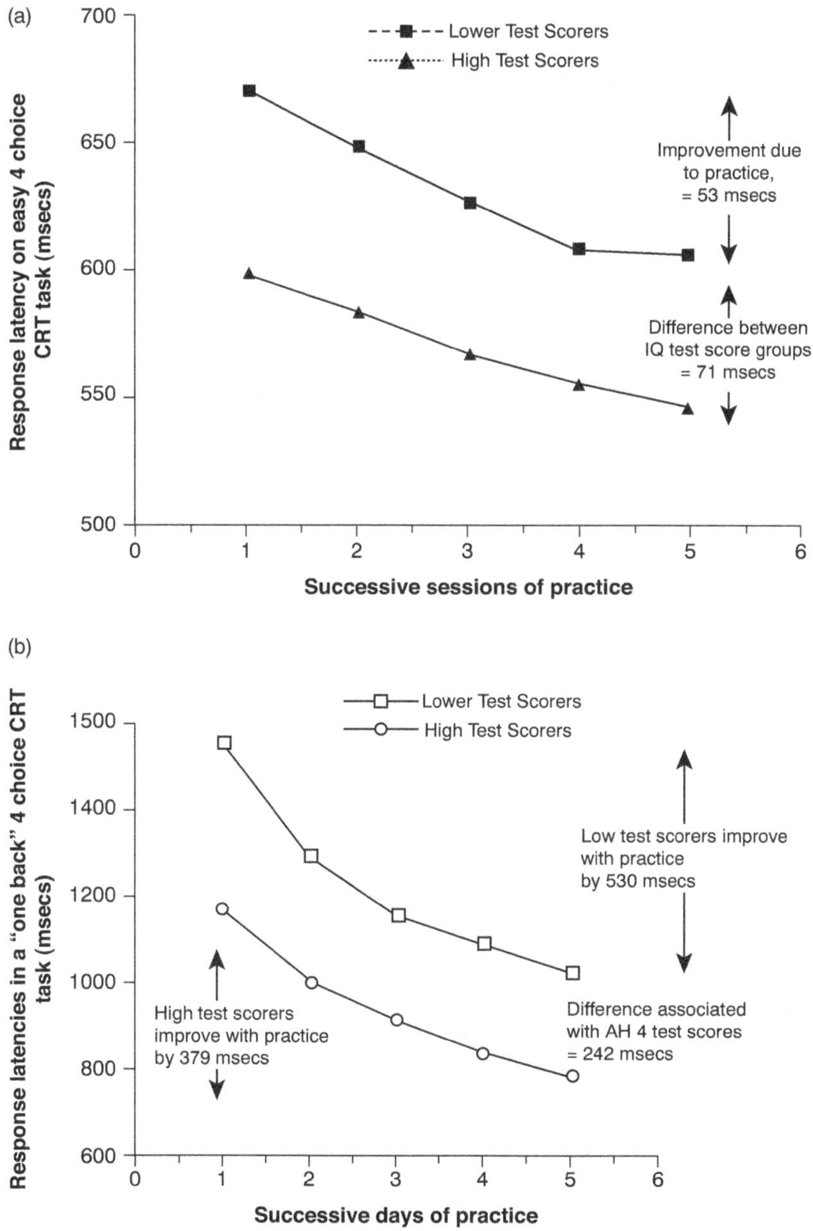

Figure 10.15 (a) Data by Stollery, Rabbit, and Moore showing effects of practice on 4-choice CRTs of groups of 46 individuals with high and with low scores on the AH 4 (1) IQ test. (b) Data by Stollery, Rabbitt, and Moore showing effects of practice on a 4-choice CRT task in which, on each trial, subjects responded not to the current, but to the previous signal. Mean CRTs for 48 individuals with high and with low scores on the AH 4 (1) IQ test.

with absolute relationships but, rather, the balance between separate, but sometimes correlated, effects. Figure 10.16a and 10.16b contrast hypothetical situations in which groups of individuals with high and low IQ test scores show asymptotic learning curves and in which the rates at which they learn a task increase with their IQ test scores. In Figure 10.16a, high test scorers constantly draw ahead of low test scorers, but as the task on which they are compared has a relatively low performance ceiling, at any given level of practice the absolute amount of improvement achieved by the low test scorers is always greater than the difference between their current level of attainment and that achieved by the high test scorers. In this particular case, if data from both groups are pooled for analysis, duration of practice will always emerge as a better predictor of performance than IQ test score. Figure 10.16b illustrates the contrasting case, in which scores are not restricted by a ceiling, so that as practice proceeds, the absolute difference in the current level of performance of the high and of the. low test scorers rapidly becomes much greater than the total improvement from baseline that the low test scorerscan achieve by the same point. As soon as the advantage for the high-test-score group exceeds the total gains from practice attained by the low-test-score group, correlation analyses must always show that test scores are more strongly determined by individual differences than by task experience.

Figure 10.17 illustrates this last point with imaginary data that might realistically reflect comparisons between the achievements of high and low test scorers at very complicated intellectual skills such as chess, music, or mathematics. Here people of high innate ability may continue to improve with practice long after people with lower ability have reached their modest limits. Novice high test scorers will, of course, initially perform much less well than "expert" low test scorers. However, the high test scorers will very rapidly improve and soon overtake the low scorers. If data from both groups are combined for analysis before this cross-over point, amount of practice will account for significantly more of the individual variance in performance than will IQ test scores. After the cross-over point these predictions will reverse, and IQ test scores will predict more individual variance than will differences in training. It is interesting to note that if, beyond the cross-over point, we again examine correlations within the *combined* data from a very highly practised low-ability group and a less practised but now much superior high-ability group, we will obtain the counter-intuitive result that attainment is *negatively* correlated with amount of practice.

Because practice markedly affects performance even on very simple cognitive tasks, no laboratory performance measure, and certainly no IQ test , can be completely "Culture Fair". Individual differences in performance will always be partly determined by individual differences in task-related experience. In very simple tasks little between-individual variance will be attributable to practice and much more to age or to other intrinsic differences. In difficult tasks the reverse will be the case, particularly because practice and intrinsic differences will interact multiplicatively rather than merely additively to increase variance.

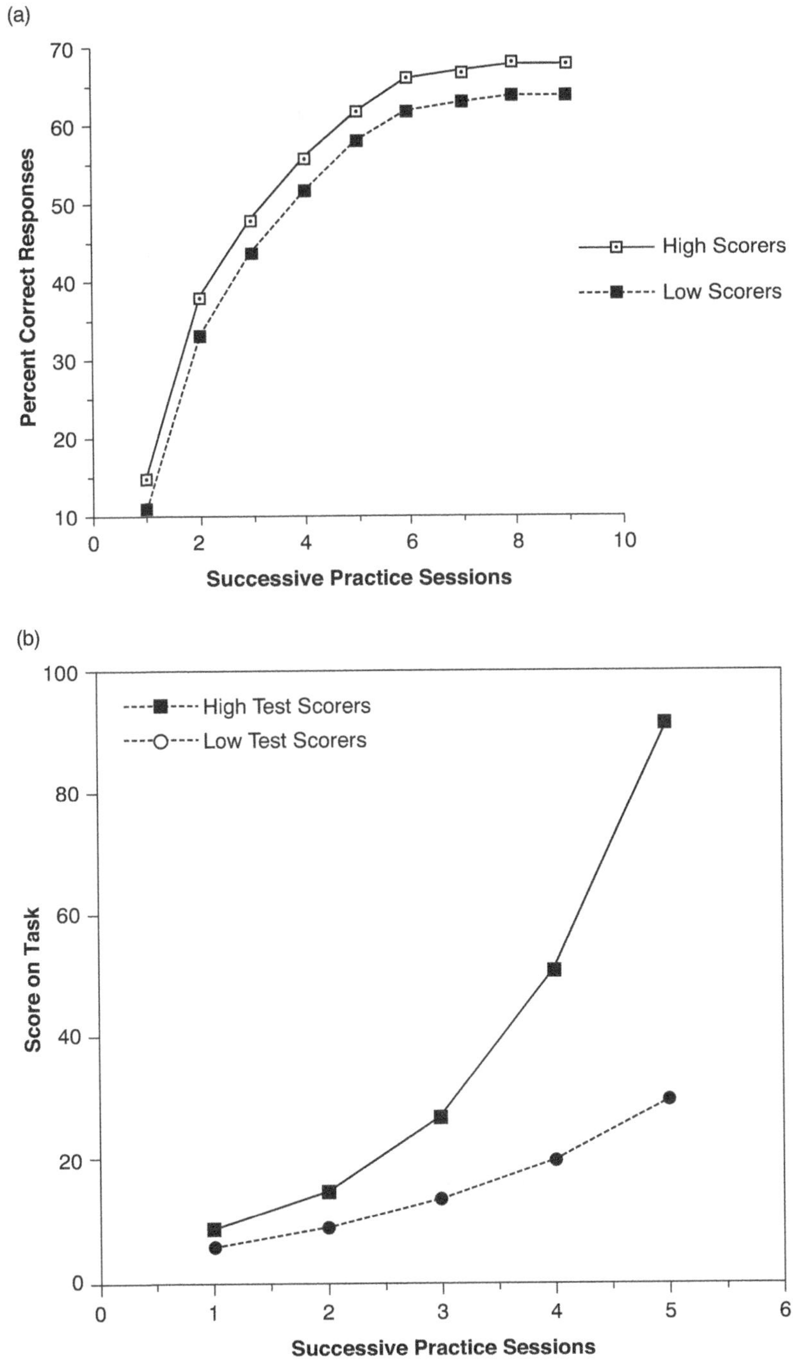

Figure 10.16 (a) Hypothetical data showing a case where individuals of high and of lower general ability rapidly converge, with practice, on the same asymptotes. (b) Hypothetical data showing a case where individuals of high and of lower general ability approach different asymptotes at different rates.

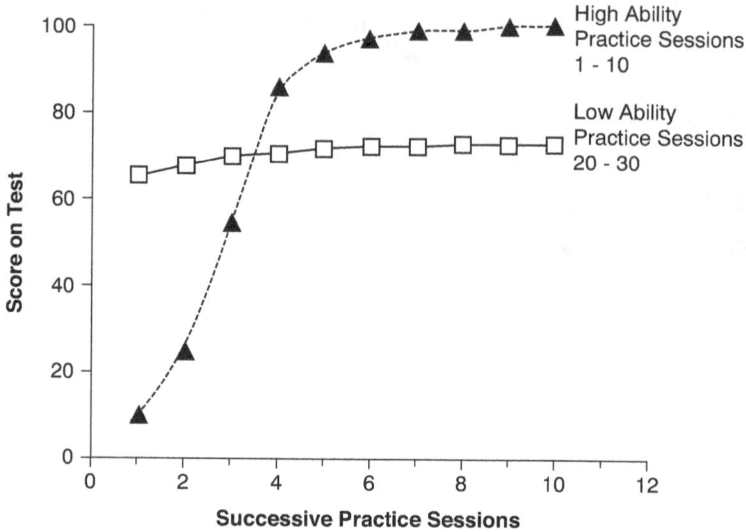

Figure 10.17 Hypothetical data showing a case in which individuals of low general ability who are practised to asymptote on a difficult skill are rapidly overtaken by high ability individuals who begin practice later.

One implication of these results is that they clarify the distinction between age effects and practice effects that we discussed earlier. Clearly the Brindley/Cerella scaling function that relates decision times of older to those of younger people across a set of tasks of different levels of difficulty must alter when they are practised. Interestingly, the way in which this function alters must vary with task difficulty. On very easy tasks, such as 4-choice CRT, the old will improve more rapidly than the young, and the slope of the Brindley/Cerella function will, accordingly, reduce with practice. In very difficult tasks the young will improve much more than the old, and the slope of the Brindley/Cerella function will markedly increase with the level of practice at which the comparison is made.

This gives us a better insight into what is going on in experiments, such as those illustrated in Figures 10.13a and 10.13b, where we measure the effects of age or ability on the relative times taken to retrieve more and less familiar (i.e. more and less practised) words or facts. In such studies it is, of course, a mistake to suppose that some Mill Hill words or Trivial Pursuit "facts" are intrinsically more "difficult" than others. There are, of course, no such intrinsic differences in difficulty, and age differences in retrieval times only reflect differences in the relative familiarity of items-that is, in the extent to which some words have been encountered and used more often during a lifetime's reading and conversation. The true conclusion to draw from Figure 10.13a is that if people of all ages were given sufficient practice on the "difficult" Mill Hill words, they would retrieve them as fast as they now access the "easy" Mill Hill words. After this practice, across all words, retrieval times for older subjects would be lagged by a constant relative to those of younger subjects. This age lag after asymptotic practice would represent an irreducible difference between retrieval times for old and young. The actual message of Figures 13a and 13b is, therefore, that when interpreting Age × Complexity effects, we must bear in mind that the multiplicative scaling age-constant that we derive from Brindley/Cerella plots operates across *durations* of processes, irrespective of the nature of other factors, such as information processing load, stimulus- response compatibility, or relative levels of practice that may determine these durations.

For the present argument, the point of more immediate interest is that if we use principal component analyses to interpret large sets of data from many tasks given to individuals who differ widely in their ages and IQ test attainments, the relative complexity of the tasks that we compare will determine the partitioning of variance at least as strongly as will the relative experience, or the intrinsic abilities, of the individuals whom we test. Thus, in the principal components analyses described by Horn (1982; 1986), it is inevitable that scores obtained from complex tasks, in which individual differences due to experience are likely to be very much greater than those associated with intrinsic differences in ability, should turn out to be poorly associated with individual differences in chronological age and IQ test scores. It is also inevitable that variance in age and IQ test scores should show commonality with scores on very simple tasks in which practice has relatively small, and intrinsic differences much larger, effects (note that in such tasks improvement due to practice may, paradoxically, correlate positively with age and negatively with IQ test score; see Figure 10.14 and Figure 10.15a). The point of the studies we have described is that we can no longer take the patterns of results discussed by Horn as evidence that a lifetime's practice changes in some radical way (i.e. "crystallizes") the *functional representations* of complex skills. We need further and different evidence to decide whether this is the case.

How Do Skills "Crystallize"? Is the Functional Mode of Representation of Skills Altered by Practice?

The most thorough investigation of the long-term preservation of practiced skills is a series of studies by Bahrick and associates (Bahrick, 1979; 1983; 1984; Bahrick, Bahrick, & Wittlinger, 1975; Bahrick, & Phelps, 1987) who have examined very long-term retention by young, middle-aged, and elderly adults of bodies of information that they had acquired as adolescents and seldom rehearsed thereafter, such as High-School Spanish, names and faces of early acquaintances, and routes around a city in which they had grown up. The general finding was that initial rapid and substantial losses are followed by an asymptotic plateau of retention, which may last for decades with little or no further detectable loss. Bahrick describes this indefinitely preserved residual information as being in "permastore". Like Horn's metaphor of "crystallization", that of "permastorage" seems to have been chosen to imply the possibility that gradual changes in the functional basis of memory representation occur with the passage of time to make "older" memories and skills increasingly resistant to forgetting and to the insults of ageing.

Neisser (1984) challenged this implication, arguing that "older" memories may be relatively robust because of differences in their informational architecture rather than in their functional representation. The term "informational architecture" refers to the particular patterns in which information is encoded, as distinct from the properties of the medium or structures in which it may be represented. So, for example, pictures or text may be translated into a variety of different codes, which may be expanded or compressed by different algorithms. These codes will be invariant whether the physical medium of storage is microscopic indentations on a compact disc read by a beam of light, patterns of polarity on a magnetic tape, or patterns of electric charges in the core memory of a computer. Neisser suggested that information in the human memory system survives longer if it has become highly "schematized" (Bartlett, 1932) and has developed a rich and highly structured network of associations with other stored data. A recent study by Conway, Cohen, and Stanhope (1991) supports this argument. They found that over a 24-month period after taking their final examinations *quondam* students of cognitive psychology rapidly and progressively forget names and isolated facts but show a markedly slower rate of loss and a higher asymptote of residual retention of abstract arguments and theories. This result cannot prove that there are no changes in the neurophysiological bases of representation of older memories, but it does show that this assumption is incomplete, and possibly superfluous, because a change in neurophysiological representation over time could not, *on its own*, explain why some *kinds* of information are selectively retained better than others. Until new evidence is available, the "schematization hypothesis" provides a sufficient explanation why some residue of information survives in memory and provides a better explanation than a metaphor of "permastorage" as to why different *kinds* of information survive and are lost. At any stage in life, fragmented bodies of information will be forgotten relatively rapidly, and as age advances this oblivescence may become increasingly rapid and will increasingly contrast with the much longer survival of bodies of information that have had to be acquired over much longer periods, which, for this reason, will probably have developed much richer patterns of mutual associations.

It still remains to be explained why "schematized" information should resist age changes in the brain. The concept of memory schematization has been very fruitful but perhaps has become so comfortably vague that it is liable to mislead us into supposing that we understand more than we can rigorously explain. The recent development of connectionist models now allows us a much more exact way to illustrate and justify the otherwise woolly concept that changes in the "informational architecture" of acquired information may damage the capacity to acquire new skills more than it affects the retention of those already learned. A trivial introductory exercise to PDP modelling is to simulate a network that can learn to reproduce any of 10 patterns of 8 binary digits, even when they are distorted on input by some random perturbation of their components. This can easily be done with an array of 8 input units, 8 output units, and an intervening set of 4 hidden units. As McClelland, Rumelhart, and PDP Research Group (1986) point out, after the network has been trained to criterion, deletion of any one of the hidden units usually has little or no effect on the efficiency with which learned patterns continue to be recognized and reproduced. However, deletion of a hidden unit greatly increases the number of trials that the network requires to learn to reproduce a new, or partially altered, set of patterns.

The point is that the *functional properties* of the units and connections in which information about the target set is stored are determined by the choice of parameters that are written into a network simulation before it is run. These need not in any way be altered by training. A pattern of representation, once established, becomes resistant to damage, which markedly reduces the efficiency with which the net can learn to represent new information. In this sense "crystallization" or "permastorage" of acquired information, contrasted with the relative lability of new information, need not imply differences in the neurophysiological or biochemical modes of representations of "old" and "new" memories. It may, rather, be a direct result of the abstract patterns of changes that occur when any information is stored in a distributed network.

This analogy between PDP networks and the human brain would be weakened if individual differences in rates of forgetting were so large that their effects swamped the benefits of practice and of long familiarity. Figure 10.18 illustrates a test of this in an experiment in which individuals aged between 50 and 81 years were divided into age-matched groups with higher and lower scores on the AH 4 IQ test and trained on a computerized CRT categorization task in which sets of target and background items were kept constant throughout 36 weekly practice sessions. Even on this relatively simple and "automatic" task, the effects of practice are three times as great as the effects of individual differences in AH 4 (1) test scores. The new point is that both high and low IQ test scorers showed equally complete retention of their gains when they were re-tested 6 months later, without any intervening practice. This, with many other studies in our laboratory, suggests that individual differences in age and in IQ test attainment markedly affect rates of learning, but even over long periods of time rates of forgetting are so slow that individual differences may have little notice-able effect on amounts retained. It follows that, even after long periods without intervening practice and even in populations of individuals aged between 50 and 80 years, gains from training may continue to overshadow individual variance in performance associated with age and IQ.

We began with the apparently simple and straightforward question of why disparities between people's levels of attainment at their various cognitive

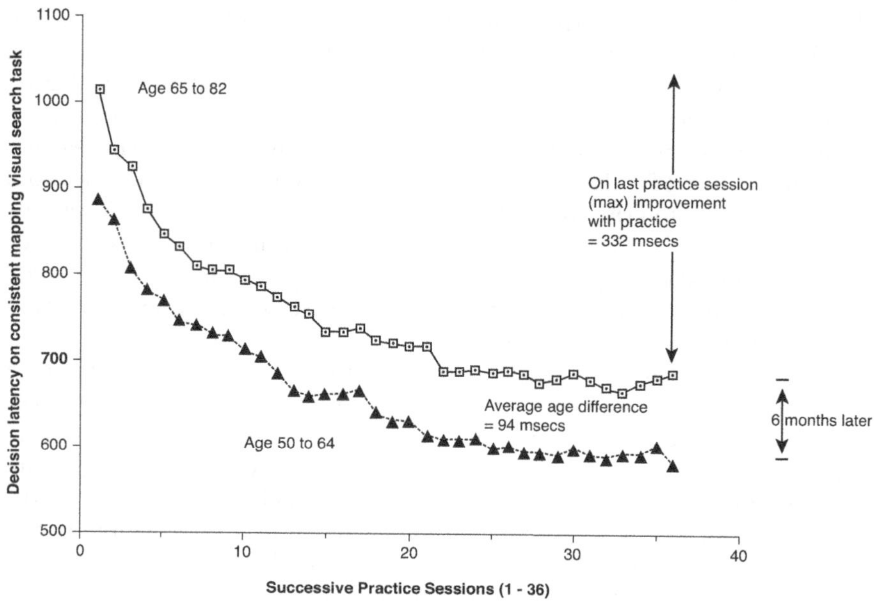

Figure 10.18 Data by Stollery, Rabbitt, and Moore showing effects of 36 sessions training on a constant-set 2 choice letter categorization task for subjects of high and of low ability on the AH 4 (1) IQ test, Also shown are latencies obtained after 6 months without further practice.

skills increase markedly as they age. We found that cognitive skills are relatively less affected by age when levels of performance are determined strongly by practice and only weakly by individual differences, and they are relatively more affected by age when the reverse is the case. We have found no evidence that extended practice produces any *qualitative* change in the way information is represented in the CNS. Thus a sufficient explanation for our data and a sufficient account of the definitions of crystallized intelligence given in the literature is that practised skills are protected against loss by a change in the informational architectures, rather than in the neurophysiological bases, of their functional representations. The next question is whether or not "fluid" skills, for which levels of attainment seem to be set by intrinsic differences between individuals rather than by duration of experience, may also vary in terms of their relative vulnerability to ageing and other neurophysiological changes.

Do All Skills Dependent on g_f "Age" at the Same Rate?

In our view, the attempt to define precisely what qualitative distinctions between different cognitive abilities may determine their relative resistance to old age becomes easier if a neglected distinction is emphasized.

In discussions by Anderson (1992), Eysenck (1986), Horn and Catteil (1967), Horn (1982; 1986), Jensen (1982a; 1982b), and, indeed, throughout this paper, an elided distinction has been that between the various *performance indices* we can obtain from psychometric tests and laboratory tasks and the *performance characteristics* that we incorporate into our hypothetical functional models of cognitive sub-systems, which we hope eventually to reify in terms of the neurophysiology of the central nervous system. Failure to keep this distinction in mind leads to further confusion when we try to use the traditional statistical technology of psychometrics, factor analyses, and principal component analyses to divide a variety of indices obtained from many different tasks into those that do and those that do not fall into common factors with chronological age. A first difficulty, that of non-commensurability of performance indices, is only part of the problem. For example, it is not rational to treat measures such as millisecond of choice reaction time, items completed per second in Ietter letter trans- formations, and numbers of items recalled from a list and total numbers of complex problems solved in psychometric tests as *equivalent performance indices.* IQ test scores are compounded measures of speed and accuracy of performance, and IQ test problems not only make demands on information processing speed but also on a variety of other system limitations such as working memory capacity, speed of retrieval from long-term memory, and dexterity of mental rotation and manipulation of images of complex figures.

A worse confusion arises if we assume that these disparate indices, and "factors" derived from associations between them, can be directly identified as *performance characteristics* of hypothetical sub-systems—e.g. that choice reaction times can be directly identified with properties of the central nervous system such as synaptic delay (Eysenck, 1986), or "level of random noise in the CNS" (Eysenck, 1986). Neglect of this distinction has become a chronic difficulty, both in ageing studies and in attempts to specify the "neurophysiological basis of intelligence".

An example of the vagueness of definition of *performance characteristics* is that we have two quite different ways of relating task performance to hypothetical neurology, which correspond to "modular" and "global" models of individual differences. A century and a half of neurophysiology has been successfully based on the premise that functions such as "memory", each of a variety of different "language functions", and "visuo-spatial ability" are anatomically localized. On this premise we might seek to relate individual differences in levels of competence across such functions to differences in the efficiency of the distinct neurophysiological "modules" that support them. Findings that age affects these functions at different times and to different degrees might be taken as evidence that these different parts of the brain "age" at different rates. We might conclude that we must try to develop "localizational' theories of cognitive ageing describing differential changes in separate brain areas and neurotransmitter systems. In this context the *"performance indices"* that we use to assess the progress of relative changes will be scores on batteries of neuropsychological tests that have been developed in clinical practice as tools for the diagnosis of local brain damage. The *"performance characteristics"* in terms of which we try to interpret our data will be derived from corresponding neuropsychological models for these local sub-systems. In view of its antiquity and continued success, it is strange that this mode of analysis has been almost entirely neglected in studies of cognitive ageing and of individual differences in intelligence (but see Horn, 1986).

A second, quite distinct approach has been to assume that *performance indices* such as "learning rate", "information processing speed", and "for- getting rate" may be directly measured and ostensively defined by particular laboratory paradigms and that they correspond as directly to the *performance characteristics* of undifferentiated neural networks (Eysenck, 1986; Salthouse, 1985). Models of this kind interpret observed patterns of individual differences or changes in *performance indices* in terms of changes in a precisely correspondent set of *performance characteristics* of the entire CNS.

These may respectively be termed the "modular" and the "global" approaches to individual differences and change.

Relating Changes in g_f to Global Ageing of the Brain: Indices, Psychometric Factors, and Hypothetical System Performance Parameters

Consider a very simple simulation involving a network that can be trained to distinguish input states and to translate them into corresponding output states. It is easy to obtain numerical data that specify how well this simulation meets particular task demands. We might time how rapidly it can produce outputs corresponding to input states, and whether and how this lag increases as the number of inputs and outputs are increased (i.e. its CRT), how many learning trials are required to achieve 100% accuracy (i.e. its learning rate), or how new learning affects the precision with which the system continues to make distinctions on which it has previously been trained (e.g. forgetting as a function of interpolated new activity, or "interference"). However, our knowledge of the structure of the simulation forces us to recognize that these *performance indices* that we measure when we run a simulation are somewhat arbitrary tests of its capabilities, and they do not map in any direct way on to the *performance characteristics* of the network, such as the "bias" of units, or the "temperature" of the system.

The *characteristics* of the simulation that determine the values of each of the *indices* we can measure will generally be multiple rather than unitary, they will seldom be directly measurable from its output, and, with very rare exceptions, they may not even be uniquely specified by any subset of many different performance indices. For example, the speed with which information is transmitted through a network will necessarily vary with the *performance characteristic* of transmission lag between individual units. However, the "information-processing rate" of the network (as of human choice reaction times) may be defined in terms of the number of different binary categorizations of input states that it can make in any unit of time, and this will vary as a function of the number of units the system contains and their degree of mutual connectivity. In all realistic simulations "units" do not simply pass on any input they receive but must learn to discriminate between input states and to inhibit, as well as facilitate, the activation of other units in the net. In some classes of simulations, and in some classes of models for human choice reaction times, it is convenient to discuss these discriminative and selective properties of information-processing sub-systems in terms of the resolution of "signal" states against "background noise". Thus the measurable *performance* indices of a network that we may refer to as its "reaction time" or "information processing rate" will not map directly on to any single *performance* characteristic and, indeed, will generally be determined by complex interactions between many different *performance characteristics*, none of which need be a uniquely direct determinant of CRT or rate of transmission.

A second directly measurable *performance index* might be the number of different input states that can be mapped on to corresponding sets of different output states. With elementary simulations of networks and with models of the nervous systems of simple organisms, we can discuss the maximum limits of the range of categorizations that can be achieved. This will not only be set by the total number of available units and their inter- connections but also, less intuitively, by the number of different types of functions that units or sub-sets of units can perform—e.g. whether units have both excitatory and inhibitory properties, whether individual units can act as "and", "or", "nand", and "nor" gates (see Arbib, 1989). It may also be limited by the sensitivity of individual units, perhaps expressed in terms of their signahoise resolving power. A different assessment of learning efficiency might be in terms of the "learning rate" of the system, expressed in terms of the *performance index* "number of trials to reach criterion". This index will, plausibly, depend on all or most of the *performance parameters* we have so far discussed but, in addition, may depend on yet another parameter—the rate at which a unit changes its threshold of activation on repeated activation by others in a Hebbian system.

A third directly measurable performance *index* might be at the rate at which a network loses information that it has learned-the rate of decline in probability that it will make a correct discrimination, either as a function of the passage of unfilled time ("forgetting rate") or as a function of the number of subsequent presentations of new patterns requiring learning of new input/output transforms ("sensitivity to retroactive interference"). Again the functional basis of individual differences or changes in this apparently simple performance index would lie in very complex interactions between the *system characteristics* that we have discussed above, and possibly with others such as the rate at which units spontaneously change their state over time.

The point of labouring the distinction between *performance indices* and *performance characteristics* in terms of several different aspects of task demands is to show that whereas some *performance characteristics, or parameters*, of a system affect only one or a few of its measurable *performance indices*, others may affect most or even all of them. This allows us to carry out the thought-experiment of repeatedly running a particular moderately complex simulation in order to accumulate, during different runs of trials, measurements of each of a variety of its different *performance indices*. If we then use the traditional technology of psychometrics to carry out multivariate and principal components analyses of relationships between these various sets of data we may find that the variance between indices is best explained by a single common factor, or by a manifold of independent factors. This will depend on the particular structure of our simulation and on the particular indices we have chosen to measure. For example, for the hypothetical network we have described, the level of random noise may so strongly affect all performance indices that they show considerable common variance. Alternatively, if learning rates and forgetting rates depend very strongly on changes in unit activation thresholds, they may share considerable variance with each other but much less variance with indices of information-processing speed. In either case, unless we have definite knowledge, or at least clear guiding hypotheses, about the functional characteristics of the system that we investigate, principal component analyses of *performance indices* will be very uncertain guides to what a system's *performance characteristics* may be, or to how they interact with each other to determine observable responses to task demands. It is almost certain to be misleading to identify a particular *performance index,* such as choice reaction time or tachistoscopic recognition threshold (inspection time), or a particular derived *factor*, in which this index is strongly represented, such as Spearman's "g", with a single hypothetical uniquely prepotent system characteristic such as "information-processing speed" (Anderson, 1992; Jensen, 1982a, 1982b) or "random noise in the system" (Eysenck, 1986).

Some Empirical Attempts to Investigate Relationships Between Performance Indices

Laboratory paradigms developed by experimental cognitive psychologists have been carefully designed to yield putatively "pure" measures of performance indices such as decision speed (information-processing rate), working memory capacity, learning rate, and forgetting rate. (Note, also, that such attributions tend to be circular, as the paradigms are actually ostensive definitions of the performance indices that they yield). In contrast, pencil-and-paper IQ tests are complex problem-solving tasks, which are often administered under speed stress, and which always make simultaneous demands on a variety of different performance indices, such as information-processing speed, speed of rotation and manipulation of visual images, working-memory capacity, and speed of retrieval from long- term memory. Thus a "total score" on an IQ test, such as the Heim AH 4 Parts 1 and 2 (Heim, 1968) represents a rough composite measure of efficiency across a very wide range of cognitive functions between which current models in cognitive psychology make very clear distinctions. Indeed, as the value of psychometric tests is judged in terms of their validity in predicting competence at meeting the complex demands of everyday life, the wider the range of different cognitive functions that a test challenges, the more likely it is to predict success in daily living.

Goward (1986) provided a simple illustration of this difference in prediction between laboratory tasks and psychometric tests in an experiment in which volunteers aged between 50 and 79 years categorized each word in 30-item lists according to semantic or surface features and then attempted to recognize them when they were presented randomly embedded among 30 distractors. The times taken to categorize words in the target list and to identify targets and distractors in the recognition list were recorded and provided measures of information-processing speed equivalent to those obtained by Jensen (1985), Vernon (1989, or Vernon and Jensen (1984) from CRT tasks. In a later replication of Goward's study, Yang Qian and Rabbitt (unpublished) measured, in addition, CRTs obtained in paradigms closely similar to those used by these authors. Experiments by Waugh and Barr (1980) lead us to expect that the faster individuals can process information, the more elaborate will be the patterns of associations that they can generate in unit time to each of the words that they inspect, and the more likely they will be to recognize them again (see also Craik & Lockhart, 1972). In agreement with these expectations, both classification times and task external CRTs did modestly predict recognition accuracy (8). As we might expect, volunteers' *d*'s were also modestly predicted by their scores on the AH 4 (1) IQ test. However, stepwise regression analyses showed that AH 4 (1) test scores predicted a significant pro- portion of individual variance in *d*' scores even after variance associated with individual differences in CRTs and classification times had been taken into consideration. In contrast, once individual differences in AH 4 test scores had been considered, "pure" measures of information-processing speed made no significant further prediction. To move from correlational data to causal speculation is always risky, but in the context of functional models for learning networks this result would mean that the speed with which a network processes information does influence the rate at which it can learn. However, as we argued above, precisely because they demand a very broad range of cognitive skills, IQ test scores do not *only* reflect individual differences in information-processing rate, but also in a number of other performance characteristics that also determine efficiency of problem solving, such as working-memory capacity and speed and accuracy of retrieval of information from long-term storage. Thus IQ test scores pick up a variety of performance characteristics that may independently influence recognition memory, among which information processing rate is only one. This opens a new question, as a simple concession that IQ test scores can pick up and reflect a *variety* of different complexly inter-related performance indices suggests that we must search further to discover whether the well-documented and marked decline of total scores on tests of "fluid" intelligence with advancing age reflects a pattern of *differential* change in different indices, rather than equal decrements in all.

To do this, it is necessary to compare old and young, and people with relatively high and low test scores on tasks in which we can independently measure individual differences not in terms of a single index but, in parallel, for two or more cognitive indices. Maylor and Rabbitt (1987) computerized the Shepherd and Teghtsoonian (1961) serial recognition paradigm so that a list of 200 words was presented one at a time, and volunteers had to press keys to signal whether each in turn was an "old" word that had previously appeared or a "new" word encountered for the first time. The probability of "old" and new items was the same for each trial, and items recurred randomly at gaps of 1, 4, 9, 19, and 49 intervening events. The programme timed and verified each response. This allowed recognition *d'* scores to be computed, both across the entire task and as a function of increasing intervals between the first and subsequent presentation of items so as to obtain measures of forgetting rate. Goward found that older individuals and those with lower IQ test scores had poorer overall recognition accuracy, but that forgetting rates, judged as the rate at which d' scores increased with the durations of intervals between successive appearances of items, were identical for all age and IQ test score groups. Decision times were directly related to subject age and inversely related to subject IQ. A replication of this experiment by Yang Qian and Rabbitt gave similar results. This suggests that age and IQ test attainment affect two different performance indices—information-processing rate and learning efficiency—but they have much less effect on a third, forgetting rate. It might have been argued that a failure to detect individual differences in forgetting rates was due to some insensitivity of the paradigm or to the testing procedure rather than to differences in the relative robustness of the performance parameters of the human cognitive system. However, Maylor and Rabbitt (1987) used the identical programme, word lists, and procedure to compare the performance of young adults who had, and who had not, recently ingested ethanol. Alcohol not only reduced the overall probability of recognition but significantly accelerated forgetting. This suggests that information-processing rate and learning rate on the one hand and forgetting rate on the other are functionally distinct performance parameters because there is evidence that they can be differentially affected by individual differences in general ability and by agents such as alcohol. To provisionally answer the main question asked in this paper, in so far as age results in a decline in IQ test performance, we may conclude that it also affects some performance parameters more severely than others.

Yang Qian and Rabbitt (presented at the July meeting of the Experimental Psychology Society, York, 1992) addressed two arithmetical ambiguities in this argument. As older individuals and those with lower IQ test scores had poorer overall performance even at the shortest inter- item intervals, the fact that their forgetting curves were thereafter parallel meant that if forgetting were assessed in terms of percentage rather than absolute change from baseline, it was indeed faster in the old and the less able. It was necessary to devise an experiment in which people of all ages and abilities began their forgetting from the same baseline. A second difficulty is that for any given number of intervening events between initial presentation and subsequent re-appearance of an item, the *elapsed time* was shorter for faster young and able than for slower old and less able individuals. Yang Qian re-analysed her data to take these time differences between groups into consideration and fouind that when the criterion of elapsed time rather than the number of intervening events was used, older individuals and those with lower IQs showed more rapid forgetting, even when absolute numbers rather than percentages of items recalled were compared. A new paradigm was necessary to check these results.

To examine the problem in a different way, Yang Qian and Rabbitt presented matrices of 9 different nouns for variable intervals of time, titrating exposure durations so that all volunteers could recall the same number of items immediately after exposure. Recall was then delayed for variable intervals of between 0 and 240 sec, during which rehearsal and further elaboration of remembered material was suppressed by an intervening task of counting backwards in 7s from 14,003. In this paradigm younger and high-scoring individuals required shorter presentation intervals in order to attain criterial levels of immediate recall and so, as usual, showed faster information-processing speeds. However, they not only showed better overall recall but slower decline of probability of recall with increasing intervals. This paradigm allowed Yang Qian and Rabbitt to use multivariate analyses to choose between the alternative possible models for individual differences in memory efficiency illustrated in Figure 10.19a-c. The results best fitted Model 39d, which assumes that age and IQ do not affect memory efficiency directly but only indirectly through their effects on information-processing rate and forgetting rate. Information-processing rate and forgetting rate, however, were uncorrelated and had separate and independent effects on the total number of items recalled. Figure 10.19d shows that the correlational structure of the data fits this particular model quite well.

These exercises show that it is possible to design paradigms to measure several performance indices simultaneously and so to discover, in the context of the same task, which of them are mutually related and which are independent. In these experiments the picture that has emerged is not that a single master performance parameter, such as information processing speed, entrains all others; rather, they suggest that subsets of the performance indices we can measure, such as learning rate and information-processing rate, may be very highly correlated with each other but not with other indices such as forgetting rate. These patterns of relationships provide us with clues against which we can check our hypotheses as to how the memory system works, what its performance parameters are, and how each of these parameters changes with age and varies between different sub-sets of individuals whom we can identify on other external criteria, such as their performance on IQ tests, their ages, their degree of fatigue, or their ingestion of particular agents.

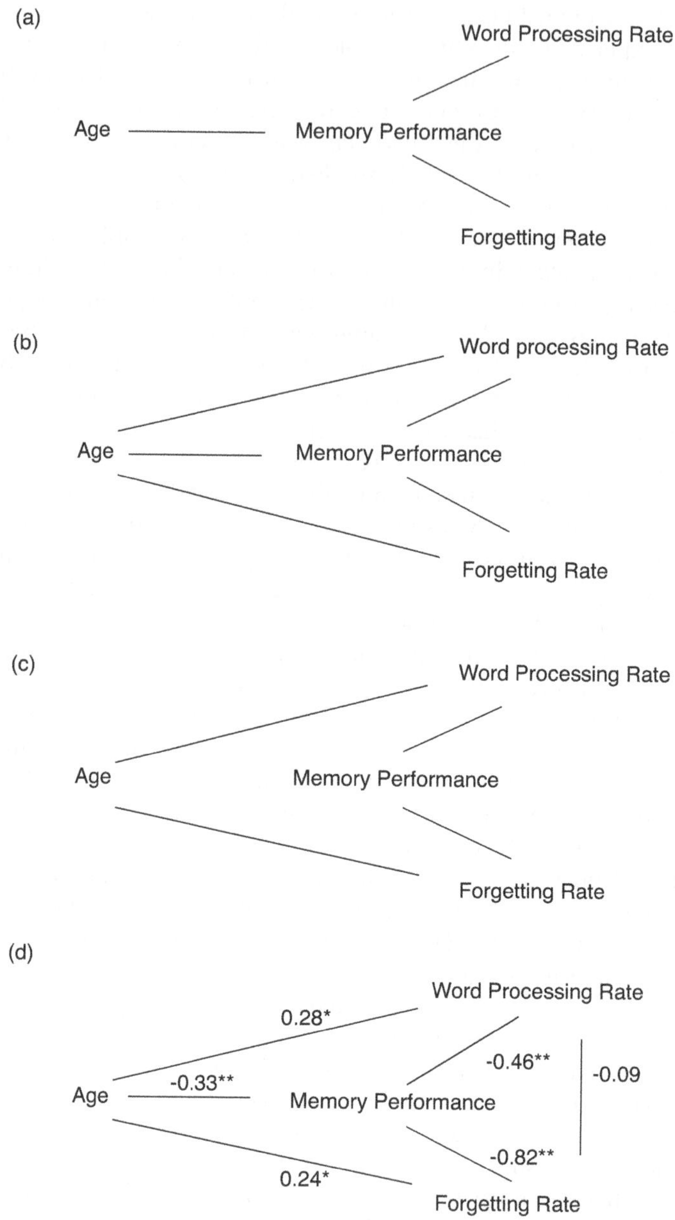

Figure 10.19 Panels a, b, and c show 3 alternative explanatory frameworks for the ways in which differences in age or general ability may affect number of items recalled; Panel d shows the correlation structure within the model that was found to fit the data best. *Significant at $p < 0.05$; ** significant at $p < 0.01$.

We know that the functional neuroanatomy and neurophysiology of the human brain is highly differentiated. It may seem to be an artificial and unpromising approach to try to interpret changes and individual differences in cognitive skills in terms of the speculative properties of an undifferentiated information-processing network. However, this is more than an intellectual exercise. First, it obliges us to consider rigorously a topic neglected in classical neuropsychology: whether diffuse changes that affect the entire CNS may selectively affect different aspects of efficiency and so potentiate with, or alter, what it has been convenient to regard as the specific effects of localized damage. Second, the only coherent theory of cognitive ageing yet available (offered by Salthouse, 1985; 1991) and one of the most widely discussed theories of the "biological bases of intelligence" (Eysenck, 1982; 1986, Jensen, 1982a; 1982b; 1985; and others) are both based on the premise that global changes in a single performance parameter entrain concomitant changes in all others. It has been necessary to take these theories seriously and to show that, even within the limited and somewhat artificial constraints in which they operate, this does not seem to be the case.

Relating Changes in g_f to Modular Ageing of the Brain

We have seen that it is risky to make inferences about the system *performance characteristics* of hypothetical information-processing networks from patterns of correlations between the *performance indices* that we derive from laboratory tasks. We are on safer ground if we can analyse scores from batteries of cognitive tests that clinical experience has found to be diagnostic of damage to particular brain structures or neurotransmitter systems. These tests, and the well-developed neuropsychological models devised to interpret them, allow a two-stage approach to cognitive ageing. By administering batteries of tests to large elderly samples and then analysing the patterns of clustering of their scores, we can test the hypo-theses that particular sub-sets of tasks reflect the integrity of particular CNS structures. If the cluster patterns we obtain make sense in terms of neuropsychological models, we can go on to determine whether levels of performance on tasks within each of these test-clusters change with age at similar rates, whereas scores on different sub-sets of tests change with age at different rates.

We administered to 375 individuals aged between 50 and 86 years a set of six tests, which, among others, have been used in our longitudinal surveys of populations in Manchester and Newcastle. One of these was the Cattell "Culture Fair" test, Sections 1 through 4. Also included were two tests of information-processing rate: a letter/letter substitution coding task and a simple visual search task in which volunteers searched sheets of random capital letters for the two targets, capital I and 0. The remaining two tests made demands on immediate memory. They were recall of names of 12 objects shown as line drawings and immediate free recall of a list of 30 words. Subjects' chronological ages were also entered with these data into a principal components analysis.

We have argued that when interpreting experimental data, it is prudent to suppose that each of the *performance indices* that we derive from experimental tasks may be determined by a sub-set of different system *performance characteristics*, and that particular *system characteristics* may deter-mine levels of more than one *performance index*. In this case levels of attainment on different performance indices would be partly determined by the same *performance characteristics*, so that we would expect modest but significant correlations between scores on most experimental paradigms. The correlations between scores on all tasks were modest but generally significant, and all these scores correlated modestly but significantly with chronological age. A preliminary cluster analysis showed that although each task within each sub-set made distinctly different demands and provided a differently derived performance index, the clustering of scores reflects an intuitively plausible separation of tasks into those that do and those that do not make direct demands on memory. All memory tasks fell into a common cluster. The tasks measuring information-processing speed also fell into another, distinct cluster. As we might expect from the psychometric analyses reported by Salthouse (1991), scores on the two IQ tests clustered with scores on information-processing tasks.

With this reassurance, a principal components analysis was made to test whether age has earlier and more severe effects on performance on memory tasks or on information-processing tasks and IQ tests. Figure 10.20 shows the factor loadings.

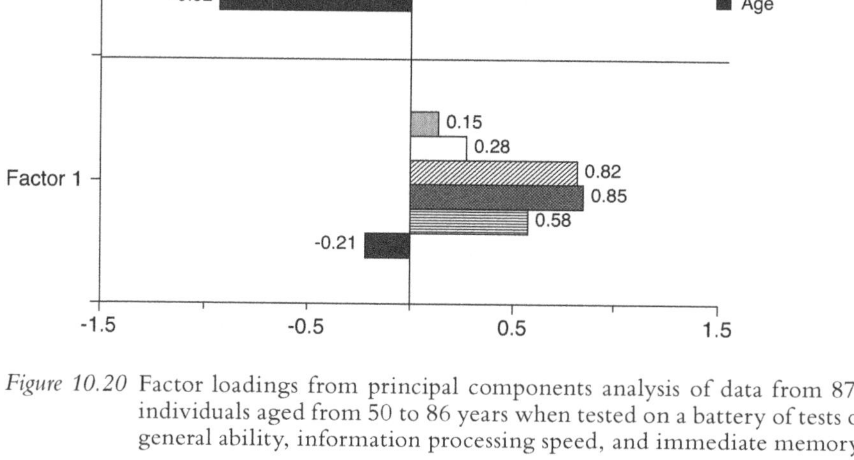

Figure 10.20 Factor loadings from principal components analysis of data from 876 individuals aged from 50 to 86 years when tested on a battery of tests of general ability, information processing speed, and immediate memory.

Consistent with earlier findings by Salthouse (1985; 1991) and suggestions by Eysenck (1986), Jensen (1982a; 1982b; 1985) and others, the dominant factor includes IQ test scores and measures of information-processing rate and accounts for about 26% of the variance. However, a powerful second factor, accounting for 24% of the variance, includes scores on a number of different memory tasks. Contrary to suggestions by Salthouse (1985; 1991) chronological age is most strongly associated with memory scores in this second factor rather than with IQ test scores and information-processing speed in the first factor. This finding does not agree with Salthouse's general theoretical position, but it does not contradict any of his published data, as memory test scores were not included in the analyses that he reports.

Principal components analyses of data from three other test batteries we have used show the same dissociation between scores on memory tasks and on information-processing tasks, and the same association of chronological age with a secondary "memory factor" rather than with the invariably dominant "intelligence and information-processing" factor. Given this evidence that cognitive change with age may be patterned rather than uniform, it is natural to ask whether different individuals may show different patterns of cognitive ageing or at least to ask the weaker question whether the dissociation between efficiency on tests of memory and on tests of intelligence and information-processing rate is larger in some individuals than in others, as well as whether, in the population at large, individuals with exceptionally large disassociations between these performance measures are more commonly found in older age groups.

To examine this, we re-analysed data from a test battery administered to 1,400 volunteers in Newcastle upon Tyne, who were then aged between 50 and 86 years. We summed normalized transforms of scores on all memory tests to obtain, for each volunteer, a composite "memory test score". We then plotted each individual's memory test score against his or her score on the AH 4 (1) IQ test. We tested the data for the best fitting regression, and found that a linear regression was superior to all others. We could then identify individuals whose composite memory test scores were 2 SD below expectation from their IQ test scores. Figures 10.21a, b and c give plots, with superimposed 2 SD limits, for volunteers aged from 50 to 59, 60 to 69, and 70+ years.

The point of interest is that the number of individuals whose memory test scores fall more than 2 SD below expectation from their IQ test scores steadily increases with group age. There were 4 such individuals in the 50–59 age group, 11 in the 6M9 age group, and 21 in the 70+ age group. Within a large population of fit elderly people, the probability of a large dissociation between memory efficiency and IQ test scores increases with age.

Groups of individuals who have been identified in this way as being "memory poor" have been intensively studied in our laboratory. Carol Holland (see Winthorpe,1989) screened a group of 72 such individuals and eliminated 36 with reported pathologies of various kinds. The remaining individuals were, as far as could be determined, quite healthy. As we might expect, they scored much more poorly than controls, who had been precisely matched for age, gender, and for vocabulary test scores, on a battery of neuropsychological

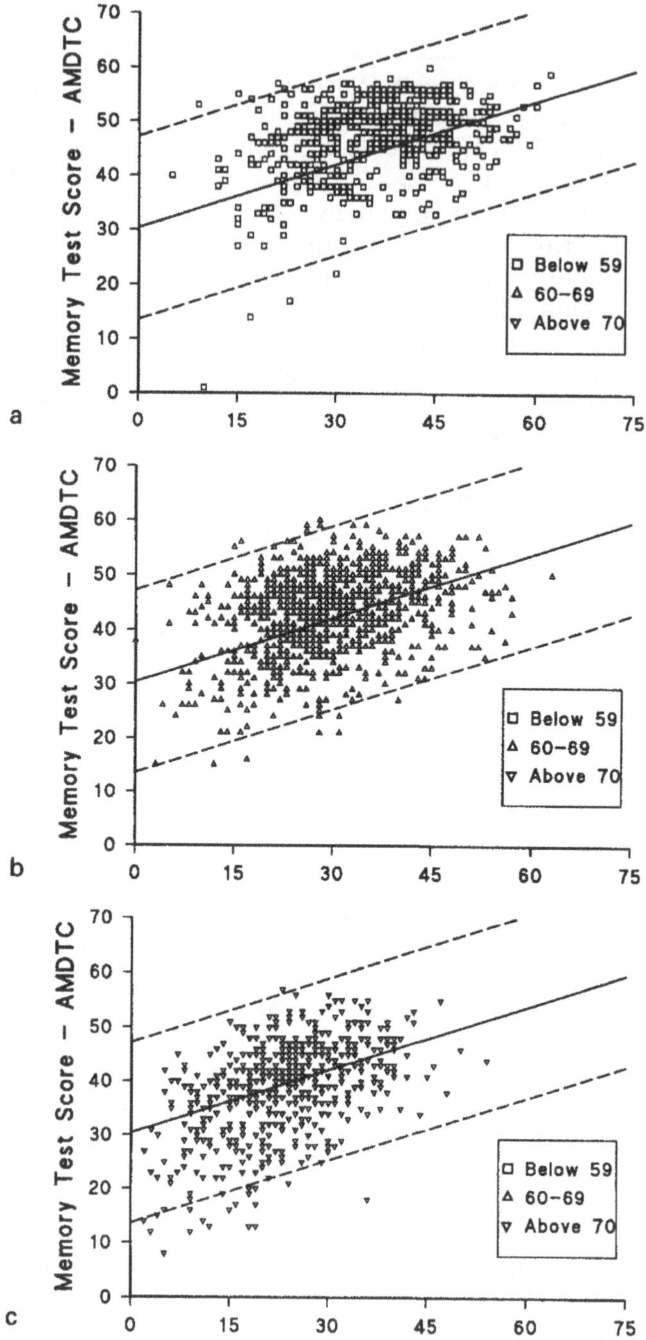

Figure 10.21 a, b, and c. Scores on a cumulative learning task plotted against scores on the AH4 (1) IQ test for 3 groups of individuals aged 50–59, 60–69, and 70–79 years. Limits of 2 SD above and below means are indicated. Manchester Data showing the regression line and 95% CI for the memory test score.

tests that are used in clinical practice to detect signs of amnesia consequent on temporal lobe damage. This confirms that scores on the sub-set of memory tests used in our longitudinal battery do have commonality with scores on a variety of clinical tests that are known to detect memory problems. Holland also compared the "memory poor" and their controls on a battery of clinical tests designed to detect cognitive impairments associated with "frontal" damage but found no differences. Nettelbeck and Rabbitt (1992) have recently published a comparison between these individuals and their matched controls on a further battery of tasks, including measures of information-processing speed. Both in a large random sample of normal elderly people and in individual matched controls for the "memory poor" sub-group, scores on laboratory measures of information-processing speed (CRT and tachisto scopic recognition threshold) correlated modestly but significantly with scores on memory tests. However, within the "memory-poor" sub-group these measures did not correlate. This is further evidence for a functional disassociation between two classes of performance measures: that, within individuals, increases in the size of this disassociation that are picked up on one of a cluster of measures (e.g. IQ test scores and memory tasks) are paralleled by disassociations between all others in this cluster (e.g. between information-processing tasks and memory tasks). In addition, it seems that within a healthy elderly population the probability of finding individuals with such disassociations increases with the age of the sample tested.

Conclusion

These data begin to give us an answer to the interesting question as to whether "it all goes together when it goes". Apparently, age changes in some aspects of cognitive performance may antidate changes in others, and the numbers of individuals in whom such disjunctions become striking increases with the age of the population we sample. The data we have discussed suggest an approach to the aetiology of these cognitive changes and directions for further work. The appearance of individuals with unusually advanced "temporal" ageing may be paralleled by the appearance of others with accelerated "frontal" changes or with other syndromes of relative loss and sparing identifiable within the framework of existing neuropsychological models. However, a new and important point is that it seems that there are also "global" changes in CNS function that may affect some parameters of performance, and so some cognitive skills, much more than others. This raises a new caveat for neuropsychological models based on single case studies, as it is very likely that all "focal" lesions will be accompanied by more or less "global" damage, which may also have markedly different effects on different cognitive skills.

However slowly and clumsily it has sometimes been approached, the main goal of research in cognitive gerontology has always been the relation of patterns of cognitive and behavioural change to corresponding alterations in brain function. We hope that these results have contributed at least some hints and the beginnings of a methodology to speed this long-awaited rapprochement.

Acknowledgements

Thanks to John Duncan and Glyn Humphreys for their most perceptive and helpful comments on earlier drafts of the paper.

References

Anderson, M. (1992). *Intelligence and development: a cognitive theory*. Oxford: Blackwells.

Arbib, M.A. (1989). *The metaphorical brain 2. Neural networks and beyond*. New York: John Wiley.

Bahrick, H.P. (1979). Maintenance of knowledge: Questions about memory we forgot to ask. *Journal of Experimental Psychology: General, 108*, 296–308.

Bahrick, H.P. (1983). The cognitive map of a city: Fifty years of learning and memory. *Psychology of Learning and Motivation, 17*, 125–163.

Bahrick, H.P. (1984). Semantic memory content in permastore: Fifty years of memory for Spanish learned at school. *Journal of Experimental Psychology: General, 113*, 1–29.

Bahrick, H.P., Bahrick, P.O., & Wittlinger, R.P. (1975). Fifty years of memory for names and faces: A cross-sectional approach. *Journal of Experimental Psychology: General, 104*, 54–75.

Bahrick, H.P., & Phelps, E. (1987). Retention of Spanish vocabulary over 8 years. *Journal of Experimental Psychology: Learning Memory and Cognition, 10*, 82–93.

Bartlett, F.C. (1932). *Remembering: A study in experimental and social psychology*. Cambridge: Cambridge University Press.

Berg, C.A., & Sternberg, R.J. (1992). Adults conceptions of intelligence across the adult lifespan. *Psychology and Aging, 7*, 221–231.

Blinkhorn, S.F., & Henderson, D.E. (1982). Average evoked responses and psychometric intelligence. *Nature, 295*, 596–597.

Brand, C.R., & Deary, I.Z. (1982). Intelligence and inspection time. In H.J. Eysenck (Ed.), *A model for intelligence (pp.* 133–148). New York: Springer Verlag.

Brindley, J.F. (1965). Cognitive sets, speed and accuracy of performance in the elderly. In A.T. Welford & J.E. Birren (Eds.), *Behaviour, aging and the nervous system (pp.* 191–216). Springfield, IL: Charles Thomas.

Cerella, J. (1985). Information processing rates in the elderly. *Psychological Bulletin, 98*, 67–83.

Conway, M., Cohen, G., & Stanhope, N. (1991). On the very long term retention of knowledge acquired through formal education: Twelve years of Cognitive Psychology. *Journal of Experimental Psychology, (General), 120*, 395–409.

Craik, F.I.M., & Lockhart, R.S. (1972). Levels of processing: A framework for memory research. *Journal of Verbal Learning and Verbal Behaviour, 11*, 671–684.

Eysenck, H.J. (1986). The theory of intelligence and the psychophysiology of cognition. In R.J. Sternberg (Ed.), *Advances in the psychology of human intelligence, Vol. 3 (pp.* 1–34). Hillsdale, NJ: Lawrence Erlbaum Associates, Inc.

Goward, L.M. (1986). An investigation of the factors contributing to scores on intelligence tests. Unpublished Ph.D. thesis, University of Manchester.

Heim, A. (1968). *The AH 4 IQ test*. Sough, U.K.: Nelson, NFER.

Holland, C.A., & Rabbitt, P.M.A. (1991). The course and causes of cognitive change with advancing age. *Reviews in Clinical Gerontology, 1*, 81–96.

Horn, J.L. (1982). The theory of fluid and crystalized intelligence in relation to concepts of cognitive psychology and aging in adulthood. In: F.I.M. Craik & S. Trehub (Eds.), *Aging and cognitive processes (pp.* 237–278). New York: Plenum.

Horn, J.L. (1986). Intellectual ability concepts. In: R.J. Sternberg (Ed.), *Advances in the psychology of human intelligence (pp.* 35–75). Hillsdale, NJ: Lawrence Erlbaum Associates, Inc.

Horn, J.L., & Cattell, R.B. (1967). Age differences in fluid and crystalized intelligence. *Acta Psychologica, 26,* 107–129.

Jensen, A.R. (1982a). Reaction time and psychometric "g". In H.J. Eysenck (Ed.), *A model for intelligence (pp.* 93–102). Heidelberg: Springer-Verlag.

Jensen, A.R. (1982b). The chronometry of intelligence. In: R.J. Sternberg (Ed.), *Advances in the study of human intelligence, Vol. 1.* Hillsdale, NJ: Lawrence Erlbaum Associates, Inc.

Jensen, A.R. (1985). The nature of the black-white difference on various psychometric tests: Spearman's hypothesis. *The Behaviourul and Brain Sciences, 8,* 193–219.

Jerison, H.J. (1982). The evolution of biological intelligence. In: R.J. Sternberg (Ed.), Handbook of *human intelligence.* Cambridge: Cambridge University Press.

Maylor, E.A., & Rabbitt, P.M.A. (1987). Effect of alcohol on rate of forgetting. *Psycho-pharmacology, 91,* 230–235.

McClelland, J.C., Rumelhart, D.E., & the PDP Research Group (1986). *Parallel distributed processing: Explorations in the microstructure of cognition.* Cambridge, MA: MIT Press.

Neisser, U. (1984). Interpreting Harry Bahrick's discovery: What confers immunity against forgetting? *Journal of Experimental Psychology, (General), 113,* 32–35.

Nettelbeck, T., & Brewer, N. (1981). Studies of mental retardation and timed performance. In: N.R. Ellis (Ed.), *International review of research on mental retardation, Vol. 10.* NY: Academic Press.

Nettelbeck, T., & Lally, M. (1981). 10 put to test. *Nature, 290,* 440.

Nettelbeck, T.. & Rabbitt, P.M.A. (1992). Age, information processing rate and intelligence. *Intelligence, 18,* 234–248.

Perfect, T.J. (1989). *Age, expertise and long term memory retrieval.* Unpublished Ph.D. thesis, University of Manchester.

Plomin, R., & McClearn, G.E. (1990). Human behavioural geneticsof aging. In: J.E. Birren & K.W. Schaie (Eds.), *Handbook of the psychology of aging,* 3rd edition. San Diego: Academic Press, Inc.

Rabbitt, P.M., & Banerji, N. (1989). How does prolonged practice affect decision speed? *Journal of Experimental Psychology, (General), 67,* 234–242.

Rabbitt, P.M., Baneji, N., & Szemanski, A. (1989). Space fortress as an IQ test? Predictors of learned and practised performance in a complex, interactive videogame. *Acta Psychologica, 71,* 243–257.

Rabbitt, P.M.A., & Goward, L.M. (in press). Age, IQ test score, practice and individual differences in reaction times. *Quarterly Journal of Experimental Psychology.*

Salthouse, T.A. (1982). Adult cognition: An experimental psychology of human aging. New York: Springer-Verlag.

Salthouse, T.A. (1985). *A theory of cognitive aging.* Amsterdam: North Holland.

Salthouse, T.A. (1988). Effects of age on verbal abilities: An examination of the psycho- metric literature. In L.L. Light & D.M. Burke (Eds.), *Language and memory in old age* (pp. 17–35). New York: Cambridge University Press.

Salthouse, T.A. (1991). *Theoretical perspectives on cognitive aging.* Hillsdale, NJ: Lawrence Erlbaum Associates, Inc.

Shepherd, R.N., & Teghtsoonian, M. (1961). Retention of information under conditions approximating to a steady state. *Journal of Experimental Psychology, 62,* 302–309.

Siegler, I.C., & Costa, P.T., Jr. (1985). Health behaviour relationships. In: J.E. Birren & K.W. Schaie (Eds.), *Handbook of the psychology of aging* (*pp.* 599–612), Washington, DC: American Psychological Association.

Spearman, C. (1904). General intelligence objectively determined and measured. American *Journal of Psychology, 15,* 201–293.

Spearman, C. (1927). *The abilities of man.* London: Macmillan.

Sternberg, R.J., & Powell, J.S. (1982). Theories of intelligence. In: R.J. Sternberg (Ed.), *Handbook of human intelligence.* Cambridge: Cambridge University Press.

Vernon, P. A. (1985). Individual differences in general cognitive ability. In: L.C. Hartledge & C.F. Telzrow (Eds.), *The neuropsychology of individual differences*: A developmental perspective (pp. 125–150). New York: Plenum.

Vernon, P.A., & Jensen, A.R. (1984). Individual and group differences in intelligence and speed of information processing. *Personality and Individual Differences, 5,* 41 1–423.

Waugh, N.C., & Barr, R.A. (1980). Memory and mental tempo. In: L.W. Poon, J.L. Fozard, L.S. Cermak, D. Arenberg, & L.W. Thompson (Eds.), *New directions in memory and aging.* Hillsdale, NJ: Lawrence Erlbaum Associates, Inc.

Winthorpe, C. (now Holland) (1988). *Patterns of change in aging memory.* Unpublished Ph.D. thesis, University of Manchester.

People inconveniently learn the tests you give them during longitudinal studies

As our longitudinal data gradually accumulated, plots of people's scores over decades made it obvious that many had improved rather than declined over successive testings. This was a practical demonstration of a theoretical problem for longitudinal data-analysis first raised by Baltes et al. (1972). They pointed out that during longitudinal studies people are repeatedly given the same tests and so may improve with practice. Their warning was not heeded by those running longitudinal studies who chose to justify their laborious activity by the assumption that if tests are repeated only at intervals of several years, practice gains must be absent or inconsequential. Our data began to make it clear that we could not justify further negligence because even on ten-minute tests of general intelligence repeated at four-year intervals, many of our volunteers improved over time.

We were rescued from our despair by an eminent statistician, Peter Diggle, who had solved the statistical problems of how to take account of, and estimate improvements with, practice when computing trajectories of age-related changes (e.g. Diggle et al., 2002). These methods also let us compare the amounts of practice improvements between older, younger and more and less intelligent volunteers and between different tasks. They showed that individuals' intelligence test scores improved even if they missed a testing session and re-encountered tests only 8 years later. The next paper describes this finding, and is also an account of our longitudinal study between 1982 and 2000.

References

Baltes, P. B., Nesselrode, K., Schaie, K. W., & Labouvie-Vief, G. V. (1972). On the dilemma of regression effects in examining ability-related differentials in ontogenetic patterns of intelligence. *Developmental Psychology*, *6*, 78–84.

Diggle, P. J., Heagerty, P. J., Liang, K.-Y., & Zeger, S. L. (2002). *Analysis of Longitudinal Data*. Oxford: Oxford University Press.

11 The University of Manchester longitudinal study of cognition in normal healthy old age, 1983 through 2003

P.M.A. Rabbitt, L. McInnes, P. Diggle, F. Holland, N. Bent, V. Abson, N. Pendleton and M. Horan

The simplest general aim of all longitudinal studies of cognitive changes in normal healthy old age has been to plot the time courses of cognitive changes, determining when they first become measurable and how rapidly they then proceed. However, because people change at very different rates as they grow older average change is less informative than marked variations in rates of change between individuals. These allow us to identify factors that slow or robustly statistically inter-dependent because all are driven, to similar extents, by the same global neurophysiological changes, or whether the functional sub-systems supporting different abilities "age" at different times and rates. This latter speculation raises the further question whether the resulting neurophysiological and consequent cognitive changes are similar for all individuals or whether people not only experience different rates but also idiosyncratic patterns or syndromes of changes.

This goal of exploring diversity of change between individuals imposes severe demands on longitudinal studies. To identify variations in rates, and possibly in patterns of changes, and to identify as wide as possible a range of factors that accelerate and retard change, samples must be as large and diverse as possible. Because age-related changes develop over decades samples must include individuals from as wide a range of ages as possible who should be followed over many years. Because many age-related changes are driven by changes in general health and by the different burdens of age-related pathologies, clinical documentation throughout the study is essential. There is evidence that not only individual differences in baseline mental ability, and also in the rates of change in mental ability are genetically determined so no study can now be considered complete unless DNA samples are obtained and archived for analysis. Because maintenance of ability in later life is strongly affected by demographic and socio economic factors such as levels of affluence, place of residence, social support and environmental challenges these factors must also be documented. These demands determined the protocol for the University of Manchester longitudinal study of cognitive ageing.

We first give details of the samples tested and the test batteries and questionnaires that constituted the longitudinally repeated core of the study, how data were collected and address some simple, but widely neglected, methodological issues, such as test sensitivity, stability and validity that must to be resolved before data can be properly interpreted. We also give details of how the sample of participants changed during the course of the study as a result of successive waves of recruitment of new participants and accelerate cognitive ageing and that prolong mental productivity happiness and duration and quality of life. Longitudinal data on individual differences in trajectories of changes also provides the best basis for generating and testing functional models for the processes of biological ageing, and especially of ageing of the brain and the Central Nervous System. For example a main issue has been whether rates of change in all mental abilities are strongly linked, and so are selective drop-out. Since data collection is now complete, and the database is currently being archived for general access, this seemed useful to other investigators who might wish to make their own analyses of the material that available. We also describe some of the attempts that have been made to address particular questions using parts of the data set. Complete descriptions of analyses are not given because in most cases they are available in published papers.

During this study theoretical insights have changed in unanticipated ways, and collection of important new kinds of data, such as DNA assays and Brain Imaging have become possible. It would not have been sensible or cost effective for the study to remain guided for 20 years by the same agenda of questions posed when it began. It is also not sensible to try to address new issues by continuously altering the batteries of longitudinally repeated tests because this would sacrifice all the advantages of longitudinal over cross-sectional comparisons. Nevertheless longitudinal studies offer a uniquely powerful way to address new theoretical issues and capitilise on methodological advances because, in addition to a cumulative database they build up the unique resource of a large sample of compliant and increasingly well-documented volunteers. This makes it increasingly useful to make focussed investigations in which the performance of sub-sets of volunteers on new tests can be related to archived data on their previous and future rates of change. We thought it helpful to other investigators to describe all of the data now available from such smaller scale studies.

The second section of the paper concerns two serious methodological problems faced by longitudinal studies. The first is that because participants repeatedly take the same batteries of tests improvements with practice can mask age related declines. Practice effects are marked, and also vary with complex interactions between the difficulty of the tasks used and participants' ages and levels of general intellectual ability (Rabbitt, 1993b; Rabbitt, Banerji, & Szemanski, 1989). A second problem is that older and less able volunteers selectively withdraw as a study progresses. However random effects models can be used to identify and study practice effects while also taking drop-out effects into consideration. Toillustrate this we describe an analysis of data from one of the two test batteries used during the course of the study and show how after practice and dropout have been taken into account it is possible to obtain clearer answers to some of the basic, substantive questions that all longitudinal studies have addressed: Do rates of cognitive changes accelerate as age increases? Do different cognitive abilities decline at different rates? What are the effects of gender, overall ability and demographics on rates of decline? What effects does increasing sample age have on the extent of variability between the individuals that it comprises?

History of study and recruitment of volunteers

The study was funded by the U.K. Social Science Research Council from 1983 to 1988, then jointly by the U.K. Medical Research Council and the Economic and Social Research Council (ESRC) from 1988 to 1993 and then by the Medical Research Council (MRC) from 1993 to 1998. From 1998 to 2003 the study continued with support from ESRC, the Welcome Trust, Unilever plc and the University of Manchester. Recruitment began in Newcastle-upon-Tyne during 1983/1984 with advertisements in local newspapers, radio and television. This attracted 2052 volunteers, 513 men aged from 49 to 86 years (mean (M) = 65.2, SD = 11.8) and 1539 women aged from 46 to 92 years (M = 67.4, SD = 14.3). All were healthy, lived independently, and were able to make their way unaided to the University of Newcastle to take two different batteries of cognitive tests. These were Test Battery A (TA) on which they were screened at recruitment and on a second visit 2 years later, and Test Battery B (TB) which, after the second visit, was alternated with TA throughout the study. From 1984 to 1986 similar advertisements recruited 2193 similar residents of Greater Manchester, 690 men aged from 45 to 93 years (M = 65.6, SD = 7.7) and 1503 women aged from 50 to 92 years (M = 64.4, SD = 7.8) who travelled independently to take the same batteries of tests at the Department of Psychology, University of Manchester. Table 11.1 shows how recruitment of new waves of volunteers continued until 1994 with biennial assessments of survivors through 2003 on two different sets of tests.

Description of batteries of cognitive tests and procedures for administration

Participants were tested in groups of 5–20. Test batteries A and B each required two, separate, 90 min sessions which were administered by two experimenters, in comfortable, quiet and well-lit rooms, not less than 1 week and not more than 4 weeks apart. Individuals with severe visual or auditory handicaps were excluded from the longitudinal study but were encouraged to participate in other, cross-sectional, projects. Individuals with mild, correctable sensory handicaps always used their prescribed lenses or hearing aids. As Tables 11.1 a and b show,

Table 11.1 Schedule of Recruitment and Testing of Volunteers (Newcastle and Manchester).

	TB1 Administered (1982–1985)	*TB1 (1985–1986)*	*Robbins & Sahakian Battery (1985–1986)*	*TB2 (1985–1991)*	*TB1 (1991–1992)*	*Currently registered*
(a) Newcastle[a]						
Waves 1–2 (1982–1985)	2052 (first test)	1578 (retest 1)	828 (first test)	1167 (first test)	977 (second test)	977
Wave 3 (1988)		629 (first test)		492 (first test)	425 (second test)	425
Wave 4 (1989–1990)				607 (first test)	601 (first test)	601
Wave 5 (1991–1992)					67 (first test)	67
		TB1 1985–1988	*TB2 October 1988–September 1990*	*TB1 October 1990–August 1992*		*Currently registered*
(b) Manchester[b]						
Wave 1-3 Recruited 1985–1988		2361	1452	1147		1147
Wave 4 Recruited 1989-1990			522 (first test)	256 (first test)		256
Wave 5 Recruited 1991-1992				104 (first test)		104

Note: [a]Total tested on at least one Battery = Waves 1 and 2 (2048)=Wave 3 (629)+Wave 4(601)+Wave 5 (67=3345).
Total retested once on Battery 1 = Wave 1 (1578) = Wave 2 (425) = 2003.
Total tested at least once on both Battery 1 and Battery 2 = Wave 1 (1167) + Wave 2 (492) = 1659.
Total still registered on panel = 2070.

[b]Total tested on at least one Battery = Waves 1–3 (2361)+522 (Wave 2)+104 (Wave 3)=2992.
Total retested once on Battery 1 (Waves 1–3) = 1147.
Total tested at least once on both Battery 1 and Battery 2=Waves 1–3 (1452)+Wave 4 (256) = 1708.
Total still registered on panel = Waves 1–3 (1147)+Wave 4 (256)+Wave 5 (104)=1507.

participants were seen, on average, every 24–30 months, and completed cycles of both TA and TB within approximately 60 months.

TA included the Heim (1970) AH4-1 and -2 intelligence tests each consisting of 65 problems. The AH4-1 consists of logic, arithmetic and completion of number series and verbal comparisons and the AH4-2 consists of non-verbal problems in which participants must select among alternative solutions the correct completions of logical series defined by progressive mental rotation, or addition and subtraction, or other comparisons of line-drawn shapes. The AH4 tests are well-standardised measures of general fluid intelligence and correlate robustly (r = .73 to .75) with instruments such as the WAIS battery (see Heim, 1970). Correlations with the Cattell and Cattell (1960) "Culture Fair" test which was also administered in Test Battery B were r = .713 (AH4-1) and r = .727 (AH4-2).

During each AH4 test experimenters guided volunteers through a set of five examples and then encouraged them to solve as many of the 65 scored problems as they could complete within 10 min. TA also included the Raven (1965) Mill Hill A vocabulary test requiring selection of the most exact synonym for each of 33 words from among 6 alternatives and the Raven's (1965) Mill Hill B vocabulary test requiring generation of an exact definition of the meaning of each of 33 words. The Mill Hill tests were administered without time limits. Scores for the AH4 and Mill Hill tests were the total numbers of correct answers and the total numbers of items attempted. TA also included three memory tests. In a Verbal Free Recall test (VFR) volunteers were shown a list of 30 six-letter nouns that had been matched for frequency (1/10,000 Kucera & Francis, 1967, norms) and for concreteness. These were projected, one at a time, at a rate of 1/1.5s by an automatically timed Kodak Carousel projector and appeared as strings of bold face Times Roman characters 150 cm long and 15 cm high on a screen located no further than 5 m from the most distant participant. Scores were the total numbers of words correctly recalled in any order. In a Cumulative Verbal Recall task (CVR) a list of 15 six-letter nouns, selected just as for the VFR task, was presented four times in the same way and at the same rate. After each cycle of presentations volunteers wrote down as many as they could remember, in any order, turning on each occasion to a new page of an answer booklet so that they could not see their previous attempts. Scores were the number of words correctly recalled after each presentation and the total number of words recalled after all four presentations. As a test of recognition memory for pictures 40 uncoloured individual frames from Schultz "Snoopy" cartoons were shown at a rate of 1/2.0s at the start of the experimental session. Frames had no dialogue or captions and were not related by theme or by actions or events portrayed. Immediately after viewing all 40 frames volunteers were shown 10 of those that they had initially seen randomly interspersed with 10 previously unseen distracters. Three further presentations of new targets and distracters were separated by intervals of approximately 20 min during which the other tests in the battery were given. Scores were the number of targets correctly identified (hits), the numbers of distracters wrongly identified (False Positives) and the numbers of targets wrongly identified as distracters (Omissions) from which values of d′ and of Beta were computed.

TB included all four parts of the Cattell and Cattell (1960) "Culture Fair" non-verbal test of general fluid intelligence. These incorporate 46 non-verbal problems. TB also included the WAIS vocabulary test (Wechsler, 1986) and three tests of information processing speed. The first was a Visual Search task in which participants were allowed 8.0 min to detect all occurrences of the letters I and O on printed pages on which all capital letters appeared equally often in random order. Scores were the numbers of targets detected and omitted (i.e. an implicit measure of scanning rate and a direct measure of accuracy). The second was the Savage (1984) Alphabet Coding Task that is derived from the widely used letter/letter coding task used in the WAIS battery (Wechsler, 1986). Volunteers encoded as rapidly as possible random sequences of 15 different letters of the alphabet using a guide printed as a heading on each score sheet. After brief unscored practice volunteers completed 4 consecutive 2 min runs during which the code remained constant. Scores were the numbers of letters correctly coded during each of these runs and also the numbers of code letters correctly recalled after all runs had been completed. Memory for code letters was also probed because previous work had shown that if participants learn even a few letter–letter pairs they need to refer less often to the guide and so work much faster. Thus this task is not only a test of information processing speed, but also of learning efficiency (Piccinin & Rabbitt, 1999). A third test involving information processing speed was the Baddeley, Emslie and Nimmo-Smith (1992) "Semantic Reasoning" task for which volunteers were given booklets containing 150 sentences, half of which were true (e.g. "Birds have wings") and half false (e.g. "Kangaroos are made of Jam"). They were allowed 2 min to verify as many sentences as possible, placing ticks against "True" and crosses against "False" propositions. Scores were the total numbers of sentences correctly and incorrectly evaluated.

TB also included five different indices of memory efficiency. One was Immediate Verbal Free Recall of a list of 10 nouns. These were selected and presented precisely as for the VFR and CVL tests in TA. Volunteers also attempted Delayed Recall of the same items after an interval of 20 min, during which other tests in the battery were completed. A test of memory for shapes and for their spatial locations required immediate recall of the names and cell locations of geometric shapes in sixteen separate 4 x 4 cell matrices. Subsets of four matrices each contained 1, 2, 3 or 4 shapes. Matrices containing 1 or 2 shapes were shown for 2 s and those showing 3 or 4 shapes for 3 s. The numbers of shapes correctly recalled, the numbers of grid cells correctly identified as having been occupied and the numbers of shapes correctly assigned to the grid cells in which they had appeared were separately scored. A test of semantic memory required immediate recall of "propositions about people". Five slides each showed the first and second name of a different one of five imaginary people with three items of information about each. Slides were each presented for 3 s. After all five had been inspected recall of items of information was prompted by visual presentation of names. Scores were the total number of items of information correctly assigned to names. In the fifth memory test volunteers were shown, for 30 s, a circle divided into 12 quadrants, in each of which appeared a line drawing of an easily nameable object. Immediately after viewing the circle they were asked to recall the names of all of the objects and to enter each into the correct one of 12 sectors of a blank circle. The total numbers of object names correctly recalled, the total numbers of filled sectors correctly identified irrespectively of name accuracy and the total number of sectors in which the correct name had been entered were separately scored.

Test/retest stability, mutual associations between measures of cognitive performance and correlations of test scores with calendar age

Age related changes in scores on cognitive tests cannot sensibly be evaluated unless the test/retest stability of measures is known. Correlations were computed from data for the Manchester sample using scores on first and second experiences of tests in TA which were, on average, 5.1 years apart and between their first and second experiences of tests in TB which were, on average, 6.3 years apart.

In TA test/retest correlations within a sample of N=1886 Manchester volunteers were AH4 (1) $r = .874$; AH4 (2) $r = .853$; Mill Hill A Vocabulary .814; Mill Hill B vocabulary .790; Verbal Free Recall $r = .607$; Cumulative Verbal Learning, .741 and Picture Recognition .581. In TB correlations for 1377 individuals were Cattell Culture Fair $r = .753$; WAIS Vocabulary $r = .759$; Letter/Letter Coding r = .892; Visual Search $r = .756$; Immediate Free Recall of 10 words $r = .247$; Delayed free recall $r = .632$; Propositions about People $r = .541$; Recall of shapes and their positions in a 4 x 4 matrix r = .536 and recall of Names of objects and their locations in a 12 sector circle $r = .357$.

A different issue when considering tests included in longitudinal batteries is their relative sensitivity to age-related changes in cognitive performance. Correlations (*r*) between scores and Calendar Age varied widely between tasks. All were negative and, except for the Mill Hill "A" and "B" vocabulary tests, all were significant. In Test Battery A they were AH4 (1), −.366; AH4 (2), −.453; Mill Hill A, −.015 (*ns*); Mill Hill B, −.026 (*ns*); Verbal Free Recall, −.323; Cumulative Learning, −.391 and Picture Recognition, −.247. In Test Battery B they were Cattell Culture Fair, −.436; WAIS vocabulary, −.156 (significant at $p = .000$); Letter/letter Coding, −.421; Visual Search, −.537; Immediate Free Recall of 10 words, −.286; Delayed Free Recall of 10 words, −.230; Propositions about people, −.262; Recall of geometric shapes and their positions in a 4 × 4 matrix, −.387 and recall of names of objects and their locations in a 12 sector circle, −.346.

These comparisons illustrate methodological points that have typically been neglected in analyses of results from longitudinal studies: Test/Retest correlations markedly vary between tasks: For well-designed psychometric instruments such as the AH4, Cattell Culture Fair and the Mill Hill and WAIS vocabulary tests, and also for the Visual Search and Letter/Letter Coding tasks, test/retest correlations are highly reliable at .753 and .874. In contrast for some memory tests reliability is low, for example .247 for immediate free recall of 10 words and .387 for recall of names of objects and of their locations in 12 sectors of a circle. If reliability is not computed, or if the implications of very wide differences in levels of reliability between measures are neglected, some of the most interesting, and apparently simplest questions about the nature of cognitive ageing cannot be answered. For example, unless analyses of longitudinal data take wide variations in test stability into account, they cannot address speculations that mental abilities decline at different rates nor accurately indicate the relative levels of association between scores on different tests and so between different mental abilities. Because these difficulties reflect inherent imprecision of measuring instruments they are not automatically resolved even by sophisticated statistical models.

Marked variations in the stability of tests and in their relative sensitivity to Age also raise uncertainties about the interpretation of many cross-sectional and longitudinal comparisons suggesting that old Age affects performance on some tasks earlier and more severely than on others. For example, scores in this study agree with compelling earlier evidence that Age affects cognitive skills that depend on knowledge about the world, and acquired techniques for problem solving ("crystallised intelligence") less than "fluid mental abilities" associated with information processing speed and the ability to solve novel problems. In this study correlations between Age and scores on the three Vocabulary tests are not significant (Mill Hill A, −.015; Mill Hill B −.026) or low (WAIS, −.156), while correlations with tests of fluid intelligence, information processing speed and cumulative learning are invariably robust (between −.326 and −.453). This is not an artefact of differences in retest stability because correlations for the WAIS (.759) the Mill Hill A (.814) and the Mill Hill B (.790) are comparable with those for tests of "fluid intelligence" (gf) such as the AH4 (1), (.874), the AH4 (2), .853 and the Cattell Culture Fair (.753) or, indeed, of simple tests of information processing speed and "fluid mental abilities" such as Visual Search (.756), Letter/letter coding (.892) or Cumulative Verbal Learning (.741).

Horn and his associates have extensively discussed the theoretical implications of these contrast (e.g. Horn, 1982, 1987; Horn, Donaldson, & Engstrom, 1981). A useful methodological consequence of differences in the rates of change in fluid and crystallised abilities is that they provide a tool to attack the substantive question whether or not individuals who have higher levels of mental ability as young adults experience slower declines in mental competence as they age. Lifespan declines in scores on tests of fluid intelligence are coupled with stability or improvement in scores on tests of vocabulary.

Young Adults' scores on vocabulary tests correlate strongly with their scores on tests of fluid intelligence (for the two Mill Hill and two AH4 tests correlations are in the range of $r = .8$ to $r = .86$). This means that individuals' vocabulary test scores in old age are good proxy measures for their fluid intelligence test scores as young adults. Rabbitt, Chetwynd, et al. (2003) used the Manchester and Newcastle data to estimate volunteers' young adult AH4-1 scores and compare these with their current, much lower, AH4-1 scores. This enabled comparisons of rates of subsequent decline between individuals with initially high and with initially low levels of attainment. Contrary to some previous suggestions (e.g. by Snowden et al., 1996) there was no evidence that individuals' levels of youthful ability affect their subsequent rates of agerelated decline.

Depression inventories, and findings on cognitive accompaniments of dysphoria

The prevalence of depression is known to be high in old age (Blazer, 1994). Studies have reported incidence of between 9% and 18% for depression of clinical relevance (e.g. Beekman, Copeland, & Prince, 1999; Beekman et al., 1995) and figures of 8% to 17% for sub-clinical depression (Beekman et al., 1999; Blazer, 1994; Tannock & Katona, 1995). Many studies show that even mild levels of induced depression impair cognitive performance in laboratory studies (e.g. Ellis, Thomas, & Rodrigez, 1984; Hertel & Hardin, 1990) and that both hospitalised patients (Ravenkilde et al.,2002) and community resident elderly depressed (McBride & Abeles, 2000) show poorer than average cognitive performance. Clearly incidence of depression contributes to variability in cognitive performance between members of ageing samples. Rabbitt, Donlan, Watson, McInnes, and Bent (1995) examined associations between cognitive test scores and scores on the Beck Depression Inventory on the first presentation of TA. In this sample Beck scores ranged from 0 to 45 ($M = 7.2$, $SD = 5.8$), with 91.7% of scores between 0 and 15 and 98.5% between 0 and 25. This means that most volunteers scored below the range considered normal for Young Adults and within a range in which differences in scores indicated relative levels of dysphoria rather than clinically significant depression. This confirms that this was an exceptionally highly motivated and healthy sample. Beck scores did not vary with Calendar Age. Women had slightly but significantly better scores than men. Dysporia varied inversely with socio-economic advantage and was greater in residents of Newcastle than in residents of Manchester. After variance associated with Age, Gender, Socio-economic advantage and City of residence had all been taken into consideration, higher Beck scores were associated with significantly poorer performance on all TA cognitive tests.

This clear association confirmed the need to continue monitoring individuals' levels of dysphoria throughout the longitudinal programme. However because some volunteers found some of the questions in the Beck inventory disturbing the Yesavage, Bruik, and Rose (1983) "Geriatric Depression Scale" (GDS) was substituted on all subsequent administrations of TB and the Beck inventory was not repeated until the final administration of TA in 2003. Analyses replicate findings of higher levels of dysphoria for women, for socially less advantaged individuals and for Newcastle residents. After all these factors have been taken into consideration there are still robust negative relationships between scores on the GDS and scores on all cognitive tests in both TB and TA. New findings are that individuals' GDS scores remain remarkably stable over periods up to 11 years so that, in the Manchester sample, GDS scores on first administration of TB significantly and negatively predict TB cognitive test scores up to 11 years later. Further analyses to examine the longitudinal associations between time trajectories of depression scores and cognitive test scores are currently in progress.

A possible explanation why negative correlations between scores on the GDS and cognitive performance endure over a decade or longer is that depression is associated with higher levels of cortisol activity. Elderly individuals with maintained high levels of cortisol are at an increased risk of brain atrophy (e.g. Lupien & McEwen, 1997) particularly of the hippocampus and amygdala, and so also to accelerated cognitive decline in later life (e.g. Belanoff, Kalchzan, Sund, Ficek, Schatzberg, 2001). Collection of blood and analyses of blood chemistry and saliva samples described below have allowed assessment of cortisol levels. Collection of salivary cortisol is described below and analyses of relationships between self-reported stress and depression and corticosteroid levels are in progress.

Another possible explanation for the long persistence of dysphoria is that levels of difficulties encountered in everyday life may be associated with unchanging aspects of lifestyle. For example the poor tend to remain poor. Scores on depression inventories may also reflect severe though relatively transitory reactions to emotionally disturbing events such as bereavement and abrupt attenuation of social support. When investigating associations between depression and cognition it is important to distinguish between the effects of lifestyle, of relatively brief episodes of depression that are reactions to traumata such as bereavement, and of more persistent depressive states that may have no ascertainable external cause. For this reason all volunteers also completed a questionnaire listing 46 different "Stressful Life Events", rating each for frequency of occurrence during the last 12 months and also, on a 5-point scale, for the relative level of stress caused. Comparisons between scores on this inventory and on the Beck and GDS now allow comparisons of the effects of reactions to transitory events and of long-lasting mood states on cognitive performance.

Other self-rating questionnaires

Longitudinal studies in cognitive gerontology would be much easier to carry out, and would yield much richer data if people could accurately report their levels of competence in their daily lives. Information on possible changes in the reliability of cognitive self-monitoring in later life would also provide direct evidence as to whether age affects this, and other, "central executive" functions (Burgess, 1997). For these reasons the first waves of recruits in both Manchester and Newcastle were given the Broadbent Cognitive Failures Questionnaire (CFQ; Broadbent, Cooper, Fitzgerald, & Parkes, 1982) and the Sunderland and Harris Memory Failures Questionnaire (MFQ; Sunderland, Harris, & Gleave, 1983). In addition 683 members of the first wave of Manchester recruits were also given the Short Inventory of Mental Lapses (SIMUL, see Reason, 1993). Scores on the CFQ and MFQ did not differ across age groups (Rabbitt & Abson, 1990) and, on the SIMUL, the numbers of reported cognitive lapses significantly declined with age (Reason, 1993). On all three questionnaires the numbers of lapses reported were unrelated to objective scores on the cognitive tests in TA, but were positively correlated with scores on the Beck depression index (Rabbitt & Abson, 1990). Volunteers' selfassessments of their cognitive competence during their daily lives seem to reflect their current levels of self-esteem and self-confidence rather than their objective levels of mental ability.

As a further check on the relationships between Age and accuracy of self-report, a subset of Newcastle volunteers who had just taken TA were asked to evaluate their levels of performance on the three memory tests that they had completed. Their self-ratings correlated modestly but significantly with their objective performance and this relationship was stronger for more able individuals with higher scores on the two AH4 intelligence tests (Rabbitt & Abson, 1991). These and other similar findings (e.g. Herrman, 1982) suggest that people cannot make accurate absolute judgements of their own abilities, but can assess themselves in respect of their own success in meeting the demands of particular tasks, or of their idiosyncratic lifestyles. They can also assess themselves relative to the observed performance of others. So, though individuals' self-ratings may provide reasonably valid assessments of their performance relative to their age-peers and to the demands of their daily lives, as they grow older their reference groups change and the demands that their lives make upon them may also alter and become more lenient. Consequently, as individuals grow older their self-ratings may remain stable or even become unrealistically optimistic although their abilities objectively decline. For similar reasons when volunteers are asked to rate their general health status on a 5-point scale from "Very Poor" to "Very Good" their subjective ratings do not change although their objectively assessed health declines (McInnes & Rabbitt, 1997). This seems to happen because people of all ages tend to evaluate their own health status against their age-peers. Since volunteers for longitudinal studies are atypically fit members of their generations, their self-ratings probably reflect a genuine relative advantage over their age-peers but do not sensitively track changes in their own status. Rabbitt, Maylor, McInnes, Bent, and Moore (1995) explored and summarised these and other limitations of self-report questionnaires as tools for studying

Table 11.2 Complete List of Self-Rating Inventories Given in Newcastle and Manchester.

Personal Detail Questionnaire
Version 1
Version 2
Version 3
Beck Depression
Broadbent Cognitive Failure
Sunderland & Harris
Self Awareness
Karasek Job Description
Negative Life Events
EPQ
Yesavage Geriatric Depression
Personality in Intellectual Aging Contexts
Education Questionnaire
Cornell Medical Index Q

cognitive changes in old age. Because their value as objective measures of competence fell into question administration of the CFQ, the MFQ and the SIMUL these questionnaires were discontinued.

To investigate how individuals in both testing centres perceived the extent of their autonomy and self-determination during their daily lives all completed the Karasek (1979) job description questionnaire. They also completed the Eysenck and Eysenck (1964) Personality Inventory. Preliminary analyses of relationships between these measures in the present and in other large longitudinal studies are described by Austin et al. (2002). Table 11.2 lists these and all other questionnaires on which data have been collected during the study.

Neuropsychological tests administered to sub-sets of participants

Models for age-related functional changes in cognitive performance have been derived from opposing premises of global and of local effects. Those predicated on the assumption that all mental abilities are affected by the same global functional changes assume that changes in some unique performance characteristic of the functional cognitive system such as information processing speed (Salthouse, 1991) or general fluid intelligence (Deary, 2000) entrain changes in all other measurable performance indices (but see commentary by Rabbitt, 1996). Modular models have been prompted by observations that old age affects particular areas of the brain, such as the hippocampus and frontal and pre-frontal cortex, earlier and more severely than others (e.g. Gur, Gur, Orbist, Skolnik, & Reivitch, 1987; Haugh & Eggers, 1991; Scheibel & Scheibel, 1975; Shaw et al., 1984). This has provoked speculations that the particular cognitive functions that these areas support must suffer earlier and more severe age related impairments. To check this, during 1989, 809

Newcastle residents who were aged from 60 to 86 years when members of the first wave of 1983/1984 recruits to the study were given the CANTAB, a battery of computerised neuropsychological tests which are designed to sensitivelydetect changes in frontal and executive function and in working memory (see Owen, Downes, Sahakian, Polkey, & Robbins, 1990; Robbins & Sahakian, 1991; Sahakian & Owen, 1992). Robbins et al. (1998) made cross-sectional comparisons between these members of the Newcastle sample and young adults and found graded agerelated declines in performance on most tests. Analyses suggested that the most substantial difference between individuals younger and older than 70 years was on an attentional shifting task, analogous to the Wisconsin Card – Sorting test, which is believed to be sensitive to frontal lobe damage. The overall age-related declines in performance on the CANTAB tests can be partly, but not entirely, explained in terms of the observed, cotemporaneous decline in scores on the AH4 intelligence tests and on the Culture Fair Test used in the longitudinal test batteries. Subsequent principal components analyses of these data by Robbins et al. (1997, 1998) identified four factors that together accounted for more than 60% of the variance. The dominant factor equated with general learning and memory ability and loaded heavily on intelligence test scores, but Age was most strongly represented in a second factor, more directly related to speed of responding.

Eleven years later during 2001/2002, 156 surviving members of this sample again took the CANTAB providing new longitudinal data on age-related changes in performance on an uniquely well validated battery of neuropsychological tests that can also be related to rates of change on all of the other cognitive measures used during the study.

Other sub-groups of individuals have been screened on other batteries of neuropsychological tests that are, purportedly, useful measures of damage to pre-frontal and medio-temporal areas of the brain. Table 11.2 shows the schedule of initial and subsequent screenings on these measures.

Screening of other large sub-sets of volunteers on further, different, physiological and cognitive measures

A substantial literature confirms modest but statistically robust associations between cognitive function in later life and simple indices of physiological efficiency, such as visual and auditory sensory acuity (Anstey, Luszcz, & Sanchez, 2001), muscle strength (Anstey, Lord, & Williams, 1997) and forced expiratory volume (Anstey, 1999). Scores on simple physiological markers can be combined to yield indices of "bioage" (Anstey & Smith, 1999). Such associations are informative because they suggest that even very simple physiological indices can act as markers for the progress of biological changes that proceed at different rates in different individuals. This makes it meaningful to distinguish between "calendar ageing" that proceeds at the same rate for all individuals and "functional ageing" that proceeds at different rates in different individuals and is jointly determined by complex interactions between genetic and environmental factors and the lifetime accumulation of pathologies and traumata (see Holland & Rabbitt, 1991; Rabbitt, 1982, 2004). Lindenberger and Potter (1998) suggest that rather than examining the relative strengths of simple correlations between age and indices efficiency it is more informative to estimate what proportion of the total, age-related variance in cognitive function between individuals is predicted by biological or other markers. They suggest a method of computing this "shared over simple variance". Baltes and Lindenberger (1997) and Lindenberger and Baltes (1994) applied this method to empirical data and found that up to 90% of the ageassociated variance in scores on tests of general fluid intelligence and up to 70% of the ageassociated variance in scores on memory tests may be predicted by scores on simple tests of vision, hearing and gait. One possible explanation for these strong associations is that even simple biological markers can be sensitive indices of changes in the central nervous system that jointly affect performance on cognitive, sensory and simple motor tasks and so of the progress of biological ageing of the brain and central nervous system.

It is important to note that however robust correlations may be they cannot uncritically be taken as evidence for functional associations. This is particularly the case in ageing research, where the passage of time can affect different aspects of performance for quite unrelated reasons. For example one explanation for Baltes and Lindenberger's (1997) finding of strong associations between hearing acuity and age-related changes in intelligence test scores might be that both are affected by the same central changes. A different explanation is that hearing losses in old age also strongly reflect mechanical damage to the cochlea hair cells cumulated over years of life, and so are functionally unrelated to the central changes that result in changes in IQ test performance. Since both factors certainly affect hearing in old age an unknown proportion of the common variance between age-related, losses in hearing and in intelligence test scores is not due to commonality of functional aetiology (see discussion of this issue by Rabbitt, 2004).

To further investigate these relationships, 600 members of the Manchester sample have been given tests of visual acuity in normal illumination, dim illumination and glare; pure tone threshold; hand grip strength; leg muscle strength measured by dynamic thrust; balance as measured both by sway on a recording platform and, independently, also by a widely used clinical test of balance and mobility in elderly people (Tinetti, 1986; Tinetti & Glinter, 1988) and a test of expelled respiratory volume. Preliminary analyses broadly replicate the conclusions of Baltes and Lindenberger (1997) and Lindenberger and Baltes (1994). All physiological tests, but especially the Tinetti (1986) clinical assessment scale of balance and mobility and simple Snellen tests of visual acuity under normal illumination proved excellent markers for age-associated change in most perceptual-motor tasks and, using Lindenberger and Potter's (1998) method of estimating age-related variance, jointly accounted for over 90% of age-associated variance in fluid intelligence. The Tinnetti test battery, a test of visual acuity and a test of expelled respiratory volume were again administered, during 2002/2003 to all 608 members of the Manchester sample who have continued with the longitudinal study since 1984/1986. The resulting data will allow measures of levels of performance on these physiological markers to be considered as end points of rates of change in cognitive function over a period of 17 years.

Measures of general health

Apart from these simple biological indices changes in volunteers' general health have been followed by biennial administrations of the Cornell Medical Index (CMI; Brodman, Erdman, & Wolff, 1949). This includes detailed checklists of symptoms of Physical and Mental pathologies. During the study CMI scores have been validated against intensive physical clinical examinations of 300 volunteers by experienced geriatricians. CMI scores correlate at $r > .7$ with scores for physical examinations (see Pendleton, Horan, Jones, McInnes, & Rabbitt, submitted). Repeated screenings on the CMI detailed in Table 11.3, have allowed computations of test/retest reliability which is found to vary between $r = .8$ and $r = .7$, understandably declining as intervals between CMI administrations increase.

A voluminous literature shows that a variety of particular pathologies, common in old age, are associated with significant, though modest, reductions in cognitive performance (see review by Holland & Rabbitt, 1991). In the present sample Bent, Rabbitt, and Metcalf (2000) found robust negative associations between the presence of late onset diabetes and cognitive function in members of the Newcastle/Manchester sample. Degrees of impact of

Table 11.3 Neuropsychological Test Batteries.

Test Battery	*1st Test N (date)*	*Retest 1 N (date)*	*Retest 2 N (date)*	*Retest 3 N (date)*
CANTAB	Total 809 (1989, 1990)			
Full Battery	268 (1989, 1990)	81 (2001–2002)		
Reduced Battery	809 (1989, 1990)	156 (2001–2002)		
Neuropsych A	277 (1992)	145 (1994)	75 (2003)	55 (2003)
Neuropsych B	277 (1994)	186 (2003)		
Neuropsych C	277 (1995)	133 (2003)		

Note: Key: Neuropsych A = Brixton Spatial Anticipation Test; Hayling Sentence Completion Test; Category Cue Memory Test; Verbal Fluency (FAS) Test; Trailmaking; Proverbs; Cognitive Estimates; People Test; Doors Test; Shapes Test; Names Test.

Neuropsych B = All Neuropsych A; Plus Cognitive Estimates; Hayling Sentence Completion; Category Cue; Verbal Fluency; Proverbs.

Neuropsych C = All Neuropsych A; Plus Memory Scan – Targets; Frontal Scanning; Rey-Osterreith Test.

diabetes on cognition varied with success of case management. Rabbitt, Bent, and McInnes (1997) also found significant negative associations between cognitive function, calendar age and self-reported general health status and with amount of use prescribed medications in a sub-set of 1100 Newcastle volunteers. CMI scores updated throughout the course of the study now allow examination relationships between changes in general health status and rates of change in cognitive function over a period of 17 years in individuals who were, on initial entry to the study, aged between 49 and 92 years.

Demographic and other background data

Descriptions of the process of cognitive ageing are incomplete without information about environmental factors that may determine both baseline levels of function and rates of decline. For example there is strong evidence that levels of socio-economic advantage and education determine longevity (e.g. Snowden, Ostwald, Kane, & Keenan, 1989). Levels of physical and social activity affect both mortality and cognitive efficiency in old age (e.g. Arbuckle, Gold, & Andres, 1986; Hayslip, 1988; Schaie, 1990). We need to determine how these factors affect trajectories of age-related change, and also how the demands of individuals' lives, and the success with which they meet them, alter as they grow older. Accordingly, when they were first recruited all volunteers completed a "Personal Details Questionnaire" (PDQ) in which they recorded their levels of education, income, household size, incidence and causes of mortality among parents and siblings, general health status and particular pathologies, accidents and traumata, history of medical treatments and of hospital attendances and surgery and their current and lifetime use of alcohol and tobacco. Volunteers have also recorded details of the daily, weekly and monthly amounts and specific kinds of physical activity and the number and nature of social interactions that they experience. They also described the number and nature of their different occupations, hobbies and pastimes and the amounts of time per week or month spent pursuing them, gave details of how they spend their time during an average day and kept diet and sleep diaries (see preliminary results by Minors, Atkinson, Bent, Rabbitt, & Waterhouse, 1998). Volunteers have updated this information approximately every 3 years throughout the study to allow investigations of longitudinal associations between changes in health, and lifestyle and in cognitive function in later life.

Collection and preliminary analyses of biological and genetic data

During 2001/2002 biological samples were collected to allow analysis of relationships between summarised levels of physiological activity across a range of regulatory systems pertinent to disease risks and contemporaneous cognitive status and previously measured rates of change over 17 years. Parameters analysed include serum total cholesterol and HDL cholesterol (markers that influence the levels of atherosclerosis); blood plasma levels of glycosylated hemoglobin (an integrated measure of glucose metabolism over time); urinary dihydroepiandrosterone sulphate (DHEA-S; a functional hypothalamo-pituitary-adrenal axis antagonist); Overnight urinary cortisol excretion (integrated measure of HPA axis activity); Overnight urinary adrenaline and noradrenaline (integrated indices of sympathetic nervous activity). These parameters are standardised to those taken from other longitudinal studies of successful ageing and can be used in the attempt to identify links between changes in cognitive and physical performance with age. In addition to these measures indices were taken of levels of plasma Il-6 (indicator of innate immune defences); differential T cell populations (ratio of CD4/ CD8 cell numbers changes with age and reflects immunosenescence); differential white blood cell count, which is a good index of general health status at time of sampling.

Elderly individuals with year-on-year increases in cortisol are at an increased risk of brain atrophy (Lupien & McEwen, 1997) With a view to examining this association investigators took diurnal measurements of salivary cortisol, the profile of which indicates a more detailed picture of HPA axis activity and complements urinary measures. These data will also enable us to correlate cognitive performance with a much more detailed picture of age-dependent physiological measures.

Collection of DNA from 2400 members of the Manchester and Newcastle samples during 1999/ 2002 has allowed analysis of relationships between genetic markers and rates of change in cognitive performance over time. This work has begun to appear (e.g. Pendleton et al., 2002).

The apolipoprotein E4 genotype has been reported to be a risk factor for development of sporadic cases of Alzheimer's disease (Wrelkin, 1996). In addition to this some recent studies suggest a relationship between the presence of apolipoprotein E4 and cognitive decline in older adults without dementia (Berr et al., 1996; Feskens et al., 1994; Jonker, Schmand, Lindeboom, Havekes, & Launer, 1998; Small, Basun, & Backman, 1998; Staehelin, Perrig-Chiello, Mitrache, Miserez, & Perrig, 1999; Yaffe, Cauley, Sands, & Browner, 1997). There is also one report relating the presence of apolipoprotein E2 genotype and protection from cognitive decline (Hyman et al., 1996). However, a number of reports find no such effect of Apolipoprotein E4 genotype on cognitive decline (Mayeux, Small, Tang, Tycko, & Stern, 2001; Small et al., 2000; Smith et al., 1998).

A group of 767 members of the Manchester sample were genotyped for apolipoprotein E (Pendleton et al., 2002). These data were related to cross-sectional and longitudinal trends in the Heim intelligence test score (AH4-1) using previously reported random-effects models (Rabbitt et al., 2001). There were no significant differences in mean scores for presence compared to absence of the apolipoprotein E4 or E2 genotypes (p = .48 and .51, respectively). This study does not demonstrate a link between intelligence and apolipoprotein E genotype in older adults.

Previous studies screening for QTLs that influence general intelligence in healthy individuals have identified four loci, two of which are located within the genes insulin-like growth factor 2 receptor (IGF2R) and the Msx1 homeobox (Chorney et al., 1998; Fisher et al., 1999). Recently we reported the finding of another QTL associated with general intelligence that is located within exon 2 of the Cathepsin D (CTSD) gene (Payton et al., 2004). In the same group of 767 healthy adults, we observed a significant association ($p = .01$) between a functional C > T (Ala > Val) transition within exon 2 of the CTSD gene that increases the secretion of pro-CTSD from the cell, and the AH4-1 score at initial testing on entry to the longitudinal study. The size of the effect was equal to a 3.3% lower intelligence test score for volunteers with the C > T transition. There was no significant effect on trend in intelligence test scores with increasing age. Interestingly CTSD is transported by IGF2R from the trans Golgi network to the lysosome.

Analyses of drop-out, and death demographic and cognitive predictors of drop-out and death

The rates of drop-out during the entire study can be followed by comparisons of the sample sizes for successive screenings on TA and TB in Table 11.1 As a guide to the extent and nature of drop-out we include results of a survey carried out in 1994. This found that rates of continuance with the study between 1983/1985 and 1994 in Newcastle had been 47% and between 1984/1985 and 1994 in Manchester had been 48%. Throughout the study whenever volunteers have declined to accept invitations to attend further testing sessions they have been warmly thanked for their previous participation and asked, as a final contribution, to give their reasons for withdrawal since these provide further important information. Table 11.4 shows a breakdown of reasons for withdrawal given by the 84% of individuals who responded to this request between 1983 and 1994.

Table 11.4 Newcastle and Manchester Panels – Totals Deceased and Withdrawn Including Withdrawal Reasons.

Total deceased	*Total withdrawn*	*1*	*2*	*3*	*4*	*5*	*6*	*7*	*8*	*9*	*10*	*11*
Newcastle												
217	1094	173	373	227	20	33	46	22	5	18	109	68
Manchester												
128	810	60	27	86	26	18	28	17	6	12	18	512

Note: Key: 1: ill health; 2: no longer interested; 3: moved away; 4: transport difficulties; 5: worsening mobility; 6: responsibilities; 7: failing eyesight; 8: failing hearing; 9: bereavement and change of lifestyle; 10: other reasons; 11: not known.

Volunteers who withdrew between 1983 and 1994, were retrospectively identified as older, from less advantaged socio-economic groups and fewer years of education than those who continued with the study. They also had lower scores on the AH4 (1) and (2) intelligence tests and on all cognitive tests (Rabbitt, Donlan, Watson, et al., 1993; Rabbitt, Watson, Donlan, Bent, & McInnes, 1994). This confirms findings from many other studies that individuals who dropout of longitudinal studies are markedly less advantaged on a number of criteria than are those who continue, so that the longer a study lasts the more likely it is that surviving participants progressively represent an elite sub-group who are more affluent, better-educated, more able and more healthy than the average for the population from which they are drawn. All longitudinal studies of cognitive change that have failed to compute the effects of drop-out have, by this token, grossly underestimated the true mean rate of decline with age. We shall also show below that neglect of drop-out grossly underestimates the marked increase in variation in cognitive performance between individuals that occurs as a population ages (see also earlier analysis by Rabbitt, Diggle, Smith, Holland, & McInnes, 2001).

In an elderly population one of the most frequent reasons for drop-out is death. In 1994 H.M. Registrar Generals' Office provided a complete census of deaths, including causes of deaths, for 463 members of the Newcastle and Manchester volunteer panels who had died since they were initially recruited in 1983. When scores on Test Battery A between 1983 and 1985 volunteers who subsequently died before 1995 had significantly higher scores on the Beck, Ward, MendelsohnMock, and Erbaugh (1961) depression scale and lower scores on all cognitive tests than their coevals who survived. This has provided the first evidence that cognitive changes can be detected up to 11 years before death (Rabbitt et al., 2002). Analyses of relationships between antecedent cognitive abilities and proximate causes of death given on Death Certificates found no significant differences between the two most common terminal conditions, cardiovascular problems and malignancies. A complete census of all deaths between 1983 and 2004 is currently in progress and is being analysed to determine the rate, and the nature, of cognitive changes during the years preceding death over a period of 20 years. Further analyses will determine how relationships between mortality, lifestyle and genetic factors affect the rates and nature of cognitive change in later life.

Development of Improved Models for Analysis of Longitudinal Data and Preliminary Findings from the University of Manchester Data-Set

Excellent longitudinal studies have estimated average trajectories for age-related changes in general intelligence, memory or information processing speed (e.g. Arenberg, 1974; Colsher & Wallace, 1991; Heron & Chown, 1967; Hertzog & Schaie, 1988; Hultsch, Hertzog, Small, McDonald-Miszczak, & Dixon, 1992; Johannsen, Zarit, & Berg, 1992; Lansen, 1997; Owens, 1953,

1966; Powell, 1994; Schaie, 1996; Schaie & Labouvie-Vief, 1974; Schaie & Strother, 1968; Schaie & Willis, 1993; Terman & Oden, 1947). However estimates of average changes in performance are of much less practical and theoretical interest than are the reasons for the marked increases in variability between individuals as a population ages (Hultsch et al., 2002; Morse, 1993; Rabbitt, 1982, 1993a; Rabbitt, Osman, Stollery, & Moore, 2001). It is widely recognized that one reason for this variability is the differential impacts on cognitive performance of factors such as educational and socioeconomic advantage (e.g. Bosworth, Schaie, & Willis, 1999; Evans et al., 1993; Forner, 1972; White, Katzman, et al., 1994); gender (e.g. Bosworth et al., 1999; Voitenko & Tokar, 1983); general health status (e.g. Bell, Rose, & Damon, 1972; Birren, Butler, Greenhouse, Sokoloff, & Yarrow, 1963; Costa & McCrae, 1980; McInnes & Rabbitt, 1997; Rabbitt et al., 1997) and specific pathologies such as diabetes (e.g. Bent et al., 2000; Hertzog, Schaie, & Gribbin, 1978; Holland & Rabbitt, 1991); degree of maintenance of physical mobility and engagement in everyday activities (e.g. Clark, 1960; Clement, 1974; Dirken, 1972; McInnes & Rabbitt, 1997). Much variation between individuals in performance in old age is, genetically determined (e.g. Bank & Jarvik, 1978; Payton, Holland, Diggle, Rabbitt, et al., 2003; Pendleton et al., 2002; Terman & Oden, 1947, 1959). Independently of these factors there are also intrinsic individual differences in variability that are inversely related to levels of general mental ability (Rabbitt, Osman, Stollery, & Moore, 2001).

Because of obvious logistic problems most studies have only compared the performance, at a single time point, of individuals of different ages who have, and who have not previously experienced a particular condition or event: for example a specific pathology. Those studies that have attempted the more difficult and informative task of determining the effects of particular factors on *rates of change over time* have sometimes acknowledged, but not yet come to terms with three pervasive methodological problems.

One issue is that it is not sufficient to simply regress performance data across successive time/ assay points. Neglect of longitudinal correlations in performance across time-points can obviously lead to incorrect inference. A second problem is that because participants in longitudinal studies must repeatedly be given the same, or very similar tests, age-related declines can be masked by marked improvements due to practice. There have been useful acknowledgements of the implications of practice effects for the interpretation of longitudinal data (e.g. Schaie, 1988) but, so far, no solutions of the statistical problem of identifying the magnitudes of practice effects and of comparing them between different tasks. Nor, more seriously, have investigators taken practice effects into account when estimating the contributions of environmental, health and genetic factors to differences in rates of change between individuals.

Neglect of practice effects does not simply lead to severe underestimations of the effects of factors that depress cognitive performance and accelerate cognitive change. A compounding difficulty is that the sizes of practice effects vary widely with complex interactions between individuals' levels of ability, and so also with the ages at which they are assessed and with the level of difficulty, and perhaps the nature of the tasks on which they are compared. For example in very easy serial choice reaction time tasks practice effects are, counter-intuitively, larger for less than for more able individuals (Rabbitt, 1993b) but, in contrast, younger and more able individuals show much faster and greater gains on difficult video-games (Rabbitt et al., 1989). Thus during longitudinal studies practice effects may mask age-related declines on the simpler tasks on which older and less able individuals show more marked improvement, but exaggerate apparent age-related impairment on difficult tasks on which younger, but not older participants improve. Analyses that do not take practice into consideration certainly underestimate the true rates of age-related decline but may also give misleading impressions that age affects different tasks to different extents, provoking unwarranted conclusions that the mental abilities supporting these tasks age at different rates.

A third problem, of selective recruitment and selective drop-out, has been very widely recognized and discussed. During any longitudinal study selective drop-out can disguise both the true extent, and the pattern, of cognitive changes over time (see Baltes, 1968; Forner, 1972; Lachman, Lachman, & Taylor, 1982; Mason & Mason, 1973; Nesselrode & Baltes, 1979; Palmore, 1978; Schaie, Labouvie, & Barrett, 1973; Schlesselman, 1973a, 1973b; Schulsinger, Knop, & Mednick, 1981). If drop-out is neglected the true rate of cognitive change in the population is underestimated. More complex misinterpretations can also occur. For example older women tend to perform better than older men on verbal learning tasks (Rabbitt, Donlan, Watson, McInnes, & Bent, 1996), and men tend to dropout of longitudinal studies earlier than their female age-peers. So, unless gender differences in drop-out are taken into consideration true rates of decline on verbal learning tasks will be underestimated.

To discover whether drop-out differentially affects apparent rates of change in different tasks a useful exploratory step is to use correlational analyses to compare cross-sectional against longitudinal trends (e.g. Sliewski & Bushke, 1999; Zelinski & Burnight, 1997; Zelinski, Gilewski, & Stewart, 1993; Zelinski & Stewart, 1998). Unfortunately this is not a complete solution. Comparisons of patterns of longitudinal and cross-sectional correlations between tasks at different time-points during a study do not testfor some interesting possibilities: For example whether substantial increases in variability between members of an ageing population have been obscured because drop-outs have not only included participants with lower overall levels of performance, but also those who have maintained high relatively high performance but with steeper trajectories of age-related decline. More directly, because drop-out reduces variance by removing poor performers, neglect of drop-out means that we fail to determine the true extent of age-related variability and, implicitly, the true sizes of the effects of variables, such as good or poor health, that retard or accelerate decline.

For these reasons, and to guide other investigators who may be interested in analysing he dataset, we thought it useful to show that interpretation of the data from the University of Manchester longitudinal study requires development of new analytic models to identify and take into consideration both practice and drop-out fects. The next section of this paper describes application of random effects analyses of the Manchester and Newcastle Test Battery A data sets to estimate, and take account of practice and drop-out effects (for a full account see Rabbitt, Diggle, Holland, et al., 2003, submitted). We also describe some new substantive findings from these analyses.

Analysis of longitudinal data from Test Battery A taking practice and drop-out effects into account

Technically, it is important to distinguish three different drop-out scenarios (Rubin, 1976):

Completely random drop-out: the drop-out process is independent of the measurement process.

Random drop-out: the drop-out process is dependent on the observed measurements prior to drop-out but is independent of the measurements that would have been observed had the participant not withdrawn.

Informative drop-out: the drop-out process is dependent on the measurements that would have been observed had the participant not dropped out. Not surprisingly analyses made under the informative drop-out assumption are fraught with difficulty. The results of such analyses typically depend on modelling assumptions that are difficult or impossible to check from observed data. This is especially the case for the kind of unbalanced data that necessarily arise in observational studies where even the identification of a firm drop-out time is extremely difficult.

At the opposite extreme analyses under the assumption of completely random drop-out are generally straightforward because no distinction need be made between measurements that are unavailable because of drop-out, and those that are unavailable because they were never intended. That is, completely random drop-out implies that the incomplete data can simply be treated as if from an unbalanced experimental design, with no commonality to the times at which measurements are made on different subjects.

The simplicity of analysis that is gained if completely random drop-out is assumed is bought at a price because, if it is invalid then so may be the resulting inferences about the measurement process. However, if likelihood-based methods of inference are used validity is retained under the weaker assumption of random drop-out. This is important because longitudinal data are typicall correlated over time and this means that even when the true drop-out process is informative the most recent measurements made on a given subject before drop-out are partially predictive of the missing measurements after drop-out. Thus by allowing for the effects of these measurements on drop-out (which is what the random drop-out assumption implies) we can partly compensate for the missing information. (See, e.g. Scharfstein, Rotnitzky, & Robins, 1999, and the associated discussion).

An important consequence is that for longitudinal data with drop-out there is no reason why a fitted mean response curve should track the observed mean response trajectory of the survivors. On the contrary, under the assumption of random drop-outs a model fitted by likelihood-based methods estimates what the mean response would have been if it had been possible to follow up the entire study population. In contrast, the observed means are estimating the mean response conditional on not dropping out before the time in question. The unconditional and conditional means coincide only if the data are uncorrelated in time, or if the drop-out process is completely random. We would argue that neither of these assumptions is plausible for the data that we analyse below. We therefore conclude that likelihood-based analyses under a random drop-out assumption give a sensible analytic strategy because they focus on the complete study population, rather than on the progressively self-selected sub-population of subjects who do not drop-out of the study.

Data from the University of Manchester longitudinal study were analysed, allowing for selective drop-out and for practice effects. This allows reassessment of the particular issue of the extent to which marked individual differences in trajectories of change result in corresponding variability between individuals increase as a population ages.

Method

Participants

The data analysed were obtained from successive assessments on Test Battery A (see above) of 5911 active community residents from Newcastle-uponTyne (n = 3265) and Greater Manchester (n = 2646) who were aged from 49 to 92 years on entry. Years of education varied from 5 to 21 (M = 11.7, SD = 4.2). Numbers of health complaints recorded on the Cornell Medical Index (Broadman et al., 1949) varied from 2 to 18 (M = 6.4, SD = 3.2). Tables 11.1 a and 1b show the time-pattern of successive waves of recruitment and the subsequent re-testing schedule by city of residence. Subjects experienced the battery between 1 and 4 times depending on when they were recruited and whether, and when, they dropped out. Demographics of this sample at the time of recruitment are given in Table 11.5.

Classification of occupation in terms of the categories used by the Office of Population Census (1980) was used as an index of relative levels of socio-economic advantage.

Table 11.5 Mean (*SD*) Percent Correct Scores at Initial Test by Selected Demographics.

	Subjects, N = 5911	*M (SD)*					
		AH4-1	*AH4-2*	*MHA*	*MHB*	*CLN*	*FR*
Sex							
Female	4176 (71%)	47.5 (17.3)	42.9 (16.2)	66.2 (14.2)	48.5 (18.5)	70.4 (14.3)	28.0 (11.1)
Male	1735 (29%)	50.8 (17.8)	49.0 (17.0)	70.5 (14.1)	52.1 (18.5)	66.4 (15.0)	25.7 (11.1)
City							
Manchester	2646 (45%)	49.7 (17.8)	45.7 (16.9)	69.8 (13.8)	54.8 (17.9)	71.2 (14.0)	28.3 (11.6)
Newcastle	3265 (55%)	47.6 (17.3)	43.8 (16.4)	65.6 (14.5)	45.4 (18.0)	67.5 (14.9)	26.4 (10.8)
Social Class							
Category 1, professional	266 (4.5%)	61.5 (13.9)	59.5 (14.9)	79.0 (11.1)	63.5 (15.7)	71.8 (13.9)	29.5 (12.2)
Category 2, intermediate	1876 (31.7%)	56.4 (16.6)	51.0 (16.0)	74.1 (12.2)	58.3 (16.6)	73.0 (13.3)	30.3 (11.8)
Category 3(N), non-manual skilled	2080 (35.2%)	48.4 (14.9)	43.6 (14.3)	66.5 (12.4)	48.1 (16.3)	70.2 (13.6)	27.4 (1.4)
Category 3(M), Manual skilled	765 (12.9%)	38.6 (15.4)	37.5 (15.3)	60.7 (13.3)	40.3 (16.7)	63.0 (14.6)	22.7 (9.5)
Category 4, party skilled or	488 (8.3%)	34.7 (14.7)	33.5 (15.1)	55.9 (13.8)	34.9 (16.4)	61.3 (15.1)	22.0 (9.2)
Category 5, unskilled	436 (7.4%)	39.7 (17.9)	38.0 (17.4)	61.4 (16.5)	42.7 (19.9)	61.4 (17.9)	24.3 (10.8)
Missing/Uncoded							
Entry Age							
49-59	1418 (24%)	55.2 (17.2)	53.0 (16.2)	68.3 (13.9)	51.4 (18.0)	75.0 (13.2)	31.6 (12.2)
60-69	2910 (49%)	49.4 (16.7)	45.3 (15.6)	67.3 (14.1)	49.4 (18.3)	69.8 (13.8)	27.6 (10.6)
70-79	1431 (24%)	41.6 (16.5)	36.6 (14.7)	67.2 (15.0)	48.3 (19.4)	64.1 (14.5)	23.5 (9.9)
80 plus	152 (3%)	33.7 (15.6)	29.6 (12.8)	68.0 (15.3)	40.4 (19.7)	56.7 (17.2)	21.2 (10.9)

Procedure and Tests

The data analysed were from the Heim (1970) AH4-1 and AH4-2 intelligence tests and the Raven (1965) Mill Hill "A" and "B" (MHA and MHB) vocabulary tests, the Cumulative Verbal Learning (CVL) task and the Verbal Free Recall (VFR) task. These have been described above. Since the various tests have total scores ranging from 30 to 65, each participant's raw scores were converted to a percentage correct to provide a common measurement scale. Mean scores at entry, broken down by the selected demographic groups, are also shown in Table 11.5.

Individual scores on all occasions for the six tasks were converted to smooth non-parametric mean response curves as functions of age within each social class, giving an informal analysis of the population average age trend, ignoring effects of practice and dropout. For all tasks more greatly advantaged socioeconomic groups had higher overall scores on all cognitive tests. The mean trajectories of age-related changes in AH4-1 and AH4-2 showed approximately parallel and declining trends. Although the average CVL scores for a given social class were over two times greater than the corresponding VFR scores, the overall rates of decline for these two tasks were also similar, with smaller effects of socio-economic advantage than for the two AH4 tests. Means of MHA and MHB scores did not change with age.

Model Specification

The general class of model used to analyse these data is illustrated by an analysis of longitudinal changes in AH4 (1) and (2) scores reported by Rabbitt, Diggle, Smith, Holland, et al. (2001). Briefly, the analysis is based on a model which, for each cognitive test under consideration, combines a conventional multiple linear regression model for the mean response with a longitudinal model for the random variation about the mean in an individual's observed response sequence over time. In the regression part we include linear and quadratic terms for the change in the mean response with age in excess of 49 years together with adjustments for the average effects of practice, sex, socio-economic status, city of residence and year of entry to the study. The decision to centre the age variable on 49 years was taken because this was the youngest age recorded in the study. The meaning of the intercept parameter in the model is then that it gives the mean response for a 49-year-old woman, resident in Manchester, with socio-economic status C1, who entered to study in 1983 and is taking the test for the first time.

In the longitudinal part, we include subject specific random intercept and slope terms, A and B, respectively, and a residual term E. The meaning of the terms A and B is that an individual subject's response trajectory with increasing age deviates from the mean response amongst their peers by an amount A + B (age – 49), where A and B are drawn from a bivariate Normal distribution with means zero, standard deviations sigma_A and sigma_B, and correlation rho_AB. Thus, for example, an individual whose personal value of A is positive will show a consistently higher response than would be predicted by the average response for their peers; similarly, an individual whose personal value of B is positive will show a slower decline with increasing age (i.e. a less negative slope) than the average for their peers. The residual term E, which is drawn from a Normal distribution with mean zero and standard deviation sigma_E, represents the combination of all sources of unpredictable variation in an individual's observed sequence of test results. Its values for an individual subject on successive test occasions are therefore assumed to be uncorrelated, in contrast with the values of A and B, which a subject carries with them for the duration of the study.

Results

Analyses of Scores from Individual Tests in TA

A total of 5894–5899 subjects with at least one response measure were included in the AH4 and MH analyses. As mentioned above, the CVL and VFR tests were performed during a second session. Because substantial numbers withdrew after the first testing session of the first data collection only 5254 subjects had a CVL or a VFR result.

AH4-1 and AH4-2 Scores

The estimated mean effects for AH4 are summarized in Tables 11.6 and Table 11.7.

The AH4-1 intercept of 66.0 was 4.9 points higher than the AH4-2 intercept. The finding that both quadratic coefficients are negative indicates accelerated cognitive decline with age on both these tests. Extrapolating from the data shown in Tables 11.5 and 11.6 considering entry scores: on AH41 the average score for a 60-year-old would be 64.6, and for a 70-year-old 58.6 (a 6 point drop), falling to 46.5 (a further 12 point fall) for an 80year-old. On the AH4-2 task the corresponding scores would be 58.2, 52.1 (6 point drop) and 38.6 (a further 13 point drop).

Tables 11.6 and 11.7 show that the average amounts of improvement with practice between the first and second testing sessions are similar for the AH4-1 and AH4-2 tests (gains of 4.5 and 5.6 points, respectively). Between the second and the fourth session the gain fell to under 2.5 on AH4-1 but for AH4-2 the gain remained above 4.5.

On average Men performed significantly better than Women on both the AH4 tests. Socioeconomic advantage had marked effects. Tables 11.6 and 11.7 show a marked declining trend in AH4 response levels relative to the baseline socioeconomic category, C1, after adjusting for the other covariates in the

Table 11.6 AH4-1 Model Estimates.

Parameter	*Estimate*	*SE*	*t value*	*p value*	*95% Confidence interval*
A. Mean response model					
Intercept	66.03	1.53	43.08	<.001	63.03 to 69.03
age 49	0.04	0.05	0.74	.459	−0.07 to 0.15
$(\text{age } 49)^2$	−0.02	0.001	−17.57	<.001	−0.03 to −0.02
Improvement					
Second vs. First	4.51	0.16	27.58	<.001	4.19 to 4.83
Third vs. Third	2.21	0.21	10.28	<.001	1.79 to 2.63
Fourth vs. Third	1.90	0.36	5.25	<.001	1.19 to 2.61
Male vs. Female	2.20	0.44	5.02	<.001	1.34 to 3.07
Socio – economic status					
C2 vs. C1	−3.77	0.96	−3.94	<.001	−5.64 to −1.89
C3(N) vs. C1	−10.53	0.98	−10.72	<.001	−12.45 to −8.60
C3(M) vs. C1	−19.94	1.04	−19.19	<.001	−21.98 to −17.91
C4/5 vs. C1	−23.20	1.13	−20.56	<.001	−25.41 to −20.99
Missing	−19.12	1.16	−16.44	<.001	−21.40 to 16.84
Newcastle vs. Manchester	−3.20	1.07	−3.00	.003	−5.29 to −1.11
Entry Year					
1984 vs. 1983	0.71	0.64	1.12	.261	−0.53 to 1.96
1985 vs. 1983	−0.82	1.25	−0.65	.515	−3.27 to 1.64
1986 vs. 1983	−0.50	1.30	−0.39	.699	−3.05 to 2.04
1987 vs. 1983	−1.54	1.33	−1.16	.245	−4.41 to 1.06
1988 vs. 1983	1.97	0.74	2.65	.008	0.51 to 3.43
1989 vs. 1983	4.64	0.89	5.24	<.001	2.90 to 6.37
1990 vs. 1983	5.37	1.47	3.65	<.001	2.49 to 8.25
1991 vs. 1983	1.19	1.84	0.65	.516	−2.41 to 4.79
1992 vs. 1983	1.64	1.55	1.06	.289	−1.39 to 4.68
B. Covariance and Residual parameter					
σ_A	15.43				14.71 to 16.18
σ_B	0.41				0.36 to 0.47
ρ_{AB}	−0.51				−0.58 to −0.44
σ_E	5.71				5.58 to 5.84

model. The largest difference was between C1 and C4/5; on both AH4 tests participants in C4/5 scored at least 20 points less on average than did those in C1. Manchester residents had significantly higher average AH41 scores than Newcastle residents but this City effect was not significant for AH4-2 scores. It is expected that Socio-Economic Advantage (SEA) should affect overall levels of performance. However because SEA entails so many factors that contribute to longevity it is unexpected that it should have no apparent effect on *rate of cognitive change over time.*

Table 11.7 AH4-2 Model Estimates.

Parameter	*Estimate*	*SE*	*t value*	*p value*	*95% Confidence interval*
A. Mean response model					
Intercept	61.12	1.44	42.57	<.001	58.31 to 63.94
age 49	−0.17	0.06	−3.01	.003	−0.28 to −0.06
$(\text{age } 49)^2$	−0.02	0.00	−15.57	<.001	−0.02 to −0.02
Improvement					
Second vs. First	5.58	0.17	32.94	<.001	5.24 to 5.91
Third vs. Third	4.72	0.22	21.07	<.001	4.28 to 5.15
Fourth vs. Third	5.88	0.38	15.34	<.001	5.13 to 6.64
Male vs. Female	5.14	0.41	12.62	<.001	4.34 to 5.93
Socio – economic status					
C2 vs. C1	−5.96	0.89	−6.73	<.001	−7.70 to −4.23
C3(N) vs. C1	−11.36	0.91	−12.50	<.001	−13.14 to −9.58
C3(M) vs. C1	−17.58	0.96	−18.25	<.001	−19.47 to −15.69
C4/5 vs. C1	−20.37	1.04	−19.50	<.001	−22.42 to −18.33
Missing	−17.56	1.08	−16.22	<.001	−19.68 to −15.44
Newcastle vs. Manchester	−0.57	0.99	−0.58	.564	−2.51 to 1.37
Entry Year					
1984 vs. 1983	0.27	0.59	−0.46	.646	−1.52 to 0.88
1985 vs. 1983	2.22	1.16	1.91	.056	−0.05 to 4.50
1986 vs. 1983	2.58	1.21	2.14	.032	0.22 to 4.94
1987 vs. 1983	2.22	1.23	1.80	.071	−0.19 to 4.94
1988 vs. 1983	3.19	0.69	4.64	<.001	1.84 to 4.54
1989 vs. 1983	9.03	0.82	11.00	<.001	7.42 to 10.64
1990 vs. 1983	8.50	1.37	6.22	<.001	5.82 to 11.17
1991 vs. 1983	7.41	1.71	4.34	<.001	4.07 to 10.75
1992 vs. 1983	4.25	1.45	2.93	<.001	1.41 to 7.08
B. Covariance and Residual parameter					
σ_A	14.63				13.94 to 15.35
σ_B	0.43				0.38 to 0.49
ρ_{AB}	−0.58				−0.63 to −0.51
σ_E	6.22				6.09 to 6.36

Cumulative Verbal Learning and Verbal Free Recall Scores

Tables 11.8 and 11.9 summarise the results for these tests. The intercept estimate of 75.6 for CVL was more than double the 35.5 point score on VFR, which was the lowest score overall.

For both these tests, just as for the AH4 responses, the quadratic term was significantly negative, indicating accelerated decline with age. However, although significant the numerical value of the estimate was close to zero and is therefore not substantively important, that is, the estimated decline with age

Table 11.8 CVL Model Estimates

Parameter	*Estimate*	*SE*	*t value*	*p value*	*95% Confidence interval*
A. Mean response model					
Intercept	75.57	1.37	55.14	<.001	72.89 to 78.26
age 49	0.07	0.06	1.06	.290	−0.06 to 0.19
$(\text{age } 49)^2$	−0.02	0.00	−13.36	<.001	−0.03 to −0.02
Improvement					
Second vs. First	0.97	0.20	4.75	<.001	0.57 to 1.37
Third vs. Third	5.51	0.28	19.50	<.001	4.95 to 6.06
Fourth vs. Third	−3.16	0.48	−6.53	<.001	−4.11 to −2.21
Male vs. Female	−4.28	0.39	−11.01	<.001	−5.04 to −3.52
Socio – economic status					
C2 vs. C1	−0.58	0.82	−0.71	.478	−2.18 to −1.02
C3(N) vs. C1	−3.76	0.84	−4.47	<.001	−5.40 to −2.11
C3(M) vs. C1	−8.63	0.90	−9.61	<.001	−10.38 to −6.87
C4/5 vs. C1	−10.88	0.98	−11.09	<.001	−12.80 to −8.96
Missing	−9.12	1.16	−7.83	<.001	−11.40 to −6.84
Newcastle vs. Manchester	−1.09	0.97	−1.12	.262	−2.98 to 0.81
Entry Year					
1984 vs. 1983	4.57	0.54	8.53	<.001	3.52 to 5.62
1985 vs. 1983	6.96	1.12	6.23	<.001	4.77 to 9.14
1986 vs. 1983	4.98	1.15	4.33	<.001	2.73 to 7.23
1987 vs. 1983	6.05	1.19	5.10	<.001	3.72 to 8.37
1988 vs. 1983	8.31	0.74	11.25	<.001	6.86 to 9.75
1989 vs. 1983	7.59	0.77	9.88	<.001	6.09 to 9.10
1990 vs. 1983	7.97	1.27	6.27	<.001	5.48 to 10.46
1991 vs. 1983	4.49	1.64	3.05	<.001	−1.78 to 8.19
1992 vs. 1983	3.87	1.37	2.83	<.001	1.19 to 6.55
B. Covariance and Residual parameter					
σ_A	10.24				9.28 to 11.29
σ_B	0.49				0.44 to 0.56
ρ_{AB}	−0.45				−0.57 to −0.32
σ_E	7.59				7.43 to 7.76

Table 11.9 FR Model Estimates.

Parameter	*Estimate*	*SE*	*t value*	*p value*	*95% Confidence interval*
A. Mean response model					
Intercept	35.46	1.07	33.10	<.001	33.36 to 37.55
age 49	0.23	0.05	−4.41	<.001	−0.34 to −0.13
$(\text{age } 49)^2$	−0.01	0.00	−4.01	<.001	−0.01 to −0.00
Improvement					
Second vs. First	0.16	0.18	−0.91	.365	−0.51 to 0.19
Third vs. Third	1.96	0.24	8.14	<.001	1.49 to 2.44
Fourth vs. Third	−0.93	0.40	−2.33	.020	−1.72 to −0.15
Male vs. Female	−2.07	0.29	−7.01	<.001	−2.65 to −1.49
Socio – economic status					
C2 vs. C1	−0.05	0.62	−0.07	.942	−1.18 to −1.27
C3(N) vs. C1	−2.99	0.64	−4.65	<.001	−4.24 to −1.73
C3(M) vs. C1	−5.83	0.68	−8.56	<.001	−7.17 to −4.50
C4/5 vs. C1	−6.71	0.75	−8.99	<.001	−8.17 to −5.25
Missing	−4.99	0.91	−5.48	<.001	−6.77 to −3.21
Newcastle vs. Manchester	−1.21	0.72	−1.68	.092	−2.61 to 0.20
Entry Year					
1984 vs. 1983	1.21	0.41	2.94	<.001	−0.41 to 2.02
1985 vs. 1983	1.35	0.84	1.61	.107	−0.29 to 3.00
1986 vs. 1983	0.52	0.86	0.61	.545	−1.17 to 2.22
1987 vs. 1983	1.06	0.89	1.18	<.237	−0.69 to 2.80
1988 vs. 1983	2.30	0.56	4.09	<.001	1.20 to 3.41
1989 vs. 1983	1.77	0.58	3.03	<.001	0.63 to 2.92
1990 vs. 1983	2.07	0.98	2.12	.034	0.15 to 3.98
1991 vs. 1983	2.11	1.26	1.67	.094	−0.36 to 4.58
1992 vs. 1983	0.11	1.05	0.10	.917	−1.95 to 2.17
B. Covariance and Residual parameter					
σ_A	9.67				8.95 to 10.46
σ_B	0.23				0.16 to 0.31
ρ_{AB}	−0.72				−0.78 to −0.65
σ_E	7.00				6.87 to 7.15

was almost linear. As an example, the average CVL entry score would be 73.6 for a 60-year-old, 68.6 for a 70-year-old, falling to 60.2 for an 80-year-old, that is, falls of 5.0 and 8.4 points. The corresponding VFR scores of 32.4, 28.6 and 23.8 points equate to declines of 3.8 and 4.8 points over the successive 10-year intervals. The average improvement on second experience of CVL was 1.0. This, although statistically significant, is slight. The difference for VFR was negative and non-significant. On the third and fourth testing occasions an improvement followed by a decline occurred for both these tests.

On both the CVL and VFR tests women performed significantly better than men. Differences in trends for socio-economic categories (Cs) were much less marked on these tests than on the AH4 tests. Again, the largest difference was between C1 and C4/5 (differences of 10.9% and 6.7% points for CVL and VFR, respectively). On CVL and VFR, as on all other tests, average scores were higher for Manchester than for Newcastle residents, but in this case these differences were not significant.

Mill Hill "A" and "B" Scores

Tables 11.10 and 11.11 show the Mill Hill results. The intercept estimate for the MHA test was 80.6, which was higher than for any other test and was 15.4 points higher than the intercept estimate of 65.1 for the MHB test.

Assuming that the age trajectories for MHA and MHB are described by a linear term there was a non-significant decline of 0.03 for MHA and a significant decline of -0.06% points per year for MHB. Assuming a mean rate corresponding to the lower confidence interval for MHB, this equates to a decline of only 1.2% over 10 years.

Tables 11.10 and 11.11 show negligible positive or negative changes of 1.5 or less on MHA at all repeat testings, and on MHB for the first and second repeat testings. The estimated improvement of 9% points on MHB on the last testing occasion is an unexplained anomaly. Scores on both the MHA and MHB tests were significantly higher for men than for women and for Manchester residents than for Newcastle residents. The differences between Socio-Economic Categories (Cs) were substantial, and were comparable in magnitude to the effect sizes for AH4. On MHA the average entry year scores from 1984 onwards were lower, but not significantly so, than was the mean score for those starting in 1983. There was no clear pattern for MHB.

Comparison of Amounts of Improvement With Practice Across Tasks

Rates of decline with age were similar for AH4-1, AH4-2 and CVL. The rate of decline was essentially linear for VFR and the mean MH scores remained stable over time.

The size of the average practice effect on the second occasion varied between tasks: gains of over 4.5% points on the AH4 tests contrast with

Table 11.10 MHA Model Estimates

Parameter	*Estimate*	*SE*	*t value*	*p value*	*95% Confidence interval*
A. Mean response model					
Intercept	80.56	1.33	60.61	<.001	77.96 to 83.16
age 49	−0.03	0.02	−1.41	.155	−0.07 to −0.01
Improvement					
Second vs. First	1.07	0.16	6.57	<.001	0.75 to 1.39
Third vs. Third	−1.48	0.21	−7.02	<.001	−1.90 to −1.07
Fourth vs. Third	1.47	0.34	4.32	<.001	0.80 to 2.131
Male vs. Female	1.89	0.39	4.82	<.001	1.12 to 2.66
Socio – economic status					
C2 vs. C1	−3.18	0.85	−3.73	<.001	−4.85 to −1.51
C3(N) vs. C1	−17.09	0.93	−18.41	<.001	−18.91 to −15.27
C3(M) vs. C1	−10.35	0.88	−11.82	<.001	−12.06 to −8.63
C4/5 vs. C1	−21.11	1.01	−20.95	<.001	−23.08 to −19.14
Missing	−16.20	1.04	−15.61	<.001	−18.23 to −14.16
Newcastle vs. Manchester	−4.21	0.96	−4.39	<.001	−6.08 to −2.33
Entry Year					
1984 vs. 1983	−0.44	0.57	−0.78	.433	−1.55 to 0.66
1985 vs. 1983	−1.44	1.12	−1.28	.200	−3.64 to 0.76
1986 vs. 1983	−1.72	1.16	−1.48	.139	−4.00 to 0.56
1987 vs. 1983	−2.15	1.19	−1.81	.071	−4.47 to 0.18
1988 vs. 1983	−0.18	0.66	−0.27	.790	−1.47 to 1.12
1989 vs. 1983	−1.24	0.79	−1.56	.120	−2.79 to 0.32
1990 vs. 1983	−1.14	1.32	−0.86	.388	−3.74 to 1.45
1991 vs. 1983	−2.56	1.65	−1.55	.121	−5.79 to 0.68
1992 vs. 1983	−2.57	1.40	−1.84	.066	−5.30 to 0.17
B. Covariance and Residual parameter					
σ_A	11.87				11.59 to 12.09
σ_E	6.07				5.97 to 6.18

Table 11.11 MHB Model Estimates.

Parameter	*Estimate*	*SE*	*t value*	*p value*	*95% Confidence interval*
A. Mean response model					
Intercept	65.13	1.59	40.91	<.001	62.01 to 68.25
age 49	−0.06	0.03	−2.35	.019	−0.12 to −0.01
Improvement					
Second vs. First	0.97	0.23	4.28	<.001	0.53 to 1.42
Third vs. Third	−1.31	0.30	−4.39	<.001	−1.89 to −0.76
Fourth vs. Third	9.31	0.49	18.93	<.001	8.34 to 10.27
Male vs. Female	0.94	0.47	2.01	.045	0.02 to 1.86
Socio – economic status					
C2 vs. C1	−4.28	1.02	−4.21	<.001	−6.27 to −2.29
C3(N) vs. C1	−13.60	1.04	−13.03	<.001	−15.64 to −11.55
C3(M) vs. C1	−21.64	1.11	−19.55	<.001	−23.81 to −19.48
C4/5 vs. C1	−26.26	1.20	−21.82	<.001	−28.62 to −23.90
Missing	−19.78	1.25	−15.88	<.001	−22.22 to −17.34
Newcastle vs. Manchester	−3.71	1.15	−3.23	.001	−5.96 to −1.46
Entry Year					
1984 vs. 1983	−2.49	0.67	−3.71	<.001	−3.81 to −1.18
1985 vs. 1983	2.32	1.35	1.72	.085	−0.32 to 4.96
1986 vs. 1983	−0.04	1.39	−0.03	.976	−2.27 to 2.69
1987 vs. 1983	0.69	1.42	0.49	.627	−2.10 to 3.48
1988 vs. 1983	0.79	0.79	1.00	.318	−0.76 to 2.33
1989 vs. 1983	−1.01	0.95	−1.06	.287	−2.87 to 0.85
1990 vs. 1983	−2.42	1.59	−1.52	.128	−5.54 to 0.70
1991 vs. 1983	−3.70	1.98	−1.86	.062	−7.58 to 0.19
1992 vs. 1983	−2.01	1.68	−1.20	.230	−5.29 to 1.17
B. Covariance and Residual parameter					
σ_A	13.53				13.22 to 13.85
σ_E	9.00				8.84 to 9.16

improvements of 1% or less on the other tasks. On the third and fourth occasion an improvement of over 4.5 was predicted for AH4-2 and CVL. This contrasts with negative estimates for several other tasks. Note that these differences may reflect a lack of fit between the quadratic and improvement parameters at older ages for which relatively few data points are available.

A secondary analysis was undertaken to examine whether the substantial practice effect of over 4.5 points on the second occasion for the AH4-1 and AH4-2 tests varied according to the interval between the initial and first re-testing. Restricting the analysis to individuals with scores at entry and at the second scheduled visit for each response, the interval between these two time-points was calculated in years. This interval ranged from 1 to 8 years. Because of small numbers in the lowest and highest categories the following categories were used: ≤2, 3, 4, 5, 6 or 7+ years. A model was fitted to each response, replacing the single-step function at the second occasion by a six-level term corresponding to the gap times. For the AH4-1 response the mean practice effects were similar across the intervals, ranging from 3.5 to 5.2 points, with no clear trend over time. The estimates were slightly more variable for AH4-2, ranging from 3.8 to 7.9. For both responses, this model provided an improvement in fit compared to the simpler model with practice at the second visit coded as a two-level factor ($p = .006$ and $p < .0001$, 5 *df*).

Discussion

The implications of possible practice and dropout in longitudinal studies have often been discussed (Schaie, 1988). The current analyses directly confirm their existence. The new estimates of the sizes of these effects allow reevaluation of some basic questions asked by previous studies. We first discuss practice and drop-out effects in turn, and then consider some substantive new information from longitudinal studies that becomes accessible when practice and drop-out have been taken into consideration.

Practice Effects

Practice effects were significant on both AH4 tests, with the greatest improvements occurring between the first and second testing sessions. Between the third and fourth testing sessions participants improved by over 4.5% points for the AH4-2 and CVL tasks. The total amount of improvement with practice is comparable to the true declines in average scores between age 60 and 70 after practice and drop-out have been taken into consideration (i.e. 6 points, from 64.6 to 58.6 on the AH4-1 and 6 points, between 58.2 and 52.1 on the AH4-2).

The sizes of the practice effects on the AH4-1 and AH4-2 tasks markedly increased with Age. Between first and second testing sessions these were over 4.5% for a 70-year-old compared with 1.5–2.5% for a 49-year-old. Practice effects also markedly varied between tasks, being much larger for the AH4-1 and -2 tests than for any others. The interaction between Age and Practice effects also varied between tasks. They were substantial in the AH4 and CVL tests small in the VFR test and negligible in the MH tests. For all tasks other than the AH4 tests they were independent of Age. Since average scores on intelligence tests decline with Age the form of this interaction between Age and Practice effects is consistent with Rabbitt's (1993b) earlier finding that practice effects are greater for less than for more able individuals, on some, but not on all tasks. Neglect of practice effects can therefore lead to many different kinds of misinterpretations. The true overall amount of Age-related cognitive change is underestimated, and acceleration of cognitive changes with age may be masked and, differences in practice effects between tasks can be misinterpreted as evidence that ageing affects some mental abilities earlier and more severely than others.

Drop-Out

These analyses again confirm that the true sizes of age-related changes are underestimated unless the effects of drop-out are taken into consideration. We have argued that these likelihood-based analyses under random drop-out assumptions allow good estimates of what actual trajectories of change would have been had drop-out not occurred. This allows more realistic estimates of how rates of age-related cognitive change differ between age groups, socio-economic groups and gender groups. Note, however, that these analyses adjust for, but do not give information about dropout effects. The relationships between volunteers' propensities to drop-out and their levels of ability, their gender, their levels of SEA or their general health status are of substantive interest, but are quite different questions that the current analyses do not resolve. We propose to investigate these relationships using informative drop-out models. The results will be reported separately in due course.

Re-Consideration of Some Familiar Questions

Analyses that take practice and drop-out into consideration now allow better answers to some of the basic substantive questions addressed by longitudinal studies: Do rates of cognitive decline accelerate as age increases? Do different mental abilities decline at different rates? How are rates of decline in scores on cognitive tests affected by individual differences in ability, by gender and by demographic factors and what is the true extent of increase in variance in cognitive performance between members of an ageing sample?

Do Rates of Cognitive Decline Accelerate as Age Increases?

After adjusting for practice and for drop-out, rates of decline were found to accelerate with Age, being greater for older than for younger participants on the two AH4 tests of general fluid intellectual ability and on the Cumulative

Verbal Learning task. Smaller declines in scores on the Verbal Free Recall task were adequately fitted by a linear function. In contrast, scores on the MHA and MHB vocabulary tests showed no age-related declines.

Do Different Cognitive Abilities Decline at Different Rates?

On the AH4-1 and -2 tests and on the CVL task, longitudinal analyses replicate previous findings of marked Age-related decline from cross-sectional comparisons (Rabbitt et al., 1996; Rabbitt, Watson, et al., 2003). A new finding is that declines on these three tasks also accelerated with Age, and at similar rates. Age-related declines in VFR scores were less marked, and were linear rather than accelerated. On the Mill Hill A and B vocabulary tests there was no overall difference between age groups and, further, no difference in longitudinal rates of decline between age cohorts. It must not be assumed that the relatively small effects of Age on the VFR and Vocabulary tests occur because of some commonality between the functional demands that these measures make. The lack of age sensitivity of the VFR task may simply reflect the fact that all participants found it relatively easy. In contrast, as in all previous studies, stability of performance on vocabulary tests in which performance is supported by "crystallised" knowledge acquired over a lifetime and maintained by practice in old age contrasts with declines in tasks that are supported by "fluid mental abilities" (Horn, 1982). The different trajectories of change for the CVL and VFR tests also confirm Horn's (1982) caution that age effects may appear to be larger on some tests of "fluid" mental abilities than on others.

Effects of Gender, Overall Ability and Demographics on Rates of Decline

On average, men performed better than women on the AH4-1, the AH4-2 and the Mill Hill A and B tests but women performed better than men on the Cumulative Verbal Learning (CVL) and on the Verbal Free Recall (VFR) tasks. These findings replicate and extend earlier cross-sectional comparisons within this sample by Rabbitt et al. (1996) and Rabbitt et al. (2002). The gender effect on CVL scores appears to be complex, because it also depends on Age. The advantage for women is relatively small at younger ages and thereafter widens. The absence of a similar Gender Age interaction for any of the other tasks questions the hypothesis that the female advantage on CVL tasks occurs only because women live longer than men and so also retain mental competence later in life. In our view this difference is quite as likely to reflect gender differences in the use of language throughout the lifespan rather than innate differences in mental abilities. These and other hints of interactions between differences in education, lifestyle and preservation of particular mental abilities in old age require further investigation.

Because the youngest volunteers were 49 when the study started it seemed reasonable to use this as the age from which to date the course of cognitive decline in this sample, and to further assumption rates of decline had been constant up to this point. On this assumption the analysis suggested that, after practice and drop-out effects had been taken into consideration, individuals who entered with lower levels of ability showed no more rapid decline than those who entered with higher levels of ability. This is consistent with recent findings, using a very different analytic model, by Rabbitt, Chetwynd, and McInnes (2003). It is not consistent with suggestions from an epidemiological study of a closed community of Nuns that higher levels of performance in young adult life may be associated with longer maintenance of ability (e.g. Snowden et al., 1996). Note, however, that the outcome of the current analysis depends on the age used for "centring" in the population. If age 65 rather than age 49 is used rates of decline do not vary with ability, and if ages older than 65 are used it appears that the less able decline more rapidly than the more able individuals. The implications of these findings with regard to methods of analysis of individual differences in the forms of trajectories of cognitive change are currently being further explored.

Cognitive performance varied markedly and directly with level of socio-economic advantage (SEA) but the size of this difference differed between tasks. Between the most and least advantaged categories it was over 20% points on the AH4 and MH tasks but 7–11% points on the CVL and VFR tasks. However although SEA affected overall level of performance there was no evidence that it differentially affected *rates of age-related decline*. This is unexpected because socio-economic advantage is a good proxy for factors such as health care, education and degree of exposure to environmental hazards that are known to markedly affect rates of biological changes (e.g. Kitagawa & Hauser, 1973). Socioeconomic disadvantage is also associated with earlier death, and immanence of death reduces cognitive performance (Berkovitz, 1965; Bosworth et al., 1999; Botwinick, West, & Storandt, 1978; Jarvik & Blum, 1971; Johannsen & Berg, 1989; Lieberman, 1965; Maier & Smith, 1999; Rabbitt et al., 2002; Reimanis & Green, 1971; Riegel & Riegel, 1972; Riegel, Riegel, & Myer, 1967; Small & Backman, 1997; Wilkie & Eisdorfer, 1974). There is also evidence that lower educational attainment associated with reduced advantage may be directly linked to prevalence of Alzheimer's disease (Bonaiuto, Rocca, & Lippi, 1995; Evans et al., 1993; Korczyn, Kahana, & Galper, 1991).

Even after the effects of SEA and gender had been taken into account Manchester residents performed significantly better than Newcastle residents on the AH4-1, MHA and MHB tests. There was no evidence of any difference in performance between Cities on the other tasks. These differences are cryptic because the City term is likely to be a proxy for a variety of unidentified factors for which the modelling process could not control.

Effects of Age on Variability Between Individuals

The standard deviation estimates provide useful insight into the amount of variability between individuals on each task. The estimated standard deviation for the linear rate of decline was similar for the AH4 and CVL tasks, ranging from 0.41 to 0.49, but was only 0.23 for VFR. The differences between the slopes for individuals give rise to increased variability in performance with age. For example, a pair of subjects with equal cognitive function on entry to the study whose slopes differed by 0.4 would differ by 4 points after 10 years and by 8 points after 20 years. Differences of this size are of practical importance since they are large enough to provide valuable insight into marked individual differences in rates of cognitive decline in old age.

There are at least two, quite separate, reasons why variability between individuals should increase with sample age. One is that trajectories of biological ageing are shaped by differences in their genetic inheritances, health histories, lifestyles and the life-events that they experience (Rabbitt, 1982, 1993a, 2001). Another is that as individuals grow older, and become correspondingly less able, their performance on any task on which they are tested becomes more variable from moment to moment. It can easily be shown that as a direct consequence their average levels of performance also vary more from session to session and from day to day (Rabbitt, 1999; Rabbitt, Osman, Stollery, & Moore, 2001). Thus lesser ability, and also greater Age, must increase not only moment to moment but also day-to-day variability in performance. Since Age increases the day-to-day variability of each member of a population the older a sample becomes, the more widely will its members differ from each other on any single assessment. The possible confound between these logically quite distinct effects raises methodological Issues.

Cross-sectional comparisons of the performance of cohorts of different ages made at particular time-points give us an inaccurate, and probably exaggerated, estimate of true differences in trajectories of cognitive ageing. To obtain more accurate estimates we need to reduce, as far as possible, the effects of session-to-session or day-to-day variability by taking several samples of performance on each task over a brief period. Use of means or medians of these samples will minimize the effects of session-to-session variability and so more clearly reveal long-term trends resulting from differences in trajectories of change. Such data will also be useful in showing the extent to which increases in the intrinsic variability of individuals' performance, as distinct from changes in their mean levels of performance, alter as they grow old.

Conclusions

The methodological and substantive conclusions of these analyses are closely interrelated. Substantive new findings that practice effects are substantial, persist for as long as 7 years and markedly differ with the ages and levels of ability of participants and between different kinds of tasks are also caveats for methodological practice in future studies. Th analyses show how practice effects can be estimated and taken into consideration. They also show how drop-out effects can be taken into consideration, but estimation of the sizes of drop-out effects and comparisons of the impacts of drop-out from different causes awaits further work. The ability to consider practice and drop-out effects allowed some substantive new findings and improved confirmation of previous results. (1) For tests of gf rates decline accelerate with increasing age. For verbal memory tasks rates of change are equally well fitted by linear as by quadratic functions. Findings that vocabulary tests show very slight or no declines are replicated. (2) These analyses provide no evidence that rates of decline are affected by overall levels of general intellectual ability. (3) While levels of socio-economic advantage directly affect overall levels of ability, counter-intuitively there is no evidence that they can affect rates of cognitive decline. (4) There is no evidence that men and women experience different rates of cognitive decline, though there are clear sex differences in overall competence at different kinds of tasks, with women showing advantages in tests of verbal memory and verbal learning contrasting with disadvantages in tests of gf and of vocabulary. (5) Perhaps the most intriguing substantive finding is that variance in cognitive performance between members of a longitudinal sample significantly increases as it ages. Evidently this marked increase in variance has been masked by practice and drop-out effects in previous studies. It is of obvious theoretical and practical importance to determine to what extent this increasing variance is due to differences in trajectories of age-related changes arising from individual differences in genetic inheritance, gender, health and demographics, and to what extent it reflects increases in variability in performance within individuals as age advances and general levels of ability decline.

References

Anstey, K., Lord, S.R., & Williams, P. (1997). Strength in the lower limbs. Visual contrast sensitivity and simple reaction time predict cognition in older women. *Psychology and Aging, 12*, 137–144.

Anstey, K., Luszcz, M.A., & Sanchez, L. (2001). A reevaluation of the common factor theory of shared variance among Age, Sensory Function and Cognitive Function in Older Adults. *Journal of Gerontology, 56B*, P3–P11.

Anstey, K., & Smith, G. (1999). Interrelationships among biological makers of Aging, Health, Activity, Acculturation and Cognitive Performance in Late Adulthood. *Psychology and Aging, 14*, 605–618.

Anstey, K.J. (1999). Sensorimotor variables and forced expiratory volume as correlates of speed, accuracy and variability in reaction time performance in late adulthood. *Aging, Neuropsychology and Cognition, 6*, 84–95.

Arbuckle, T.Y., Gold, D., & Andres, D. (1986). Cognitive functioning of older people in relation to social and personality variables. *Psychology and Aging, 1, 55–62.*

Arenberg, D. (1974). A longitudinal study of problem solving in adults. *Journal of Gerontology, 29*, 650–658.

Austin, E.J., Deary, I.J., Whiteman, M.C., Fowkes, F.G.R., Pedersen, N.L., Rabbitt, P.M.A., Bent, N.C., & McInnes, L. (2002). Relationships between ability and personality: Does intelligence contribute positively to personal and social adjustment? *Personality and Individual Differences, 32*, 1391–1411.

Baddeley, A.D., Emslie, H., & Nimmo-Smith, I. (1992). *The Speech and Capacity of Language Processing* (SCOLP) Test. Bury St Edmunds: Thames Valley Test Company.

Baltes, P.B. (1968). Longitudinal and cross-sectional sequences in the study of age and generation effects. *Human Development, 11*, 145–171.

Baltes, P.B., & Lindenberger, U. (1997). Emergence of a powerful connection between sensory and cognitive functions across the lifespan: A new window to the study of cognitive aging? *Psychology and Aging, 12*, 12–21.

Bank, L., & Jarvik, L.F. (1978). A longitudinal study of aging human twins. In E.L. Schneider (Ed.), *The genetics of aging* (pp. 303–333). New York: Plenum Press.

Beck, A.T., Ward, C.H., Mendelsohn, M., Mock, J., & Erbaugh, J. (1961). An inventory for measuring depression. *General Archives of Psychiatry, 4*, 561–571.

Beekman, A.T.F., Copeland, J.R.M., & Prince, M. (1999). Review of community prevalence of depression in later life. *British Journal of Psychiatry, 174*, 307–311.

Beekman, A.T.F., Deeg, D.J.H., Tilburg, T. van, Smit, J.H., & Tilburg, W. van. (1995). Major and minor depression in later life: A study of prevalence and risk factors. *Journal of Affective Disorders, 65*, 65–75.

Belanoff, J.K., Kalchzan, M., Sund, B., Ficek, S.K., & Schatzberg, A.F. (2001). Cortisol activity and cognitive changes in psychotic major depression. *American Journal of Psychiatry, 158*, 1612–1616.

Bell, B., Rose, C.L., & Damon, A. (1972). The normative aging study: Interdisciplinary and longitudinal study of health and aging. *Aging and Human Development, 3*, 5–17.

Bent, N.C., Rabbitt, P.M.A., & Metcalf, D. (2000). Diabetes mellitus and the rate of cognitive change. *British Journal of Clinical Psychology, 39*, 349–362.

Berr, C., Dufouil, C., Brousseau, T., Richard, F., Amouyel, P., Marceteau, E., & Alperovitch, A. (1996). Early effect of ApoE-epsilon 4 allele on cognitive results in a group of highly performing subjects: The EVA study. Etude sur le Vieillissement Arteriel. *Neuroscience Letters, 218*, 9–12.

Birren, J.E., Butler, R.N., Greenhouse, S.W., Sokoloff, L., & Yarrow, M.R. (1963). *Human aging* (No. 986). Washington, DC: U.S. Government Printing Office Publication.

Blazer, D.G. (1994). Epidemiology of late-life depression. In L.J. Schneider, C.F. Reynolds III, B.D. Leibowitz, & A.J. Friedhoff (Eds.*), Diagnosis and treatment of late-life depression: Results of the* NIH *consensus development conference* (pp. 9–21). Washington: APA.

Bonaiuto, S., Rocca, W.A., Lippi, A., Giannandra, E., Mele, M., Cavarzeram, F., & Amaducci, I. (1995). Education and occupation as risk factors for dementia: A population-based case-control study. *Neuroepidemiology, 14*, 101–109.

Bosworth, H.B., Schaie, K.W., & Willis, S.L. (1999). Cognitive and sociodemographic risk factors for mortality in the Seattle Longitudinal Study. *Journal of Gerontology: Psychological Sciences, 54B*, P273–P282.

Botwinick, J., West, R., & Storandt, M. (1978). Predicting death from behavioral test performance. *Journal of Gerontology, 33*, 755–776.

Broadbent, D.E., Cooper, P.T., Fitzgerald, P., & Parkes, K.R. (1982). The cognitive failure questionnaire (CFQ) and its correlates. *British Journal of Clinical Psychology, 25*, 1–16.

Brodman, K., Erdmann, A.J., Jr., & Wolff, H.G. (1949). *Manual for the Cornell medical index, health questionnaire.* New York: Cornell University Medical College.

Burgess, P.W. (1997). Theory and methodology in executive function research. In P.M.A. Rabbitt (Ed.), *Methodology of frontal and executive function* (pp. 81–116). Psychology Press: Hove.

Cattell, R.B., & Cattell, A.K.S. (1960). *The Individual or Group Culture Fair Intelligence Test.* Champaign, IL: IPAT.

Chorney, M.J., Chorney, K., Seese, N., Owen, M.J., Daniels, J., McGuffin, P., Thompson, L.A., Detteman, D.K., Benbom, C.P., Lubinsky, D., Eley, T.C., & Plumin, R. (1998). A quantitative trait locus associated with cognitive ability in children. *Psychological Sciences, 9*, 159–166.

Clark, J.W. (1960). The ageing dimension. A factorial analysis of individual differences with age on psychological and physiological measurement. *Journal of Gerontology, 15*, 183–187.

Clement, F.J. (1974). Longitudinal and cross-sectional assessments of age-changes in physical strength as related to sex, social class and mental ability. *Journal of Gerontology, 15*, 183–187.

Colsher, P.L., & Wallace, R.B. (1991). Longitudinal application of cognitive measures in a defined population of community dwelling elders. *Annals of Epidemiology, 3*, 71–77.

Costa, P.T., & McCrae, R.R. (1980). Somatic complaints in males as a function of age and neuroticism: A longitudinal analysis. *Journal of Behavioral Medicine, 3*, 245–253.

Dewy, I.J. (2000). *Looking down on human intelligence: From psychometrics in the brain.* Oxford: Oxford University Press.

Dirken, J.M. (1972). *Functional age of industrial workers.* Groningen: Wolters-Noordhof.

Ellis, H.C., Thomas, R.L., & Rodriguez, L.A. (1984). Emotional mood states and memory: Elaborative encoding, semantic processing and cognitive effort. *Journal of Experimental Psychology: Learning, Memory and Cognition, 1*, 501–518.

Evans, D.A., Beckett, L.A., Albert, M.S., Hebert, L.E., Scherr, P.A., Funkenstein, H.H., & Taylor, J.O. (1993). Level of education and change in cognitive function in a community population of olderpersons. *Annals of Epidemiology, 3*, 71 77.

Eysenck, H.J., & Eysenck, S.B.G. (1964). *The Eysenck personality questionnaire.* London, UK: University of London Press.

Feskens, E.J.M., Havekes, L.M., Kalmijn, S., de Knijff, P., Launer, L.J., & Kromhout, D. (1994). Apolipoprotein e4 allele and cognitive decline in elderly men. *British Medical Journal, 309*, 1202–1206.

Fisher, P.J., Turic, D., Williams, N.M., McGuffin, P., Asherson, P., Ball, D., Craig, I., Eley, T., Hill, L., Chorney, K., Chorney, M.J., Benbom, C.P., Lubinsky, D., Plumin, R., & Owens, M.J. (1999). DNA pooling identifies QTLs on chromosome 4 for general cognitive ability in children. *Human Molecular Genetics, 8*, 915–922.

Forner, A. (1972). *Aging and society* (Vol. III). New York: Russell-Sage Foundation.

Gur, R.C., Gur, R.E., Orbist, W.D., Skolnik, B.E., & Reivitch, M. (1987). Age and regional cerebral blood flow at rest and during cognitive activity. *Archives of General Psychiatry, 44*, 617–621.

Haugh, H., & Eggers, R. (1991). Morphometry of the human cortex cerebri and cortex striatum during aging. *Neurobiology of Aging, 12*, 336–338.

Hayslip, B., Jr. (1988). Personality–ability relationships in aged adults. *Journal of Gerontology, 45*, 116–127.

Heim, A.W. (1970). AH4 *group test of general intelligence*. Windsor, UK: NFER-Nelson.

Heron, A., & Chown, S. (1967). *Age and function. London*: Churchill.

Herrman, D. (1982). Know thy memory: The use of questionnaires to assess and study memory. *Psychological Bulletin, 92*, 434–452.

Hertel, P.T., & Hardin, T.S. (1990). Remembering with and without awareness in a depressed mood. Evidence of deficit in initiative. *Journal of Experimental Psychology: General, 119*, 45–59.

Hertzog, C., & Schaie, K.W. (1988). Stability and change in adult intelligence. 2. Simultaneous analysis of longitudinal means and covariance structures. *Psychology and Aging, 3*, 122–130.

Hertzog, C., Schaie, K.W., & Gribbin, K. (1978). Cardiovascular disease and changes in intellectual function from middle to old age. *Journal of Gerontology, 33*, 872–883.

Holland, C.M., & Rabbitt, P.M.A. (1991). The course and causes of cognitive change with advancing age. *Reviews in Clinical Gerontology, 1*, 81–96.

Horn, J.L. (1982). The theory of fluid and crystallized intelligence in relation to concepts of cognitive psychology and aging in adulthood. In F.I.M. Craik & S. Trehub (Eds.), *Aging and cognitive processes* (pp. 127–183). Boston, Plenum.

Horn, J.L., Donaldson, G., & Engstrom, R. (1981). Application, memory and fluid intelligence decline in adulthood. *Research on Aging, 3*, 33–84.

Hultsch, D.F., Hertzog, C., Small, B.J., McDonaldMiszczak, L., & Dixon, R.A. (1992). Short-term longitudinal change in cognitive performance in later life. *Psychology and Aging, 7*, 571–584.

Hyman, B.T., Gomez-Isla, T., Briggs, M., Chung, H., Nichols, S., Kohout, F., & Wallace, R. (1996). Apolipoprotein E and cognitive change in an elderly population. *Annals of Neurology, 40*, 55–65.

Jarvik, L., & Blum, J.E. (1971). Cognitive declines as predictors of mortality in twin pairs. In E. Palmore & F. Jeffers (Eds.), *Prediction of life-span* (pp. 199–211). Lexington: D.C. Heath.

Johannsen, B., & Berg, S. (1989). The robustness of the terminal decline phenomenon: Longitudinal data from the digit-span memory test. *Journal of Gerontology, Psychological Sciences, 44*, 184–186.

Johannsen, B., Zarit, S.H., & Berg, S. (1992). Changes in cognitive function of the oldest old. *Journal of Gerontology, Psychological Sciences, 47*, 75–80.

Jonker, C., Schmand, B., Lindeboom, J., Havekes, L.M., & Launer, L.J. (1998). Association between apolipoprotein E epsilon4 and the rate of cognitive decline in community-dwelling elderly individuals with and without dementia. *Archives of Neurology, 55*, 1065–1069.

Karasek, R.A., Jr. (1979). Job demands, job decision latitude and mental implications for job design. *Administrative Science Quarterly, 24*, 33–56.

Kitagawa, E.M., & Hauser, P.M. (1973). *Differential mortality in the United States: A study in socioeconomic epidemiology*. Cambridge, MA: Harvard University Press.

Korczyn, A.D., Kahana, E., & Galper, Y. (1991). Epidemiology of dementia in Ashkelon, Israel. *Neuroepidemiology, 10*, 100.

Kucera, H., & Francis, N. (1967). *Frequency and word association norms*. Providence: Brown University Press.

Lachman, R., Lachman, J.L., & Taylor, D.W. (1982). Reallocation of mental resources over the productive lifespan: Assumptions and task analyses. In F.I.M. Craik & S. Trehub (Eds.), *Aging and the cognitive process* (pp. 22–76). New York: Plenum Press.

Lansen, P. (1997). The impact of aging on cognitive functions: An 11-year follow up study of four age cohorts. *Acta Neurologica Scandinavica Supplimentum, 96*, 172.

Lieberman, M.A. (1965). Psychological correlates of impending death: Some preliminary observations. *Journal of Gerontology, 20*, 181–190.

Lindenberger, U., & Baltes, P.B. (1994). Sensory functioning and intelligence in old age: A strong connection. *Psychology and Aging, 9*, 339–355.

Lindenberger, U., & Potter, U. (1998). The complex nature of unique and shared effects in hierarchical linear regression: Implications for developmental psychology. *Psychological Methods, 3*, 218–230.

Lupien, S.J., & McEwen, B.S. (1997). The acute effects of corticosteroids on cognition: Integration of animal and human model studies. *Brain Research Reviews, 24*, 1–27.

Maier, H., & Smith, J. (1999). Psychological predictors of mortality in old age. *Journal of Gerontology: Psychological Sciences, 54B*, P44–P54.

Mason, K., & Mason, W. (1973). Some methodological issues in cohort analysis of archival data. *American Sociological Review, 38*, 242–258.

Mayeux, R., Small, S.A., Tang, M., Tycko, B., & Stern, Y. (2001). Memory performance in healthy elderly without Alzheimer's disease: Effects of time and apolipoprotein-E. *Neurobiology of Aging, 22*, 683–689.

McBride, A.M., & Abeles, N. (2000). Depressive symptoms and cognitive performance in older adults. *Clinical Gerontologist, 21*, 27–47.

McInnes, L., & Rabbitt, P.M. (1997). The relationship between functional ability and cognitive ability among elderly people. In *Facts and research in gerontology* (pp. 34–45). Paris: Serdi.

Minors, D., Atkinson, G., Bent, N., Rabbitt, P., & Waterhouse, J. (1998). The effect of age upon some aspects of lifestyle and implications for studies on circadian rhythmicity. *Age and Ageing, 27*, 67–72.

Morse, C.K. (1993). Does variability increase with Age? An archival study of cognitive measures. *Psychology and Aging, 8*, 156–164.

Nesselrode, J.R., & Baltes, P.B. (1979). *Longitudinal research in the study of behaviour and development*. New York: Academic Press.

Office of Population Censuses and Surveys. (1980*). Classification of occupations 1980.* London, UK: Her Majesty's Stationery Office.

Owen, A.M., Downes, J.J., Sahakian, B.J., Polkey, C.E., & Robbins, T.W. (1990). Planning and spatial working memory following frontal lobe lesions. *Neuropsychologia, 27*, 1329–1344.

Owens, W.A. (1953). Age and mental abilities: A longitudinal study. Genetic *Psychological Monographs, 48*, 3–54.

Owens, W.A. (1966). Age and mental abilities: A second adult follow-up. *Journal of Educational Psychology, 57*, 311–325.

Palmore, E. (1978). When can age, period and cohort be separated? *Soc. Forces, 57*, 282–295.

Payton, A., Holland, F., Diggle, P., Rabbitt, P., Horan, M., Davidson, Y., Gibbons, L., Worthington, J., Ollier, W., & Pendleton, N. (2004). Cathepsin D exon 2 polymorphism associated with general intelligence in a healthy older population. *Molecular Psychiatry, 8*, 14–18.

Pendleton, N., Horan, M., Jones, M., McInnes, L., & Rabbitt, P.M.A. (submitted). Concordance of Cornell medical index (CMI) self-reports to structured clinical assessment for the identification of physical health status. *Archives of Gerontology and Geriatrics.*

Pendleton, N., Payton, A., Boogerd, E.H., Holland, F., Diggle, P., Rabbitt, P.M.A., Horan, M.A., Worthington, J., & Ollier, W.E.R. (2002). Apolipoprotein E genotype does not predict decline in intelligence in healthy older adults. *Neuroscience Letters, 324*, 74–76.

Piccinin, A.M., & Rabbitt, P.M.A. (1999). Contribution of cognitive abilities to performance and improvement on a substitution-coding task. *Psychology and Aging, 14*, 539–551.

Powell, D.H. (1994). *Profiles in cognitive aging.* Cambridge, MA: Harvard University Press.

Rabbitt, P., Bent, N., & McInnes, L. (1997). Health, age and mental ability. *The Irish Journal of Psychology, 18*, 104–131.

Rabbitt, P., Diggle, P., Smith, D., Holland, F., & McInnes, L. (2001). Identifying and separating the effects of practice and of cognitive ageing during a large longitudinal study of elderly community residents. *Neuropsychologia, 39*, 532–543.

Rabbitt, P.M., Chetwynd, A., & McInnes, L. (2003). Do clever brains age more slowly? Further exploration of a nun result. *British Journal of Psychology, 94*, 63–71.

Rabbitt, P.M., Watson, P., Donlan, C., Bent, L., & McInnes, L. (1994). Subject attrition in a longitudinal study of cognitive performance in community-based elderly people. In *Facts and research in gerontology* (pp. 203–207). Paris: Serdi.

Rabbitt, P.M.A. (1982). Cognitive psychology needs models for old age. In A.D. Baddeley & J. Long (Eds.), *Attention and performance* (Vol. IX, pp. 209–340). Hove, UK: Erlbaums.

Rabbitt, P.M.A. (1993a). Does it all go together when it goes? *Quarterly Journal of Experimental Psychology, 46*, 385 433.

Rabbitt, P.M.A. (1993b). Crystal quest: An examination of the concepts of "fluid" and "crystallised" intelligence as explanations for cognitive changes in old age. In A.D. Baddeley & L. Weiskrantz (Eds.), *Attention, selection, awareness and control* (pp. 125–212). Oxford: Oxford University Press.

Rabbitt, P.M.A. (1999). Measurement indices, functional characteristics and psychometric constructs in cognitive ageing. In T.J. Perfect & E.A. Maylor (Eds.), *Models of cognitive aging* (Chap. 6). Oxford: Oxford University Press.

Rabbitt, P. (2004). Ageing and cognition. In H. Pashler (Ed.), *Stevens handbook of experimental psychology*, 3rd ed., Vol. 4 (pp. 793–860). Chichester: John Wiley.

Rabbitt, P.M.A., & Abson, V. (1990). Lost and found: Some logical and methodological limitations of self-report questionnaires as tools to study cognitive ageing. *British Journal of Psychology, 81*, 1–16.

Rabbitt, P.M.A., & Abson, V. (1991). Do older people know how good they are? *British Journal of Psychology, 81*, 137–151.

Rabbitt, P.M.A., Banerji, N., & Szemanski, A. (1989). Space fortress as an IQ test? Predictions of learning and of practised performance in a complex video game. *Acta Psychologica, 71*, 243–257.

Rabbitt, P., Diggle, P., Holland, F., & McInnes, L. (2004). Practice and drop-out effects durin a 17-year longitudinal study of cognitive aging. *J. Gerontol.* (B). *Psychol. Sci. Social Sciences, 59*, 84–97.

Rabbitt, P.M.A., Donlan, C., Watson, P., McInnes, L., & Bent, N. (1996). Unique and interactive effects of depression, age socio-economic advantage and gender on cognitive performance of normal healthy older people. *Psychology and Aging, 10*, 221–235.

Rabbitt, P., Donlan, C., Bent, N., McInnes, L., & Abson, V. (1993). The University of Manchester Age and Cognitive. Performance Center and NorthEast Age Research Longitudinal Programmes, 1982–1997. *Zeitschrift Gerentol., 26*, 176–183.

Rabbitt, P.M.A., Maylor, E.A., McInnes, L., Bent, N., & Moore, B. (1995). What goods can self-assessment questionnaires deliver for cognitive gerontology? *Journal of Applied Psychology, 9*, S127–S152.

Rabbitt, P.M.A., Osman, P., Stollery, B., & Moore, B. (2001). There are stable individual differences in performance variability, both from moment to moment and from day to day. *Quarterly Journal of Experimental Psychology, 54A*, 981–1003.

Rabbitt, P.M.A., Watson, P., Donlan, C., McInnes, L., Horan, M., Pendleton, N., & Clague, J. (2002). Effects of death within 11 years on cognitive performance in old age. *Psychology and Aging, 17*, 468–481.

Raven, J.C. (1965). *The Mill Hill vocabulary scale*. London: H.K. Lewis.

Ravenkilde, B., Videbech, P., Clemmensen, K., Egander, A., Rasmussen, N., & Rosenberg, R. (2002). Cognitive deficits in major depression. *Scandinavian Journal of Psychology, 43*, 239–251.

Reason, J. (1993). Self-report questionnaires in cognitive psychology: Have they delivered the goods? In A.D. Baddeley & L.S. Weiskrantz (Eds.), *Attention, selection, awareness and control* (pp. 406–439). Oxford: Oxford University Press.

Reimanis, G., & Green, R. (1971). Immanence of death and intellectual decrement in the aging. *Developmental Psychology, 5*, 270–272.

Riegel, K.F., & Riegel, R.M. (1972). Development, drop and death. *Developmental Psychology, 6*, 308–316.

Riegel, K.F., Riegel, R.M., & Myer, G. (1967). A study of the drop-out rates in longitudinal research on aging, and the prediction of death. *Journal of Personality and Social Psychology, 4*, 342–348.

Robbins, T.W., James, M., Owen, A.M., Sahakian, B.J., Lawrence, A.D., McInnes, L., & Rabbitt, P.M.A. (1998). A study of performance on tests from the CANTAB battery sensitive to frontal lobe dysfunction in a large sample of normal elderly volunteers: Implications for theories of executive functioning and cognitive ageing. *Journal of the International Neurophysiological Society, 4*, 474–490.

Robbins, T.W., James, M., Owen, A.M., Sahakian, B.J., McInnes, L., & Rabbitt, P. (1997). A neural systems approach to the cognitive psychology of ageing: Studies with CANTAB on a large sample of the normal elderly population. In P. Rabbitt (Ed.), *Methodology of frontal and executive function* (pp. 215–238). Hove, UK: Psychology Press.

Robbins, T.W., & Sahakian, B.J. (1991). Computerised testing in dementia. In J.R.M. Copeland, M.T. Abou-Saleh, & D.G. Blazer (Eds.), *Handbook of geriatric psychiatry*, Chichester: Wiley.

Rubin, D.B. (1976). Inference and missing data. *Biometrika, 63*, 581–592.

Sahakian, B.J., & Owen, A.M. (1992). Computerised assessment in neuropsychiatry using CANTAB. *Journal of the Royal Society of Medicine, 85*, 399–402.

Salthouse, T.A. (1991). Theoretical perspectives on *cognitive aging*. Hillsdale, NJ: Erlbaum.

Savage, R.D. (1984). *Alphabet coding task-15*. Perth, W. Australia: Murdock University.

Schaie, K.W. (1990). Intellectual development in adulthood. In J.E. Birren & K.W. Schaie (Eds.), *Handbook of the psychology of aging* (3rd ed., pp. 89–126). San Diego, CA: Academic Press.

Schaie, K.W. (1996). *Intellectual development in adulthood: The Seattle longitudinal study.* New York: Cambridge University Press.

Schaie, K.W., Labouvie, G.V., & Barrett, T.J. (1973). Selective attrition effects in a fourteen-year study of adult intelligence. *Journal of Gerontology, 28*, 328–334.

Schaie, K.W., & Labouvie-Vief, G. (1974). Generational versus ontogenetic components of change in adult cognitive functioning: A fourteen-year cross-sequential study. *Developmental Psychology, 10*, 305–320.

Schaie, K.W., & Strother, C.R. (1968). A crosssequential study of age changes in cognitive behaviour. *Psychological Bulletin, 70*, 671–680.

Schaie, K.W., & Willis, S.L. (1993). Age difference patterns of psychometric intelligence in adulthood: Generalizability within and across ability domains. *Psychology and Aging, 8*, 44–55.

Scharfstein, D.O., Rotnitzky, A., & Robins, J.M. (1999). Adjusting for non-ignorable drop-out using semiparametric non-response models (with Discussion). *Journal of the American Statistical Association, 94*, 1096–1120.

Scheibel, M.E., & Scheibel, A.B. (1975). Structural changes in the aging brain. In H. Brody, D. Harmon, & J.M. Ordy (Eds.), *Aging* (Vol. 1, pp. 11–37). New York: Raven Press.

Schlesselman, J.J. (1973a). Planning a longitudinal study. I. Sample size determination. *Journal of Chronic Diseases, 26*, 532–560.

Schlesselman, J.J. (1973b). Planning a longitudinal study. II. Frequency of measurement and study duration. *Journal of Chronic Diseases, 26*, 561–570.

Schulsinger, F., Knop, J., & Mednick, S.A. (1981). *Longitudinal research.* MA: Hingham.

Sliewinski, M., & Buschke, M. (1999). Cross-sectional and longitudinal relationships among age, cognition and information processing speed. *Psychology and Aging, 14*, 18–33.

Small, B.J., & Backman, L. (1997). Cognitive correlates of mortality: Evidence from a populationbased sample of very old adults. *Psychology and Aging, 12*, 309–313.

Small, B.J., Basun, H., & Backman, L. (1998). Three year changes in cognitive performance as a function of apolipoprotein E genotype: Evidence from very old adults without dementia. *Psychology and Aging, 13*, 80–87.

Small, B.J., Graves, A.B., McEvoy, C.L., Crawford, F.C., Mullan, M., & Mortimer, J.A. (2000). Is APOE – epsilon4 a risk factor for cognitive impairment in normal aging? *Neurology, 54*, 2082–2088.

Smith, G.E., Bohac, D.L., Waring, S.C., Kokmen, E., Tangalos, E.G., Ivnik, R.J., & Petersen, R.C. (1998). Apolipoprotein E genotype influences cognitive 'phenotype' in patients with Alzheimer's disease but not in healthy control subjects. *Neurology, 50*, 355–362.

Snowden, D.A., Kemper, S.J., Mortimer, J.A., Greinier, L.H., Wekstein, D.R., & Markesbery, W.R. (1996). Linguistic ability in early life and cognitive function and Alzheimer's disease in later life. Findings from the Nun study. *Journal of American Medical Association, 21*, 528–532.

Snowden, D.A., Ostwald, S.K., Kane, R.E.L., & Keenen, N.L. (1989). Years of life with good and poor mental function in the elderly. *Journal of Clinical Epidemiology, 42*, 1055–1066.

Staehelin, H.B., Perrig-Chiello, P., Mitrache, C., Miserez, A.R., & Perrig, W.J. (1999). ApolipoproteinE genotypes and cognitive functions in healthy elderly persons. *Acta Neurologica Scandinavica, 100,* 53–60.

Sunderland, A., Harris, J.E., & Gleave, J. (1983). Memory failures in everyday life following severe head injury. *Journal of Clinical Neuropsychology, 6,* 127–142.

Terman, L.M., & Oden, M.H. (1947). *Genetic studies of genius. The gifted child grows up* (Vol. 4). Stanford, CA: Stanford University Press.

Terman, L.M., & Oden, M.H. (1959). *Genetic studies of genius. The gifted group at mid life* (Vol. 5). Stanford, CA: Stanford University Press.

Tinetti, M.E. (1986). Performance-oriented assessment of mobility problems in elderly patients. *Journal of the American Geriatric Society, 34,* 119–126.

Tinetti, M.E., & Glinter, S.F. (1988). Identifying mobility problems in elderly patients. *Journal of the American Medical Association, 259,* 1190–1193.

Voitenko, V.P., & Tokar, A.V. (1983). The assessment of biological age and sex differences of human aging. *Experimental Aging Research, 9,* 239–244.

Wechsler, D. (1986). *The Wechsler Adult Intelligence Test – Revised.* New York: The Psychological Corporation.

White, L.R., Katzman, R., Losonczy, K., Salive, M., Wallace, R., Berkman, L., Taylor, J., Fillenbaum, G., & Havlik, R. (1994). Association of education with incidence of cognitive impairment in three established populations for epidemiological studies of the elderly. *Journal of Clinical Epidemiology, 47,* 363–374.

Wilkie, F., & Eisdorfer, C. (1974). Terminal changes in intelligence. In E. Palmore (Ed.), *Normal aging* (Vol. II, pp. 178 199). Durham, NC: Duke University Press.

Wrelkin, N. (1996). Consensus statement apolipoprotein E genotyping in Alzheimer's disease. *Lancet, 347,* 1091–1099.

Yaffe, K., Cauley, J., Sands, L., & Browner, W. (1997). Apolipoprotein E phenotype and cognitive decline in a prospective study of elderly community women. *Archives of Neurology, 54,* 1110–1114.

Yesavage, J.A., Bruik, T.L., & Rose, T.L. (1983). Development and validation of a geriatric depression screening scale: A preliminary report. *Journal of Psychiatric Research, 17,* 37–49.

Zelinski, E.M., & Burnight, K.P. (1997). Sixteen-year longitudinal and time lag changes in memory and cognition in older adults. *Psychology and Aging, 12,* 503–513.

Zelinski, E.M., Gilewski, M.J., & Stewart, K.W. (1993). Individual differences in cross-sectional and 3 year longitudinal memory performance across the adult life span. *Psychology and Aging, 8,* 176–186.

Zelinski, E.M., & Stewart, S.T. (1998). Individual differences in 16-year memory changes. *Psychology and Aging, 13,* 622–630.

Using longitudinal data to explore causes of cognitive changes

Peter Diggle's statistics were not just a methodological advance that solved the problem of distinguishing between the effects of practice and of age-related decline. They also allowed a substantive discovery that even ten minutes spent on a simple intelligence test can improve performance four, or even eight years later. This suggests a need to review some assumptions in the psychometric literature. For example, Jim Flynn (2007) has spent much of his illustrious career analyzing data from many countries to show that population averages of intelligence test scores have slightly, but steadily, improved over many decades. He has vigorously challenged nearly all plausible explanations for this, such as world-wide improvements in nutrition and in general health, in education and the cognitive demands of living in increasingly literate, educated and technologically challenging societies. It is certainly cheeky, and probably also rash, to suggest that a different contributing factor that Flynn was unable to assess is that during the twentieth century it became increasingly likely that individuals would encounter intelligence tests on more than one occasion and also that they would benefit from increasing familiarity with the general styles of problems encountered in different intelligence tests.

A persistent finding in the Manchester/Newcastle study, as in many others, is that individuals' scores on tests of fluid intelligence, (*gf*) predict both their contemporary levels of performance and their rates of future learning on other cognitive tasks, such as memory or decision speed. Volunteers who had higher intelligence test scores on entry to studies are faster learners and so experience greater practice gains, not only when they again take the same intelligence tests, but also on most other measures of cognitive ability. Unless we take into consideration relationships between level of intelligence on entry to a study and all subsequent changes in test scores over time, our estimates of how other factors affect the rate of change of mental competence in later life will be wrong.

This issue affects our interpretation of classical studies that have found accelerating declines in mental competence preceding deaths ("terminal drops", e.g. Kleemeir, 1962; Palmore & Cleveland, 1976). Earlier investigators had no way to separate the opposing effects of declines caused by pathologies terminating in death and of practice gains during longitudinal assessments. A related issue is that in order to discover how declines in mental ability are related to distance from death, we must also recognize that not all volunteers continue to attend testing sessions until death closes their records. Many participants drop out of longitudinal studies due to increasing frailty, boredom, development of new interests, or changes of residence. If their records are not separated from those of survivors, the effects of terminal decline will be wrongly estimated (Rabbitt, Lunn & Wong, 2005; 2006; Rabbitt et al., 2008). The next study reported the first estimate of terminal decline after both practice and dropout had also been considered.

References

Flynn, J. R. (2007). *What is Intelligence? Beyond the Flynn Effect*. New York: Cambridge University Press.

Kleemeier, R. W. (1962). Intellectual changes in the senium. In *Proceedings of the social statistics section of the American statistical association* (Vol. 1, pp. 290–295).

Palmore, E., & Cleveland, W. (1976). Aging, terminal decline, and terminal drop. *Journal of Gerontology, 31*(1), 76–81.

Rabbitt, P., Lunn, M., & Wong, D. (2005). Neglect of dropout underestimates effects of death in longitudinal studies. *The Journals of Gerontology Series B: Psychological Sciences and Social Sciences, 60*(2), P106–P109

Rabbitt, P., Lunn, M., & Wong, D. (2006). Understanding terminal decline in cognition and risk of death. *European Psychologist, 11*(3), 164–171.

Rabbitt, P., Lunn, M., Wong, D., & Cobain, M. (2008). Age and ability affect practice gains in longitudinal studies of cognitive change. *The Journals of Gerontology Series B: Psychological Sciences and Social Sciences, 63*(4), P235–P240.

12 Death, dropout, and longitudinal measurements of cognitive change in old age

P.M.A. Rabbitt, M. Lunn and D. Wong

Many studies of changes preceding death in old age have found that individuals who are between 18 months and 11 years from death score less well on tests of mental abilities than survivors do (e.g., Johansson & Berg, 1989; Lieberman, 1965; Palmore & Cleveland, 1976; Rabbitt, Watson, Donlan et al. 2002; Reimanis & Green, 1971; Riegel & Riegel, 1972; Riegel, Riegel, & Meyer, 1967; Siegler & Botwinick, 1979; Small, Fratiglioni, von Strauss, & Backman, 2002). The typical methodology has been to assess participants only once and to compare the scores of survivors and decedents at a later, arbitrary, census date. This underestimates the effects of death, because younger decedents are compared against younger survivors who will survive longer beyond the census date whereas elderly decedents are compared against elderly survivors who are likely to die soon after census (Rabbitt, Lunn, & Wong, 2005; Rabbitt, Watson, Donlan, Bent, & McInnes, 1994). This explains the otherwise paradoxical findings that differences in ability between deceased persons and survivors are larger in younger than in older samples (e.g., Riegel & Riegel; Riegel et al.).

Longitudinal studies in which participants are repeatedly assessed over many years avoid these problems but encounter other methodological difficulties. Participants improve with practice as a result of repeated testing (Rabbitt, Diggle, Holland, McInnes, Bent, et al., 2004); recruitment cohorts may markedly differ in ability; and participants typically drop out of studies because of deteriorating health and survivors become increasingly elite and able (Lachman, Lachman, & Taylor, 1982; Rabbitt, Watson, Donlan, Bent, & McInnes, 1994; Schaie, Labouvie, & Barrett, 1973). Thus, if scores of decedents are compared against those of all survivors, including less able dropouts, then the effects of approaching death are underestimated (Rabbitt et al., 2005). Demographic factors must be taken into consideration. Women, the socioeconomically advantaged, and the most able live longer, so deaths selectively alter sample composition (Hart et al., 2003). More and less advantaged individuals tend to die from different causes and so experience different patterns and rates of terminal declines in health and cognition (Nagi & Stockwell, 1973; Pincus, Callahan, & Birkhauser, 1987; Snowden, Ostwald, Kane, & Keenan, 1989). Differences in age must be considered because, independent of approach to death, age accelerates the rate of change in performance over time; the effects of pathologies, and so of approaching death, may also alter as age advances (Rabbitt, Diggle, Holland, & McInnes, 2004).

Data from the University of Manchester Longitudinal Study, described in detail elsewhere (Rabbitt, Diggle, Holland, McInnes, Bent, et al., 2004), allowed us to make analyses of rates of change preceding death and dropout after the effects of practice, age, cohort effects, and demographics had also been considered.

Methods

Participants and Procedure

A panel of 5,842 volunteers, that is, 2,615 residents of Greater Manchester and 3,227 residents of Newcastle-upon Tyne, United Kingdom, were all sufficiently healthy and motivated to travel independently to the University of Newcastle-upon-Tyne or the University of Manchester, where they were given cognitive tests in groups of 10 to 20. There were 1,711 men aged between 49 and 93 years ($M = 65.6$, $SD = 7.7$) and 4,131 women aged between 49 and 92 years ($M = 64.4$, $SD = 7.8$). They were each paid £5 (UK) per session to cover expenses. A search by Her Majesty's Registry Office UK obtained exact dates and proximate causes for all 2,342 deaths between 1983, when the study began, and the census date, July 2004. Of 3,204 dropouts, 1,208 also died before the census date. Most dropouts only appeared as failures to answer invitations for testing and so could only be dated from the last session attended. Consequently, to compare rates of changes preceding dropout and death, we had to use the same dating. We could not compare changes preceding dropouts from different causes because many participants did not reveal them. However, a previous survey found that, although most respondents before 1993 cited poor health as their reason for dropping out, many cited positive reasons such as taking up new employment (Rabbitt et al., 1994). Thus, data pooled overall dropouts underestimates the effects of illness and increasing frailty. The remaining 1,996 participants did not drop out before July 2003 and also survived the July 2004 census of deaths. During the course of the study from 1983 to 2004, 7 participants were identified as suffering from dementias, either by death certificates or information from relatives, and we excluded these. Since 2004, all survivors have been screened every 6 months on the Mini-Mental State Examination and other assessment protocols for dementias, and so far nine cases have been identified. We have also retrospectively excluded these. Although it is impossible to be certain that no individuals contributing data did not also suffer from dementia, the latter figure suggests that the incidence was sufficiently low as to have hardly any effect on the comparisons described.

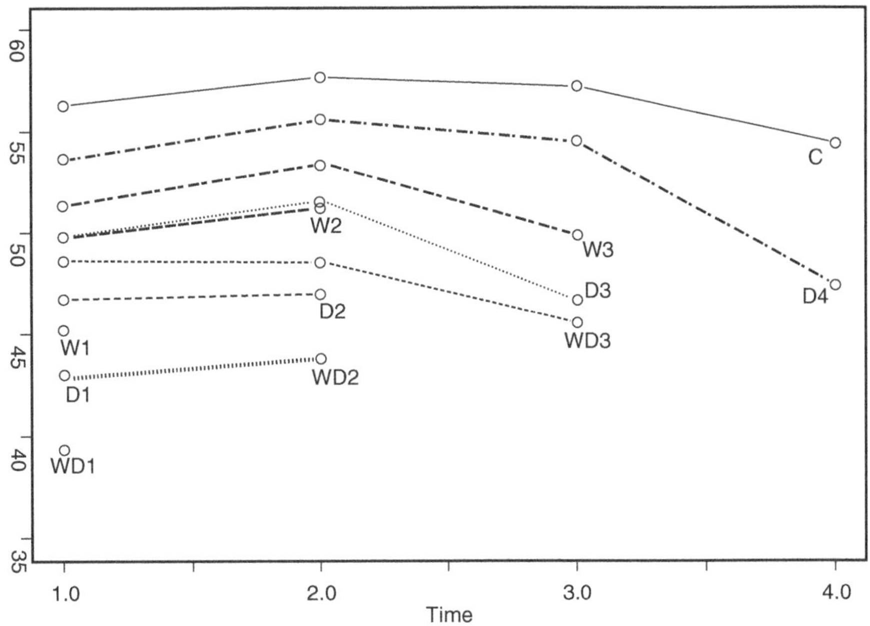

Figure 12.1 Profiles of percentage scores on the Heim AH4-1 test (AH41) of fluid intelligence across testing sessions for survivor (C), death (D), and dropout (W) groups.

Materials

Some of us have given details of the entire study elsewhere (Rabbitt, Diggle, Holland, McInnes, Bent, et al., 2004). The data analyzed here are from tests of general fluid intelligence, that is, the Heim (1970) AH4-1 intelligence test; of vocabulary, that is, the Raven (1965) Mill Hill B Vocabulary Test; and cumulative verbal learning, that is, the Cumulative Verbal Learning task (CVL task) administered on four successive occasions at 4-year intervals between 1983–1985 and 2003. The AH4-1 test consists of 64 logic, verbal comparisons, and arithmetic problems. Scores are the percentages of correct answers given within 10 minutes. The Mill Hill B Vocabulary Test requires correct definitions for each of 34 words with no time limit. For the CVL task, 15 three-syllable words matched for frequency (1/100,000) and concreteness are projected, one at a time, on a screen at a rate of 1/1.5 s. Participants recall as many words as possible and the words are then shown three times in different random orders and recalled without sight of previous attempts. Scores are percentages of correct answers.

Levels of socioeconomic advantage (SEA) are indexed by the Office of Population Censuses and Surveys (1980) in their classification of occupational

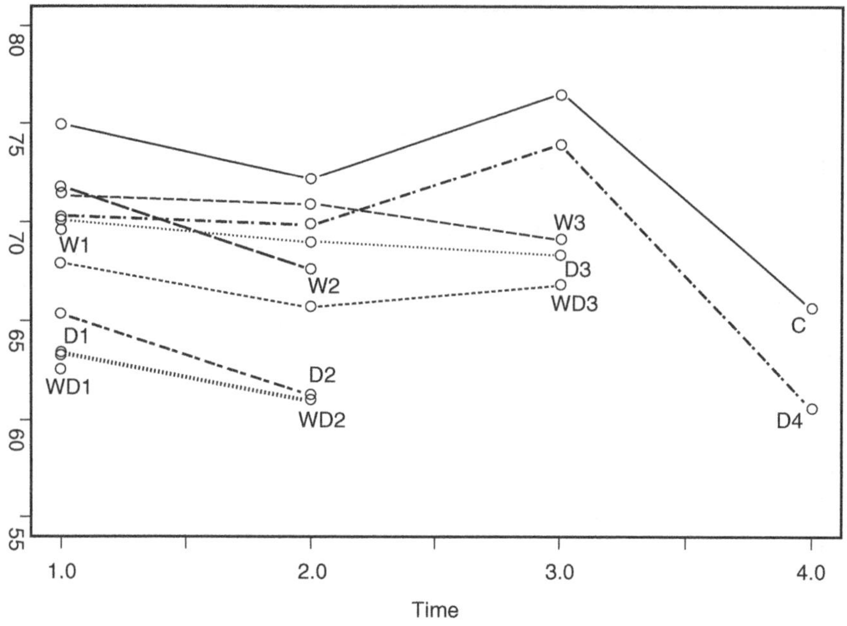

Figure 12.2 Profiles of percentage scores on the Cumulative Verbal Learning task across testing sessions for survivor (C), death (D), and dropout (W) groups.

categories. These categories are as follows: C1, made up of professionals such as doctors, lawyers, senior managers, and academics; C2, which consists of other professionals such as schoolteachers, junior managers, and pharmacists; C3N, made up of skilled nonmanual workers such as secretaries and clerical workers; C3M, consisting of skilled manual workers such as plumbers, craftsmen, joiners, fitters, and machinists; C4, made up of nonskilled, nonmanual workers such as security guards; and C5, which consists of nonskilled manual workers such as cleaners. We categorized those participants who did not reveal occupations as nonresponders (labeled NR). We include SEAs, city of residence, gender, and recruitment cohort in all analyses.

We divided participants into 11 groups according to their histories of survival, dropout, and death, logged with respect to the four quadrennial assessment time points: T1, T2, T3, and T4. The groups, labeled as D (for death), W (for withdrawal), or WD (for withdrawal followed by death), are as follows: D1 completed T1 but died before T2; D2 completed T1 and T2 but died before T3; D3 completed T1, T2, and T3 but died before T4; D4 completed T1, T2, T3, and T4 but died before the close of the census of deaths in 2004; WD1 completed T1 but withdrew before T2 and also died before the 2004 census; WD2 completed T1 and T2 but withdrew and then died before the 2004 census; WD3 completed T1, T2, and T3 but withdrew and then died before the 2004 census; W1 completed T1 and withdrew before T2 but survived the 2004 census; W2 completed T1 and T2, withdrew before T3, but survived the 2004 census; W3 completed T1, T2, and T3, withdrew before T4, but survived the 2004 census. Group C was a control group whose members completed all four assessments and survived the 2004 census.

The average raw scores for each of these death and dropout groups at each of the four testing occasions, that is, T1, T2, T3, and T4, are plotted for the AH4-1 test in Figure 12.1, for the CVL task in Figure 12.2, and for the Mill Hill B Vocabulary Test in Figure 12.3. Note that we have not taken effects of differences in age, recruitment cohort, and demographics into consideration. Although these means illustrate the logic of grouping individuals in this way, they only provide very approximate indications of specific comparisons between data points. Results of comparisons between these means, after age, cohort, and demographics have been considered, are described in the following paragraphs.

Figure 12.1, 12.2, and 12.3 show that, for all tests, and most clearly for the AH4-1, there is a clear vertical separation between most groups from Group C through Group WD3. We exploit this in the pattern-mixture mixed-effects model by introducing an indicator for the group to which the individual belongs.

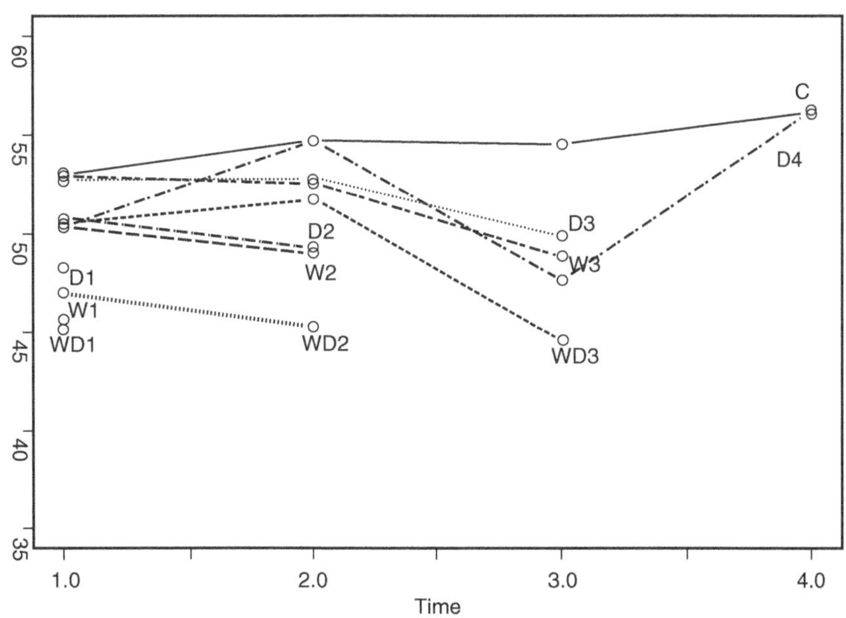

Figure 12.3. Profiles of percentage scores on the Mill Hill B Vocabulary Test (MHB) across testing sessions for survivor (C), death (D), and dropout (W) groups.

Results

Table 12.1 show details of the demographic and age categories, and death and withdrawal categories, and mean scores of these subgroups on the AH4-1 test, the Mill Hill B Vocabulary Test, and the CVL task.

Analyses

Methodology. —Our analyses were based on the models described by some of us elsewhere (Rabbitt, Diggle, Smith, Holland, & McInnes, 2001; Rabbitt, Diggle, Holland, McInnes, Bent, et al., 2004; Rabbitt et al., 2005). We consider age, gender, socioeconomic status, and whether participants are taking the test for the first, second, third, or fourth time (the practice effect). We also include cities of residence and years of recruitment of cohorts to adjust for

Table 12.1 Means and standard deviations of scores on intelligence, verbal learning, and vocabulary tests for age and demographic groups

Subset	*M(SD) AH4-1*	*M(SD) CVL*	*M(SD)MHB*
Manchester (2,615)	49.6 (17.7)	71.6 (13.9)	54.8 (17.9)
Newcastle (3,227)	47.5 (17.3)	67.5 (14.8)	45.2 (17.9)
Men (1,711)	50.9 (17.4)	66.2 (15.1)	52.1 (18.4)
Women (4,131)	47.4 (17.4)	70.4 (14.2)	48.5 (18.5)
Oclass C1 (261)	61.1 (14.0)	72.2 (13.4)	63.3 (15.8)
Oclass C2 (1,849)	56.2 (16.6)	73.1 (13.4)	58.3 (16.6)
Oclass C3(NM)(2,061)	48.4 (14.9)	70.1 (13.6)	48.1 (16.2)
Oclass C3M (771)	39.2 (15.8)	63.0 (14.4)	40.6 (16.7)
Oclass C4 (433)	34.4 (14.0)	61.7 (14.7)	35.3 (16.3)
Oclass C5 (47)	31.0 (16.6)	55.5 (17.4)	29.9 (16.7)
Oclass Na (420)	40.5 (18.3)	62.6 (18.0)	42.7 (20.1)
Age 49–60 (1,347)	55.4 (17.1)	75.5 (12.9)	51.7 (18.0)
Age 61–70 (2,849)	49.5 (16.6)	69.7 (13.8)	49.4 (18.2)
Age 71–80 (1,477)	41.8 (16.5)	63.5 (14.7)	48.1 (19.4)
Age 80+(169)	33.7 (15.5)	57.5 (16.7)	47.8 (20.0)
Pattern			
C (1,504)	56.3 (16.2)	74.9 (12.1)	53.0 (17.4)
D1 (365)	43.0 (17.4)	63.4 (16.8)	48.3 (19.4)
D2 (408)	46.7 (16.6)	65.3 (14.5)	50.8 (19.2)
D3 (246)	49.9 (14.8)	70.1 (12.7)	52.8 (18.7)
D4 (115)	53.6 (16.3)	70.2 (12.9)	50.4 (19.5)
WD1 (745)	39.4 (17.5)	62.5 (15.9)	45.2 (19.4)
WD2 (354)	42.9 (15.4)	63.2 (14.8)	47.0 (19.4)
WD3 (109)	48.7 (16.0)	67.9 (14.1)	50.5 (19.5)
W1 (1,013)	45.2 (17.1)	69.6 (14.3)	45.6 (18.2)
W2 (595)	49.8 (16.8)	71.7 (13.2)	50.4 (17.8)
W3 (388)	51.4 (15.6)	71.4 (13.3)	52.9 (16.6)

Note: AH4-1 = Heim AH4-1 test of fluid intelligence; CVL = Cumulative Verbal Learning task; MHB = Mill Hill B Vocabulary Test; Oclass = occupational class (see text for details on the C designations). For patterns, C = control, D = death, and W = withdrawal (see text for particular designations).

unidentified confounding factors. The model can be considered in two parts: a model for the average response over time for a subject with given values of all explanatory variables, and a model for the random variation about the main response.

The aim is to determine the effect of imminent death on a participant's cognitive performance. However, some participants who withdraw survive beyond the census date whereas others do not, giving three mechanisms by which they fail to complete the tests: death, withdrawal, and withdrawal followed by death. The statistical method determines whether or not these three mechanisms have similar effects on the test scores.

There are at least two possible approaches to handling missing data. One uses a selection model, and the other uses a pattern-mixture model. We are interested in a retrospective analysis of the effects of death and dropout, and so a pattern mixture model is an ideal tool. The probability density function is factored as $f(y, d) = f(y|d)f(d)$, where y represents the response and d represents the dropout data. We will be interested in the first factor on the right-hand side of the equation, which represents the response conditional on the dropout pattern. In this data set, dropouts occur between test sessions or between the last session and the end of the study, but they are also of three types: death, dropout followed by death, and dropout with survival after census. We can thus classify volunteers into groups by dropout type or pattern. We model the conditional density as we did in Rabbitt and colleagues (2001), that is,

$$Y_{ij} = \mu_{ij} + A_i + B_i x_{ij1} + E_{ij},$$

where the mean value of Y_{ij} is given by

$$\mu_{ij} = \beta_0 + \beta_1 x_{ij1} + \beta_2 x_{ij2} + \ldots + \beta_p x_{ijp} + \gamma_2 g_{i2} + \ldots + \gamma_r g_{ir}.$$

Index i is the identifier of the volunteer, index j gives the occasion of the test ($j = 1, \ldots, 4$), and x_{ijk} denotes the values of the explanatory variables, where k runs from 1 to p and g_{im} is an indicator, a value 1 denoting to which of r type or pattern groups the ith volunteer belongs. Only one of these indicators is nonzero. The first two variables x_{ij1} and x_{ij2} are related to age and age squared, with a value of zero corresponding to age 49, which is close to the mean age.

As in Rabbitt and colleagues (2001), the random effects (Level 2) are given by $A_i + B_i x_{ij1}$, where (A_i, B_i) are bivariate normal with a mean of zero and covariance matrix

$$\Sigma = \begin{pmatrix} \sigma_A^2 & \sigma_{AB} \\ \sigma_{AB} & \sigma_B^2 \end{pmatrix}$$

and are independent of the Level 1 error, E_{ij}, which follows a univariate normal distribution with a mean of zero and variance σ_E^2.

This allows us to quantify the mean effect of death or withdrawal, including also the test occasion by which this has occurred. It also allows us to make a direct comparison of the effects of death and of withdrawal, as we shall see.

We have also considered interactions between the various explanatory variables and these are included in the final models.

Analysis of AH4-1 intelligence test scores. —To illustrate general trends common to all tasks, we give analyses of AH4-1 scores in detail. Scores for vocabulary and cumulative learning are jointly discussed in the subsequent text. Table 12.1 shows results from a linear mixed-effects pattern-mixture model comparing percentages of correct unadjusted AH4-1 scores for the death and dropout groups after the effects of age, gender, occupational category, city of residence, recruitment cohort, and practice are considered. Age was centered at 49, the lowest recorded in the study. Variance between individuals has been modeled with random effects because these are longitudinal data and measurements from the same individual are correlated.

Significant linear and quadratic terms show an accelerating decline in mean scores with increasing age. Because there is no Age × Death or Age × Dropout Group interaction, there is no evidence that the cognitive effects of death or dropout differ with the ages at which they occur. There is no interaction between group and any of the variables of age, gender, city, occupational class, or cohort (entry year), but there is a significant constant effect of group at each session time, as seen in the plot of the raw data. (It is not possible to look for an interaction with session time because these regression coefficients would be unidentifiable.)

There are, however, some significant interactions of age with practice gains. The interaction between age and the difference between scores at T1 and T2 is not significant, but the interactions between age and the T3 versus T1 difference ($p = .0086$) and between age and the T4 versus T1 difference ($p = .0089$) are significant. In survivors, deceased individuals, and dropouts alike, the effect of age on test scores increases with the interval over which it is measured. Overall, men ($M = 50.9$, $SD = 17.7$) scored higher than women did ($M = 47.4$, $SD = 17.4$). The significant Age × Sex interaction shows that even when longevity has been taken into account, women decline less as they age. Mancunians or persons from Greater Manchester ($M = 49.6$, $SD = 17.7$) score higher than Novocastrians or persons from Newcastle ($M = 47.5$, $SD = 17.3$). Scores range from 61.1, $SD = 14.0$, for C1 (the most advantaged SEA group), to 31.0, $SD = 16.6$, for SEA C5. This is reflected in the main model, shown in Table 12.2. There, we can see that the mean score of C5 is over 14% lower than that of C3 (both C3N and C3M), the baseline class, and that of C1 is 9.5% higher than C3 (C3N and C3M). There are significant differences between recruitment waves with performance for entry years 1990 and 1992 that are greater than those for 1985 (baseline). There is a highly significant practice gain between T1 and T2 followed by rather less substantial gains (less than 2%) between T2 and T3 and between T3 and T4.

Table 12.2 Model for Analysis of Scores on the AH4-1 Intelligence Test

Item	*CE*	SE	df	t	P
(Intercept)	53.63	0.75	6732	70.68	<.0001
Age	−0.77	0.04	6732	−19.16	<.0001
Age^2	−0.014	0.00	6732	−5.78	<.0001
Gender	−2.25	0.44	5814	−5.09	<.0001
City	−1.42	0.66	5814	−2.13	.03
Oclass C1	9.58	0.96	5814	9.91	<.0001
Oclass C2	6.14	0.46	5814	13.26	<.0001
Oclass C3M	−8.56	0.60	5814	−14.09	<.0001
Oclass C4	−11.96	0.74	5814	−16.06	<.0001
Oclass C5	−14.85	2.07	5814	−7.14	<.0001
Oclass Na	−5.42	0.79	5814	−6.78	<.0001
T2	3.71	0.18	6732	20.43	<.0001
T3	3.54	0.29	6732	19.08	<.0001
T4	7.22	0.52	6732	13.78	<.0001
Entry year					
1982	2.49	1.73	5814	0.28	.7737
1983	−1.86	0.89	5814	−2.09	.0365
1984	−1.16	0.85	5814	−1.36	.1713
1986	−0.27	0.68	5814	−0.40	.6884
1987	−1.59	1.10	5814	−1.43	.1502
1988	−0.55	0.74	5814	−0.74	.4552
1990	9.28	2.79	5814	3.32	.0009
1991	1.86	0.86	5814	2.16	.0305
1992	3.08	0.82	5814	3.72	.0002
Pattern					
D1	−7.22	0.87	5814	8.21	<.0001
D2	−5.03	0.79	5814	−6.31	<.0001
D3	−3.71	0.96	5814	−3.86	.0001
D4	0.41	1.34	5814	0.31	.7569
WD1	−9.93	0.69	5814	−14.28	<.0001
WD2	7.24	0.85	5814	−8.47	<.0001
WD3	3.43	1.38	5814	−2.48	.0129
W1	−8.15	0.60	5814	−13.45	<.0001
W2	−4.71	0.68	5814	−6.85	<.0001
W3	−2.46	0.80	5814	−3.07	.0021
Interactions					
Age × Gender	0.08	0.03	6732	2.66	.0076
Age × T2	−0.04	0.02	6732	−1.82	.0686
Age × T3	−0.12	0.04	6732	−2.62	.0086
Age × T4	−0.20	0.07	6732	−2.61	.0089

Residual standard deviations: Levels 1 and 2

Level		*SD*	Correlation with intercept
2	Intercept	13.086	
2	Age	0.389	0.05
1	Residual	5.467	

Note: CE = coefficient; T1–T4 = Times 1–4; Oclass = occupational class (see text for details on the C designations); Oclass Na = occupational class not specified. For patterns, D = death and W = withdrawal (see text for particular designations).

After we consider these effects and interactions, then we compare the death, withdrawal, or death followed by withdrawal groups against those for the control group of survivors, Group C. Table 12.3 compares average scores throughout the study between Group C survivors and all others by using t values computed from the main model. Group C survivors score higher than any of the members of the death and withdrawal groups except Group D4, whose members also completed all four assessments but then died within the 12 months before the death census in July 2004. Table 12.3 shows comparisons by two tailed *t* tests between all other death and withdrawal groups. After applying a Bonferroni correction for multiple testing, we take the threshold level for significance for these multiple comparisons as $p = .001$.

Comparing the effects of death and dropout.—Specific comparisons using *t* tests (calculated from the main model) compared differences in the amounts of practice gains between survivors and death and withdrawal groups. After correction the threshold for significance is $p = .001$. Persons in Group D2 completed assessments at T1 and T2 but then died before T3. From the raw data their nonsignificant gain in average scores between T1 and T2 was 0.03 points. Again from the raw data, members of Group C, who completed all four assessments and survived the census date, shows a gain of 1.34 points between test sessions T1 and T2. From the main model, over all test sessions, we see that Group D2 and Group C have significantly different mean scores (5%), $p < .0001$. Similarly, Group D1 and Group C have significantly different scores (7%), $p < .0001$, with a rather larger loss of score than Group D2, as would be expected from their more imminent time of death. Group D3 again has a significant loss as compared with Group C but with a smaller mean difference than those of D1 and D2.

Table 12.3 Specific Comparisons of Mean AH4-1 Intelligence Test Scores Between Death and Dropout Groups

AH4-1	*D1*	*D2*	*D3*	*D4*	*W1*	*W2*	*W3*	*WD1*	*WD2*	*WD3*
C	.0001	.0001	.0001		.0001	.0001		.0001	.0001	
D1				.0001			.0001		.001	
D2				.0002						
D3										
D4										
W1						.0001	.0001			.0009
W2										
W3										
WD1										.0001

Note: Values of *t* statistics are derived from the main model. After correction, $p < .001$ is taken as the threshold for significance. C = control group; D = death and W = withdrawal (see text for particular designations).

Similar results can be seen for comparisons between Group C and (dropout and survivor) Groups W1 through W3. Rather more pronounced results of a similar nature are also seen with Groups WD1 through WD3 (participants who dropped out and subsequently died).

Both from the raw data (Figure 12.1) and from the main model (Table 12.2), we see that death, dropout, and dropout with sub- sequent death persons do indeed model in much the same way as do overall survivors who did not withdraw.

Analyses for cumulative verbal learning and vocabulary.—Tables 12.4 and 12.5 and Tables 12.6 and 12.7 show the same analyses for correct percentage scores on the CVL task and Mill Hill B Vocabulary Test, respectively.

For the CVL task, significant linear and quadratic age terms show that mean decline accelerates as calendar age increases over all survival, dropout, and death groups. In the Mill Hill B Vocabulary Test, the mean effects of age and of age squared are not significant. In both tests, because age does not significantly interact with death or withdrawal group membership, there is no evidence that approaching death causes more rapid decline in older than in younger participants. Women score higher than men on the CVL task, but a similar result on the Mill Hill B Vocabulary Test has only a 5% significance level. On both tasks there are no significant Sex × Age interactions and so there is no evidence that men and women decline at different rates. Mancunians score significantly higher than Novocastrians on the Mill Hill B Vocabulary Test, but persons from the different cities do not differ on the CVL task. Greater SEA (occupational class) is associated with better overall performance but there is no Occupational Class × Test Sessions interaction and so no evidence that occupational class affects rates of decline. On both

Table 12.4 Model for Analysis of Scores on the Cumulative Verbal Learning Task

Item	*CE*	SE	df	t	P
(Intercept)	68.96	0.70	5603	97.93	<.0001
Age	−0.82	0.04	5603	−19.06	<.0001
Age^2	−0.01	0.01	5603	−3.95	.0001
Gender	4.18	0.46	4774	10.28	<.0001
City	−0.53	0.76	4774	−0.70	.4824
Oclass C1	3.14	0.90	4774	3.48	.0005
Oclass C2	2.93	0.41	4774	7.12	<.0001
Oclass C3M	−4.59	0.55	4774	−8.23	<.0001
Oclass C4	−6.09	0.68	4774	−8.87	<.0001
Oclass C5	−11.44	1.95	4774	−5.85	<.0001
Oclass Na	−3.17	0.93	4774	−3.38	.0007
T2	−0.56	0.24	5603	−2.32	.0202
T3	4.79	0.35	5603	13.57	<.0001
T4	−0.21	0.60	5603	−0.35	.7237

(*Continued*)

Item	*CE*	SE	df	t	P
Entry year					
1982	−1.77	1.53	4774	−1.15	.2490
1983	−5.68	0.87	4774	−6.52	<.0001
1984	−1.23	0.85	4774	−1.45	.1468
1986	−1.41	0.59	4774	−2.37	.0176
1987	−0.59	0.98	4774	−0.60	.5479
1988	0.48	0.71	4774	0.68	.4957
1991	0.62	0.97	4774	0.63	.5237
1992	0.75	1.49	4774	0.50	.6138
Pattern					
D1	−5.25	0.93	4774	−5.64	<.0001
D2	−4.56	0.77	4774	−5.91	<.0001
D3	−0.78	0.92	4774	−0.84	.4004
D4	0.17	1.18	4774	−0.14	.8811
WD1	−7.05	0.68	4774	−10.34	<.0001
WD2	−6.06	0.75	4774	−8.06	<.0001
WD3	−2.40	1.16	4774	− 2.06	.0391
W1	−4.78	0.58	4774	−8.22	<.0001
W2	−2.56	0.60	4774	−4.24	<.0001
W3	−1.58	0.65	4774	−2.41	.0157
Interactions					
Age × City	0.36	0.03	5603	10.41	<.0001
Age × T2	−0.08	0.03	5603	−2.46	.0137
Age × T3	−0.18	0.05	5603	−3.25	.0012
Age × T4	−0.36	0.09	5603	−3.92	.0001

Residual standard deviations: Levels 1 and 2

Level		*SD*	Correlation with intercept
2	Intercept	10.607	
2	Age	0.444	0.533
1	Residual	7.433	

Note: CE = coefficient; T1–T4 = Times 1–4; Oclass = occupational class (see text for details on the C designations); Oclass Na = occupational class not specified. For patterns, D = death and W = withdrawal (see text for particular designations).

Table 12.5 Specific Comparisons of Mean CVL Task Scores Between Death and Dropout Groups

CVL	*D1*	*D2*	*D3*	*D4*	*W1*	*W2*	*W3*	*WD1*	*WD2*	*WD3*
C	.0001	.0001			.0001	.0001		.0001	.0001	
D1			.0002	.0004		.0066	.0003			
D2			.0005	.0009			.0007			
D3										
D4										
W1						.0007	.0001			
W2										
W3										
WD1										.0002
WD2										

Note: Values of *t* statistics are derived from the main model. After correction, p < .001 is taken as the threshold for significance. CVL task = Cumulative Verbal Learning task; C = control group; D = death and W = withdrawal (see text for particular designations).

Table 12.6 Model for Analysis of Scores on the Mill Hill B Vocabulary Test

Item	*CE*	SE	df	t	P
(Intercept)	57.88	0.82	6797	70.51	<.0001
Age	0.01	0.04	6797	0.02	0.97
Age^2	−0.01	0.01	6797	−0.87	.3789
Gender	1.02	0.47	5837	−2.12	.0339
City	−6.08	0.72	5837	−8.48	<.0001
Oclass C1	12.67	1.03	5837	12.24	<.0001
Oclass C2	8.91	0.49	5837	18.06	<.0001
Oclass C3M	−7.36	0.65	5837	−11.21	<.0001
Oclass C4	−11.69	0.80	5837	−14.46	<.0001
Oclass C5	−16.88	2.26	5837	−7.46	<.0001
Oclass Na	−3.57	0.86	5837	−4.12	<.0001
T2	0.13	0.26	6797	0.51	.6039
T3	−1.40	0.37	6797	−3.70	.0002
T4	3.24	0.66	6797	4.89	<.0001
Entry year					
1982	1.82	1.83	5837	0.99	.3210
1983	0.07	0.95	5837	0.08	.9331
1984	−2.36	0.90	5837	−2.59	.0094
1986	−1.81	0.74	5837	−2.45	.0141
1987	−3.75	1.18	5837	−3.18	.0015
1988	−0.12	0.80	5837	−0.15	.8751
1990	1.05	2.94	5837	0.35	.7209
1991	−3.34	0.93	5837	−3.56	.0004
1992	−3.06	0.90	5837	−3.38	.0007
Pattern					
D1	−5.41	0.98	5837	−5.51	<.0001
D2	−3.57	0.85	5837	−4.20	<.0001
D3	−2.31	1.01	5837	−2.27	.0227
D4	−1.02	−0.73	5837	1.39	.4652
WD1	−7.90	0.76	5837	−10.29	<.0001
WD2	−6.09	0.92	5837	−6.61	<.0001
WD3	−1.78	1.47	5837	−1.21	.2239
W1	−7.26	0.65	5837	−11.09	<.0001
W2	−4.67	0.72	5837	−6.48	<.0001
W3	−1.73	0.84	5837	−2.05	.0402
Interactions					
Age × T2	−0.01	0.03	6797	−0.41	.6755
Age × T3	−0.04	0.06	6797	−0.72	.4687
Age × T4	−0.31	0.09	6797	−3.25	.0011

Residual standard deviations: Levels 1 and 2

Level		*SD*	Correlation with intercept
2	Intercept	13.513	
2	Age	0.097	0.845
1	Residual	9.163	

Note: CE = coefficient; T1–T4 = Times 1–4; Oclass = occupational class (see text for details on the C designations); Oclass Na = occupational class not specified. For patterns, D = death and W = withdrawal (see text for particular designations).

Table 12.7 Specific comparisons of MHB scores between death and dropout groups

MHB	*D1*	*D2*	*D3*	*D4*	*W1*	*W2*	*W3*	*WD1*	*WD2*	*WD3*
C	.0001	.0001			.0001	.0001		.0001	.0001	
D1							.001			
D2										
D3										
D4										
W1						.0002	.0001			.0009
W2							.001			
W3										
WD1										.0004
WD2										
WD3										

Note: Values of *t* statistics are derived from the main model. After correction, $p <.001$ is taken as the threshold for significance. MHB = Mill Hill B Vocabulary Test; C = control group; D = death and W = withdrawal (see text for particular designations).

tasks, members of Group C, who continued and survived the census date, have a mean score that is higher than that of all other groups. Differences in mean gains again reflect the time to death or withdrawal.

Tables 12.5 and 12.7 show the results when t values from the main models for the CVL task and the Mill Hill B Vocabulary Test are used to compare overall scores between all death or withdrawal groups throughout the study. The corrected threshold for significance is $p =.001$.

For the CVL task, Tables 12.4 and 12.5 show that overall average scores for the D3 and D4 groups are significantly higher than for the D1 and D2 groups and that the D2 group scores higher than the D1 group, although this last item is not significant at the corrected level of $p = .001$. In other words, mean declines in verbal learning scores accelerate as death approaches. There are similar graded effects of dropout, with scores for the W3 group being higher than those for the W2 or W1 group and scores for the W2 group being higher than those for W1. The D1 and the W1 groups do not differ, suggesting that over this brief interval the effects of impending withdrawal are as severe as those of impending death. For the Mill Hill B Vocabulary Test, Table 12.6 shows that the mean differences follow similar patterns. Even scores on a test of crystallized intelligence, production vocabulary, fall as death approaches. There are no differences between those groups who drop out and then die shortly thereafter and those who die without first dropping out.

General Discussion

These analyses replicate the main findings of Rabbitt and colleagues (2005) for AH4-1 intelligence test scores on a much larger sample, extend and compare these to the CVL task and production vocabulary (Mill Hill B Vocabulary

Test), and examine the time courses of changes in greater detail, con- cluding that mean scores on all analyzed cognitive tests decline according to nearness of death or dropout.

Time Courses of Effects of Death and Dropout

There are significant declines up to 8 years preceding death, but participants who survived for more than 8 years after their first assessment (T1) performed almost as well as those who survived the final testing session. Because there is no Age × Death or Age × Dropout interaction, there is no evidence, in this study of atypically healthy participants, of change in the sizes or the time courses of the cognitive effects of approaching death between the ages of 49 and 93 years.

A new finding is that amounts of decline preceding dropout closely resemble those before death in all tests. Because only some participants gave reasons for dropout, we could not compare the decline of individuals who dropped out for different reasons. However, some of us (Rabbitt et al., 1994) found that the group of dropouts who gave reasons for withdrawal included relatively healthy and able people who withdrew for reasons such as employment. Because these analyses include such "robust dropouts," the actual similarity of declines preceding dropout caused by illness or frailty to those preceding death must be even closer than these analyses suggest. The finding that amounts of declines preceding impending death and dropout are so strikingly similar suggests that they are both caused by declining health. On this interpretation, death and dropout are empirically useful, but rough and indirect, markers for worsening health. The effects of approach to death, on their own, tell us little about the functional causes of cognitive decline. To learn more we must study precisely how particular terminal illnesses affect our brains and central nervous systems.

Are Different Cognitive Abilities Differentially Affected by Death and Dropout?

Declines with age for production vocabulary (Mill Hill B Vocabulary Test) are much less (and nonsignificant) than those for intelligence and cumulative verbal learning. Vocabulary, a skill crystallized because it is acquired early in life and maintained by continual practice into old age (Horn, 1987; Horn, Donaldson, & Engstrom, 1981), is not only relatively resistant to "normal" aging but also to the pathologies that accompany aging and that may terminate in death. The effect of death or withdrawal group is also weaker in Mill Hill B Vocabulary Test.

This result differs from previous findings that vocabulary test scores may be especially sensitive to approaching death (Berg, 1987; Birren, 1965; Siegler, McCarty, & Logue, 1982). It is noteworthy that these previous studies were cross-sectional and used relatively elderly samples and brief census periods of 24 months or less. It is therefore possible that participants in these studies were quite near to their deaths but that this could not be observed because the census periods were so short. It is therefore plausible that declines in vocabulary only become marked very shortly before death and so were less pronounced in the present study, in which the times of measurement were 4 years or longer. It seems likely that individuals who are, as yet, only experiencing declines in so-called fluid abilities are relatively further from death than those whose terminal pathologies have become severe enough to affect even their crystallized abilities. Accepting this context declines in vocabulary are particularly sensitive markers of approaching death.

Effects of Gender and Demographic Variables

Women perform better than men on the CVL task and on the Mill Hill B Vocabulary Test (the latter at a marginal significance level), and men perform better than women on the AH4-1 intelligence test. On the AH4-1 task, although women score lower on average than men do, they also decline more slowly as they grow older. This is informative because the effects of differences in death and dropout have been taken into consideration, as the slower declines of women of advancing age cannot be attributed simply to their greater longevity or lower dropout rate. This raises a fruitful topic for further investigation. It is possible that examining the differences in the nature of terminal pathologies in men and women would be informative.

A different point is that significant gender advantages in baseline scores are opposite on different cognitive tests. This means that if we do not take into account the typical progressive, age-related increases in the proportion of women to men during longitudinal studies, then our speculations as to which cognitive abilities are most and least sensitive to age and pathology will be insecure.

Recruitment cohorts differ markedly in cognitive test score and, as exploratory analyses show, also in average levels of SEA. Because mortality is strongly associated with level of general intellectual ability (Hart et al., 2003) and with SEA (e.g., Nagi & Stockwell, 1973), it is essential that researchers check for differences between recruitment cohorts when analyzing the effects of impending death on cognitive performance.

Methodological Issues

Most studies have found that particular pathologies that become common in later life, such as diabetes (e.g., Bent, Rabbitt, & Metcalf, 2000), hypertension and other cardiovascular problems (Fahlander et al., 2000; Hertzog, Schaie, & Gribbin, 1978; Lopez et al., 2003), respiratory problems (Holland & Rabbitt, 1991), and undifferentiated health problems (McInnes & Rabbitt, 1997), have significant but surprisingly small effects on cognitive performance. Most studies have compared patients and healthy controls only at a single time point, and the few longitudinal studies have ignored death and dropout. The current analyses suggest that if individuals in so-called patient groups who die or withdraw are not included in comparisons against healthy controls, then the true effects of pathologies must be severely underestimated. If dropouts and deaths are excluded from analyses then the comparisons will involve only patients whose conditions are, as yet, relatively mild. The effects of terminal declines and of early stages of pathologies can only be compared if all deaths and dropouts are logged and taken into account.

References

Bent, N., Rabbitt, P. M. A., & Metcalf, D. (2000). Diabetes mellitus and the rate of cognitive change. *British Journal of Clinical Psychology, 39*, 349–362.

Berg, S. (1987). Intelligence and terminal decline. In G. Maddox and E. W. Busse (Eds.), *Aging: The universal human experience* (pp. 234–259). New York: Springer.

Birren, J. E. (1965). Age changes in speed of behavior: Its critical nature and physiological correlates. In A. T. Welford and J. E. Birren (Eds.), *Behavior, aging and the nervous system* (pp. 171–189). Springfield, IL: Charles C Thomas.

Fahlander, K., Wahlin, A., Grut, M., Forsell, Y., Hill, R. D., Winblad, B., et al. (2000). The relationship between signs of cardiovascular deficiency and cognitive performance in old age. *Journal of Gerontology: Psychological Sciences, 55B*, P259–P265.

Hart, C. L., Taylor, M. D., Davey-Smith, G., Whalley, L. J., Starr, J. M., Hole, D. J., et al. (2003). Childhood IQ, social class, deprivation and their relationships with mortality risk in later life: Prospective observational study linking the Scottish Mental Survey 1932 and the Midspan Studies. *Psychosomatic Medicine, 65*, 877–883.

Hertzog, C., Schaie, K. W., & Gribbin, K. (1978). Cardiovascular disease and changes in intellectual functioning from middle to old age. *Gerontology, 33*, 872–883.

Holland, C. M., & Rabbitt, P. M. A. (1991). The course and causes of cognitive change with advancing age. *Reviews in Clinical Gerontology, 1*, 81–96.

Horn, J. L. (1987). A context for understanding information processing studies of human abilities. In P. A. Vernon (Ed.), *Speed of information processing and intelligence* (pp. 201–238). Norwood, NJ: Ablex.

Horn, J. L., Donaldson, G., & Engstrom, R. (1981). Application, memory and fluid intelligence decline in adulthood. *Research on Aging, 3*, 33–84.

Houx, P. J. (1991). Rigorous health screening reduces age effects on a memory scanning task. *Brain and Cognition, 15*, 246–260.

Johansson, B., & Berg, S. (1989). The robustness of the terminal decline phenomenon: Longitudinal data from the digit-span memory test. *Journal of Gerontology: Psychological Sciences, 44B*, P184–P186.

Kleemeier, R. W. (1962). Intellectual changes in the senium. *Proceedings of the Social Statistics Section of the American Statistical Association, 23*, 290–295.

Lachman, R., Lachman, J. L., & Taylor, D. W. (1982). Reallocation of mental resources over the productive lifespan: Assumptions and task analyses. In F. I. M. Craik & S. Trehub, (Eds.), *Aging and the cognitive process* (pp 304–350). New York: Plenum Press.

Lieberman, M. A. (1965). Psychological correlates of impending death: Some preliminary observations. *Gerontology, 20*, 181–190.

Lopez, O. L., Jagust, W. J., Dulberg, C., Becker, J. T., De Kosky, S. T., Fitzpatrick, A., et al. (2003). Risk factors for mild cognitive impairment in the Cardiovascular Health Study cognition study. *Archives of Neurology, 60*, 1394–1399.

McInnes, L., & Rabbitt, P. M. (1997). The relationship between functional ability and cognitive ability among elderly people. In *Facts and research in gerontology* (pp. 34–45). Paris: Sardi.

Nagi, M. H., & Stockwell, E. G. (1973). Socioeconomic differentials in mortality by cause of death. *Health Services Reports, 88*, 449–456.

Office of Population Censuses and Surveys. (1980). *Classification of occupations 1980.* London, England: Her Majesty's Stationery Office.

Palmore, E., & Cleveland, W. (1976). Aging, terminal decline and terminal drop. *Gerontology, 31*, 76–81.

Pincus, T., Callaghan, L. F., & Birkhauser, R. V. (1987). Most chronic diseases are reported most frequently by individuals with fewer than 12 years formal education in the age 18–64 US population. *Journal of Chronic Disorders, 40*, 865–874.

Rabbitt, P. (2002). Cognitive gerontology. In H. Pashler & J. Wixted (Eds.), *Stevens' handbook of experimental psychology* (Vol. 4., pp. 203–254). New York: Wiley.

Rabbitt, P., Diggle, P., Holland, F., & McInnes, L. (2004). Practice and drop-out effects during a 17-year longitudinal study of cognitive aging. *Journal of Gerontology: Psychological Sciences, 59B*, P84–P97.

Rabbitt, P., Diggle, P., Smith, D., Holland, F., & McInnes, L. (2001). Identifying and separating the effects of practice and of cognitive ageing during a large longitudinal study of elderly community residents. *Neuropsychologia, 39*, 532–543.

Rabbitt, P., Lunn, M., & Wong, D. (2005). Neglect of dropout underestimates effects of death in longitudinal studies. *Journal of Gerontology: Psychological Sciences, 60B*, P106–P109.

Rabbitt, P., Watson, P., Donlan, C., Bent, N., & McInnes, L. (1994). Subject attrition in a longitudinal study of cognitive performance in community resident elderly people. In B. J. Vellas, J. L. Albarende, & P. J. Garry (Eds.), *Facts and research in gerontology: Epidemiology and aging* (pp. 29–34). Paris: Serdi.

Rabbitt, P., Watson, P., Donlan, C., McInnes, L., Horan, M., Pendleton, N., et al. (2002). Effects of death within 11 years on cognitive performance in old age. *Psychology and Aging, 17*, 1–14.

Rabbitt, P.M.A., Diggle, P., Holland, F., McInnes, L., Bent, N., Abson, V., et al. (2004). The University of Manchester longitudinal study of cognition in normal healthy old age, 1983 through 2003. *Aging, Neuropsychology and Cognition, 11*, 245–279.

Raven, J. C. (1965). *The Mill Hill Vocabulary Scale.* London: Lewis.

Reimanis, G., & Green, R. (1971). Immanence of death and intellectual decrement in the aging. *Developmental Psychology, 5*, 270–272.

Riegel, K. F., & Riegel, R. M. (1972). Development, drop and death. *Developmental Psychology, 6*, 306–319.

Riegel, K. F., Riegel, R. M., & Meyer, G. (1967). A study of the drop-out rates in longitudinal research on aging and the prediction of death. *Journal of Personality and Social Psychology, 5*, 342–348.

Roth, M. (1986). The association of clinical and neuropsychological findings and its bearing on the classification and etiology of Alzheimer's disease. *British Medical Bulletin, 42*, 42–50.

Schaie, K. W., Labouvie, G. V. & Barrett, T. J. (1973). Selective attrition effects in a fourteen-year study of adult intelligence. *Gerontology, 28*, 328–334.

Siegler, I. C., & Botwinick, J. (1979). A long-term longitudinal study of intellectual ability of older adults: The matter of selective subject attrition. *Gerontology, 34*, 242–245.

Siegler, I. C., McCarty, S. M., & Logue, P. E. (1982). Wechsler Memory Scale scores: Selective attrition and distance from death. *Gerontology, 37*, 176–181.

Small, B. J., Fratiglioni, L., von Strauss, E., & Backman, L. (2003). Terminal decline and cognitive performance in very old age. *Psychology and Aging, 18*, 193–202.

Snowden, D. A., Ostwald, S. K., Kane, R. E. L., & Keenan, N. L. (1989). Years of life with good and poor mental and physical functions in the elderly. *Journal of Clinical Epidemiology, 42*, 1055–1066.

Van Boxtel, M. P. J., Buntink, F., Houx, P. J., Metsemakers, J. F. M., Knottmerus, A., & Jolles, J. (1998). The relation between morbidity and cognitive performance in a normal aging population. *Journal of Gerontology: Medical Sciences, 55A*, M147–M154.

Relating declining mental abilities to gross brain changes

Rabbitt, Lunn and Wong (2006) showed that reluctance or inability to continue with a study is associated with increasing frailty and so is a marker of cognitive decline. If we include "dropouts" in comparison groups of survivors we will underestimate the amounts of "terminal drops" in performance preceding deaths (e.g. Kleemeir, 1962; Palmore & Cleveland, 1976). We see that assessments of longitudinal declines are unreliable unless both practice and dropouts are considered (Rabbitt, Lunn and Wong, 2006). If we take this into consideration, we can also check whether deaths from different pathologies are preceded by different, and characteristic amounts and rates of cognitive declines. For example, Rabbitt et al. (2011) showed that the time-courses of cognitive changes before deaths from cancers are briefer than from cardiovascular disease or diabetes. The latter affect cognitive abilities over many years before they end life. Aichele, Rabbitt and Ghisletta (2015) used improvements in statistical methods to gain more cheerful insights. After taking into consideration effects of other significant factors, such as amounts of engagement in everyday life, amounts of physical activity, and the incidence of specific pathologies, they found that the most powerful predictors of volunteers' survival in the Manchester/Newcastle sample were their subjective self-assessments of their own health and objective measures of their decision speeds.

Now improved statistical methods not only allow us to compare average rates of age-related decline but also the relative proportions of declines between mental abilities within and between individuals. Ghisletta et al. (2012) found that after controlling for practice, city of residence, sex and socio-economic advantage group, average performance on tests of all abilities declined with age, but more for some abilities than others. Individual differences in amounts of decline were marked on all but picture-memory and vocabulary. Fifty per cent of the variance in baseline level of performance was shared across tasks and this proportion increased to 66% for individual differences in amounts of change. General level of performance and amounts of change correlated positively, showing that patterns of declines across abilities do significantly differ between individuals but, in contrast, amounts and rates of declines in different mental abilities within individuals are also significantly associated.

This is consistent with evidence from brain scans that show both gross overall age-related changes and marked individual differences in patterns of change across different brain areas (Raz et al., 2005). That is, within any individual, gross age-related changes affect all, or most, areas of the brain and so account for correlations between amounts of decline in different abilities over time. There are idiosyncratic patterns of change in different brain areas of different individuals and these manifest as differences in the patterns of change in the behavioural measures of the particular, distinct cognitive abilities that these areas support.

In 1982, when we obtained initial support for a longitudinal study, brain-imaging was hard to access, expensive and, because image interpretation was a new art, not very informative. Consequently, all we could do was to collect data on self-report questionnaires, intelligence tests (estimating *gf*) and behavioural tests of memory and decision speed. During the 1990s, costs of imaging fell and image-interpretation improved so that by 2002 it was no longer disingenuous to request support to carry out MRIs on a subset of 150 volunteers who had already been assessed on behavioural tests since 1983.

Our scanning data were limited in two ways: we could scan volunteers only once and so could not record changes over time, and the images we could obtain provided only gross measures of brain health: age-related losses of brain volume (ARLBV) since early maturity; efficiency of carotid blood flow (CBF) and global rather than local white matter lesion prolifration (WMLP). Our first tasks were to check how these coarse measures related to volunteers' current scores on cognitive tests and also to their trajectories of longitudinally assessed changes in performance on these same measures over the previous 20 years.

Measures of ARLBV, WMLP and CBF all robustly and negatively predicted their current scores on tests of *gf*, speed and memory. This allowed us to further explore what had been a logically enigmatic finding. Brauer, Woollacott and Shumway-Cook (2001), Hofer, Berg and Era (2003) and many other investigators had found that scores on tests of balance positively correlate with scores on measures of cognitive ability, particularly of *gf*. Comprehensive reviews of the literature had confirmed that elderly individuals' scores on tests of visual acuity, balance and intelligence all correlate with each other and with their ages (Anstey, Lord & Williams, 1997). Unfortunately, we cannot interpret these reliable results as evidence that these diverse changes in performance are brought about by the same changes in the central nervous system. They may be temporal coincidences of independent processes: as time passes, cataracts progressively reduce visual acuity, death of cochlea hair cells impair hearing, mechanical joint damage and changes in the vestibular system progressively impair balance and, quite independently of these peripheral failures, age-related changes in the brain progressively impair mental abilities. Correlations between acuity, balance and cognition must at least partly reflect parallel progress of functionally unrelated declines. To correctly interpret correlations between markers of diffuse brain changes and measures of cognitive performance, we must estimate how much of the common variance between them reflects only temporal synchronicities of changes. To take this into account we need to enter individuals' ages as an additional predictor of their scores on cognitive tests. This allows us to re-assess relationships between changes in particular system performance characteristics: in this case balance and intelligence, after the effects of the passage of time on all other performance characteristics have been taken into consideration.

We became involved with this issue through applied work to discover behavioural markers for driving ability in old age during which we found that average score on a simple assessment of balance, the Tinnetti test (Köpke & Meyer, 2006) is a good marker for intelligence but, more pertinently, the best predictor we could find for current driving ability in older motorists. Our newly acquired direct measurements of gross brain changes allowed us to test whether age-related neurophysiological changes cause both losses in balance and in mental abilities. The next paper reproduced describes our results.

References

Aichele, S., Rabbitt, P., & Ghisletta, P. (2015). Life span decrements in fluid intelligence and processing speed predict mortality risk. *Psychology and Aging, 30*(3), 598–612.

Anstey, K. J., Lord, S. R., & Williams, P. (1997). Strength in the lower limbs, visual contrast sensitivity, and simple reaction time predict cognition in older women. *Psychology and Aging, 12*(1), 137–144.

Brauer, S. G., Woollacott, M., & Shumway-Cook, A. (2001). The interacting effects of cognitive demand and recovery of postural stability in balance-impaired elderly persons. *The Journals of Gerontology Series A: Biological Sciences and Medical Sciences, 56*(8), M489–M496.

Ghisletta, P., Rabbitt, P., Lunn, M., & Lindenberger, U. (2012). Two thirds of the age-based changes in fluid and crystallized intelligence, perceptual speed, and memory in adulthood are shared. *Intelligence, 40*(3), 260–268.

Hofer, S. M., Berg, S., & Era, P. (2003). Evaluating the interdependence of aging-related changes in visual and auditory acuity, balance, and cognitive functioning. *Psychology and Aging, 18*(2), 285–305.

Kleemeier, R. W. (1962). Intellectual changes in the senium. In *Proceedings of the Social Statistics Section of the American Statistical Association* (Vol. 1, pp. 290–295).

Köpke, S., & Meyer, G. (2006). The Tinetti test. *Zeitschrift für Gerontologie und Geriatrie, 39*(4), 288–291.

Palmore, E., & Cleveland, W. (1976). Aging, terminal decline, and terminal drop. *Journal of Gerontology, 31*(1), 76–81.

Rabbitt, P., Lunn, M., Pendleton, N., & Yardefagar, G. (2011). Terminal pathologies affect rates of decline to different extents and age accelerates the effects of terminal pathology on cognitive decline. *The Journals of Gerontology Series B: Psychological Sciences and Social Sciences, 66*(3), 325–334.

Rabbitt, P., Lunn, M., & Wong, D. (2006). Understanding terminal decline in cognition and risk of death. *European Psychologist, 11*(3), 164–171.

Raz, N., Lindenberger, U., Rodrigue, K. M., Kennedy, K. M., Head, D., Williamson, A., ... & Acker, J. D. (2005). Regional brain changes in aging healthy adults: General trends, individual differences and modifiers. *Cerebral cortex, 15*(11), 1676–1689.

13 Balance marks cognitive changes in old age because it reflects global brain atrophy and cerebro-arterial blood-flow

P.M.A. Rabbitt, M. Scott, N. Thacker, C. Lowe, M. Horan, N. Pendleton, D. Hutchinson and A. Jackson

Introduction

As individuals age they experience very different rates of physiological and neurophysiological changes and so show markedly different trajectories of cognitive decline (Rabbitt Diggle, Holland, & McInnes, 2003). Because of this divergence in their trajectories of change individuals' calendar ages become increasingly imprecise indices of differences in their mental abilities. It is both practically useful and theoretically informative to find simple markers that directly index age-related changes in neurophysiological integrity and so also age-related differences in cognitive performance.

Within samples of older people many different indices of general physiological fitness correlate with individual differences in cognitive performance. Heron and Chown (1967) find negative correlations between elderly individuals' levels of visual and auditory acuity and their scores on a range of cognitive tests. Anstey, Stankov, and Lord (1993) report positive associations between scores on intelligence tests and measures of body sway, quadriceps strength, vibration sense, and visual acuity. Anstey, Lord and Williams (1997) have found associations between leg muscle strength and cognitive function. Salthouse, Hancock, Meinz, and Hambrick (1996) find correlations between visual acuity and some tests of cognitive function. Anstey (1999) reports correlations between expelled respiratory volume, visual acuity, and vibration detection threshold and both speed and variability of choice reaction times. Anstey and Smith (1999) report negative correlations between performance on a variety of cognitive tests and a composite index of "bioage" derived from measures of vision, hearing, expiratory volume, and grip strength. Li, Jordonova, and Lindenberger (1998) report positive associations between visual acuity and intelligence. Anstey, Luszcz, and Sanchez (2001) find that longitudinally assessed amounts of declines in vision and leg muscle strength predict declines in memory. Lindenberger and Baltes (1994) and Baltes and Lindenberger (1997) used a novel extension of multiple regression analysis, described by Lindenberger and Potter (1998), to show that simple measures of gait and of visual and auditory acuity can account for over 80% of that particular proportion of variance in ability between individuals that is associated with differences in their calendar ages.

A plausible explanation for these pervasive associations is that indices of physiological integrity as diverse as sensory acuity, gait, and postural stability, muscle strength and expelled respiratory volume are all, to varying degrees, biomarkers for the declines in general physiological efficiency that accompany advancing age and worsening health (Balin, 1994; Voitenko & Tokar, 1983). Insofar as these general changes in efficiency also affect the brain and Central Nervous System, biomarkers will also predict performance on tests of cognitive abilities such as intelligence, memory, and information processing speed.

A logical problem with this explanation is that simple correlations are not sufficient evidence for functional relationships. This is particularly true for correlations between the time courses of age-related changes because, even if co-temporaneous processes are functionally independent their rates of progress will be correlated because they act as independent "clocks" measuring the same periods of time. For example age-related hearing losses are partly due to cumulative mechanical damage to cochlea hair cells by lifetime exposure to noise (Corso, 1987) and age-related changes in gait, balance, and postural stability at least partly reflect cumulative mechanical damage to leg joints. Thus, within an elderly population, levels of hearing loss and of balance are likely to be significantly correlated although their causes may be unrelated. For the same reasons some proportion of shared variance between biomarkers such as sensory acuity and balance and scores on cognitive tests must at least partly, and may possibly entirely, reflect temporal synchrony of functionally independent changes. To verify that any of the shared variance between biomarkers and cognitive test scores is due to their common dependence on neurophysiological function we need to examine their separate and common associations with direct measures of neurophysiological integrity.

Recent studies show that measures of cognitive performance in old age, such as scores on tests of intelligence, information processing speed and memory, are predicted by levels of global and local brain atrophy (Raz, 2000; Raz, Gunning-Dixon, Head, Dupuis, & Acker, 1998), by age related losses of brain volume, by reductions in carotid and basilar artery blood flow (cerebro-arterial blood flow, CBf (Rabbitt, Scott et al., in press) and by the incidence and location of diffuse white matter abnormalities (Breteler, van Amerongen et al., 1994; Breteler, van Swieten et al., 1994; Deary, Leaper, Muray, Staff, & Whalley, 2003; de Groot et al., 2000; de Leuw et al., 2001; Gunning-Dixon & Raz, 2000; Leaper et al., 2001). By examining the variance shared between these indices of gross age related neurophysiological changes, biomarkers such as balance, and performance on cognitive tests we can determine to what extent correlations between biomarkers and cognitive test scores reflect associations between biomarkers and direct indices of the extents of age related neurophysiological changes which may, for convenience, be termed "neuromarkers".

Experimental

Tests of associations between balance and cognitive performance in old age

Method

The particular biomarker investigated in this study is balance indexed by the total score on all elements of the Tinetti test battery for balance and postural stability (Tinetti, 1986; Tinetti & Glinter, 1988). The version used in this study requires a trained observer to instruct participants to carry out the following actions: sitting down, rising, immediate standing, standing with eyes closed, turning, standing on one leg, regaining stability after a nudge, backward extension and freedom of neck movement. Each of these actions is rated on a 3-point scale and the scores analysed are the sums of ratings for all actions. We have not found previous reports of associations between Tinetti scores and cognitive test scores. However, in our own laboratory, we examined this relationship within a sample of 501 citizens of Greater Manchester, UK, 251 women and 250 men aged from 50 to 90 years (mean 68.8, S.D. 7.2). All led independent lives in the community and were active volunteer members of the University of Manchester Longitudinal Research panel who independently made their way to the University of Manchester Age and Cognitive Performance Research Centre where they were tested, individually, by an experienced experimenter during two 1-h experimental sessions. The measures of cognitive performance were total numbers of problems correctly solved on the Cattell and Cattell (1960) "Culture Fair" intelligence test, completion times for each of three conditions of the colour/word Stroop test, word reading (Stroop 1), colour naming (Stroop 2) and word reading in the colour/word conflict condition (Stroop 3), and completion times for two conditions of a modified "Trails" test (Trails 1 and Trails 2) and scores on the Raven (1965) Mill Hill "A" and "B" Vocabulary tests.

Results

Table 13.1 shows correlations between volunteers' scores on each of these eight cognitive tests and their summed scores on the Tinetti balance scale.

Tinetti scores correlate significantly and positively with scores on the Culture Fair Intelligence Test and negatively with completion times on all conditions of the Stroop and Trails tests, but not with scores on the Mill Hill A and B vocabulary tests. It seems that within an elderly sample Tinetti scores are a marker for individual differences in cognitive performance, and most particularly for decision speed. It cannot yet be argued that these correlations reflect functional relationships rather than temporal synchrony since the age-related changes in neurophysiological integrity that affect cognitive performance may only be cotemporaneous with, but not functionally related

Table 13.1 Correlations between scores on eight cognitive tests and summed scores for all items on the Tinetti balance and mobility test

Cognitive tests	*Correlations with scores on the Tinetti Balance test*
Stroop 1	−0.175**
Stroop 2	−0.326**
Stroop 3	−0.257**
Trails 1	−0.264
Trails 2	−0.250**
Cattel "Culture Fair" Intelligence Test	0.178**
Mill Hill A Vocabulary Test	−0.007
Mill Hill B Vocabulary Test	0.07

** $P < 0.01$

to, progress of arthritis and of mechanical damage to joints and declines of muscle strength that also affect balance. To establish functional relationships it is necessary to show association between balance and cognitive test scores and direct measures of neurophysiological integrity ("neuromarkers").

Experimental

Test of relationships between balance, cognitive performance, and measures of age-associated loss of brain volume (atrophy) and cerebro-arterial blood flow

Method

A different group of 69 volunteers, 29 men and 40 women aged from 62 to 83 years (mean 73.2, S.D. 8.1) had participated in the University of Manchester 1984–2003 longitudinal study of healthy old age (for details see Rabbitt, McInnes et al., in press). Volunteers were selected on the criteria that they had all been continuously documented during this study for at least 13 years and that they were willing to undertake an additional, taxing, cognitive testing programme and to volunteer for Brain Imaging. Thus they are unusually highly motivated, and relatively mobile and healthy sample of elderly people. However their mean ages, and co-temporaneously obtained mean Ages, AH4-1 intelligence test scores and Ravens' (1960) Mill Hill A vocabulary test scores did not differ from those for the entire sample of 2046 participants in the University of Manchester longitudinal study. These were, respectively, 73.2 (S.D. 5.5) and 72.46 (S.D. 6.1) years; 39.3 (S.D. 10.4) and 36.5 (S.D. 11.0) points and 23.8 (S.D. 3.8) and 24.0 (S.D. 4.1) points. Cognitive test scores used in the present analyses are for three different tests of general fluid intelligence (gf): the Heim (1970) AH4-1 and AH4-2 intelligence tests and the Cattell and Cattell (1960) "Culture Fair" intelligence test (CF). Three tests of decision speed (1) a visual search task (VS) in which they scanned sheets of random capital letters of the alphabet to identify as many instances of the target letters I and O as possible in 2 min. (2) A version of the WAIS letter/letter substitution coding test (L/L Coding) in which they encoded as many letters as possible in four runs of 1 min each. (3) The Baddeley, Emslie and Nimmo-Smith (1992) "SCOLP" test of speed of semantic processing in which they evaluated the truth values of as many printed propositions as possible in 2 min. They also completed a test of "memory for objects and locations" (OL) in which they attempted to recall both the names and the relative spatial locations of 12 line drawings of common objects, each of which appeared in a different one of 12 equal sectors of a circle.

Within 6 months of taking these tests structural brain images were obtained to assess gross age-related changes in brain volume (Atrophy) by volumetric measurement of cranial fluid using MR image volumes from a coronal fast spin echo inversion recovery images (TR 6850 ms, TE 18 ms, TI 300 ms, echo train length = 9). Contiguous 3 mm slices were obtained throughout the brain with an in-plane resolution of 0.89 mm^2 (matrix 256 × 204, field of view 230 mm × 184 mm). These data were analysed using a fully automated technique that produced a binarised CSF volume analysed in a standardised co-ordinate frame. The data were rotated so that axes of symmetry of the brain in the coronal and axial views were aligned to the vertical and horizontal planes. The midsagittal slice was then rotated to align the horizontal axis with the ventral surface of the genu of the corpus callosum and the junction of the corpus callosum with the body of the fornix. Eyes and sinuses were removed and the data were then partitioned into 12 equal sized rectangular regions, computed by dividing the volume defined by the maximal extent of the cranial fluid space, equally left to right and top/bottom, and in three front-to-back. The 12 measurements are truly volumetric, unlike results obtained from techniques such as Voxel Based Morphometry that are influenced strongly by topological change. Thus the present technique allows conclusions to be drawn from relatively small data samples (Thacker, Varma, Bathgate, Stivaros et al., 2002). Note that measurements were normalized for differences in skull size and, by measuring cranial fluid, quantify the decrease in brain tissue since early adulthood. The correlations between these measurements can be analysed using pattern recognition techniques based upon comparison to reference data sets. The full method, which is capable of discriminating and quantifying correlated changes in brain shape and volume in a variety of dementing disorders, is described elsewhere (Thacker, Varma, Bathgate, Stivaros et al. 2002). It should be emphasised that, in this context, atrophy is an age related measure, the values of which reflect individual differences in percentage amounts of age-related loss of brain volume rather than of individual differences in lifespan brain volume, or in absolute brain volume at the time of measurement.

Measurements of Carotid and Basilar arterial flow (CBf) were made using a cardiac gated phase contrast quantitative flow sequence (TE=3ms,

TR = 6 ms, Flip angle = 15°, in-plane resolution = 1.17 mm × 1.17 mm, slice thickness = 5 mm). The arteries were imaged in one slice perpendicular to the direction of greatest blood flow. Fifteen temporal positions of the arteries were imaged, spanning one heartbeat. Magnitude and quantitative flow images were obtained for each time point. For each artery under consideration the first magnitude image of the sequence was normalized to 1 using the maximum value in that artery, and the image was thresholded at 0.5 to obtain a mask of that artery. The mask was then applied to all of the quantitative flow images and the cumulative flow calculated. Note that it is valid to apply the mask from the first image to all of the images, as the arteries are constrained by the skull and hardly move. Absolute flow in the arteries can also be calculated as the heart rates of subjects were also recorded.

CBf indexes level of arterial blood supply to the brain. Declines in CBf accompany constriction of the arteries and accompany cerebrovascular insufficiencies that become increasingly common in an elderly population. It is therefore not unexpected that in this sample CBf negatively correlated with age ($R = 244$, $p < 0.05$). Even when measured at a single time point a low value of CBf is a risk factor chronic insufficiency of blood supply that may result in diffuse damage to neurones. Consistent with this possibility CBf correlated negatively with amount of age-related atrophy ($R = 0.361$, $p < 0.001$).

Results

Correlations between biomarkers and neurological markers and comparisons of their predictions of performance on cognitive tests

In this sample summed Tinetti Balance test scores were negatively correlated with age ($R = 0.271$, $p < 0.01$) and with age-associated atrophy ($R = 0.246$, $p < 0.05$) and positively correlated with CBf ($R = 0.268$, $p < 0.01$). Age correlated negatively with balance scores ($R = 0.271$, $p < 0.01$), and with CBf ($R = 244$, $p < 0.05$) and positively with atrophy ($R = 0.449$, $p < 0.000$).

Table 13.2 shows simple correlations between summed scores on the Tinetti Balance battery, measures of age-related atrophy and of CBf and scores on the seven cognitive tests. Tinetti scores significantly and positively correlate with scores on all the cognitive measures Both age-related atrophy and CBf correlate significantly and negatively with speed on Letter/Letter coding, Visual Search and Semantic Reasoning and with scores on the OL memory test, but not with scores on any of the three intelligence tests. These findings replicate previous findings on a smaller subset of participants (Rabbitt, Scott et al., in press).

In interpreting these analyses, and also those that follow, it should be noted that estimates of relationships between variables must certainly be weakened by unknown measurement errors in Tinetti scores and also indices of atrophy and CBf. Further, in this elite sample, it is likely that correlations are weakened by the relatively high and narrow range of scores on the cognitive,

Table 13.2 Correlations of Tinetti Balance scores, age-associated atrophy and cerebral blood flow with scores on cognitive tests

Cognitive task	*Correlations with Tinetti Balance test scores*	*Correlations with age-associated atrophy*	*Correlations with basilar and carotid artery blood flow*
CCF	0.38***	0.04	0.04
AH4-1	0.34***	0.09	0.17
AH4-2	0.37***	0.04	0.14
Letter/Digit Coding	0.31**	0.45***	0.40***
Visual search	0.26**	0.26*	0.29**
Semantic processing	0.27**	0.38**	0.26**
Memory for objects and locations	0.26*	0.26*	0.22***

* $P < 0.05$.
** $P < 0.01$.
*** $P < 0.001$.

neurophysiological, and balance tests. We might therefore expect associations in an epidemiologically normal population to be stronger than those observed here.

Shared variance between balance and neuromarkers in predictions of age-related variance in cognitive tests

The simple associations shown in Table 13.2 are not sufficient evidence for functional relationships. To prove functional causality it is necessary to test how far associations between Tinetti scores and Cognitive test scores reflect associations between Tinetti scores and Neuromarkers. To do this hierarchical multiple regression analyses are performed to examine, in the first models, the values of R^2 for predictions of Cognitive Test Scores from the two neuromarkers, atrophy and blood flow and then, in the second phase of the analysis, the new values of R^2 when scores for the biomarker, Balance, are also entered. The amounts and levels of significance of changes in R^2 are also computed to test whether entry of Balance scores dose, or does not account for significant additional variance in cognitive test scores. The logic is that since Balance scores made significant, simple, predictions of all test scores, a finding that they no longer make any additional significant contribution after the variance associated with neuromarkers has been taken into consideration must mean that Balance and Neuromarkers share significant common variance in predictions of cognitive performance (Table 13.3).

Examination of the data reveal 0–3 cases of outliers for regressions predicting performance of individual cognitive test scores but, as deletion of these cases do not affect the results, data from all participants are included in all the

Table 13.3 R^2 and R2 change when atrophy and CBf are used to predict cognitive test scores and after Balance is then included

Cognitive test	*R^2 for model 1 with atrophy and CBf as predictors*	*R^2 for model 2 with balance added*	*Change in R^2 between models 1 and 2*
CCF	0.008 (p = 0.76)	0.330 (p = 0.009)	0.10 (p = 0.05)
AH4-1	0.075 (p = 0.075)	0.398 (p = 0.049)	0.0371 (p = 0.102)
AH4-2	0.038 (p = 0.280)	0.398 (p = 0.010)	0.121 (p = 0.003)
Letter/ Letter Coding	0.271 (p = 0.000)	0.303 (p = 0.033)	0.033 (p = 0.115)
Visual search	0.161 (p = 0.003)	0.186 (p = 0.024)	0.026 (p = 0.115)
Semantic reasoning	0.158 (p = 0.008)	0.207 (p = 0.005)	0.049 (p = 0.07)
Object location	0.037 (p = 0.292)	0.281 (p = 0.089)	0.046 (p = 0.1)

Joint and independent predictions of cognitive test scores from Tinetti balance test scores and from measures of age adjusted atrophy and summed carotid and basilar artery blood flow (CBf).

analyses described below. Non-linear relationships are examined by testing whether additions of power-functions of the variables lead to increases in R^2 but these are not significant.

Neuromarkers significantly predict scores on the three speed tests and on the memory test but not on any of the three intelligence tests. Inclusion of Tinetti scores result in significant joint predictions for all three intelligence tests, and in significant increases in R^2 for Cattell Culture Fair and for AH4-2 scores, but not for AH4-1 scores. For two of the three speed tests, Letter/ Letter Coding and Visual Search, inclusion of Tinetti scores results in significant joint predictions but not in a significant increase in R^2. For the third speed test, Semantic Processing, the increase in R2 approaches, but falls short of, conventional criteria for significance ($p = 0.07$). For the Object Memory test inclusion of Balance results in a significant joint prediction but not a significant increase in R^2.

Discussion

Scores on a particular biomarker, the Tinetti balance test, when taken alone, significantly predict scores on three different intelligence tests, on three tests of decision speed and on a complex memory task. Tinetti balance scores also significantly predict levels of two different indices of gross neurophysiological integrity, global age-related brain atrophy and CBf. Atrophy and CBf both predict performance on the three speed tests and on the memory test but not on any of the three intelligence tests. This disassociation between predictions from these neuromarkers of performance on tests of intelligence and on tests of information processing speed replicates findings in another study (Rabbitt, Scott et al., in press). In this earlier study atrophy accounted for up to 80% of age-related variance in performance on tests of speed and on a test of executive function but gave no significant prediction for scores on intelligence tests after the effects of Age had been taken into consideration. Nevertheless, the marked decline of intelligence with age must also be due to age-related neurophysiological changes. It follows that while atrophy and CBf are effective markers for those particular neurophysiological changes that affect memory and information processing speed, they are not markers for some, different, neurophysiological changes that affect intelligence. This, incidentally makes the point that the functional systems that support intelligence must be different from those that support information processing speed and at least one form of complex episodic memory.

The present paper addresses the different, and simpler question whether Tinetti scores predict cognitive performance in old age because balance is a marker for neurophysiological integrity, or only because functionally independent changes in balance and in neurophysiological integrity progress over the same periods of time. To test this, hierarchical regressions were performed to check whether entry of Balance makes any significant improvement in prediction after variance associated with these particular neuromarkers, atrophy and CBf, have been taken into consideration. Atrophy and CBf do not significantly predict scores on any of the three intelligence tests, but Balance does. When Balance is entered there is a significant increase in R^2 and the joint prediction is also significant. We infer that for intelligence tests balance scores clearly reflect individual differences in neurophysiological integrity other than those that are associated with atrophy and CBf. Associations between intelligence test scores and age are all robustly significant and negative (for the Cattell test. $R = 0.491$, $p = 0.01$; for the AH4-1, $R = 0.469$, $p = 0.01$ and for AH4-2, $R = 0.500$, $p = 0.01$). Thus it follows that while there obviously must be age-related neurophysiological changes that affect intelligence, these are functionally different from the particular changes that are associated with progress of atrophy and decline of CBf. However the present data cannot tell us whether Balance scores significantly predict Intelligence test scores because Balance is sensitive to these, other, neurophysiological changes, or simply because although declines in both Balance and Intelligence are driven by functionally independent processes, they occur over the same periods of time.

For the three Speed tests and the Memory test inclusion of Balance into the regression models does not result in significant increases in R^2. Nevertheless Balance, on its own, significantly predicts performance on all these tests. We conclude that this must be because it shares common variance with atrophy and CBf. This is what would occur if the neurophysiological changes marked by atrophy and CBf also affect Balance, so that Balance is a significant marker for levels of atrophy and CBf. So, at least for these particular tests, these findings do offer support for the "common cause hypothesis": some biomarkers predict individual differences in cognitive performance in old age because they mark the progress of age-related changes in the brain and central nervous system (see Anstey, 1999). Nevertheless, it is important to note that these relationships are likely to vary between different combinations of biomarkers, neurophysiological indices and behavioural tests. Balance marks differences in atrophy, in CBf, and in all of the behavioural tests examined here. In contrast differences in atrophy and CBF are surprisingly specific because, while they mark differences in information processing speed and memory, they do not mark differences in intelligence. Balance may possibly be affected by neurophysiological changes other than those that are associated with increases in global atrophy and declines in CBf. It is equally possible that different biomarkers may be especially sensitive to some neurophysiological changes but insensitive to others. Finally some unknown proportion of the prediction by biomarkers of cognitive performance or, indeed, of neurophysiological status must often, and perhaps always, also reflect the co-temporaneous progress of functionally independent processes.

Nevertheless, bearing these caveats in mind, the present analyses do show that at least one biomarker, balance, predicts individual differences in performance on some behavioural tasks because it is affected by the progress of diffuse, global, age-related changes in the brain.

References

Anstey, K. J. (1999). Sensorimotor variables and forced expiratory volume as correlates of speed, accuracy and variability in reaction time performance in late adulthood. *Aging, Neuropsychology and Cognition, 6*, 84–95.

Anstey, K., Lord, S. R., & Williams, P. (1997). Strength in the lower limbs. Visual contrast sensitivity and simple reaction time predict cognition in older women. *Psychology & Aging, 12*, 137–144.

Anstey, K., & Smith, G. A. (1999). Interrelationships among biological markers of aging, health, activity, acculturation and cognitive performance in late adulthood. *Psychology & Aging, 14*, 605–618.

Anstey, K., Stankov, L., & Lord, S. (1993). Primary aging, secondary aging and intelligence. *Psychology & Aging, 8*, 562–570.

Anstey, K., Luszcz, M. A., & Sanchez, L. (2001). A re-evaluation of the common factor theory of shared variance among age, sensory function and cognitive function in older adults. *Journals of Gerontology*, 56B, P3–P11.

Baddeley, A. D., Emslie, H., & Nimmo-Smith, I. (1992). *The speech and capacity of language processing (SCOLP) test.* Busy St. Edmunds:Thames Valley Test Company.

Balin, A. K. (1994). *Practical handbook of biological age-determination.* Boca Raton, FL: CRC Press.

Baltes, P. B., & Lindenberger, U. (1997). Emergence of a powerful connection between sensory and cognitive functions across the lifespan: A new window to the study of cognitive aging? *Psychology & Aging, 12*, 12–21.

Breteler, M. M. B., van Amerongen, N. M., van Swieten, J. C., Claus, J. J., Grobbee, D. E., Vangijn, J., et al. (1994). Cognitive correlates of ventriculat enlargement and cerebral whie matter lesions on magnetic resonance imaging, The Rotterdam Study. *Stroke, 25*, 1109–1115.

Breteler, M. M. B., van Swiewten, J. C., Bots, M. L., Grobbee, D. E., Claus, J. J., cvan der Hout, J. H. W., et al. (1994). Cerebral white matter lesions, vascular risk factors and cognitive function in a population-based study. *Neurology, 44*, 1246–1252.

Corso, J. F. (1987). Sensory-perceptual processes and aging. In K. W. Schaie (Ed.), *Annual review of gerontology and geriatrics* (pp. 29–55). New York: Springer.

Deary, I. J., Leaper, S. A., Murray, A. D., Staff, R. T., & Whalley, L. J. (2003). Cerebral white mater abnormalities and lifetime cognitive change: A 67-year follow-up of the Scotish Mental Survey off 1932. *Psychology & Aging, 18*, 140–148.

de Groot, J. C., de Leeuw, F. E., Oudkerk, M., van Gijn, J., Hofman, A., Jolles, J., et al. (2000). Cerebral white matter lesions and cognitive e function: The Rotterdam Scan Study. *Journal of Neurology, Neurosurgery and Psychiatry, 70*, 9–14.

de Leuw, F. E., de Groot, J. C., Achten, E., Oudkerk, M., Ramos, L. M. P., Heijboer, R., et al. (2001). Prevalence of cerebral white matter lesions in elderly people: A population-based magnetic imaging study. The Rotterdam Scan Study. *Journal of Neurology, Neurosurgery and Psychiatry, 70*, 9–14.

Gunning-Dixon, F. M., & Raz, N. (2000). The cognitive e correlates of white matter abnormalities in normal aging: A quantitative review. *Neuropsychology, 14*, 224–232.

Heim, A. W. (1970). *AH4 group test of general intelligence*. Windsor, U.K.: NFER-Nelson.

Heron, A., & Chown, S. (1967). *Age and function*. London: Churchill.

Li, S.-C., Jordanova, M., & Lindenberger, U. (1998). From good senses to good sense: A link between tactive information processing and intelligence. *Intelligence, 26*, 99–122.

Lindenberger, U., & Baltes, P. B. (1994). Sensory functioning and intelligence in old age: A strong connection. *Psychology and Aging, 9*, 339–355.

Lindenberger, U., & Potter, U. (1998). The complex nature of unique and shared effects in hierarchical linear regression: Implications for developmental psychology. *Psychological Methods, 3*, 218–230.

Leaper, S. A., Murray, A. D., Lemmon, H. A., Staff, R. T., Deary, I. J., Crawford, J. R., et al. (2001). Neuropsychological correlates of brain white matter lesions: The 1921 Aberdeen Birth Cohort. *Radiology, 221*, 51–55.

Raz, N. (2000). Aging of the brain and its impact on cognitive performance: Integration of structural and behavioural findings. In F. I. M. Craik & T. Salthouse (Eds.), *Handbook of aging and cognition* (2nd ed., pp. 1–90). Mahwah, NJ: Lawrence Erlbaum.

Rabbitt, P. M. A., McInnes, L., Diggle, P., Holland, F., Bent, N., Abson, V., et al. (in press). The University of Manchester Longitudinal Study of Cognition in Normal Healthy Old Age, 1983 through 2003. *Age, Neuropsychology and Cognition.*

Rabbitt, P. M. A., Scott, M., Thacker, N., Lowe, C, Jackson, J., Horan, M. et al. (in press). Losses in gross brain volume and cerebral blood flow account for age-related differences in speed but not in gf. *Neuropsychology.*

Raz, N., Gunning-Dixon, F. M., Head, D. P., Dupuis, J. H., & Acker, J. D. (1998). Neuroanatomical correlates of cognitive aging: Evidence from structural MRI. *Neuropsychology, 12*, 95–114.

Salthouse, T. A., Hancock, H. E., Meinz, E. J., & Hambrick, D. Z. (1996). Interrelations of age, visual acuity and cognitive functioning. *Journal of Gerontology: Psychological Sciences, 51B*, P317–P330.

Thacker, Varma, Bathgate, Stivaros, et al. (2002). Dementing disorders: Volumetric measurement of cerebrospinal fluid to distinguish normal from pathologic findings – Feasibility study. *Radiology, 224*, 278–285.
Tinetti, M. E. (1986). Performance-oriented assessment of mobility problems in elderly patients. *Journal of the American Geriatric Society, 34*, 119–126.
Tinetti, M. E., & Glinter, S. F. (1988). Identifying mobility problems in elderly patients. *Journal of the American Medical Association, 259*, 1190–1193.
Voitenko, V. P., & Tokar, A. V. (1983). The assessment of biological age and sex differences of human aging. *Experimental Aging Research, 9*, 239–244.

How some gross brain changes affect mental abilities in old age

We were now secure that our gross measures of age-related brain changes predict volunteers' current performance on a variety of tests of mental ability. For interpretation of 20 years of longitudinal data the urgent question was whether the age-related brain changes that volunteers had experienced during their adult lifetimes retrospectively predicted their declines in performance on the mental tests that they had repeatedly taken during the previous 8 to 20 years. The next paper reports this analysis.

14 Age-associated losses of brain volume predict longitudinal cognitive declines over 8 to 20 years

P.M.A. Rabbitt, S. Ibrahim, M. Lunn, M. Scott, N. Thacker, C. Hutchinson, M. Horan, N. Pendleton and A. Jackson

There is evidence that markers for the diffuse and complex brain changes that occur in old age, such as incidence of white matter lesions (WMLs) or age-related reduction of global brain volume, are associated with both general and specific decrements in cognitive performance. Even healthy non-dementing older adults experience increasing incidence of (WMLs) as they age, and this change is associated with poorer performance on a variety of cognitive tasks (e.g., Breteler, 1994; De Groot, de Leeuw, & Breteler, 1998; de Leeuw et al., 2001; Hickie et al., 1995; Longstreth et al., 1996; Schmidt et al., 1993; van Swieten, Staal, Kappelle, Derix, & van Gijn, 1996; Ylikoski et al., 1995). There is evidence that WMLs have selective as well as global effects and impair speed of information processing more than they affect memory, learning, or executive functions (e.g. De Groot et al., 2000; Junque et al., 1990; Ylikoski et al., 1993). Differences in gross brain volume among older adults are also associated with differences in performance on a variety of cognitive tasks (e.g., MacLullich et al., 2002; Raz, 2000; Raz, Gunning-Dixon, Head, Dupuis, & Acker, 1998). As in the case of WMLs, there is also evidence that differences in brain volume may affect information-processing speed more than other parameters of cognitive performance (Rabbitt & Anderson, 2006; Walhovd et al., 2005). However, analyses to date have been incomplete in two ways:

People of all ages differ markedly in skull size and also in brain volume. Consequently comparisons of brain volume between older adults reflect lifelong differences as well as differences in the proportional losses that they have experienced as they have grown old. This raises the question, To what degree do individual differences in the relative amounts of brain volume that older adults have lost during their lifetimes account for that proportion of the variance in cognitive performance among them that is associated with differences in their ages?

To address this issue, we need a measure of proportional change in brain volume. The difference between the volumes of the unchanging skull and diminished brain, estimated from the volume of cerebrospinal fluid (CSF), indexes the absolute amount of brain volume that people have lost as they have grown old. Since interior skull volume does not change with age, proportional change can be estimated by adjusting for head size. Correlations between this index and scores on cognitive tests can then show how differences in performance between older adults relate to proportional differences in volume loss that they have experienced since they were young adults.

Another limitation of previous analyses is that they have been based on cross-sectional comparisons between individuals made at a single time point. This means that the effects of differences in brain volume may have been confounded with other individual differences that also affect cognitive performance. Only longitudinal comparisons within the same individual can provide reliable evidence about relationships between amounts of losses of volume and of cognitive decline.

Ideal data would come from a study in which losses of brain volume adjusted for head size and scores on a wide range of tests of different parameters of cognitive performance are both measured, contemporaneously, on several successive occasions over many years. Such comparisons are hard to achieve because of the logistical difficulties of longitudinal studies and because the necessary imaging techniques have only recently become available. A simpler alternative is to measure proportional loss of brain volume on a single occasion for participants who have repeatedly been assessed on the same cognitive tests over many years. On the plausible assumption that brain shrinkage proceeds gradually, so that individuals who have experienced greater proportional losses have also experienced more rapid cognitive declines, this allows analyses of relationships between estimates of age-associated losses of brain volume obtained after the end of the longitudinal study and previous rates of cognitive changes. Data enabling such analyses became available from the University of Manchester longitudinal study of cognitive change in healthy old age (Rabbitt, Diggle, Holland, Bent, McInnes, Abson, et al., 2004).

Method

Participants

In 2003, a subset of 93 volunteers in the University of Manchester Longitudinal Study, 39 men ages 65 to 81 years and 54 women ages 63 to 86 years, who had all repeatedly been assessed on the same battery of cognitive tests over periods of 8 to 20 years, volunteered to undergo brain imaging. The number of times that individuals had taken the battery varied with their dates of entry to the study and with occasional missed testing sessions. All 93 participants had taken the battery on 2 occasions, 97% on three occasions and 69% on four occasions. Within 6 months of their scans all were given detailed physical examinations by experienced geriatricians (Michael Horan and Neil Pendleton). None of the participants showed any symptoms of severe health problems, dementias or other neurological problems. Scans also confirmed absence of neurological signs. No participants had suffered unusually rapid declines in cognition because, on all tests, their rates of change during the longitudinal study fell within the range of −0.5 *SD* to +1.5 *SD* of the means for a larger sample of 768 volunteers from which they were drawn.

Cognitive Tests

Detailed schedules of recruitment and assessment and descriptions of the tests and their administration are given by Rabbitt, Diggle, Holland, Bent, McInnes, Abson, et al. (2004). Tests included one test of general fluid intelligence (gf; the Cattell & Cattell, 1960, Culture Fair Intelligence Test). Additionally, participants took two tests of information-processing speed: (a) a visual search task in which they scanned printed sheets, in which all capital letters of the alphabet appeared in random order and with equal frequency detecting as many instances of two target letters, I and O as they could within 2 min and (b) a Letter–Letter Coding test in which they used a guide printed at the head of the answer sheet to substitute code letters for other target letters printed in random order and in upper case. Also included were the Wechsler Adult Intelligence Scale Vocabulary subtest (Wechsler, 1981) and three tests of Memory: "Propositions about People (PAP), requiring recall of three items of information about each of five imaginary persons; Circle Object Memory, requiring recall of the names and locations of 12 line drawings of objects each located in 1 of 12 sectors of a circle; Immediate Free Recall of 10 three–syllable nouns (matched for frequency [1/10,000] and imageability and visually presented at a rate of 1 per 1.5 s). Normative data for the entire longitudinal study are given in Rabbitt, Diggle, Holland, and McInnes (2004).

Brain Imaging

Anatomical images, from which a measure of age-related loss of brain volume could be obtained were acquired using an axial fast spin-echo inversion recovery sequence (repetition time [TR] = 6,850 ms; echo time [TE] 18 ms; inversion time [TI] 300 ms; echo train length = 9). Contiguous 3-mm slices were obtained throughout the brain with an in-plane resolution of 0.89 mm^2 (matrix 256 × 204, field of view 230 mm × 184 mm). Age-related brain atrophy can be estimated using the volume of CSF as a surrogate. Because the volume of CSF increases as the brain shrinks, measurement of CSF volume, normalized to skull size, gives a good indication of relative loss of brain volume over the life span.

CSF volume was obtained using a fully automated procedure. The anatomical images were initially registered into a standard coordinate frame where the interhemispheric fissure was aligned to the plane passing through the vertical axis (of the standard coordinate frame). The mid-sagittal slice was rotated to align the horizontal axis with the ventral surface of the genu of the corpus callosum, and the junction of the corpus callosum, with the body of the fornix. The CSF in the images was segmented with a Bayesian approach, and a mask was applied to remove the eyes and sinuses from the images, as these structures exhibit comparable voxel intensities to the CSF. Previously, this technique has been used to partition the bounding box of the interior of the skull into 12 equal-sized cuboids (left–right, top–bottom, and front–middle–back). This provides 12 true volumetric estimates of CSF, unlike the statistical measures resulting from techniques such as VBM, which themselves are strongly influenced by topological change. Because the brain can move within the head, volumetric estimates of CSF must be analyzed as a correlated set of measurements. This method was developed as a tool for decision support rather than for investigation of regional tissue loss. However because our interest was in a global measure of atrophy, we used only the total CSF, which is independent of regional tissue loss. Persons with larger heads, and hence more brain tissue as young adults, might be expected to experience more absolute atrophy (assuming a constant average population rate of atrophy) than those with smaller heads. CSF volume is therefore corrected for head size using the volume of the bounding box of the interior surface of the skull. This allows quantification of the loss of brain tissue since early adulthood. The full method, which is capable of discriminating and quantifying correlated changes in brain shape and volume in a variety of dementing disorders, is described elsewhere (Scheltens, Barkhof, & Leys, 1993; Thacker et al., 2002). It should be emphasized that in this context, brain volume is an age-related measure that reflects individual differences in total amounts of age-related loss. Losses measured in this way will reflect not only the progress of the "normal" aging process but also any additional cause of loss of volume sustained throughout the participant's lifetime.

Statistical Modeling

A linear-mixed model with random effects was fitted to the data for each test in turn. This estimated the average rate of change in scores over successive testing sessions for an individual, taking into account a set of explanatory demographic variables—age, sex, socioeconomic status—as well as the proportional loss of brain volume (PLBV). A general linear model would be adequate if only a single measure on the dependent variable had been recorded, but with longitudinal data it is important that the method also takes into consideration the fact that successive measurements on an individual are positively correlated and not independent (Armitage, Berry, & Matthews, 2002; Diggle, Heagerty, Liang, & Zeger, 2002). The model fitted was similar to the one used by Rabbitt, Diggle, Smith, Holland, and McInnes (2001). Age was coded in years over the minimum age at entry in the data, which was 52 years, and the age effect was modeled as a quadratic effect [i.e., $(\text{age} - 52)^2$]. A variable for time point of assessment (i.e., occasion 1, 2, 3, or 4), was included to reveal practice effects that occur due to repeated testing during longitudinal studies (see Rabbitt, Diggle, Holland, & McInnes, 2004). However practice effects were significant only in some of the analyses described below.

Because the model fits were better without them, they were excluded from the final versions except where indicated below.

Rabbitt, Diggle, Holland, and McInnes (2004) found that scores on all of the cognitive tests analyzed in their study markedly increased with level of socioeconomic advantage (SEA), as indexed by Her Majesty's Registrar-General's Index of Occupational Classifications (Office of Population Censuses and Surveys, 1980). Levels of SEA were therefore included in the model. Sex was also included because Rabbitt, Diggle, Holland, and McInnes (2004) had found significant differences between men and women on some tests.

Random effects were used to indicate a random intercept and slope. This showed a quadratic time trend for each participant and the age – 52 variable denoted the random slope. The model in algebraic form is described in detail by Rabbitt et al. (2001).

Modeling was carried out within the statistical software R (R Foundation for Statistical Computing).[1] The method of restricted maximum likelihood (REML) was applied with the linear mixed effects model, computed as lme ( ) function in R. Examination of the residuals through histograms and normal plots was carried out for model diagnostic checks.

Summary Statistics

Column 1 of Table 14.1 gives a breakdown of the sample in terms of age decade, sex, and SEA assessed by the HM Registrar General's Index of Occupational Classification (Office of Population Censuses and Surveys, 1980). Column 2 shows levels of PLBV, and Columns 3 through 9 give means and standard deviations of their scores on the seven cognitive tests.

A linear mixed model with random effects was fitted to the data separately for each test administered. In all analyses except where stated, the plot of standardized residuals against fitted values, histogram of residuals, and normal probability plot were examined for normality and outliers. The model fits were reasonable, and no unusual patterns of behavior were discovered. Table 14.2 shows summarized data giving parameter estimates for mean total test scores for linear and quadratic effects of age and for effects of PLBV. Complete estimate for effects of sex and SEA, and for practice, with standard deviations (δ) for the distribution of random effects and residual error are available for each test separately in the associated Supplemental Data online.

Analysis for Cattell Culture Fair Intelligence Test

Effects of sex, practice, and interactions between age, sex, CSF volume, and SEA were not significant and were excluded from the final model because this improved the fit. Mean Cattell Culture Fair Intelligence Test scores significantly increased with level of SEA, so this variable was retained. The quadratic effect of age was significant, indicating that declines in Cattell scores accelerate as age increased. Standard deviations for the distributions of

Table 14.1 Summary of Demographic Variables and Mean Scores on Tests at the Initial Time Point

Variable	*Total participants n (%)*	*Proportion of CSF M (SD)*	*Cattell Culture Fair Intelligence Test total correct M (SD)*	*Visual search mean total correct of 316 M (SD)*	*Coding/ Letter-Letter Substitution M (SD)*	*WAIS –III Vocabluray subtest M (SD)*	*Propositions About People Memory Test M (SD)*	*Memory Circle Test M (SD)*	*Free recall M (SD)*
Sex									
Male	39 (41.9%)	0.09 (0.019)	31.4 (5.45)	205.6 (42.8)	212.7 (50.4)	56.2 (9.53)	4.67 (1.94)	8.59 (1.43)	6.85 (1.44)
Female	54 (59.1%)	0.076 (0.02)	31.0 (4.84)	209.6 (39.8)	248.7 (41.6)	56.5 (8.37)	6.24 (2.39)	9.04 (1.48)	7.22 (1.69)
Socioeconomic status									
Class 1, professional	14 (15.1%)	0.087 (0.018)	33.7 (3.54)	230.0 (50.6)	237.1 (57.6)	60.9 (7.24)	6.00 (2.42)	9.21 (1.05)	7.36 (1.28)
Class 2, intermediate	38 (40.9%)	0.083 (0.02)	32.2 (4.18)	216.1 (40.1)	232.0 (37.0)	59.7 (7.92)	5.61 (2.56)	8.74 (1.48)	6.89 (1.81)
Class 3N, nonmanual skilled	8 (8.6%)	0.074 (0.02)	28.4 (6.65)	200.1 (44.8)	226.5 (61.04)	54.0 (6.78)	5.25 (2.12)	8.50 (1.77)	6.63 (2.07)
Class 3M, manual skilled	23 (24.7%)	0.082 (0.023)	30.61 (5.36)	192.3 (32.5)	243.8 (53.6)	52.2 (8.00)	5.83 (2.27)	8.87 (1.60)	7.30 (1.18)
Class 4, part skilled	6 (6.5%)	0.077 (0.027)	24.8 (5.67)	189.5 (24.1)	199.8 (59.7)	47.5 (7.69)	4.67 (2.07)	8.83 (1.72)	7.17 (1.94)
Class 5, unskilled	1 (1.1%)	0.054 (.)	28.0 (.)	199.0 (.)	215 (.)	46.0 (.)	3.00 (.)	9.00 (.)	8.00 (.)
Age at initial test									
52–59 years	19 (20.4%)	0.073 (0.023)	33.42 (4.06)	214.8 (47.2)	261.8 (52.2)	59.4 (9.46)	6.05 (2.01)	9.53 (1.07)	7.47 (1.35)
60–69 years	60 (64.5%)	0.081 (0.019)	30.7 (5.15)	209.1 (37.8)	227.5 (46.8)	56.2 (8.40)	5.50 (2.51)	8.72 (1.51)	7.05 (1.66)
70–79 years	14 (15.0%)	0.095 (0.022)	30.1 (5.42)	193.6 (44.5)	225.2 (40.7)	53.2 (9.22)	5.29 (2.02)	8.50 (1.56)	6.57 (1.55)
Overall age	$M = 63.5$ (SD = 5.40)	0.082 (0.021)							
Total	$N = 93$		31.1 (5.08)	207.9 (40.9)	233.8 (48.6)	56.4 (8.83)	5.58 (2.34)	8.85 (1.47)	7.06 (1.59)

Note: Empty parentheses indicate that a function or expression of choice can be inserted here. CSF = cerebrospinal fluid; WAIS-III = Wechsler Adult Intelligence Scale—Third Edition.

Table 14.2 Parameter Estimates for Mean Correct Responses on the Cattell Culture Fair Intelligence Test, Model, With Random Effects and Residual Error

Variable	*Estimate*	*Standard error*	*t*	*p*	*95% Confidence interval*
Cattell Culture Fair Intelligence Test					
Intercept	38.61	2.42	15.98	<.0001	33.92 to 43.31
Age 52 years	0.10	0.13	0.75	.45	−0.15 to 0.34
(Age 52 years)^2	−0.01	0.003	−2.29	.022	−0.01 to −0.001
PLBV	−46.83	22.06	−2.12	.037	−90.09 to −3.56
Coding / Letter-Letter Substitution					
Intercept	265.45	27.86	9.53	<.0001	210.56 to 320.33
Age 52 years	0.59	0.87	0.68	.5	−1.12 to 2.30
(Age 52 years)^2	−0.07	0.02	−2.84	.005	−0.11 to −0.02
PLBV	−736.93	214.52	−3.44	.001	−1163.69 to −310.18
Visual Search Test					
Intercept	271.86	19.82	13.72	<.0001	232.81 to 310.92
Age 52 years	0.43	0.7	0.61	.54	−0.95 to 1.81
(Age 52 years)^2	−0.03	0.02	−1.85	.06	−0.07 to 0.002
PLBV	−518.15	188.68	−2.75	.007	−893.42 to −142.88
WAIS – III Vocabulary subtest					
Intercept	70.5	3.84	18.37	<.0001	62.9 to 78.06
Age 52 years	−0.27	0.17	−1.58	.11	−0.60 to 0.06
(Age 52 years)^2	0.0007	0.005	1.46	.15	−0.002 to 0.02
PLBV	−83.7	38.65	−2.17	.03	−160.58 to −6.83
Free Recall Test					
Intercept	6.07	0.94	6.47	<.0001	4.21 to 7.91
Age 52 years	0.106	0.056	1.88	0.06	−0.005 to 0.216
(Age 52 years)^2	−0.004	0.001	−2.82	.005	−0.007 to 0.001
PLBV	−7.25	7.56	−0.96	.34	−22.27 to 7.76
Proposition About People Memory Test					
Intercept	3.34	1.24	2.69	.008	0.90 to 5.78
Age 52 years	0.11	0.06	1.80	.07	−0.01 to 0.23
(Age 52 years)^2	−0.005	0.001	−3.15	.002	−0.009 to 0.002
PLBV	−6.29	9.36	−0.67	.503	−24.92 to 12.33
Memory Circle Test					
Intercept	8.87	0.88	10.14	<.0001	7.15 to 10.60
Age 52 years	0.032	0.045	0.703	.48	−0.057 to 0.12
(Age 52 years)^2	−0.003	0.001	−2.52	.01	−0.006 to −0.0007
PLBV	−8.59	6.87	−1.25	.21	−22.23 to 5.05

Note: PLBV = proportional loss of brain volume. WAIS-III = Wechsler Adult Intelligence Scale—Third Edition.

random intercept and age were 5.05 and 0.24, respectively. The true effect of the estimate δ(age − 52) is taken when multiplied by age in the model. Therefore, a difference of 0.24 in the linear rates of decline between two participants with equal Cattell scores at initial test result in a difference of 4.8 (95% confidence interval [CI] = 3.2 to 7.0) total correct score after 20 years in the study.

Amounts of decline over time increased significantly with levels of PLBV. Thus individuals with higher current levels of PLBV had experienced larger declines in Cattell scores during longitudinal assessment.

Analysis for the Letter–Letter Coding Task

The effects of practice were not significant and were excluded from the final model because this improved fit stability. A significant quadratic term for age indicated that decline in performance accelerated as age increased. There was a significant effect of sex, with men performing better than women. The effects of SEA were highly significant. After all of these factors had been taken into consideration, the amounts of decline in scores on the WAIS Letter–Letter Coding subtest were found to significantly increase with amounts of PLBV.

Analysis for the Visual Search Task

Effects of sex and practice were not significant and so were omitted from the final model. Though the effect of age was not significant, this variable was retained because inclusion improved model fit. Visual search Test score (number of target items correctly identified) significantly increased with SEA and declined with PLBV. For an individual, Visual Search Test score was estimated to improve by four additional target letters identified (95% CI = 0.5 to 7.9 correct scores) for every 0.01 reduction in PLBV. The standard deviations for the distributions of random intercept and age were 36.62 and 1.13, respectively. The true effect of the estimate δ (age − 52) is taken when multiplied by age in the model. Therefore, a difference of 1.13 in the linear rates of decline between 2 participants with equal cognitive ability at initial test results in a difference of a score of 22.6 (95% CI = 10.6 to 48.2) after 20 years in the study.

The diagnostic plots showed five outlying observations. In these cases, scores at the final longitudinal assessment and values of PLBV, taken after this assessment, were less than the sample means (0.08). Four of the 5 individuals were part of the two most advantaged SEA groups. When their final assessment scores were compared with scores at their previous visits, they were found to have scored lower than expected. A sensitivity analysis was carried out, and found that exclusion of the outliers did not alter the significance of the variables but improved the model fit. In the new model, without outliers, the effect of age became significant at the 10% but not at the 5% level. The effect of PLBV was greater than that of age, as for every 0.01 increase in PLBV, the Visual Search Task score was estimated to fall by 5 (95% CI = 1.4 to 8.9). There was an interaction between PLBV and SEA such that the effects of SEA increased as PLBV diminished. It seems that on this task, the effects of loss of brain volume are significantly modified by SEA.

Analysis for the WAIS Vocabulary Test

The effects of practice were not significant and were omitted to improve model fit. The linear effect of age approached significance at $p = .08$, but the quadratic term was not significant. The effects of sex were not significant. As might be expected from differences in educational and employment opportunities, the effects of SEA are highly significant. The effect of PLBV approached significance at $p = .09$. In sum, there are weak indications that WAIS Vocabulary scores may decline with increasing age and with increasing PLBV.

Analysis for the Immediate Free Recall Task

Effects of SEA and its interactions were not significant and were omitted from the final model. Significant practice improvements appeared between assessments 1 and 2 and 1 and 3. Accordingly, practice was retained in this model. A significant quadratic term for age indicated that the amount of decline in immediate free recall scores accelerated as age increased. The estimate for sex was significant, with women performing slightly but significantly better than men. Current levels of PLBV showed no detectable relationship with amounts of previous decline.

The standard deviations for the distributions of random intercept and age were 1.37 and 0.06, respectively. The estimates of the random effects were small because the maximum possible score was only 10. The true effect of the estimate δ (age – 52) is taken when multiplied by age in the model. Therefore, a difference of 0.06 in the linear rates of decline between 2 participants with equal cognitive ability at initial test result in a difference of 1.2 (95% CI = 0.6 to 2.6) total correct score after 20 years in the study.

Analysis for the Propositions About People Memory Task

PLBV was not significant but, as it is the main factor of interest, was retained in the model. Interactions and practice effects were not significant and thus were excluded. Parameter estimates, standard deviations (δ) for the distribution of random effects, and residual error are shown in Table G in the Supplemental Data online.

A significant quadratic term indicated accelerating decline with age. Women performed significantly better than men by an average of 2 correct responses (95% CI = 1.3 to 2.9 correct). The standard deviations for the distributions of random intercept and age were 1.35 and 0.05, respectively. The true effect of the estimate δ (age – 52) is taken when multiplied by age in the model. Therefore, a difference of 0.05 in the linear rates of decline between 2 participants with equal cognitive ability at initial test result in a difference of 1 (95% CI = 0.2 to 3.6) total correct score after 20 years in the study.

Analysis for the Circle–Object Memory Task

There were no significant effects of PLBV. Effects of practice and SEA, as well as all interactions, were not significant and were excluded because this improved model fit. Parameter estimates for mean total correct scores, the standard deviations (δ) for the distribution of random effects, and residual error are shown in Table H. A significant quadratic term indicates that declines in scores, though small, significantly accelerated with age. Women performed slightly better than men, and this difference was marginally significant at $p = .05$.

The standard deviations for the distributions of random intercept and age were 0.83 and 0.05, respectively. The estimates of the random effects were small because the maximum possible score was only 12. The true effect of the estimate δ(age – 52) is taken when multiplied by age in the model. Therefore, a difference of 0.05 in the linear rates of decline between 2 participants with equal cognitive ability at initial test result in a difference of 1 (95% CI = 0.2 to 3.6) total correct score after 20 years in the study.

Discussion

These results extend information based on absolute differences in brain volume by considering the effects of proportional losses of brain volume. The variety of different, diffuse, age-related brain changes that are marked by *global loss* of brain volume account for significant proportions of the variance between individuals that are related to differences in their age. Further, longitudinal comparisons show that amounts of age-related losses of brain volume significantly predict amounts of previous decline in cognitive performance over periods of 8 to 20 years on tests of information- processing speed, on the Cattell Culture Fair Intelligence Test and, marginally, on the WAIS Vocabulary subtest. However, predictions for declines in scores on three different memory tasks are not significant. Nevertheless, on all of these three memory tests, scores significantly declined as age increased.

When interpreting these results, it is essential to bear in mind that both PLBV and calendar age must certainly be effective statistical markers for many different kinds of neurophysiological changes associated with brain aging. On the Cattell Culture Fair Intelligence Test, the WAIS Letter–Letter Coding subtest, and the Visual Search Task, both age and PLBV make significant independent predictions of amounts of change in test scores over time. The weak predictions from both age and PBLV for vocabulary are expected, as Vocabulary scores show little or no change with age (e.g., see Rabbitt, Chetwynd, & McInnes, 2003). In contrast, on the three memory tasks, age predicted rate of decline, but PLBV did not. The differing predictions from age and PLBV suggest that PLBV marks some, but not all, of the age-related neurophysiological changes that affect cognition. However, findings that PLBV predicts losses in general fluid intelligence and in information processing speed, but that age and not PLBV predicts losses in memory test performance, should not, as yet, be taken as evidence that these two markers are associated with different kinds of functional neurophysiological changes. An adequate test of this possibility would require a larger sample of participants and concomitant more stringent confidence levels. Nevertheless, we suggest that these contrasts between effects of PLBV on different parameters of cognitive function are an incentive for larger and more detailed studies.

Another finding meriting further investigation is that, for Visual Search Task scores, there was a significant interaction between PLBV and SEA such that the effects of SEA increased as PLBV reduced. This is an intriguing suggestion that the effects of age-related neurophysiological changes may be offset, or moderated, by sociocultural and demographic factors. The present finding is difficult to interpret because SEA, as indexed in this study, is a strong statistical proxy measure for a very wide variety of different factors, including higher mental ability (see analysis of Cattell Culture-Fair Intelligence Test scores and Rabbitt, Diggle, Holland, & McInnes, 2004) as well as better education and greater lifelong professional demands and probably also for better access to health care and better self-maintenance. For instance, further investigations should take into account that because the Visual Search Task required rapid scanning of pages of random letters, performance may well have varied with long acquired skills at reading and scanning of printed text, which, like vocabulary, may be maintained by continued practice in old age.

The power of the present comparisons is adequate to establish that the amounts of loss of brain volume that individuals have experienced at a particular point in time and thus, inferentially, the rates of loss of brain volume that they have experienced as they have grown older, significantly predict their individual rates of loss in intelligence and in information-processing speed over previous periods of 8 to 20 years. We accordingly suggest that measurements of PLBV may be useful clinical tools for estimation of the amounts of cognitive impairment that individuals have experienced as they have aged and also as predictors of their expected future rates of change.

Acknowledgments

The entire study was funded by a grant from the Wellcome Trust. Work on the development of the cerebrospinal fluid volume estimation technique was supported by the United Kingdom's Engineering and Physical Sciences Research Council Inter-disciplinary Research Consortium (From Medical

Images and Signals to Clinical Information) grant. Software and details of the technique can be found on the website: www.tina-vision.net.

Note

1 R Statistical Software is available from http://www.r-project.org/foundation/

References

Armitage, G., Berry, P., & Matthews, J. N. S. (2002). *Statistical methods in medical research*. Malden, MA: Blackwell.

Breteler, M. M., van Amerongen, N. M., van Swieten, J. C., Claus, J. J., Grobbee, D. E., van Gijn, J., Hofman, A., & van Harskamp, F. (1994). Cognitive correlates of ventricular enlargement and cerebral white matter lesions on magnetic resonance imaging: The Rotterdam study. *Stroke, 25*, 1109–1115.

Cattell, R. B., & Cattell, A. K. S. (1960). *Handbook for the individual or group Culture Fair Intelligence Test*. Champaign, IL: IPAT.

De Groot, J. C., de Leeuw, F. E., & Breteler, M. M. B. (1998). Cognitive correlates of cerebral white matter changes. *Journal of Neural Transmission Supplement, 53*, 41–67.

De Groot, J. C., de Leeuw, F-E., Oudkerk, M., van Gijn, J., Hoifman, A., Jolles, J., & Breteler, M. M. B. (2000). Cerebral white matter lesions and cognitive function: The Rotterdam study. *Annals of Neurology, 47*, 145–151.

de Leeuw, F.-E., de Groot, J. C., Achten, E., Oudkerk, M., Ramos, L. M. P., Heijboer, R., Hofman, A., Jolles, J., van Gijn, J., & Breteler, M. M. B. (2001). Prevalence of cerebral white matter lesions in elderly people: A population based magnetic resonance imaging study. The Rotterdam Scan Study. *Journal of Neurology, Neurosurgery, and Psychiatry, 70*, 9–14.

Diggle, P. J. Heagerty, P., Liang, K. Y., & Zeger, S. L. (2002). *Analysis of longitudinal data* (2nd ed.). Oxford, England: Oxford University Press.

Hickie, I., Scott, E., Mitchell, P., Wilhelm, K., Austin, M.-P., & Bennet, B. (1995). Subcortical hyperintensities on magnetic resonance imaging: Clinical correlates and prognostic significance in patients with severe depression. *Biological Psychiatry, 37*, 151–160.

Junque, C., Pujol, J., Vendrell, P., Bruna, O., Jodar, M., Ribas, J. C., et al. (1990). Leuko-araiosis on magnetic resonance and speed of mental processing. *Archives of Neurology, 47*, 151–156.

Longstreth, W. T., Jr., Manolio, T. A., Arnold, A., et al. (1996). Clinical correlates of white matter findings on cranial magnetic resonance imaging of 3301 elderly people: The Cardiovascular Health Study. *Stroke, 27*, 1274–1282.

MacLullich, A. M. J., Ferguson, K. J., Deary, I. J., Seckl, J. R., Starr, J. M., & Wardlaw, J. M. (2002). Intracranial capacity and brain volumes are associated with cognition in healthy elderly men. *Neurology, 59*, 169–174.

Office of Population Censuses and Surveys. (1980). *Classification of occupations 1980*. London, United Kingdom: Her Majesty's Stationery Office.

Rabbitt, P. M. A., & Anderson, M. (2006). The lacunae of loss: Age and the differentiation of cognitive abilities. In F. I. M. Craik & E. Bialostok (Eds.), *Models for aging and development* (pp. 331–343). New York: Wiley.

Rabbitt, P. M. A., Chetwynd, A., & McInnes, L. (2003). Do clever brains age more slowly? Further exploration of a nun result. *British Journal of Psychology, 94*, 63–71.

Rabbitt, P. M. A., Diggle, P., Holland, F., Bent, N., McInnes, L., Abson, V., Pendleton, N., & Horan, M. (2004). The University of Manchester Longitudinal Study of Cognition in Normal Healthy Old Age, 1983 through 2003. *Aging, Neuropsychology, and Cognition, 11*, 245–279.

Rabbitt, P., Diggle, P., Holland, F., & McInnes, L. (2004). Practice and drop-out effects during a 17-year longitudinal study of cognitive aging. *Journal of Gerontology Series B: Psychological Sciences and Social Sciences, 59*, P84 –P97.

Rabbitt, P., Diggle, P., Smith, D., Holland, F., & McInnes, L. (2001). Identifying and separating the effects of practice and of cognitive aging during a large longitudinal study of elderly community residents. *Neuropsychologia, 39*, 532–543.

Raz, N. (2000). Aging of the brain and its impact on cognitive performance: Integration of structural and behavioural findings. In F. I. M. Craik and T. Salthouse (Eds.), *Handbook of Aging and Cognition* (2 nd ed., pp. 1–90). Mahwah, NJ: Lawrence Erlbaum.

Raz, N., Gunning-Dixon, F. M., Head, D. P., Dupuis, J. H., & Acker, J. D. (1998). Neuroanatomical correlates of cognitive aging: Evidence from structural MRI. *Neuropsychology, 12*, 95–114.

Scheltens, P., Barkhof, F., & Leys, D. (1993). A semiquantitative rating scale for the assessment of signal hyperintensities on magnetic resonance imaging. *Journal of the Neurological Sciences, 114*, 7–12.

Schmidt, R., Fazekas, F., Offenbacher, H., Dusek, T., Zach, E., Reinhart, P., et al. (1993). Neuropsychologic correlates of white matter hyperintensities: A study of 150 normal volunteers. *Neurology, 43*, 2490–2494.

Thacker, N. A., Varma, A. R., Bathgate, D., Stivaros, S., Snowden, J. S., Neary, D., & Jackson, A. (2002). Dementing disorders: Volumetric measurement of cerebrospinal fluid to distinguish normal from pathologic findings—Feasibility study. *Radiology, 224*, 278–285.

van Swieten, J. C., Staal, S., Kappelle, L. J., Derix, M. M. A., & van Gijn, J. (1996). Are white matter lesions directly associated with cognitive impairments in patients with lacunar infarcts? *Journal of Neurology, 243*, 196–200.

Walhovd, K. B., Fjell, A. M., Reinvang, I., Lundervold, A., Fischl, B., Salar, D., Quinn, B., Makris, N., & Dale, A. M. (2005). Cortical volume and speed of processing are complementary in predicting performance intelligence. *Neuropsychologia, 43*, 704–713.

Wechsler, D. (1981). *Wechsler Adult Intelligence Scale Revised Manual.* New York: Psychological Corporation.

Ylikoski, A., Erkinjuntti, T., Raininko, R., Sarna, S., Sulkava, R., & Tilvis, R. (1995). White matter hyperintensities on MRI in the neurologically nondiseased elderly: Analysis of cohorts of consecutive subjects aged 55 to 85 years living at home. *Stroke, 26*, 1171–1177.

Ylikoski, R., Ylikoski, A., Erkinjuntti, T., Sulkava, R., Raininko, R., & Tilvis, R. (1993). White matter changes in healthy elderly persons correlate with attention and speed of mental processing. *Archives of Neurology, 50*, 818–824.

Does it all go together when it goes?

One of our three measures of age-neurophysiological changes, Age Associated Loss of Brain Volume (AALBV), a rough measure of loss of brain tissue since young adulthood, robustly predicted the amounts and rates of declines in intelligence test scores (*gf*) that volunteers had experienced over the last eight to 20 years. The first of further questions was whether a different measure of gross brain efficiency, Cerebral Blood Flow (CBF), also marks declines in mental abilities and whether this measure of brain health is associated with similar patterns of changes across behavioural measures as is AALBV. To examine this Rabbitt et al. (2008) analyzed relationships between volunteers' current levels of both AALBV and CBF and their most recent scores on our longitudinal test battery, i.e. three tests of fluid intelligence (*gf*) (the AH 4-1 and AH 4-2, and the Cattell Culture Fair Test); three vocabulary tests (Mill Hill A and B, and adult WAIS); two tests of verbal memory; and two tests of information processing speed (letter/letter substitution coding and simple visual search). We also included scores on tests of working, of episodic memory and four tests of frontal lobe function that had been taken contemporaneously with MRI scans.

By including a wide range of behavioural measures we could test whether AALVB and CBF are associated with the same patterns of change across all cognitive tests and also compare the proportions of scores on these measures that were associated with differences in age with those associated with AALVB and CBF. Individuals' levels of AALVB accounted for 8% to 15%, CBF for 2% to 9% and their calendar ages for 20.4% to 22.6% of differences between their scores in the three intelligence tests. AALVB is a stronger predictor of current fluid intelligence than CBF but neither measure accounts for the entire variance in *gf* scores associated with individuals' ages. The same pattern of predictions maintained for scores on tests of memory and of frontal and executive function. In contrast, predictions from AALBF for scores on the two speed tests were as strong as those for age (21.4% and 12.6% as against 17.3% and 13.8%). CBF made weaker predictions of speed scores (5.5% and 4.4%). The striking finding that individual differences in AALBV account for as high a proportion of variance in speed between individuals as do differences in their ages prompted us ask whether variance in AALBV between individuals accounts for all, or only for some, of the variance in speed between individuals that is associated with their ages. We used hierarchical regressions to estimate the overlap of the variance associated with neurophysiological indices with each other and with age. After non-significant differences associated with sex had been taken into account, AALBV accounted for 38.4% to 60.7% and CBF for 10.3% and 24% of that part of the variance in *gf* scores between individuals that was associated with differences in their ages. For scores on tests of speed, the corresponding estimates for AABLV were 67.3% and 78.0% and for CBF 33.7% and 36.3%. For tests of frontal and executive function, predictions of age-related performance from neurophysiological measures were also robust (AALBV 50.4% to 83.0%; CBF 18.0% to 32.5%), but for memory tests predictions were relatively weak (AALBV 46.2% and 58.7%; CBF 13.4% and 21.8%).

This pattern of results seemed theoretically interesting because it bears on two widely espoused assumptions. The first is that speed of simple decisions, measured by CRTs or inspection times, is a direct measure of the "biological basis of (fluid) intelligence (*gf*)" because it indexes the speed of neurophysiological processes – possibly even a parameter as basic as neuronal conduction time (e.g. Eysenck, 1988; Jensen & Whang, 1993; Engel & Henderson, 1973; Reed & Jensen, 1992; Robinson et al., 1984). Our results now suggested that the relationship between decision speed and intelligence cannot be so simple and direct. Individual differences in extent of age-related neurophysiological changes, AALBV and CBF, do affect both speed and *gf*, but to different degrees. Both AABLF and CBF affect speed more than *gf*.

Another popular theory is that age-related brain changes affect speed more than any other index of mental ability and that the resulting "global slowing" has strong knock-on effects on most, or even on all, other measures of mental abilities – especially memory and probably also intelligence (Salthouse, 1996; 2000). In our analyses, ARLBV and CBF are, indeed, quite sensitive markers for the neurophysiological changes that contribute to slowing in old age, but they are relatively weak markers for the changes that impair memory and *gf*.

This result suggested that it is simplistic to suppose that age-related neurophysiological changes in the brain affect all, or most, behavioural measures of mental abilities *solely* because they bring about "global slowing". AALBV and CBF have quite modest effects, accounting for only a third of age-related variance in speed. But AALBV and CBF are, arguably, not the most sensitive measures of slowing associated with age-related brain changes. Our third index of global age-related brain changes, White Matter Lesion Prevalence (WMLP) has a convincing track record from large population studies for predicting levels of speed more strongly than levels of performance on tests of most other mental abilities (de Groot al., 2000; de Leeuw et al., 2001). Because WMLP is an exceptionally strong neurophysiological marker for mental slowing, we examined how well our volunteers' levels of WMLP predicted age-related differences in their scores on behavioural tests of mental abilities.

References

De Groot, J. C., de Leeuw, F. E., Oudkerk, M., Van Gijn, J., Hofman, A., Jolles, J., & Breteler, M. M. (2000). Cerebral white matter lesions and cognitive function: The Rotterdam Scan Study. *Annals of Neurology: Official Journal of the American Neurological Association and the Child Neurology Society*, *47*(2), 145–151.

De Leeuw, F. E., de Groot, J. C., Achten, E., Oudkerk, M., Ramos, L.M.P., Heijboer, R., ... & Breteler, M.M.B. (2001). Prevalence of cerebral white matter lesions in elderly people: A population based magnetic resonance imaging study. The Rotterdam Scan Study. *Journal of Neurology, Neurosurgery and Psychiatry*, *70*(1), 9–14.

Engel, R., & Henderson, N. B. (1973). Visual evoked responses and IQ scores at school age. *Developmental Medicine and Child Neurology, 15*(2), 136–145.

Eysenck, H. J. (1988). The biological basis of intelligence. In S. H. Irvine & J. W. Berry (Eds), *Human Abilities in Cultural Context* (pp. 87–104). New York: Cambridge University Press.

Jensen, A. R., & Whang, P. A. (1993). Reaction times and intelligence: A comparison of Chinese-American and Anglo-American children. *Journal of Biosocial Science, 25*(3), 397–410.

Rabbitt, P., Ibrahim, S., Lunn, M., Scott, M., Thacker, N., Hutchinson, C., ... & Jackson, A. (2008). Age-associated losses of brain volume predict longitudinal cognitive declines over 8 to 20 years. *Neuropsychology, 22*(1), 3–9.

Reed, T. E., & Jensen, A. R. (1992). Conduction velocity in a brain nerve pathway of normal adults correlates with intelligence level. *Intelligence, 16*(3–4), 259–272.

Robinson, D. L., Haier, R. J., Braden, W., & Krengel, M. (1984). Psychometric intelligence and visual evoked potentials: A replication. *Personality and Individual Differences, 5*(4), 487–489.

Salthouse, T. A. (1996). The processing-speed theory of adult age differences in cognition. *Psychological Review, 103*(3), 403–428.

Salthouse, T. (2000). *A Theory of Cognitive Aging* (Vol. 28). Amsterdam: North-Holland.

15 White matter lesions account for all age-related declines in speed but not in intelligence

P.M.A. Rabbitt, M. Scott, M. Lunn, N. Thacker, C. Lowe, N. Pendleton, M. Horan and A. Jackson

Diffuse and global age-related changes in the brain impair cognitive performance, but the functional specifics of these relationships are still unclear. One widely held view is that the main behavioral effect of diffuse brain changes is to slow information processing speed and that this functionally drives changes in all, or almost all, other mental abilities (Salthouse, 1985, 1991, 1996a, 1996b). An even more radical hypothesis is that individual differences in information-processing speed are the functional bases of differences in general fluid intelligence in young adults (Vernon & Jensen, 1994) and that slowing of information-processing speed is a main cause of declines in general fluid intelligence and in other mental abilities in old age (Deary, 2001). This theoretical context makes it important to find more direct evidence that, in later life, global and diffuse brain changes affect information-processing speed more than they do other aspects of cognitive performance.

One marker for diffuse age-related changes in the brain is the increase in white matter lesion prevalence (WMLP). Many studies of healthy, nondementing elderly people confirm that WMLP increases in old age and report negative correlations between WMLP and scores on a variety of tests of cognitive performance (e.g., Breteler, van Amerongen, & van Swieten, 1994; de Groot, de Leeuw, & Breteler, 1998; Deary, 2001; Deary, Leaper, Murray, Staff, & Whalley, 2003; de Groot et al., 2000; de Leeuw et al, 2001; Hickie et al., 1995; Junque et al., 1990; Longstreth et al., 1996; Schmidt et al., 1993; van Swieten, Staal, & Keppelle, 1996; A. Ylikoski et al., 1995; R. Ylikoski et al., 1993). Some studies also find that measures of WMLP correlate more strongly with scores on tests of information processing speed than on tests of memory, frontal and executive function, or intelligence (e.g., de Groot et al., 2000; Junque et al., 1990; R. Ylikoski et al., 1993). These differences in the strengths of simple correlations between WMLP and test scores have been taken as support for the hypothesis that the diffuse age-related brain changes marked by WMLP cause declines in most aspects of cognitive performance mainly, or even solely, because they slow the speed of information processing on which nearly all other mental abilities, and particularly fluid intelligence, functionally depend.

A weakness in this attractively parsimonious account is that simple correlations do not provide sufficient evidence to test it. Failure to recognize this has vitiated attempts to test hypotheses about the relationship between changes in the brain and changes in cognitive performance in old age. The issue cuts deeper than the familiar truism that correlations between variables do not necessarily prove functional relationships. The crux is, rather, that investigators have not recognized that because correlations between time-linked variables are an interesting special case their interpretation requires particular caution. This is because within any complex system that degrades over time the amounts of changes in the properties of the system, and so in its performance characteristics, will necessarily be significantly correlated even if they are actually functionally independent. For example, there is excellent empirical evidence that, in elderly samples, individuals' scores on tests of visual acuity, balance, and intelligence all correlate with each other and with their ages (Anstey, Lord, & Williams, 1997). This does not necessarily mean that they must all have a "common functional cause" in the sense that they are brought about by the same changes in the brain or central nervous system. As age advances, for example, cataracts may progressively reduce visual acuity, mechanical joint damage may progressively impair balance, and age-related changes in the brain may progressively impair cognition. Significant correlations between acuity, balance, and cognition must at least partly, and possibly entirely, reflect the parallel progress of functionally unrelated changes. Without more direct evidence than simple correlations between balance, acuity, and cognition, it is prudent to assume that some proportion of the variance that they share may be due to age-related changes in brain systems that affect all of them but that some different and additional proportion of their common variance must reflect temporal coincidences of processes of change in functionally unrelated systems.

By the same logic, in order to correctly interpret correlations between markers of diffuse changes in the brain, such as WMLP, and measures of cognitive performance, such as scores on tests of information-processing speed, we need to find out how much of the common variance between them is due to simple synchronicity and how much to functional codependence. If we cannot do this, then however robust may be the correlations between WMLP and scores on tests of information-processing speed, we cannot be sure that the particular age-related brain changes that are marked by WMLP actually do affect information-processing speed. The functionally effective changes may not be marked by WMLP but merely take place over the same time span. It follows that it is also insecure to argue, just from simple correlations between measures of WMLP and of cognitive performance, that levels of WMLP functionally affect information-processing speed either more or less than they affect other aspects of cognitive performance, such as intelligence, frontal and executive function, or memory.

To find out what is actually happening, we need to examine associations between individuals' scores on cognitive tests and their levels of WMLP after the effects of the passage of time have also been taken into consideration. Perhaps the simplest way to do this is to enter individuals' ages as an additional predictor of their scores on cognitive tests. The rationale is that healthy older individuals' ages provide a rough index of differences in the amounts of all changes in all parts of their brains that have occurred during their lifetimes. Although this must be true in general terms, it is important to note that longitudinal studies show that people experience markedly different trajectories of age-related changes (see Rabbitt, Diggle, Holland, & McInnes, 2004). Consequently, differences in their birthdays can only be rough indices of the different amounts of brain changes, and so of the amounts and kinds of cognitive changes that they have suffered. Nevertheless, by entering people's ages together with measures of their levels of WMLP into regression equations to predict their cognitive test scores we can at least determine whether WMLP accounts for all, some, or none of the age-related differences in performance between members of a sample of older individuals.

Within this framework there are four possible hypotheses as to why levels of any marker of diffuse age-related brain changes, such as WMLP, may correlate with scores on particular cognitive tests. Fortunately, it is possible to choose between them, because each hypothesis makes a different prediction of outcomes when age is entered as an additional predictor of test performance.

The first hypothesis is that WMLP predicts age differences on a particular cognitive test simply because it acts as a "clock" measuring the passage of time during which the other, functionally effective, brain changes occur. In this case we would expect that both WMLP and age will individually correlate with test scores but that when age is also entered as a joint predictor the correlation with age will remain significant but the correlation with WMLP will disappear. In this case the appropriate interpretation would be that, because age-related changes in task performance are brought about by age-related changes in brain systems different from those that are marked by WMLP, the simple correlation between WMLP and task scores occurs only because of temporal coincidence. Note that such a finding, if for only one cognitive task but not for others, would be strong empirical evidence that correlations between measures of brain integrity and cognitive performance sometimes represent temporal synchrony of independent processes rather than functional associations between them. A demonstration of this promotes the logical pitfalls of neglecting synchronicity from a pedantic anxiety to an obligatory guideline for correct interpretation of associations between measures of brain integrity and cognition.

A second hypothesis is that differences in WMLP account for all of the age-related variance between individuals in scores on a particular test and that performance on this test is not affected by any other age-related brain changes that WMLP does not mark. In this case, when both age and WMLP are entered as predictors of test scores, their joint prediction will be significant but their independent predictions will not.

A third hypothesis is that WMLP accounts for all of the age-related variance between individuals in performance of a particular task but that it also accounts for additional variance that differences in ages do not predict. In this case we would expect that after age is entered the correlation with WMLP will remain significant but a previously significant simple correlation with age will now disappear. The interpretation would be that there is no evidence that age-related changes in performance are brought about by any other brain changes than those for which WMLP is a marker. It would also mean that, because people age at very different rates, differences in their ages are only a rough index of the progress of brain changes that affect task performance, so that age is a much more coarse measure of WMLP than are direct measures of neurophysiological integrity, such as brain scans.

The remaining hypothesis is that age-related changes in performance are partly due to age-related brain changes for which WMLP is a marker but are also partly due to other changes in the brain that WMLP does not mark. In this case we would expect that, after age is entered, correlations between both age and test scores and WMLP and test scores should remain significant. We would also expect that the joint prediction from both age and WMLP should account for more of the variance in performance between individuals than either factor on its own. The appropriate interpretation would be that task performance is affected both by age-related changes that are marked by WMLP and also by other changes that WMLP does not mark.

All these hypotheses assume that, because WMLP may mark specific brain changes that affect performance on some kinds of tests but not on others, inclusion of age as an additional predictor may have different outcomes for different cognitive tests. For this reason, in order to test these hypotheses it is essential to include as wide a range of cognitive tests as possible. This also allows a test of the widely held assumption that WMLP is more closely associated with information-processing speed than with memory, fluid intelligence, or frontal and executive performance, and it further allows a test of the more radical idea that individual differences in information-processing speed are the functional bases for differences in general fluid intelligence (Eysenck, 1988; Jensen, 1982; Vernon & Jensen, 1994). If this latter idea is correct, then WMLP should account, to an equal or at least to a similar extent, for age-related differences in speed and intelligence. If this does not turn out to be the case, then we must conclude that age-related changes in speed and intelligence are caused by different kinds of functional changes in the brain.

To test between these possibilities, we obtained levels of WMLP with MRI scans of 65 healthy elderly people who were contemporaneously given 17 different cognitive tests, including measures of general fluid intelligence, vocabulary, speed, working memory, and frontal and executive function. Simple and joint predictions of test scores based on their ages and WMLPs were then examined.

Method

Participants included 40 women and 25 men ages 64 – 85 years (M = 73.1, SD = 5.3). All were independently dwelling community residents of Greater Manchester, United Kingdom, who had been members of the University of Manchester longitudinal research panel for 11–17 years preceding this experiment. Detailed descriptions of recruitment and of conduct of the longitudinal study are given by Rabbitt, McInnes, et al. (2004). Participants' levels of general fluid and crystallized intellectual ability were indexed by their scores on three tests of general fluid intelligence and on three vocabulary tests administered between 12 and 18 months before brain scans were performed. Table 15.1 gives the means and standard deviations of these scores. Levels of performance on these tests make it very unlikely that any participants are suffering from dementias or serious neurological problems. This conclusion is reinforced by clinical judgments made during complete physical and neurological examination by two experienced geriatricians (Neil Pendleton and Mike Horan) and by the fact that scans found no neurological abnormalities.

The three tests of general fluid intelligence included Cattell and Cattell's (1960) Culture Fair and the Alice Heim (1970) AH4–1 and AH4–2. The AH4–1 is composed of 65 problems involving verbal comparisons, logical reasoning, and mental arithmetic. The AH4–2 involves 65 nonverbal problems requiring deduction of logical sequences derived by mental superposition, subtraction, and rotation of line-drawn shapes. Scores on each of the AH4 tests are based on the total number of items correctly coded within a 10-min time limit. The Culture

Table 15.1 Means and Standard Deviations of Scores on 17 Cognitive Tests

Test type and cognitive test	*M*	*SD*
General fluid intelligence		
Culture Fair	29.6	6.4
AH4-1	39.2	9.9
AH-4-2	38.2	10.9
Vocabulary		
WAIS Vocabulary	55.5	11.0
Mill Hill "A"	23.9	3.9
Mill Hill "B"	18.8	5.4
Immediate and working memory		
Forward Digit Span	6.2	1.3
Backward Digit Span	4.5	1.6
Word Span	2.3	2.0
Complex episodic memory		
Proposition about People	4.8	2.1
Circle/Object	7.2	2.6
Speed		
Visual Search	108.8	19.1
Letter/Digit Substitution Coding	63.7	12.2
Frontal/executive		
Phonemic Fluency	15.2	3.7
Category Fluency	20.9	4.6
Brixton	18.7	7.3
ROCF Immediate Recall	23.0	7.8

Note: WAIS = Wechsler Adult Intelligence Scale; ROCF = Rey–Osterrieth Complex Figure.

Fair is a nonverbal test in which participants must deduce rules to correctly recognize and insert missing elements in 50 different line-drawn matrices. The three vocabulary tests included the Raven (1965) Mill Hill "A" and "B" tests and the Wechsler Adult Intelligence Scale (WAIS) Vocabulary Test (Wechsler, 1955). The Mill Hill "A" requires selection of the closest synonym for each of 32 different words from 6 alternatives provided in each case. The Mill Hill "B" requires production of exact definitions for each of 32 different seldom-used words. The WAIS Vocabulary Test requires selection of the appropriate definition out of 4 possibilities supplied for each of 64 words. All vocabulary test scores are based on the number of correctly identified synonyms or definitions.

The three tests of immediate and working memory included Forward Digit Span, Backward Digit Span, and Word Span for lists of randomly selected, unrelated bisyllabic words. Scores are based on the number of lists in which all items are recalled in the order presented or required. For one of two complex episodic memory tasks, Propositions about People (PaP), participants are visually shown the names of five different imaginary individuals with three items of information about each. They are then immediately cued by the names to recall as many items of information about each person as they can. Scores are based on the total number of items of information correctly identified with the appropriate names. In the Circle/Object Task, participants are given 15 s to inspect a circle divided into 12 equal sectors, each of which contains a line drawing of an easily nameable common object. Participants then turn over an answer sheet and write within the appropriate sectors of a blank circle the names of as many objects as they can remember. Scores are based on the total number of correct object names entered into the correct sectors. One of two tests for information-processing speed is Visual Search, in which participants scan sheets of all capital letters of the alphabet, printed in random order and with equal frequency, to locate and mark as many instances of I and O as they can during a period of 2 min. Scores are based on the number of letters, up to and including the last target, correctly identified. The second speed test is a Letter/Digit Substitution Coding Task adapted from the WAIS battery. Scores are based on the number of items correctly coded during a single run of 1 min. One test of "frontal" or "executive" abilities is a Phonemic Fluency Test requiring participants to write down as many words beginning with the letter F as they can generate within 2 min, and another is a Category Fluency Task requiring them to write down as many names of animals as they can within 2 min. Scores are based on the total number of correct, nonrepeated items. Two further executive tests are the Shallice and Burgess (1991) Brixton Test and the Immediate Recall of the Rey-Osterrieth Complex Figure Test (Shin, Park, Park, Seol, & Kwon, 2006).

Participants were all able to travel independently to the University of Manchester Age and Cognitive Performance Research Centre, where they were tested individually by the same investigator (Christine Lowe) in a quiet room. Testing required two 75-min sessions. Both sessions took place within a period of 6 weeks. Participants were each paid an honorarium of £10 (about US $20) per session to cover their travel expenses.

Within 6 weeks of completing the cognitive tests, all participants underwent cranial MRI. The project was approved by the Central Manchester Local Research Ethics Committee, and all participants gave informed consent at least 24 hr before scanning. Scanning was performed with a 1.5 Tesla whole-body scanner (Philips ACS PT 6000 NT, Philips Medical Systems; Best, Netherlands) with a quadrature birdcage head coil. Imaging was parallel to a plane connecting the lower borders of the genu and the splenium of the corpus callosum, and images covered the whole brain from the vertex to the foramen magnum. Axial Fluid Attenuated Inversion Recovery (TR/TE/TI = 11,000/140/2,600 ms) images and Axial T1 Weighted Inversion Recovery (TR/TE/TI = 6,850/18/300 ms) images were acquired. For both scans, 51 slices of 3.0 mm, with no interslice gap, were obtained, using a matrix of 256 × 256 mm and a field of view of 230 × 230 mm.

WMLP was assessed by an experienced neuroradiologist (Alan Jackson) using EFilm (EFilm Medical Ltd.; Toronto, Ontario, Canada). Alan Jackson's reliability measured against other experienced practitioners is 87%. WMLP is assessed from the matched T1 inversion recovery and Axial Fluid Attenuated Inversion Recovery images with the Scheltens scale (Scheltens, Barkhof, & Leys, 1993). Cortical deep white matter lesions are assessed on a scale of 0–6 in the frontal, parietal, occipital, and temporal lobes, and these values can be summed up to give a total lesion load (0–24), as was done in this case.

Results

Table 15.1 gives the means and standard deviations of participants' scores on all tests. Table 15.2 gives results of simple regressions with participants' ages and their total WMLP scores as predictors of their performance on each of the 17 cognitive tests. As might be expected from nearly all earlier studies, participants' WMLPs correlated significantly and positively with their ages ($R = .376$; $N = 65$; $p = .003$).

Participants' scores on all three intelligence tests correlated robustly with their ages, but only their AH4–1 test scores correlated with their WMLP scores. Among the vocabulary tests, WAIS scores were modestly predicted by WMLP but not by age. Mill Hill "A" and "B" vocabulary test scores were not predicted by either age or by WMLP. Episodic Memory scores were predicted by both age and WMLP. Among the working memory tasks, Forward Digit Span was marginally predicted by both age and WMLP, but Backward Digit Span and Word Span were predicted by WMLP and not by age. Scores on both speed tasks were robustly predicted by both age and WMLP. Among executive tests, scores on the Category Fluency and Rey-Osterrieth tests were robustly predicted by both age and WMLP, scores on Phonemic Fluency were only marginally predicted by age and by WMLP, and scores on the Brixton frontal test were robustly predicted by age but only marginally predicted by WMLP.

The aim was to determine what proportion of the total variance between individuals that was related to differences in their ages could also be accounted for by individual differences in WMLP and vice versa. One way to do this

Table 15.2 R Values for Simple Correlations Between Participants' Ages and WMLP Scores and Their Scores on 17 Cognitive Tests

Test type and cognitive test	*R for age*	*R for WMLP*
General fluid intelligence		
Culture Fair	−.411***	−.175
AH4-1	−.414***	−.271*
AH4-2	−.481***	−.201
Vocabulary		
WAIS Vocabulary	−.206	−.281*
Mill Hill "A"	−.159	−.128
Mill Hill "B"	−.158	−.208
Immediate and working memory		
Forward Digit Span	−.211 (p = .08)	−.212 (p = .08)
Backward Digit Span	−.194	−.335**
Word Span	−.168	−.236*
Complex episodic memory		
Propositions about People	−.290**	−.310**
Circle/Object	−.516***	−.338**
Speed		
Visual Search	−.306**	−.384***
Letter/Digit Substitution Coding	−.329**	−.440***
Frontal/executive		
Phonemic Fluency	−.215 (p = .08)	−.218 (p =.07)
Category Fluency	−.349**	−.380**
Brixton	.369**	.217 (p = .08)
ROCF Immediate Recall	−.555***	−.332**

Note: WMLP = white matter lesion prevalence; WAIS = Wechsler Adult Intelligence Scale; ROCF = Rey-Osterrieth Complex Figure. *$p < .05$. **$p < .01$. ***$p < .001$.

was to use hierarchical regressions in which participants' WMLP scores were entered first and their ages second. This showed the amount and significance of any increase in R^2 when age was entered and allowed values of betas for age and for WMLP to be compared. Table 15.3 shows R^2 for WMLP, the ΔR^2 when age was entered, and betas for WLMP scores and age for each of the 17 tests.

Age and WMLP jointly made significant predictions of scores on all tasks except the three vocabulary tests (*ns*), Forward Digit Span (nonsignificant at p = .06), and Phonemic Fluency (*ns*).

Intelligence Tests

For all three tests, age produced a highly significant increase in R^2 over that for WMLP. In the joint models, betas for age were highly significant for all three intelligence tests, but betas for WMLP were not significant for any.

Table 15.3 Results of Hierarchical Multiple Regressions With WMLP and Age Successively Entered

Test type and cognitive test	*R^2 for WMLP*	*ΔR^2 when age is added*	*WLMP β*	*Age β*
General fluid intelligence				
Culture Fair	.03	.139**	−.103	−.367***
AH4-1	.07	.191**	−.023	−.492***
AH4-2	.04	.191**	−.023	−.492***
Vocabulary				
WAIS Vocabulary	.08	.008	−.236 (p = .08)	−.098
Mill Hill "A"	.02	.013	−.07	−.129
Mill Hill "B"	.043	.005	−.171	−.079
Immediate and working memory				
Forward Digit Span	.045 (p = .08)	.016	−.146	−.144
Backward Digit Span	.112**	.002	−.312*	−.052
Word Span	.056*	.006	−.201	−.087
Complex episodic memory				
Propositions about people	.096*	.028	−.224 (p = .08)	−.188
Circle/Object	.115**	.165***	−.130	−.456***
Speed				
Visual Search	.147***	.021	−.309**	−.164
Letter/Digital Substitution Coding	.194***	.021	−.366**	−.162
Frontal executive				
Phonemic Fluency	0.48 (p =.07)	.0.17	−.151	−.146
Category Fluency	.144**	.039	−.278*	−.222
Brixton	.046 (p =.08)	.092**	.061	.341*
ROCF Immediate Recall	.110**	.205***	−.099	−.510*

Note: WMLP = white matter lesion prevalence; WAIS = Wechsler Adult Intelligence Scale; ROCF = Rey-Osterrieth Complex Figure. *p < .05. **p < .01. ***p < .001.

Vocabulary Tests

R^2 for WMLP was nonsignificant only for the WAIS (p = .08). Entry of age into the model did not significantly increase the R for any test. In the joint models, the beta for WMLP approached significance for the WAIS (p = .08), but the beta for age was not significant for any vocabulary test.

Episodic Memory Tests

The R^2 for WMLP was significant for both the PaP and Circle/Object tests. For the PaP test, entry of age did not significantly increase R^2. In the joint model, beta for WMLP approached significance, but beta for age did not.

For the Circle/Object test, entry of age resulted in a highly significant increase in R^2, and in the joint model, the beta for age was highly significant, but the beta for WMLP was not.

Working Memory Tests

For Forward Digit Span, the R^2 WMLP approached significance (p =.08), but entry of age did not significantly increase R^2, and in the joint model, betas for neither WMLP nor age were significant. For Backward Digit Span, the R^2 for WMLP was significant, there was no significant increase in R^2 when age was entered, and the beta for WMLP was significant but the beta for age was not. For Word Span, the R^2 for WMLP was significant, entering age did not significantly increase this R^2, and in the joint model, betas for neither WMLP nor age were significant.

Frontal and Executive Tests

For Phonemic Fluency, the R^2 for WMLP approached significance, entry of age did not significantly increase the R^2, and in the joint model, betas for neither WMLP nor age reached significance. For Category Fluency, the R^2 for WMLP was robustly significant, entry of age did not significantly increase this R^2, and the beta for WMLP was significant but the beta for age was not. For the Brixton test, the R^2 for WMLP was nonsignificant and was significantly increased by entry of age. In the joint model, the beta for age was significant, but the beta for WMLP was not. For the Immediate Recall of the Rey-Osterrieth figure, the R^2 for WMLP was significant, entry of age resulted in a highly significant increase in R^2, and in the joint model, the beta for age was significant but the beta for WMLP was not.

Discussion

The results show that although WMLP accounts for all of the age-related variance in some tasks, it accounts for only some or for none of the age-related variance in others. This empirically underwrites the logical point that, when interpreting associations between measures of brain status and scores on cognitive tests, it is crucial to recognize that simple correlations can reflect functionally unrelated associations. It also shows that by entering age as an additional predictor we can obtain useful new information about the actual functional relationships between indices of age-related neurophysiological changes and measures of cognitive performance. The finding that entering age as an additional predictor to WMLP has markedly different effects for different tasks is new because it shows that the effects of WMLP are very much more selective than has previously been thought. WMLP accounts for all of the age-related variance in some tasks, such as the tests of speed, but for none of the age-related variance in others, such as intelligence tests. In particular, entry of age as an additional predictor allows us to discover which of four possible hypotheses best describes the relationship between WMLP and performance for any particular task.

One possibility is that, at least for some tasks, simple correlations between WMLP and scores are significant only because the increase in WMLP as age advances acts as a "clock" measuring the same passage of time during which other, functionally unrelated brain changes actually do the business. In this case, when age is entered it should make a significant independent contribution to WMLP, but WMLP should make no significant prediction additional to that made by age. This pattern of results appears for the AH4–1 intelligence test, the Circle/Object episodic memory task, and immediate reproduction of the Rey-Osterrieth figure. It follows that, for these tests, there is no evidence that simple correlations with WMLP reflect anything other than the temporal synchrony of functionally unrelated processes of change in the aging brain. This also shows that correlations between indices of brain status and of cognitive performance can be seriously misinterpreted unless the possibility of this disassociation is taken into consideration.

A second possibility is that differences in WMLP may account for all of the variance in scores between individuals that is associated with differences in their ages, but not for any additional variance that age differences do not detect. Because age and WMLP account for precisely the same variance in test scores, we would expect that when either is entered as an additional predictor to the other their joint prediction remains significant, but their independent predictions no longer are. No clear instances of this pattern of results were found in this experiment.

A third possibility is that differences in WMLP may account for all of the age-related variance in test scores between individuals and, in addition, for further variance that differences in their ages do not predict. In this case we would expect that after age is entered the correlation with WMLP would remain significant but a previously significant simple correlation with age would disappear. This would mean that there is no evidence that age-related changes in performance are brought about by any other brain changes than those for which WMLP is a marker. This finding also provides corroborative evidence that, because people age at very different rates, differences in their ages can only be rough indices of the extent of brain changes and so of the cognitive changes that they have experienced. WMLP is a much more direct measure of age-related neurophysiological change than is calendar age. However, it is crucial to note that, as these analyses show, it marks some changes but not others. The results for the two speed tasks, Letter/Digit Coding and Visual Search, and for the Category Fluency Task are clear evidence that this pattern of relationships does occur. For these particular tasks, individual differences in WMLP account for not only all age-related differences in performance but also for additional variance that differences in age do not pick up.

A final possibility is that, for some tasks, age-related changes in performance are partly due to age-related brain changes for which WMLP is a marker but are also partly due to other changes in the brain that WMLP does not mark. In this case we expect that entry of age into regression equations should significantly improve the correlation with WMLP alone and that correlations between both age and test scores and WMLP and test scores should remain significant. The interpretation would be that age brings about changes in the brain, and so in task performance, that are different from and additional to those that are associated with increases in WMLP. However, because age is only a rough measure of the extent of changes in individuals, WMLP is a more direct and so more sensitive measure of differences in the progress of the particular brain changes for which it is a marker. No clear instances of this pattern appeared.

The analyses also incidentally tested the hypothesis that individual differences in information-processing speed are the functional bases of differences in general fluid intelligence (e.g., Eysenck, 1988; Jensen, 1982; Vernon & Jensen, 1994) and that, because of this, age-related declines in intelligence and in speed must be driven by the same changes in the aging brain (Deary, 2001). WMLP accounted for all of the age-related variance between individuals in both measures of information-processing speed, Letter/Digit Coding and Visual Search, but for none of the variance in scores on three different intelligence tests, the AH4–1 and AH4–2 and Cattell and Cattell's (1960) Culture Fair. Because brain changes marked by WMLPs affect speed but not intelligence, it follows that intelligence and speed are not supported by identical functional processes in the brain. Indeed, these data provide no evidence for any commonality.

This disassociation is theoretically interesting but is also an important methodological warning of the risks of concluding that just because different behavioral measures correlate robustly they must necessarily be supported by the same functional neuropsychological systems. The hypothesis that general fluid intelligence and speed are supported by the same systems (Eysenck, 1988; Jensen, 1982) is based on a voluminous and uncontroversial body of reliable findings of robust correlations between intelligence test scores and measures of speed. The further hypothesis that agerelated declines in information-processing speed drive declines in most or all other performance characteristics of the cognitive system (Deary, 2001; Salthouse, 1985, 1991, 1996a, 1996b) is based on equally good evidence that, for nearly all cognitive measures tested, differences in age no longer make any prediction when scores on tests of speed, such as Letter/Digit Coding or Visual Search, are entered as copredictors (Rabbitt & Anderson, 2006; Salthouse, 1985, 1991, 1996). The present results do not, of course, contradict this body of data, but they do radically question the interpretations that have been derived from it. In doing this they also, very strongly, make the point that it is unsafe to try to derive models of brain function entirely from patterns of shared variance between behavioral measures.

With regard to the specific associations between WMLP and cognitive performance in old age, the present analyses suggest the following summary. As people age they experience a number of different changes in their brains and central nervous systems. Though many of these changes may be functionally associated with each other, some are functionally independent. In any particular elderly person, different kinds of brain changes will have progressed over the same periods of time, and different brain changes may also have different time courses. Individuals' current ages are proxy measures for the progress of all the brain changes that they have as yet experienced, but because trajectories of cognitive aging markedly differ between individuals (Rabbitt, Diggle, et al., 2004), differences in their ages are only very rough measures of the different amounts, and perhaps also of the different kinds, of age-related brain changes that have occurred during their lives. Another way to put this is that trajectories of change in old age are determined by a wide range of different factors that affect individuals to different degrees. For example, trajectories of change are accelerated by pathology and by approaching death, and longevity is affected by socioeconomic advantage and geographical location of residence, by birth weight, by lifetime health status, and by greater or lesser burdens of pathologies (see, for example, Rabbitt, Lunn, & Wong, 2005, 2006). Individual differences in exposure to these changes imply corresponding individual differences in "biological age" and so "neurophysiological age."

The present analyses confirm that these brain changes that occur with age, but at different rates in different individuals, include some that are significantly correlated with a particular marker of neurophysiological status, WMLP, but also include others that WMLP marks only weakly or not at all. However, although individuals' birthdays are imperfect indices of the extent of the age-related brain changes that they have experienced during their lifetimes, entry of their calendar ages as an additional predictor with a measure of brain status, such as WMLP, implies entry of an approximate proxy measure both of the progress of age-related brain changes that are marked by WMLP and of the other agerelated brain changes that are not marked by WMLP. The present data show that for particular tasks, such as measures of information-processing speed, entry of age results in no significant improvement in prediction over WMLP alone and, moreover, does not affect the strength of the prediction from WMLP. Here we can conclude that levels of WMLP reflect the amounts of age-related changes in all brain systems that support the particular cognitive performance parameters that are indexed by these tasks, information-processing speed. Further, we find no evidence that task performance is affected by other brain changes that WMLP does not mark. This is an advance on previous knowledge because it leads to much stronger conclusions than does the previous consensus that WMLP correlates more strongly with measures of information-processing speed than with many other measures of cognitive performance. The gain is illustrated by the finding that for other, different tasks, such as intelligence tests, significant predictions from WMLP disappear when age is entered. This shows that the simple correlations between intelligence test scores and WMLP that have been noted in earlier studies are not reliable evidence for any functional association. It seems likely that they occur only because brain changes affecting intelligence proceed during the same periods of time as do increases in WMLP. We cannot speculate on the functional etiology of these changes without more evidence than we currently have. Finally, these analyses show that entry of age into regression equations as a joint predictor with particular neurophysiological markers, such as WMLP, not only guards against some misinterpretations of functional associations between brain markers and cognition but also gives us rough, but empirically useful, estimates of how much of age - related variance in cognitive performance different, particular markers of brain status can account for.

Acknowledgments

We thank the Wellcome Trust for funding the entire study.

References

Anstey, K. J., Lord, S. R., & Williams, P. (1997). Strength in the lower limbs: Visual contrast sensitivity and simple reaction time predict cognition in older women. *Psychology and Aging, 12,* 137–144.

Breteler, M. M. B., van Amerongen, N. M., & van Swieten, J. C. (1994). Cognitive correlates of ventricular enlargement and cerebral white matter lesions on magnetic resonance imaging: The Rotterdam study. *Stroke, 25,* 1109–1115.

Cattell, R. B., and Cattell, A. K. S. (1960). *Handbook for the individual or group Culture Fair Intelligence Test.* Champaign, IL: Institute for Personality and Ability Testing.

Deary, I. (2001). *Looking down on human intelligence.* Oxford, England: Oxford University Press.

Deary, I. J., Leaper, S. A., Murray, A. D., Staff, R. T., & Whalley, L. J. (2003). Cerebral white matter abnormalities and lifetime cognitive change: A 67-year follow-up of the Scottish Mental Survey of 1932. *Psychology and Aging, 18,* 140–148.

de Groot, J. C., de Leeuw, F. E., & Breteler, M. M. B. (1998). Cognitive correlates of cerebral white matter changes. *Journal of Neural Transmission Supplement, 53,* 41–67.

de Groot, J. C., de Leeuw, F. E., Oudkerk, M., van Gijn, J., Hoifman, A., Jolles, J., & Breteler, M. M. B. (2000). Cerebral white matter lesions and cognitive function: The Rotterdam study. *Annals of Neurology, 47,* 145–151.

de Leeuw, F. E., de Groot, J. C., Achten, E., Oudkerk, M., Ramos, L. M. P., Heijboer, R., et al. (2001). Prevalence of cerebral white matter lesions in elderly people: A population based magnetic resonance imaging study: The Rotterdam Scan Study. *Journal of Neurology, Neurosurgery, and Psychiatry, 70,* 9–14.

Eysenck, H. J. (1988). The concept of "intelligence": Useful or useless? *Intelligence, 12,* 1–16.

Heim, A. (1970). *The AH4 intelligence tests.* Slough, United Kingdom: NFER/Nelson.

Hickie, I., Scott, E., Mitchell, P., Wilhelm, K., Austin, M.-P., & Bennet, B. (1995). Subcortical hyperintensities on magnetic resonance imaging: Clinical correlates and prognostic significance in patients with severe depression. *Biological Psychiatry, 37,* 151–160.

Jensen, A. R. (1982). Reaction time and psychometric *g.* In H. J. Eysenck (Ed.). A *model for intelligence* (pp. 221–278). Berlin, Germany: Springer-Verlag.

Junque, C., Pujol, J., Vendrell, P., Bruna, O., Jodar, M., Ribas, C., et al. (1990). Leuko-araiosis on magnetic resonance and speed of mental processing. *Archives of Neurology, 47,* 151–156.

Longstreth, W. T., Jr., Manolio, T. A., Arnold, A., Burke, G. L., Bryan, N., Jungreis, C. A., et al. (1996). Clinical correlates of white matter findings on cranial magnetic resonance imaging of 3301 elderly people: The Cardiovascular Health Study. *Stroke, 27,* 1274–1282.

Rabbitt, P., & Anderson, M. (2006). The lacunae of loss? Aging and the differentiation of cognitive abilities. In E. Bialostok and F. I. M. Craik (Eds.), *Lifespan cognition: Mechanisms of change* (pp. 331–343). New York: Oxford University Press.

Rabbitt, P., Diggle, P., Holland, F., & McInnes, L. (2004). Practice and drop-out effects during a 17-year longitudinal study of cognitive aging. *Journal of Gerontology, Series B: Psychological Sciences and Social Sciences, 59*, 84–97.

Rabbitt, P., McInnes, L., Diggle, P., Holland, F., Bent, N., Abson, V., et al. (2004). The University of Manchester longitudinal study of cognition in normal healthy old age, 1983 through 2003. *Aging, Neuropsychology and Cognition, 11*, 245–279.

Rabbitt, P., Lunn, M., & Wong, D. (2005). Neglect of dropout underestimates effects of death in longitudinal studies. *Journal of Gerontology, Series B: Psychological Sciences and Social Sciences, 60*, 106–109.

Rabbitt, P., Lunn, M., & Wong, D. (2006). Understanding terminal decline in cognition and risk of death. *European Psychologist, 11*, 164–171.

Raven, J. C. (1965). *The Mill Hill Vocabulary Scale.* London: Lewis.

Salthouse, T. A. (1985). *A cognitive theory of aging.* Berlin, Germany: Springer-Verlag.

Salthouse, T. A. (1991). *Theoretical perspectives on cognitive aging.* Hillsdale, NJ: Erlbaum.

Salthouse, T. A. (1996a). General and specific speed mediation of adult age differences in memory. *Journal of Gerontology, Series B: Psychological Sciences and Social Sciences, 51*, 30–42.

Salthouse, T. A. (1996b). The processing-speed theory of adult age differences in cognition. *Psychological Review, 103*, 403–428.

Scheltens, P., Barkhof, F., & Leys, D. (1993). A semiquantitative rating scale for the assessment of signal hyperintensities on magnetic resonance imaging. *Journal of the Neurological Sciences, 114*, 7–12.

Schmidt, R., Fazekas, F., Offenbacher, H., Dusek, T., Zach, E., Reinhart, B., et al. (1993). Neuropsychologic correlates of MRI white matter hyperintensities: A study of 150 normal volunteers. *Neurology, 43*, 2490–2494.

Shallice, T., & Burgess, P. W. (1991). Higher-order cognitive impairments and frontal lobe lesions in man. In H. S. Levin, H. M. Eisenberg, & A. L. Benton, (Eds.), *Frontal lobe function and dysfunction* (pp. 34–75). New York: Oxford University Press.

Shin, M.-S., Park, S.-Y., Park, S.-R., Seol, S.-H., and Kwon, J.-S. (2006). Clinical and empirical applications of the Rey-Osterrieth Complex Figure Test, *Nature Protocols, 1*, 892–899.

van Swieten, J. C., Staal, S., & Keppelle, I. J. (1996). Are white matter lesions directly associated with cognitive impairments in patients with lacunar infarcts? *Journal of Neurology, 243*, 196–200.

Vernon, P. A., & Jensen, A. R. (1994). Individual and group differences in intelligence and speed of information processing. *Personality and Individual Differences, 5*, 411–423.

Wechsler, D. (1955). *Wechsler Adult Intelligence Scale.* New York: Psychological Corporation.

Ylikoski, A., Erkinjuntti, T., Raininko, R., Sarna, S., Sulkava, R., & Tilvis, R. (1995). White matter hyperintensities on MRI in the neurologically nondiseased elderly: Analysis of cohorts of consecutive subjects aged 55 to 85 years living at home. *Stroke, 26*, 1171–1177.

Ylikoski, R., Ylikoski, A., Erkinjuntti, T., Sulkava, R., Raininko, R., & Tilvis, R. (1993). White matter changes in healthy elderly persons correlate with attention and speed of mental processing. *Archives of Neurology, 50*, 818–824.

How brain changes affect speed and intelligence

We found strong relationships between WMLP and scores on speed tests. This agreed with similar findings from much larger studies (de Groot al., 2000; de Leeuw et al., 2001). Our new finding was that when we entered both WMLP and age as joint predictors of behavioural test scores, WMLP accounted for all of the variance in speed between individuals that was associated with differences in their ages (Rabbitt et al. 2006; 2007). At first this seems a neat confirmation of Salthouse's (1996; 2000) proposals that scores on simple tests of decision speed are sensitive markers for the age-related neurophysiological changes that cause "global slowing" and so account for all or much of the age-associated variance in performance on all behavioural tests of mental abilities, especially on memory tests. In the event, we found that while WMLP accounts for all of the age-related variance in performance on speed tests, it accounts for none of the age-related variance in scores on intelligence tests (*gf*). For two of the memory tests, after differences in WMLP had been considered, age still accounted for significant additional variance. The relationship of WMLP to age-related changes in scores on tests of mental abilities are more complex than we would expect if WMLP marked only a single factor, "global slowing", that drives declines in performance on all tests of other mental abilities. WMLP has significant effects on mental abilities that do not seem to be merely secondary consequences of its effects on speed. The proposal that age-related declines in *gf* and memory are *solely* caused by the same age-related neurophysiological changes that affect speed of decisions during easy behavioural tasks seems an over-simplification. This finding also makes a wider a methodological point that hypotheses of "global age-related slowing" of all neurophysiological functions are unreliable if, as in the studies cited by Salthouse (1996; 2000), they are entirely derived from correlations between scores on behavioural tasks.

To explore these issues as far as our data allowed, we used Structural Equation Models to examine patterns of relationships between our three indices of age-related neurophysiological changes and scores on different categories of behavioural tasks. We also hoped to determine whether the degree to which the effects of neurophysiological changes on some mental abilities, such as memory and intelligence, can be entirely explained as consequences of their effects on other mental abilities, such as decision speed. To do this we combined scores on our three neurophysiological markers of brain changes into a single entity, "Neuro", and calculated how this index related to individual differences in scores on 20 different tests of information processing speed, *gf*, frontal and executive function, and of vocabulary – which has been taken to be a good measure of crystallized intelligence (Horn, 1972).

References

De Groot, J. C., de Leeuw, F. E., Oudkerk, M., Van Gijn, J., Hofman, A., Jolles, J., & Breteler, M. M. (2000). Cerebral white matter lesions and cognitive function: The Rotterdam Scan Study. *Annals of Neurology: Official Journal of the American Neurological Association and the Child Neurology Society, 47*(2), 145–151.

De Leeuw, F. E., de Groot, J. C., Achten, E., Oudkerk, M., Ramos, L.M.P., Heijboer, R., ... & Breteler, M.M.B. (2001). Prevalence of cerebral white matter lesions in elderly people: A population based magnetic resonance imaging study. The Rotterdam Scan Study. *Journal of Neurology, Neurosurgery and Psychiatry, 70*(1), 9–14.

Horn, J. L. (1972). State, trait and change dimensions of intelligence. *British Journal of Educational Psychology, 42*(2), 159–185.

Rabbitt, P., Scott, M., Thacker, N., Lowe, C., Jackson, A., Horan, M., & Pendleton, N. (2006). Losses in gross brain volume and cerebral blood flow account for age-related differences in speed but not in fluid intelligence. *Neuropsychology, 20*(5), 549–557.

Rabbitt, P., Scott, M., Lunn, M., Thacker, N., Lowe, C., Pendleton, N., ... & Jackson, A. (2007). White matter lesions account for all age-related declines in speed but not in intelligence. *Neuropsychology, 21*(3), 363–370.

Salthouse, T. A. (1996). The processing-speed theory of adult age differences in cognition. *Psychological Review, 103*(3), 403–428.

Salthouse, T. (2000). *A Theory of Cognitive Aging* (Vol. 28). Amsterdam: North-Holland.

16 Effects of global atrophy, white matter lesions, and cerebral blood flow on age-related changes in speed, memory, intelligence, vocabulary, and frontal function

P.M.A. Rabbitt, O. Mogapi, M. Scott, M. Thacker, C. Lowe, M. Horan, N. Pendleton, A. Jackson and D. Lunn

As they grow old, even exceptionally healthy and able people experience some decline of cognitive performance (Houx, 1991; Rabbitt, Diggle, Holland, McInnes, Bent, et al., 2004). A key issue is the relationship between these behaviorally assessed losses and aging of the brain and central nervous system. The classical methodology for investigating relationships between brain and behavior has been to seek associations between losses of specific cognitive abilities and focal brain lesions. This is of limited use in cognitive gerontology because the brain changes that occur in normal, healthy older people are global, varied, and diffuse rather than local and specific, and it is unclear whether they affect all cognitive abilities to the same or to different extents. For example, within samples of healthy older people without dementia, a marker for diffuse neurophysiological changes, incidence of white matter lesions (WMLs), is associated with poorer performance on tests of a wide variety of different cognitive abilities (e.g., Breteler, Van Amerongen, & Van Swieten, 1994; de Leeuw et al., 2001; Hickie et al., 1995; Longstreth et al., 1996; Van Swieten et al., 1996; Ylikoski et al., 1995). However, there is also evidence that WMLs affect the speed with which older people can make simple decisions more than they affect other parameters of cognitive performance (e.g., de Groot et al., 2000; Junque et al., 1990; Ylikoski et al., 1993). Similarly, other markers for diffuse neurophysiological changes, global age-associated losses of brain volume (AALBV) and carotid and basilar artery blood flow (CBF), are correlated with each other and with WML incidence and are also associated with losses on many different parameters of cognitive performance, but particularly with slowing of information processing speed (McLullich et al., 2002; Rabbitt et al., 2006).

Markers for global and diffuse age-related changes in the brain such as levels of WMLs, AALBV, or CBF reflect many diverse age-related neuroanatomical, neurophysiological, and neurochemical changes that are still incompletely understood. Consequently, it is currently more prudent not to frame hypotheses about precise functional relationships between age-related changes in WML, AALBV, and CBF and age-related changes in particular cognitive abilities but rather, for the moment, to treat these indices simply as statistical markers for the extents of some, as yet unspecified, age-related neurophysiological changes. Because levels of WML, AALBV, and CBF account only for part, but certainly not for all, of that proportion of the variance in cognitive test scores between individuals that is associated with differences in their calendar ages (Rabbitt et al., 2006), they certainly do not mark all of the brain changes that alter cognitive performance in old age. Cognitive performance must also be affected by other age-related neurophysiological changes for which WMLs, AALBV, and CBF are not sensitive markers.

A different reason for caution in inferring specific functional relationships between diffuse, global brain changes and particular mental abilities is that, as Weiskrantz (1992) remarked, "There is no such thing as a pure (behavioural) test" (p. 6). This is because *mental abilities* are ill-defined, logical entities because they are defined in terms of scores on particular laboratory tests that reflect competence on a variety of hypothetically different functions such as, for instance, attention, memory, and information processing speed. This has become a particular problem for aging studies because individuals' scores on tests of information processing speed (Cerella, 1990) or of intelligence predict most, or all, of the variance between them on most other behavioral tests of cognitive performance (Rabbitt & Anderson, 2006). Numerous similar findings have encouraged an influential hypothesis that age-related declines in performance on tests of memory are functionally driven by slowing of information processing speed (Salthouse, 1985, 1991, 1996a, 1996b). A more radical hypothesis is that, at any age, individual differences in information processing speed are the functional causes of differences in general fluid intelligence (Anderson, 1988; Deary, 2001; Eysenck, 1986; Jensen, 1982). On these assumptions, findings that levels of indices of diffuse brain changes such as WML incidence, AALBV, and CBF account for most of the age-related slowing of information processing speed would mean that, if only for this reason, they must also be associated with impairments of other cognitive abilities such as memory and intelligence.

This raises a series of further questions: One is whether gross neurophysiological markers such as WMLs, AALBV, and CBF account for a large proportion of the age-related variance in all cognitive abilities—such as information processing speed, memory, intelligence, and frontal and executive function or vocabulary—or only in some of them and not in others. A second is whether WMLs, AALBV, and CBF affect particular cognitive abilities because they have direct effects on the particular functional systems that support these abilities or because they cause global slowing of information processing speed that affects all cognitive abilities. To address these questions, we obtained brain images giving measures of WML incidence, AALBV, and CBF from a group of 133 elderly individuals who had contemporaneously been given three different tests of general fluid intelligence, three different vocabulary tests, two tests of information processing speed, four tests of frontal and executive function, and eight different memory tests. Structural equation modeling (SEM) was used to derive a statistical construct, neurophysiology (neuro), from measures of WML, AALBV, and CBF and constructs representing intelligence, vocabulary, speed, frontal, and memory from cognitive test scores. A series of models compared the direct and indirect predictions of individuals' performance on each of these cognitive constructs from their ages and from their scores on the neuro construct (Bollen, 1989).

Method

Participants were 63 men and 70 women aged between 61 and 85 years (M = 73.7, SD = 12.4). They were selected because they were free of any symptoms of neurological problems or pathologies likely to affect the central nervous system after complete physical examinations and record of medical histories by two experienced geriatricians (MH and NP). These criteria were subsequently confirmed by structural brain imaging. All participants attended the University of Manchester Age and Cognitive Performance Centre where, during two 90-min testing sessions, they completed 20 tests. The three intelligence tests were Heim's (1970) AH4-1 and AH4-2 and Cattell and Cattell's (1960) Culture Fair Test; three vocabulary tests, including Raven's (1965) Mill Hill A and B tests and the Wechsler Adult Intelligence Scale vocabulary test (Wechsler, 1955); two tests of information processing speed, consisting of a letter–letter substitution coding task (in which participants followed a guide printed at the head of an answer form to encode target letters printed in random order below during work periods of 2 min) and a visual search task; and four tests of frontal and executive function, including the Phonemic Fluency, Category Fluency, Brixton (Shallice & Burgess, 1991), and Rey–Osterrith immediate recall tests. Eight tests of immediate and intermediate term memory were the following: (a) the Baddeley Doors and (b) Names tests; (c) a computerized Delayed Matching to Sample test from the Robbins' Cambridge Neuropsychological Test Automated Battery; (d) a test of memory for propositions about people (PAP), in which they attempted to recall three items of information about each of five imaginary people, cued by surnames; (e) immediate free recall of a list of 10 threesyllable words; (f) a circle–object (CO) test, in which they were shown, for 15 s, a circle divided into 12 sectors within each of which there was a line drawing of a common, easily named object, and then immediately attempted recall of the names of all of the objects and the sectors of the circle in which they had been located; (g) Immediate Backward Digit Span; and (h) Immediate Word Span. Participants were tested, one at a time, by an experienced experimental psychologist (CL). Travel expenses were reimbursed at a flat rate of 5 pounds (United Kingdom) per session.

Within the same period of 6 weeks during which participants completed all 20 behavioral tests, they also underwent magnetic resonance brain scans. All gave informed consent at least 24 hours prior to imaging, and the protocol was approved by the local research ethics committee.

Anatomical images were acquired using an axial fast spin–echo inversion recovery sequence (return time [TR] = 6,850 ms, echo time [TE] = 18 ms, TI = 300 ms, echo train length = 9). Contiguous 3-mm slices were obtained throughout the brain with an in-plane resolution of 0.89 mm^2 (matrix, 256 × 204; field of view, 230 × 184 mm). Age-related losses of brain volume can be estimated using the volume of cerebrospinal fluid (CSF) as a surrogate. As the brain shrinks, the volume of CSF increases. Thus, measurement of CSF volume, normalized to skull size, gives a good indication of relative brain volume loss over the life span.

CSF volume was obtained using a fully automated procedure. The anatomical images were initially registered into a standard coordinate frame, where the interhemispheric fissure was aligned to the plane passing through the vertical axis (of the standard coordinate frame). The midsagittal slice was rotated to align horizontal axis with the ventral surface of the genu of the corpus callosum and the junction of the corpus callosum with the body of the fornix. The CSF in the images was segmented using a Bayesian approach (Pokric, Thacker, Scott, & Jackson, 2001), and a mask was applied to remove the eyes and sinuses from the images, as these structures exhibit comparable voxel intensities to the CSF. Previously, this technique has been used to partition the bounding box of the interior of the skull into 12 equal-sized cuboids (left–right, top–bottom, and front–middle–back). This provides 12 true volumetric estimates of CSF, unlike techniques such as VBM, which is strongly influenced by topological change. However, because our interest was in a global measure of atrophy, here only the total CSF was used. Persons with larger heads, and hence more brain tissue as young adults, might be expected to undergo more absolute atrophy (assuming a constant average population rate of atrophy) than those with smaller heads. CSF volume is therefore corrected for head size using the volume of the bounding box of the interior surface of the skull. This allows quantification of loss of brain tissue since early adulthood. The full method, which is capable of discriminating and quantifying correlated changes in brain shape and volume in a variety of dementing disorders, is described elsewhere (Thacker et al., 2002). It should be emphasized that in this context volume is an age-related measure that reflects individual differences in total amounts of age-related loss. Losses measured in this way reflect not only the normal aging process but also any additional cause of atrophy sustained throughout the participant's lifetime.

Measurements of CBF were made using a cardiac-gated phase contrast quantitative flow sequence (TE = 3 ms, TR = 6 ms, flip angle = 15 degrees, in-plane resolution = 1.17 × 1.17 mm, slice thickness = 5 mm). The arteries were imaged in one slice perpendicular to the direction of greatest flow. Fifteen temporal positions of the arteries were imaged, spanning one heartbeat, the duration of which was known. Magnitude and quantitative flow images were obtained for each time point. For each artery under consideration, the first magnitude image of the sequence was normalized to 1 using the maximum value in that artery, and the image thresholded at 0.5 to obtain a mask of that artery. The mask was then applied to all of the quantitative flow images, and the cumulative absolute flow was calculated. It is valid to apply the mask from the first image to all of the images as the arteries are constrained by the skull and do not move. The total blood flow into the head via the left and right carotid arteries and basilar artery was calculated as the sum of the three, and this value was normalized to the volume of the bounding box of the interior of the skull. It is acknowledged that there should be some sort of dependency of blood flow on head size, but dividing total blood flow by the volume of the bounding box of the interior of the skull resulted in a significant negative linear correlation of corrected CBF against skull size ($p = .01$, $R^2 = .094$). The less severe two-thirds correction resulted in a nonsignificant correlation of corrected CBF against skull volume ($p = .277$, $R^2 = .018$), and so this scale factor was used. One potential explanation for using a two-third dependency on skull size is that the grey matter makes by far the greatest demand on the blood supply to the brain. The thickness of the grey matter cortex appears invariant to head size (unpublished 2 observation), and so one might expect a dependency of demand on the surface area of the grey matter. Grey matter surface area should be proportional to the skull bounding box.

Results

SEM was used to examine the relative effects on information processing speed, memory, intelligence, frontal and executive function, and vocabulary of individuals; calendar ages; and a construct neuro derived from their levels of AALBV, CBF, and WMLs. The first five models examined the joint and separate associations among age; neuro; and constructs for speed, frontal and executive function, fluid intelligence, vocabulary, and memory derived from cognitive test scores.

Model 1: The Effects of Age and Neuro on Speed

The result of applying SEM to ascertain the effects of age and neuro on speed is shown in Figure 16.1.

Because the relationship between performance on speed tests and neurophysiological variables has nonsignificant overall likelihood chi-square p value of .64, the SEM is acceptable. The values of GFI (0.99) and root-mean-square error of approximation (RMSEA; 0.000) also support model adequacy. As expected, neuro had a negative loading of −0.32 for WMLs and −0.63 for loss of global brain volume (AALBV), but there was a positive loading of 0.75 for

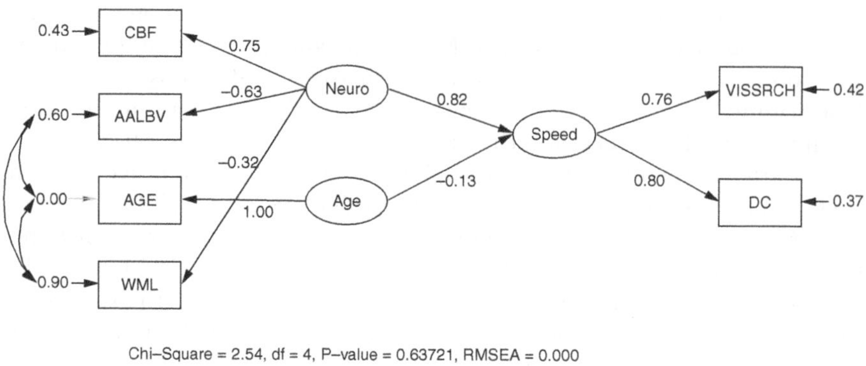

Figure 16.1 Path diagram for speed, age, and neurophysiological (neuro) constructs. CBF = carotid and basilar artery blood flow; AALBV = global age-associated losses of brain volume; WML = white matter lesion; VISSRCH = visual search; DC = digit coding; RMSEA = root-mean-square error of approximation.

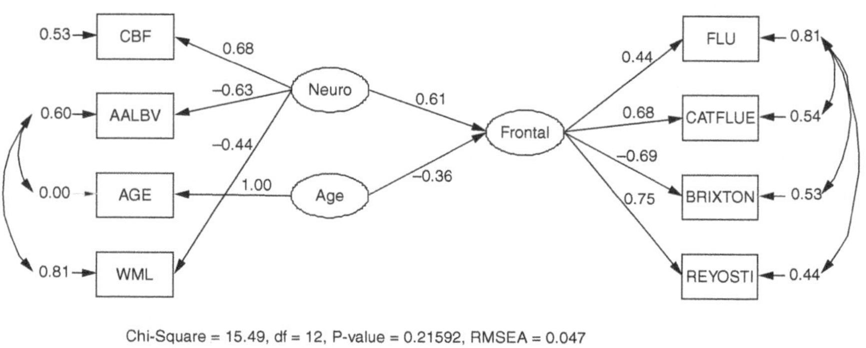

Figure 16.2 Path diagram for frontal, age, and neurophysiological (neuro) constructs. CBF = carotid and basilar artery blood flow; AALBV = global age-associated losses of brain volume; WML = white matter lesion; FLU = verbal fluency; CATFLUE = category fluency; BRIXTON = Brixton; REYOSTI Rey–Osterrith figure recall test; RMSEA = root-mean-square error of approximation.

blood flow (CBF). The loadings of speed variables VISSRCH (0.76) and DC (0.80) are almost the same. Note that the loadings measure the extent of the relationship between a latent variable and its manifest variables. They can be interpreted as regression coefficients for the manifest variables on their latents. From Figure 16.2, we also learn that although AALBV, AGE, and WML are significantly correlated, as one might expect, there is no apparent significant correlation between the speed variables. The structural relationship among neuro, speed and age has R^2 of 80%, and Table 16.1 shows a highly significant direct effect of neuro on speed and an insignificant direct effect of age on speed. In other terms, although very many experiments have shown (e.g., Salthouse, 1991, 1996b) that individuals' ages are robustly corre-lated with

Table 16.1 The Structural Model of Neurophysiological (Neuro) and Age Constructs With Five Categories of Cognitive Tests

Construct	*Direct effects*	
	Estimate	*P*
Speed		
Neuro	0.82	.000
Age	−0.13	.082
Frontal		
Neuro	0.61	.002
Age	−0.36	.000
Intelligence		
Neuro	0.30	.023
Age	−0.12	.004
Vocabulary		
Neuro	0.24	.031
Age	−0.12	.145
Memory		
Neuro	0.30	.032
Age	−0.37	.022

the speed with which they make simple decisions, when neuro is entered into the model it accounts for nearly all of the variance in speed that is associated with differences in age.

Note that all latent variables are standardized to have a variance of one so that their unit of measurement is in standard deviation terms. The relationship between neuro and speed is also supported by a positive correlation of .89, whereas age and speed have a smaller negative correlation of −.46. Thus, more variation in speed is accounted for by neuro than by age. However, the correlation between age and neuro is −.40, which suggests that even though age is not a crucial marker for speed, it does affect neuro to influence speed. This is expected because increasing age results in increases in WMLs and AALBV and declines in CBF. Thus, the functional interpretation is that the neurophysiological differences among participants that are marked by WMLs, AALBV, and CBF are related to their ages and that these neurophysiological differences entirely account for all individual differences in speed.

Model 2: The Effects of Age and Neuro on Frontal and Executive Tasks

As with the previous model, there is no reason for rejection (p = .22, GFI = 0.97, RMSEA = 0.047).

The measurement model on frontal variables shows a negative loading of −0.69 for Brixton and positive loadings for verbal fluency (noun generation cued by initial letter F, A, and S; 0.44), category fluency (noun generation cued by a superordinate category such as "animal names"; 0.68), and Rey–Osterrith figure recall test (0.75). Furthermore, verbal fluency is significantly correlated with the other frontal variables. Figure 16.3 also shows, once again, that AALBV is correlated with age and WML. The structural model on frontal, neuro, and age has an R^2 of 72%. Table 16.1 shows that the direct effects of neuro and age on the frontal construct are both significant.

The correlation between neuro and frontal is .78 and between age and frontal is −.65. Thus, both neuro and age serve as markers for levels of frontal and executive functions. Age has relatively large correlation with neuro of −.47, which can be interpreted as in the model for speed. In sum, both age and neuro account for a significant proportion of variance among individuals in performance on frontal and executive tasks.

Model 3: The Effects of Age and Neuro on Fluid Intelligence

The overall likelihood chi-square p value (.07), GFI (0.96), RMSEA (0.07), and standardized root-mean-square residual (SRMR) (0.049) are all within acceptance limits. As expected from the classical analyses by Spearman (1927), a separate principal components analysis shows that up to 70% of the variance among individuals on the three unadjusted intelligence test scores can be explained by a single factor. The variable communalities are Culture Fair Test (Cattell & Cattell, 1960; 58.8%), AH4-1 (79.5%), and AH4-2 (71.3%). Loadings of intelligence variables on its constructs are positive and large as shown in Figure 16.3.

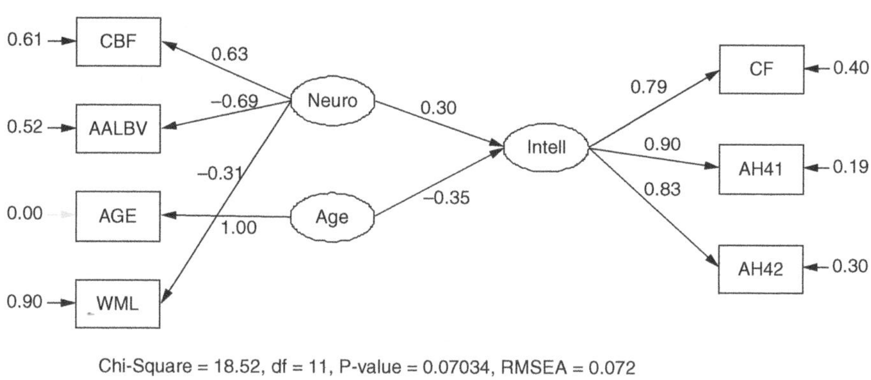

Figure 16.3 Path diagram for intelligence (intell), age, and neurophysiological (neuro) constructs. CBF = carotid and basilar artery blood flow; AALBV = global age-associated losses of brain volume; WML = white matter lesion; CF = Culture Fair Test; AH41 and AH42 = Heim's (1970) tests; RMSEA = root-mean-square error of approximation.

We found large loadings for CBF (0.63) and AALBV (−0.69) on neuro but less loading for WML (−0.31). The structural relationship among neuro, age, and fluid intelligence is significant (see Table 16.1).

The similar levels of the correlations between age and intelligence (–.54) and between neuro and intelligence (.52) confirm that both age and neuro make similar contributions to fluid intelligence. However, although the direct effects of both neuro and age on fluid intelligence are important there is nevertheless a joint R^2 of 34%, which suggests that a combination of the age-related individual differences in neurophysiological integrity that are directly marked by WMLs, AALBV, and CBF, and by the other neurophysiological differences that are associated with differences in age between 61 and 83 years, account for a relatively small proportion of the total variance in intelligence test scores among individuals. This is to be expected because there are very marked lifelong individual differences in intelligence among individuals of all ages.

Model 4: The Effects of Age and Neuro on Vocabulary

The likelihood chi-square p value (.15), GFI (0.97), SRMR (0.052), and RMSEA (0.072) are all acceptable.

Figure 16.4 shows the loadings for each variable on its latent variables. The loadings of vocabulary on its constructs are high, with the lowest being 0.87 (see Table 16.1).

Here, neuro has a significant but modest effect on vocabulary, but age does not. The effect of neuro can be mainly attributed to the correlation between WML and AALBV. Despite good overall fit, R^2 is 11% for the structural model, which is very low. The correlation between age and neuro (–.57) is double that

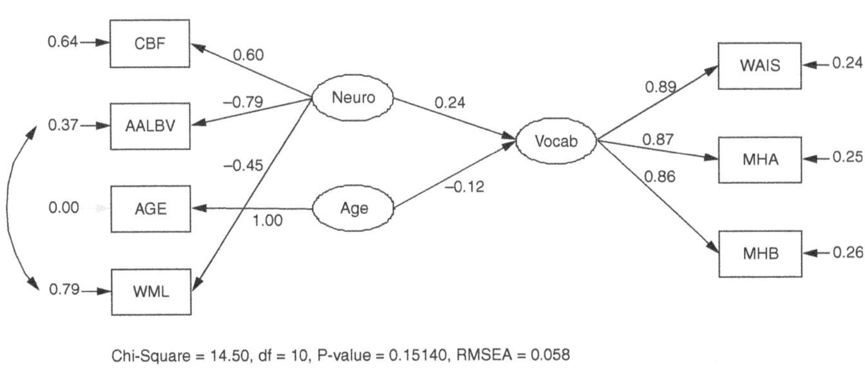

Figure 16.4 Path diagram for vocabulary (vocab), age, and neurophysiological (neuro) constructs. CBF = carotid and basilar artery blood flow; AALBV = global age-associated losses of brain volume; WML = white matter lesion; WAIS = Wechsler Adult Intelligence Scale (Wechsler, 1955); MHA = Mill Hill A; MHB = Mill Hill B; RMSEA = root-mean-square error of approximation.

of age and vocabulary (–.26). This suggests that although individual differences in age are associated with individual differences in neuro, differences in age alone do little to predict vocabulary. This is in agreement with many earlier findings (such as Horn, 1982, 1987; Horn, Donaldson, & Engstrom, 1991; Rabbitt, Chetwynd, & McInnes, 2003) that vocabulary test scores are only slightly, or not at all, affected by calendar age. There is reason to think that neuro might act as a mediator of age on vocabulary; that is, even though age on its own does not directly affect vocabulary, the construct neuro, which is of course strongly associated with the construct age, does affect vocabulary. The model adds the new information that such changes in vocabulary as do occur with age are associated with age-related changes in gross neurophysiological indices rather than with the simple passage of time. A plausible interpretation is that because cognitive, and inferentially neurophysiological, age-related changes occur at markedly different rates in different individuals (Rabbitt, Diggle, Holland, McInnes, Bent, et al., 2004), variance in direct indices of global neurophysiological integrity among individuals mark these changes more sensitively than do individual differences in calendar age.

Model 5: The Effects of Age and Neuro on Memory

The chi-squared *p* value (0.098), RMSEA (0.048), (0.048), SRMR (0.050), and GFI (0.94) are all acceptable, R^2 was 35% for the structural model when age and neuro were both entered as predicttors (see Figure 16.5).

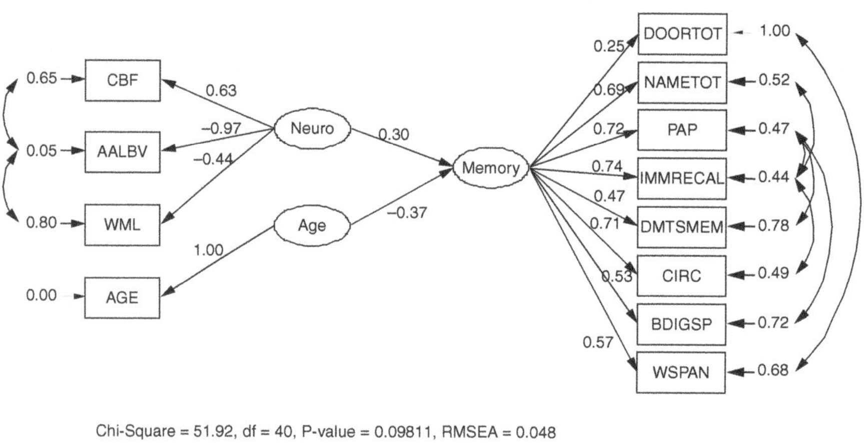

Figure 16.5 Path diagram for memory, age, and neurophysiological (neuro) constructs. CBF = carotid and basilar artery blood flow; AALBV = global age-associated losses of brain volume; WML = white matter lesion; DOORTOT = total score on Baddeley Doors test; NAMETOT = total score on Baddeley Names test; PAP = propositions about people test; IMMRECAL = immediate free recall; DMTSMEM = delayed matching to sample in CANTAB battery; CIRC = Circle Item Spatial Recall Test (Rabbitt et al., 2004); BDIGSP = Backward Digit Span; WSPAN = Word Span; RMSEA = root-mean-square error of approximation.

The model shows higher loadings for PAP (0.72) and immediate free recall (0.74) and a small loading for the Baddeley Doors test (0.25) on the memory construct. Both the memory variables and the neurophysiological variables are correlated among themselves. The direct effect of neuro on memory is positive but, as expected, loadings of WML and AALBV on neuro are negative, with positive loading for CBF. R^2 was 35% for the model. Although neuro interacts with age to modestly affect memory, in this particular model the relationship between neuro and age is not very strong (see Table 16.1).

In sum, both individual differences in age and individual differences in neuro affect memory, and these effects seem to be in large part independent of each other.

These analyses addressed the issue of how far individual differences in age and neuro accounted for individual differences in five areas of cognitive performance: speed, frontal and executive function, fluid intelligence, vocabulary, and memory. The next task was to discover how far the predictions from age and neuro of individual differences in memory, frontal and executive function, and fluid intelligence are mediated by individual differences in speed. SEM analyses testing this are described in the next section.

Model 6: Speed as an Intervening Variable in the Effects of Age and Neuro on Memory

The overall model for age, neuro, and memory is nonsignificant (p = .111). However, after differences in speed are taken into account neuro has no significant direct effect on memory, and the direct effect of age on speed is also not significant. This is expected from the results of the previous analysis summarized in Table 16.1. Specifically, the direct effect of neuro on memory is 0.024 (p = .45) and the direct effect of age on speed is −0.042 (p = .41). The indirect effect of age on memory mediated by speed is also not significant, and the indirect effect of neuro is only marginally significant.

The direct effects of age on memory and speed are very small compared to other effects in the model. We therefore drop the direct effects of age on speed and the direct effect of neuro on memory in a further analysis. The p value for the chi-squared value increased to .153, and all other goodness-of-fit measures support adequacy of the model (GFI = 0.93, RMSEA = 0.037, SRMR = 0.053).

Figure 16.6 shows that DOORTOT has the smallest loading of 0.24 on memory, and the highest loading is achieved by PAP with 0.76. The DC variable for speed has higher loading of 0.85 on speed, and VISSRCH loads 0.70 on speed. As expected, the neurophysiological variables are correlated with a negative loading of WML on neuro, whereas both AALBV and CBF have positive loadings.

Table 16.2 shows that there are significant direct effects of both age and speed on memory. With the insignificant direct effect of neuro dropped from this model, we now see that the indirect effect of neuro on memory, which is mediated through speed, is highly significant (p = 0.000). This is supported

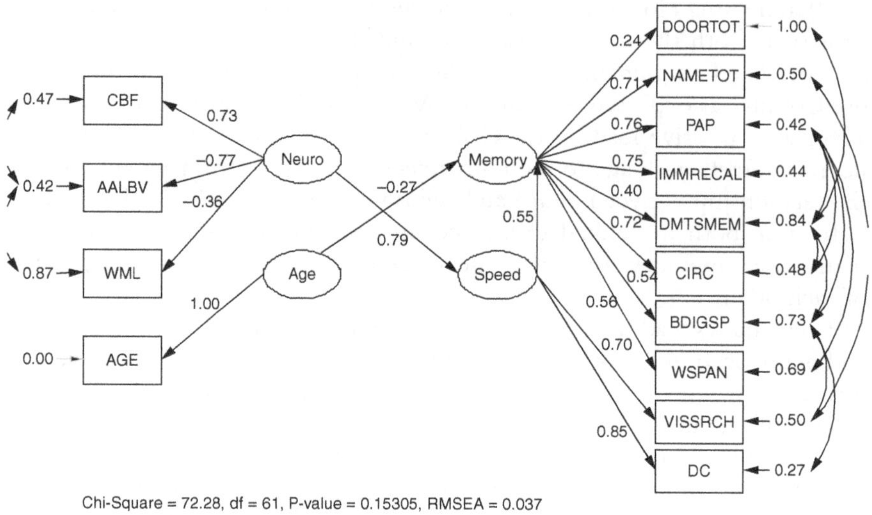

Figure 16.6 Path diagram of the relationship of age, neurophysiology (neuro), speed, and memory with omitted direct effects of age on speed and memory. CBF = carotid and basilar artery blood flow; AALBV = global age-associated losses of brain volume; WML = white matter lesion; DOORTOT = total score on Baddeley Doors test; NAMETOT = total score on Baddeley Names test; PAP = propositions about people test; IMMRECAL = immediate free recall; DMTSMEM = delayed matching to sample in CANTAB battery; CIRC = Circle Item Spatial Recall Test; BDIGSP = Backward Digit Span; WSPAN = Word Span; VISSRCH = visual search; DC = digit coding; RMSEA = root-mean-square error of approximation.

Table 16.2 The Structural Model for the Age, Neurophysiological (Neuro), Speed, and Memory Constructs With Omitted Direct Effects of Age on Speed and Memory

Construct	*Direct effects*			*Indirect effects*
	Age	*Neuro*	*Speed*	*Neuro*
Memory	−0.27		0.55	0.79
SE	0.14		0.23	0.12
p	.025		.009	.000
Speed		0.79		
SE	—	0.12		
p	—	.000		

Note: Dashes indicate values that were omitted because computation was uninformative.

by high construct correlations between neuro and speed (0.79) and between speed and memory (0.67). Thus, the most concise description is that age has a significant direct effect on memory but has no indirect effect on memory, mediated by speed. This is because, as we have seen, individual differences in neuro account for all age-related differences in speed. Conversely, neuro has no significant direct effect on memory but has a highly significant indirect effect that is mediated through speed.

Model 7: Speed as an Intervening Variable Between Age, Neuro, Intelligence, and Frontal and Executive Function

A *p* value of .055 gives only marginal support for the adequacy of the model, but with RMSEA (0.051), SRMR (0.053), and GFI (0.93), it could be argued that the model is still useful. The overall model R^2 is 91% on frontal, 60% on intelligence, and 68% on speed (see Figure 16.7 and Table 16.3).

Intelligence (0.70) and neuro (0.37) have significant direct effects on frontal test scores, but age (–0.0075) does not. Speed (0.88) and age (–0.42) do have significant direct effects on intelligence test scores but were only marginally significant (p = .063). The effect of neuro (–0.47) is not significant. Neuro (0.85) but not age (0.0045) has a significant direct effect on speed. Like previous analyses, this indicates that the effects of age on speed are no longer significant if direct indices of age-related neurophysiological changes are also entered into the model. We can interpret this as evidence that all of

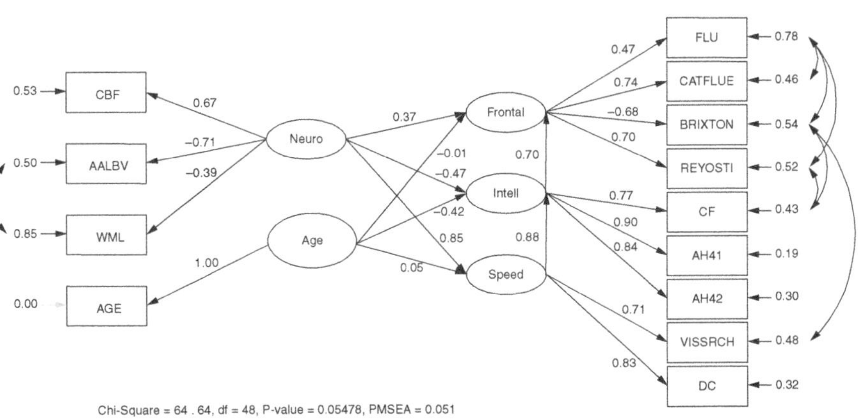

Figure 16.7 Path diagram of the relationship of age, neurophysiology, speed, intelligence (intell), and frontal function. CBF = carotid and basilar artery blood flow; AALBV = global age-associated losses of brain volume; WML = white matter lesion; FLU = verbal fluency; CATFLUE = category fluency; BRIXTON = Brixton; REYOSTI = Rey–Osterrith figure recall test; CF = Culture Fair Test; AH41 and AH42 = Heim's (1970) tests; VISSRCH = visual research; DC = digit coding; RMSEA = root-mean-square error of approximation.

Table 16.3 The Structural Model for Relationships Among Age, Neurophysiological (Neuro), Speed, Intelligence (Intell), and Frontal Constructs

Latent variable	*Direct effects of latent variable on others*				*Indirect effects of latent variable on others*		
	Age	*Neuro*	*Intell*	*Speed*	*Age*	*Neuro*	*Speed*
Frontal ($R^2 = .91$)	−0.0075	0.37	0.70	–	−0.27	0.19	0.62
SE	0.075	0.12	0.15	–	0.10	0.09	0.24
p	.115	.000	.000	–	.004	.022	.005
Intell ($R^2 = .60$)	−0.42	−0.47	–	0.88	0.04	0.74	
SE	0.12	0.31	–	0.29	0.11	0.30	
p	.000	.063	–	.001	.36	.007	
Speed ($R^2 = .68$)	0.045	0.85					
SE	0.12	0.16					
p	.36	.000					

Note: Dashes indicate values that were omitted because computation was uninformative.

the age-related changes in speed that affect frontal and executive function are accounted for by age-related changes in the three markers of global neurophysiological changes examined in this study. The indirect effects of neuro and age on the frontal construct are also significant when mediated by speed. Thus, the effects of both neuro and age on frontal tasks are largely mediated through their effects on speed.

The construct correlation between age and intelligence is −.55 and between neuro and intelligence is .50. Thus, both age and neuro have similar effects on intelligence. Note, however, that age and neuro affect intelligence in different ways. When speed is included in the model, neuro no longer has any direct effect on intelligence, but age still does. In other words, although the effect of neuro on intelligence is entirely due to its effect on speed, the effect of age on intelligence is only partially due to its effect on speed and is also partially related to other age-related neurophysiological changes that are not associated with speed. The correlation between speed and neuro is .82, whereas that between speed and age is −.47. As in all previous analyses, neuro has a much stronger association with speed than does age. The path diagram also shows that scores on the frontal and executive tests are significantly correlated with each other and with scores on the speed tests.

Speed emerges as an important factor mediating the effects of both neuro and age on frontal and on intelligence. However, the model also suggests that the influence of speed on frontal is mediated by intelligence. The indirect effect of speed on frontal is 0.62, which is highly significant ($p = .005$). Further, the construct correlation between intelligence and the frontal construct is .90, indicating that the relationship between them is so strong that for practical purposes we may assume a one-to-one relationship between these constructs. This is theoretically important because it seems that individuals' levels of intelligence are much more powerful determinants of their performance on frontal tasks than are their levels of speed. The strong relationship between intelligence test scores and performance on frontal tasks is completely consistent with suggestions by Duncan and associates (Duncan, Burgess, & Emslie, 1995; Duncan & Owen, 2000; Duncan, Emslie, Williams, Johnson, & Freer, 1996; Duncan et al., 2000) that problems derived from intelligence tests, specifically from Cattell and Cattell's (1960) Culture Fair Test, are exceptionally sensitive tests of frontal and executive functions.

General Discussion: Relationships Between Neuro, Age, and Scores on Five Categories of Cognitive Tests

For tests of speed, all age-related performance can be accounted for by differences in WML incidence, AALBV, and CBF. For tests of intelligence, frontal and executive performance, and memory, both age and neuro make significant direct predictions. Vocabulary scores are not predicted by age but are weakly predicted by neuro. These findings are summarized in Table 16.4.

For intelligence, frontal executive function, and memory, neuro has direct effects that are independent of age. Differences in calendar age also predict significant proportions of the variance in test scores that neuro does not predict. Predictions from neuro independent of those made by age and predictions from age independent of those made by neuro are interpreted in different ways.

Although neuro is robustly associated with age, it also makes additional and independent predictions of cognitive performance. To interpret this, we must bear in mind that individuals experience markedly different trajectories of cognitive changes over time (see Rabbitt, Diggle, Holland, McInnes, Bent, et al., 2004) so that their calendar ages are only approximate indices for individual differences in the amounts of age-related neurophysiological, and so also cognitive, changes that they have experienced as they have grown older (we may term individual differences in the extent of these changes *neurophysiological ages*). Because the construct neuro is derived from direct brain measurements, it is a more sensitive index of the progress of some part of individuals' neurophysiological aging than is calendar age. A concrete

Table 16.4 Summary of Results of Separate Analyses of the Effects of Age and Neurophysiological (Neuro) on Five Different Subsets of Cognitive Tests

Cognitive performance construct	*Direct effect of age*	*Direct effect of neuro*
Speed	None	Significant
Intelligence	Significant	Significant
Frontal	Significant	Significant
Memory	Significant	Significant
Vocabulary	None	Significant

example is that age makes no prediction, but neuro makes a weakly significant prediction for differences in vocabulary. The lack of prediction from age is expected because vocabulary test scores are well known to change very little or not at all in old age (Horn, 1982, 1987; Horn et al., 1981; Rabbitt, Chetwynd, and McInnes, 2003). The weak prediction from neuro suggests that nevertheless, vocabulary is modestly affected by neurophysiological aging, marked by more direct indices of neurophysiological integrity such as WMLs, AALBV, and CBF.

A different hypothesis is needed to explain why individuals' ages account for significant amounts of variance additional to that which is associated with levels of neurophysiological markers: Only three neurophysiological markers, WMLs, AALBV, and CBF were measured. Participants evidently experienced other ageassociated neurophysiological changes for which these three are not sensitive indices. These unmarked neurophysiological changes must account for the additional variance associated with differences in individuals' calendar ages.

Age makes no further prediction of speed after neuro has been taken into consideration, whereas neuro makes strong predictions of speed independent of those made by age. Although the pattern of relationships between age and speed is similar to that between age and vocabulary, it cannot be interpreted in the same way. All studies agree that decision speed is exceptionally sensitive to aging, whereas vocabulary is not. It must therefore follow that all, or very nearly all, of those particular age-related neurophysiological changes that affect speed of performance in old age are sensitively marked by levels of WMLs, AALBV, and CBF. This is theoretically interesting because all studies over the last 50 years suggest that loss of information processing speed is probably the most sensitive index of the progress of age-related cognitive changes. There is also evidence that after individual differences in speed have been taken into consideration, the effects of differences in age on tests of memory (Salthouse, 1985, 1991, 1996a; Rabbitt & Anderson, 2006), frontal and executive function (Verhaegen & De Meersman, 1998), and intelligence (Deary, 2001; Rabbitt & Anderson, 2006) are entirely abolished or greatly attenuated. These pervasive relationships in behavioral data have encouraged the hypothesis that the effects of age on most cognitive abilities can be explained in terms of its effects on information processing speed (Deary, 2001; Salthouse, 1985; 1991, 1996a, 1996b).

A radical extension of this hypothesis has been that individual differences in intelligence, not simply those that are associated with differences in age in later life, but also between children (Anderson, 1988, 1992) and young adults (Deary, 2001; Eysenck, 1986; Jensen, 1982) are strongly associated with, and perhaps functionally mediated by, individual differences in speed. A different view, derived from elegant empirical evidence by Duncan and associates (Duncan et al., 1995; Duncan et al., 2000), is that scores on intelligence tests are strongly associated with frontal and prefrontal cortical function but are not necessarily, functionally, primarily dependent on speed.

The present analyses of relationships between age and neuro and each of the five categories of cognitive tasks summarized in Table 16.4 suggest a different interpretation because they show that the neurophysiological determinants of age-related individual differences in information processing speed are, to a considerable extent, different from the determinants of age-related individual differences in memory, frontal and executive function, and intelligence. This raises the further question whether the relationships among neuro and memory, frontal and executive function, and intelligence are entirely, or mainly, mediated by their effects on information processing speed.

The idea that age-related slowing of information processing speed functionally determines corresponding declines in other cognitive abilities has entirely been based on behavioral investigations of speed as an intervening factor in the effects of age on memory (Salthouse, 1985, 1991). Because the construct memory used in this study was derived from scores on eight different memory tests, the present data provide a reasonable basis for checking how far associations of memory with age and neuro are mediated by information processing speed.

Both age and neuro have significant direct effects on memory, when speed is omitted. However, when speed is included neuro no longer has a significant direct effect. A second model omits the direct effect of age on speed and the direct effect of neuro on memory. In this model, there is a significant direct effect of age and the highly significant indirect effects of neuro on memory are entirely mediated by speed. This pattern of results can be interpreted as evidence that the particular neurophysiological changes marked by WMLs, AALBV, and CBF affect memory only because they slow information processing. However, it is important to note that because age has direct effects on memory that are not mediated by speed, these must be due to other age-related neurophysiological changes in the brain that are different from those marked by WMLs, AALBV, and CBF and that are also independent of slowing of information processing speed.

For intelligence and frontal functions, the overall model including neuro, age, and speed is marginally acceptable. As we have shown, neuro markedly affects speed, but the robust correlation between age and speed disappears when neuro is entered. This once again suggests that all of the observed age-related slowing in speed can be accounted for by the particular age-related neurophysiological changes that are marked by WMLs, AALBV, and CBF. Although intelligence and neuro both have significant direct effects on frontal tasks, age does not. The indirect effects of both neuro and age on frontal tasks are significant when mediated by speed. Both speed (0.88) and age (–0.42) also have significant direct effects on intelligence, but neuro (–0.47) does not. The indirect effects of neuro on intelligence are modulated through speed, but the indirect effects of age on intelligence are not modulated by speed. Fitting the model without the direct effect of age on speed and the direct effect of age on frontal achieves a larger likelihood p value of .07, and the RMSEA declines to 0.048. It is reasonable to drop these direct effects because we would not expect age to be mediated by speed on any latent variables when it actually has an insignificant direct effect. Neuro achieves marginal significance, but the indirect effect of neuro on intelligence is significant when the direct effects of age on speed and frontal are ignored. A plausible interpretation is that the effect of age on frontal is mediated by the effects of age on intelligence, but the effect of neuro on frontal is jointly mediated by both speed and intelligence.

All this suggests that the particular brain changes that are marked by AALBV, CBF, and WMLs affect both intelligence and frontal and executive performance solely because they slow information processing speed. However, increasing age also entails other brain changes that are not well marked by neuro, and these changes have significant effects on both intelligence and on frontal executive function that are not modulated by their effects on speed. For instance, the effect of age on frontal is modulated by intelligence. Thus, the first conclusion from these results is that cognitive slowing is not responsible for all of the changes in cognitive performance that occur with advancing age. The second stronger and more general conclusion is that intelligence, frontal and executive function, and speed are not all supported by identical functional neurophysiological systems.

The present data are, of course, quite insufficient to provide a detailed model for the functional bases of memory, intelligence, frontal and executive functions, and information processing speed. Apart from the issue of sample size which, though relatively large for imaging studies, is only modest for SEM, the neurophysiological indices are markers for diffuse and global changes rather than for the more local and specific changes that future models must incorporate. Nevertheless, they do test and disconfirm the hypothesis that information processing speed is a master system performance characteristic that determines age-related individual differences in performance on all, or nearly all, cognitive tasks. Memory, intelligence, and frontal performance are affected by agerelated brain changes that are not marked by AALBV, CBF, and WML incidence and are not mediated by slowing of information processing speed. In contrast, those age-related changes that are marked by AALBV, CBF, and WML incidence account for all of age-related changes in speed. The effects of AALBV, CBF, and WML on memory are entirely mediated by their effects on speed, and the effects of AALBV, CBF, and WML on intelligence and frontal function are also partly mediated by their effects on speed. However AALBV, CBF, and WML also have direct effects on fluid intelligence and frontal function that are not mediated by speed. It follows that a significant proportion of the effects of the age-related brain changes marked by AALBV, CBF, and WML incidence on intelligence and frontal function are independent of their effects on global slowing.

The findings of strong correlations between intelligence and frontal constructs are entirely consistent with recent evidence that intelligence tests, such as Cattell and Cattell's (1960) Culture Fair Test used in the current study, are as sensitive, or even more sensitive, indicators of frontal and executive function than are the frontal and executive laboratory tests used in this study or than are other diagnostic instruments for frontal damage that have been developed in clinical practice (Duncan et al., 1995; Duncan et al., 2000). According to Duncan et al.'s (2000) hypothesis, performance on intelligence tests is supported by the prefrontal cortex. There is considerable evidence that the frontal and prefrontal cortex is earlier and more severely affected by age-associated loss of volume than other parts of the brain (e.g., Albert, 1993; Haugh & Eggers, 1991; Mittenberg, Siedenberg, O'Leary, & Di Ginlio, 1989; Raz, 2000; Raz, Gunning-Dixon, Head, Dupuis, & Acker, 1998; Uylings & de Braboder, 2002) and also that CBF is earlier and more severely affected in the frontal lobes than in other parts of the brain (Gur, Gur, Orbist, Skolnik, & Reivitch, 1987). Taking these two lines of evidence together, it is reasonable to suppose that age-associated losses of intelligence should be less strongly associated with the progress of gross global losses of brain volume than with specific and local age-related changes in the frontal lobes. Thus, the relative effects of brain aging on frontal and executive tasks, intelligence tests, and other cognitive tests must vary among individuals, as some complex function of the ratio of local frontal to global and diffuse age-related changes that they have experienced. Further, although there is convincing behavioral evidence that people's scores on pencil and paper intelligence tests are indeed robustly correlated with the speed with which they can make simple decisions (Deary, 2001), the present results now radically qualify this conclusion. Although the effects of ageassociated brain changes marked by AALBV, CBF, and WML on intelligence are indeed partly mediated by their effects on speed, they also have direct effects that are additional to and independent of speed. This contradicts the view that fluid intelligence is only a direct function of mental speed and that speed is the (sole) "biological basis of intelligence" (Eysenck, 1986, p. 79).

References

Albert, M. (1993). Neuropsychological and neurophysiological changes in healthy adult humans across the lifespan. *Neurobiology of Aging, 14*, 623–631.

Anderson, M. (1988). Inspection time, information processing and the development of intelligence. *British Journal of Developmental Psychology, 6*, 43–57.

Anderson, M. (1992). *Intelligence and development: A cognitive theory.* Oxford: Blackwell.

Bollen K. A. (1989). *Structural equations with latent variables.* New York: Wiley-Interscience.

Breteler, M. M. B., Van Amerongen, N. M., & Van Swieten, J. C. (1994). Cognitive correlates of ventricular enlargement and cerebral white matter lesions on magnetic resonance imaging: The Rotterdam study. *Stroke, 25*, 1109–1115.

Cattell, R. B., & Cattell, A. K. S. (1960). *Handbook for the individual or group culture fair intelligence test.* Champaign, IL: IPAT.

Cerella, J. (1990). Aging and information processing rate. In J. E. Birren & K. W. Schaie (Eds.), *Handbook of the psychology of aging* (3rd ed., pp. 201–221). San Diego, CA: Academic Press.

Deary, I. (2001). *Looking down on human intelligence.* Oxford: Oxford University Press.

De Groot, J. C., de Leeuw, F.-E., Oudkerk, M., van Gijn, J., Hoifman, A., Jolles, J., & Breteler, M. M. B. (2000). Cerebral white matter lesions and cognitive function: The Rotterdam study. *Annals of Neurology, 47,* 145–151.

de Leeuw, F.-E., de Groot, J. C., Achten, E., Oudkerk, M., Ramos, L. M. P., Heijboer, R., et al. (2001). Prevalence of cerebral white matter lesions in elderly people: A population based magnetic resonance imaging study. The Rotterdam Scan Study. *Journal of Neurology, Neurosurgery, and Psychiatry, 70,* 9–14.

Duncan, J., Burgess, P., & Emslie, H. (1995). Fluid intelligence after frontal lobe lesions. *Neuropsychologia, 33,* 261–268.

Duncan, J., Emslie, H., Williams, P., Johnson, R., & Freer, C. (1996). Intelligence and the frontal lobe: The organisation of goal-directed behaviour. *Cognitive Psychology, 30,* 257–303.

Duncan, J., & Owen, A. (2000). Common regions of the human frontal lobe recruited by diverse cognitive demands. *Trends in Neurosciences, 23,* 475–483.

Duncan, J., Seitz, R. J., Kolodny, J., Bor, D., Herzog, H., Ahmed, A., et al. (2000, July 21). A neural basis for general intelligence. *Science, 289,* 457–460.

Eysenck, H. J. (1986). The theory of intelligence and the psychophysiology of cognition. In R. J. Sternberg (Ed.), *Advances in the psychology of human intelligence* (Vol. 3, pp. 173–191). Hillsdale, NJ: Erlbaum.

Gur, R. C., Gur, R. E., Orbist, W. D., Skolnik, B. E., & Reivitch, M. (1987). Age and regional cerebral blood flow at rest and during cognitive activity. *Archives of General Psychiatry, 44,* 617–621.

Haugh, H., & Eggers, R. (1991). Morphometry of the human cortex cerebri and cortex striatum during aging. *Neurobiology of Aging, 12,* 336–338.

Heim, A. (1970). *The AH4 intelligence tests.* Windsor, England: NFER– Nelson.

Hickie, I., Scott, E., Mitchell, P., Wilhelm, K., Austin, M.-P., & Bennet, B. (1995). Subcortical hyperintensities on magnetic resonance imaging: Clinical correlates and prognostic significance in patients with severe depression. *Biological Psychiatry, 37,* 151–160.

Horn, J. L. (1982). The theory of fluid and crystallized intelligence in relation to concepts of cognitive psychology and aging in adulthood. In F. I. M. Craik & S. Trehub (Eds.), *Aging and cognitive processes* (pp. 127–183). Boston: Plenum.

Horn, J. L. (1987). A context for understanding information processing studies of human abilities. In P. A. Vernon (Ed.), *Speed of information processing and intelligence* (pp. 201–238). Norwood, NJ: Ablex.

Horn, J. L., Donaldson, G., & Engstrom, R. (1981). Application, memory and fluid intelligence decline in adulthood. *Research on Aging, 3,* 33–84.

Houx, P. J. (1991). Rigorous health screening reduces age effects on a memory scanning task. *Brain and Cognition, 15,* 246–260.

Jensen, A. R. (1982). Reaction time and psychometric *g*. In H. J. Eysenck (Ed.), *A model for intelligence.* Berlin: Springer-Verlag.

Junque, C., Pujol, J., Vendrell, P., Bruna, O., Jodar, M., Ribas, J. C., et al. (1990). Leuko-araiosis on magnetic resonance imaging and speed of mental processing. *Archives of Neurology, 47,* 151–156.

Longstreth, W. T., Jr., Manolio, T. A., Arnold, A., Burke, G. L., Bryan, N., Jungreis, C. A., et al. (1996). Clinical correlates of white matter findings on cranial magnetic resonance imaging of 3301 elderly people: The Cardiovascular Health Study. *Stroke, 27,* 1274–1282.

McLullich, A. M. J., Ferguson, K. J., Deary, I. J., Seckl, J. R., Starer, J. M., & Wardlaw, J. M. (2002). Intracranial capacity and brain volumes are associated with cognition in healthy elderly men. *Neurology, 59*, 169–197.

Mittenberg, W., Siedenberg, M., O'Leary, D. S., & Di Ginlio, D. V. (1989). Changes in cerebral function associated with normal aging. *Journal of Clinical and Experimental Neuropsychology, 11*, 918–932.

Pokric, M., Thacker, N. A., Scott, M. L. J., & Jackson, A. (2001). Multi-dimensional medical image segmentation with partial voluming. In N. Thacker (Ed.), *Proceedings of medical imaging, understanding and analysis* (pp. 77–81). New York: Wiley.

Rabbitt, P. M. A., & Anderson, M. (2006). The lacunae of loss: Age and the differentiation of cognitive abilities. In F. I. M. Craik & E. Bialostok (Eds.), *Models for aging and development* (pp. 130–139). New York: Wiley.

Rabbitt, P. M. A., Chetwynd, A., & McInnes, L. (2003). Do clever brains age more slowly? Further exploration of a nun result. *British Journal of Psychology, 94*, 63–71.

Rabbitt, P. M. A., Diggle, P., Holland, F., McInnes, L., Bent, N., Abson, V., et al. (2004). The University of Manchester Longitudinal Study of Cognition in Normal Healthy Old Age, 1983 through 2003. *Aging, Neuropsychology and Cognition, 11*, 245–279.

Rabbitt, P. M. A., Scott, M., Thacker, N., Lowe, C., Jackson, A., Horan, M. & Pendleton, N. (2006). Losses in gross brain volume and cerebral blood flow account for age-related differences in speed but not in gf. *Neuropsychology, 20*, 224–239.

Raven, J. C., (1965). *The Mill Hill Vocabulary Scale.* London: H. K. Lewis.

Raz, N. (2000). Aging of the brain and its impact on cognitive performance: Integration of structural and behavioural findings. In F. I. M. Craik & T. Salthouse (Eds.), *Handbook of aging and cognition* (2nd ed., pp. 1–90). Mahwah, NJ: Erlbaum.

Raz, N., Gunning-Dixon, F. M., Head, D. P., Dupuis, J. H., & Acker, J. D. (1998). Neuroanatomical correlates of cognitive aging: Evidence from structural MRI. *Neuropsychology, 12*, 95–114.

Salthouse, T. A. (1985). *A cognitive theory of aging.* Berlin: Springer Verlag.

Salthouse, T. A. (1991). *Theoretical perspectives in cognitive aging.* Hillsdale, NJ: Erlbaum.

Salthouse, T. A. (1996a). General and specific speed mediation of adult age differences in memory. *Journal of Gerontology Series B: Psychological Sciences and Social Sciences, 51*, P30–P42.

Salthouse, T. A. (1996b). The processing-speed theory of adult agedifferences in cognition. *Psychological Review, 103*, 403–428.

Shallice, T., & Burgess, P. W. (1991). Higher-order cognitive impairments and frontal lobe lesions in man. In H. S. Levin, H. M. Eisenberg, & A. L. Benton, (Eds.), *Frontal lobe function and dysfunction* (pp. 34–75). New York: Oxford University Press.

Spearman, C. (1927). The *abilities of man.* New York: Macmillan.

Thacker, N. A., Varma, A. R., Bathgate, D., Stivaros, S., Snowden, J. S., Neary, D., & Jackson, A. (2002). Dementing disorders: Volumetric measurement of cerebrospinal fluid to distinguish normal from pathologic findings—Feasibility study. *Radiology, 224*, 278–285.

Uylings, N. B. M., & de Braboder, J. M. (2002). Neuronal changes in normal human aging and Alzheimer's disease. *Brain and Cognition, 49*, 268–276.

Van Swieten, J. C., Staal, S., Keppelle, I. J., Derix, M. M., & van Gijn, J. (1996). Are white matter lesions directly associated with cognitive impairment in patients with lacunar infarcts? *Journal of Neurology, 243*, 196–200.

Verhaegen, P., & De Meersman, L. (1998). Aging and the Stroop effect: A meta-analysis. *Psychology and Aging, 13*, 120–126.

Wechsler, D. (1955). *The Wechsler Adult Intelligence Scale.* New York: Psychological Corporation.

Weiskrantz, L. (1992). Introduction: Dissociated issues. In A. D. Miller, & M. D. Rugg (Eds.), *The neuropsychology of consciousness: Foundations of neuropsychology* (p. 6). London: Academic Press.

Ylikoski, A., Erkinjuntti, T., Raininko, R., Sarna, S., Sulkava, R., & Tilvis, R. (1995). White matter hyperintensities on MRI in the neurologically nondiseased elderly: Analysis of cohorts of consecutive subjects aged 55 to 85 years living at home. *Stroke, 26*, 1171–1177.

Ylikoski, R. Ylikoski, A., Erkinjutti, T., Sulkava, R., Raininko, R., & Tilvis, R. (1993). White matter changes in healthy elderly persons correlate with attention and speed of mental processing. *Archives of Neurology, 50*, 818–824.

Task performance indices, hypothetical functional characteristics, psychometric constructs and neurophysiological markers

Combined scores on three gross measures of age-related neurophysiological changes, AALBV, WMLP and CBF ("neuro") accounted for all of the age-related variance between individuals on measures of "speed". Neuro also directly predicts significant variations between individuals in scores on tests of frontal function and intelligence but, in both cases, age also makes significant additional and independent predictions. Neuro also predicts individual variance in scores on vocabulary tests, but age does not. On this point, gratifyingly, the data seem to agree with common sense: there is no reason why living longer should reduce the number of words we can remember. On the contrary, we should expect our vocabularies to increase, or at least to be preserved by additional years for experience and practice unless, and only if, neurophysiological changes intervene to diminish our lexicons.

Age directly accounts for a small but significant proportion of variance in memory test scores. Neuro has no significant direct effect on memory but does have highly significant indirect effects mediated through its effects on speed. This, of course, agrees with Salthouse's (1996) finding that scores on a letter/letter substitution coding task account for all age-related variance in memory, and prompted his idea that that age-related brain changes affect memory only, or mainly because they slow information processing speed. Neuro has significant direct effects on intelligence (*gf*), but these are much weaker than its indirect effects, which are modulated through speed scores. Interestingly, while variance on frontal tests is strongly related to age-related variance in intelligence, the reverse is not the case. At first sight this seems to conflict with convincing arguments by Duncan and associates (Duncan, Burgess and Emslie, 1995; Duncan et al., 1996) proposing strong links between frontal function and *gf*. However we must note that our data concern the effects of gross age-related neurobiological changes in an elderly sample while Duncan explored relationships in young adults with healthy brains.

These patterns of associations are hard to interpret because they clearly reflect complex entrainments between logically quite different classes of variables. They do suggest some conclusions about the functional relationships between brain ageing and changes in cognitive function. Gross indices of brain ageing are much more strongly associated with declines in speed than in other mental abilities. To interpret this comparison we must consider whether "decision speed" is a particular "mental ability" in the same sense as are "memory", "frontal function" or "*gf*". Scores of memory, frontal function and *gf* are derived from behavioural tasks that can provide only two directly measurable indices of competence: how fast and how accurately we can do things. Rabbitt et al., (2007) and Salthouse (1996; 2000) used the same task to measure "mental speed": letter/letter substitution coding in which memory efficiency plays some part because performance markedly improves as the volunteers become more familiar with the vocabulary of codes (Piccinin & Rabbitt, 1999). Rabbitt et al. (2007) used, in addition, times for simple visual search for capital letters O and I among all other letters in the alphabet. Intelligence tests and tests of frontal and executive function are more complex and make a much greater variety of demands on both short-term and long-term memory. However, a critical issue is that scores on these more complex tasks are also, incidentally, measures of information processing speed. In our data scores on intelligence tests were the numbers of problems that volunteers can solve within a set time limit. For this reason alone, and irrespective of the functional relationships involved, it is inevitable that scores on intelligence tests should be strongly related to scores on simple tests of mental speed. It can be argued that scores on our memory tasks were similarly restricted by time since volunteers had to complete inspection and rehearsal of material to be remembered within a set period of time. Since we inhabit a universe in which events can only happen in time, I find it impossible to think of a behavioural test in which correct performance is entirely independent of time and so, however indirectly, a measure of rate.

Because duration is an attribute of any process that occurs over time, it is trite to conclude that process duration, aka "speed" of task completion, is a basic, or "global", functional characteristic of the human cognitive system. Our results suggest that the speed with which we can perform very simple tasks sensitively mirrors the progress of global age-related brain changes. Even so, if we include both global neurophysiological measures and speed as predictors, we find that measures of speed do not account for *all* of the variance in performance on tests of memory, intelligence and frontal abilities that are associated with levels of AALBV, WMLP and CBF. It seems that these neurophysiological indicators also mark age-related changes in functional processes that support abilities, such as memory and fluid intelligence but for which speed measures are not the most sensitive indices of age-related differences.

Though the concept of "mental speed" seems too simple to be ambiguous, I think that models for age-related cognitive changes have elided four different ways in which it has been used. One usage of "mental speed" is as a directly measured index of performance in simple behavioural tasks – for example Choice Reaction Times measured in milliseconds, or numbers of symbols scanned, or letter/letter codes completed or, indeed, numbers of intelligence test problems solved in unit time.

A second use of "speed" is as a derived value that is not directly measured but is derived in terms of the particular assumptions of a particular, hypothetical, model for the functional processes supporting a task. An example is the Baddeley/Hitch (1974) model in which capacity of one (among many different!) systems supporting "working memory" – the capacity of the "articulatory loop" system – is determined by trade-off between the rates of decay over time of items held in it and the speed with which they can be dynamically cycled through the system (see Rabbitt and Goward, 1994 for a discussion of how estimates of these hypothetical system parameters change with age).

A third use of "speed" is as a hypothetical property of the central nervous system. This may be as straightforward and capable of direct measurement as speed of nerve conduction, behaviourally measured by comparing RTs to touches on the jaw and foot in Helmholtz's classic experiments. It may also be a much more complex property of nerve networks within which speeds of transactions are not solely, or even mainly determined by transmission times through separate single chains of single neurones but by the varying numbers of elements, or nodes, in branching, densely inter-connected webs involved in the transactions whose durations we record.

A fourth, and different use of speed is as a psychometric variable derived from performance or more than one task – as in the Structural Equation Models derived by Rabbitt et al. (2007), reproduced above, or the "global slowing" model proposed by Salthouse (1996). A caveat when using speed as a psychometric variable is that it may be derived from estimates derived from one, two or more of the levels of description described above; for example, from both direct measurements of RTs or items processed in unit time, from measurements derived from particular models of the functional perceptual motor system – that, consequently, depend on the reliability of these models, from even more than one psychometric proxies for "speed" computed in different ways, and from results of different kinds of tests.

Consequently, although this is a seductive simplification, it is unwise to conclude that estimates of gross age-related brain change, such as WMLP, directly determine "global system speed" in the brain and, consequently, also affect mental abilities, such as working memory, that are supported by functional processes whose efficiency partly, or entirely, depends on "global speed". WMLP, AALBV and CBS may all affect the efficiency of cognitive sub-systems in other ways than by slowing their operation. These gross measures may also have different and unequal effects on brain systems that support particular functions and this may result in correspondingly local, and so sometimes patterned, losses of the cognitive abilities that they support. Happily, huge improvements in the precision with which brain images can be obtained and interpreted return us to recall Paul Broca's insight that cognitive functions can be quite markedly localized, and that ageing of the brain can have unequal effects on local, semi-independent systems and on the systems of connections between them.

References

Baddeley, A. D., & Hitch, G. (1974). Working memory. In G. H. Bower (Ed.), *Psychology of Learning and Motivation* (Vol. 8, pp. 47–89). New York: Academic Press.

Duncan, J., Burgess, P., & Emslie, H. (1995). Fluid intelligence after frontal lobe lesions. *Neuropsychologia, 33*(3), 261–268.

Duncan, J., Emslie, H., Williams, P., Johnson, R., & Freer, C. (1996). Intelligence and the frontal lobe: The organization of goal-directed behavior. *Cognitive Psychology, 30*(3), 257–303.

Piccinin, A. M., & Rabbitt, P. (1999). Contribution of cognitive abilities to performance and improvement on a substitution coding task. *Psychology and Aging, 14*(4), 539–551.

Rabbitt, P., & Goward, L. (1994). Age, information processing speed, and intelligence. *Quarterly Journal of Experimental Psychology Section A, 47*(3), 741–760.

Rabbitt, P., Mogapi, O., Scott, M., Thacker, N., Lowe, C., Horan, M., ... & Lunn, D. (2007). Effects of global atrophy, white matter lesions, and cerebral blood flow on age-related changes in speed, memory, intelligence, vocabulary, and frontal function. *Neuropsychology, 21*(6), 684–695.

Salthouse, T. A. (1996). The processing-speed theory of adult age differences in cognition. *Psychological Review, 103*(3), 403–428.

Salthouse, T. (2000). *A Theory of Cognitive Aging* (Vol. 28). Amsterdam: North-Holland.

Overview and some personal reflections

To publish a review of some of a lifetime's work is an act of vanity. I have grown intensely to regret this as re-reading what I have written over the last 60 years provokes humiliating hindsights of fumbles and misunderstandings, of imprecisions in the questions asked and, even more painful, exasperation at the better questions missed. Nothing is more tedious for readers or writers than a catalogue of regrets. It seems best to end by trying to chart the wider intellectual contexts of the work on which I spent my working life. A good start is to illustrate the intellectual climate of this half century with a sketch of the far more distinguished careers of my excellent mentors.

In 1958, when I began my working life as his research student, Donald Broadbent published *Perception and Communication*, his first and most famous book that made him the medium for the zeitgeist of British Psychology for the next 20 years. Donald had just become Director of the Cambridge Applied Psychology Research Unit, set up by Sir Frederick Bartlett to work on applied problems for the military. The investment was considered successful and peacetime funding was continued through the UK Medical Research Council.

Applied military work in the Second World War transformed the intellectual lives of distinguished psychologists in the UK and in the USA. On one hand, the obligation to find workable solutions to practical problems stretched their minds by forcing them to consider data they would not otherwise have collected and to try to derive models to generalize from provocative unexpected observations. Donald's achievement was to develop a theoretical structure and language to make useful generalizations from the huge legacy of unanticipated experimental results that became available during and immediately after the Second World War. For example, it is often said that Donald's greatest contribution was to the study of selective attention by showing how it could be used to choose between, or combine, simultaneous messages delivered to the two ears. A historical footnote is that an excellent experimenter and, alas, his bitter career rival, Christopher Poulton, published observations on binaural selection before Donald (i.e. Poulton, 1953; Broadbent 1954; 1956). The difference between these studies is that Poulton meticulously and unsensationally described a new phenomenon, while Donald invented a new framework in which this could be discussed, and suggested a testable model that launched not only his own career but the work of a new generation of brilliant younger people he attracted to the study of selective attention. These included Anne Triesman (then Taylor) and Neville Moray in the UK and many others in the USA and elsewhere. *Perception and Communication* also provided a theoretical context for other legacies from military applications, such as Norman Mackworth's pioneering studies of vigilance during watchkeeping.

Donald's next book during this, his most luminous period, seems intended to be polemical rather than synthetic. His *Behaviour* is a critical review of the models derived from "rat psychologists" such as Hull and Skinner (Tolman comes out rather better). This spirited and necessary intervention did much to undermine the credibility of the clumsily proliferating models based on rat-maze-running in university laboratories. Studying how animals cope with the demands of their natural environments rather than the artificial constraints of the mini-worlds we constructed for them completed this process.

Fourteen years later, at an uncomfortable point in his life and career trajectory, Donald tried to repeat the brilliant achievement of *Perception and Communication*. The first chapters of *Decision and Stress* present a detailed, intelligent, complete and fair account of a huge body of experimental results that had accumulated since 1958. This is intended to set a scene for a new theoretical framework to do what *Perception and Communication* had achieved for a comparatively modest legacy of wartime work. I have never been able to deconstruct his theoretical manifesto, based on a (to me incomprehensible) distinction between "pigeonholing" and "categorization" of perceived information. The disappearance of this model beneath the silence of my colleagues somewhat eases my feelings of personal inadequacy that I still cannot get its point.

This is not an attempt to record a stumble of a very distinguished intellect. I believe that the problem was that during the late 1960s and 1970s measurements of human performance in a vast range of situations, in and out of laboratories, massively accumulated, but the richness and diversity of this new information began to show us that models based solely on behavioural data had ceased to raise or answer useful questions. I can think of few scientists more able or original than Donald, but his next assay into model generation does support this view of a fruitless struggle to develop models based on behavioural evidence alone. His "Maltese Cross Model of Memory" (Broadbent, 1984) is a lucid and intellectually powerful account of an arbitrary and, in my view, untestable model. It is ingenious, internally consistent and, as far as I know, incapable of tested prediction. It would be mean-spirited and redundant to document the scores of much weaker models by much frailer intellects than Donald's. Collectively, these illustrate that the increasing sophistication of technologies for presenting information and recording responses was beginning to provide fascinating new data that could not be explained in terms of models based on behavioural evidence alone.

During the 1980s, the "Maltese Cross" model and less intelligent attempts by other colleagues confirmed my growing scepticism as to whether it is useful to try to use behavioural data alone to understand individual differences in performance associated with ageing, or indeed any other source of cognitive variation between individuals. In retrospect, it seems significant that neither of my extraordinarily warm and gifted gerontological mentors, Jim Birren and Alan Welford, ever attempted a model, far less a "theory" of cognitive ageing. As we have noted, Alan's early career in gerontology was in applied research on how older workers could be better assimilated into industry. Jim Birren set himself a wider remit, and forged fruitful working relationships with medical geriatricians, insurance actuaries, sociologists and demographers, but was much too savvy of the limitations of behavioural data to venture a grand theory of ageing or even a comprehensive model for age differences in efficiency on any particular behavioural task.

This grumpy commentary is not intended as a criticism of Donald for constructing brilliant intellectual edifices that have proved to have no practical applications, nor to blame Alan Welford, Jim Birren and Chris Poulton for their patient and clever progress from one specific task-related problem to another without attempting to construct a general frame of reference for their scores of useful and provocative findings. The most gifted experimentalists are, perhaps, more keenly aware of the limitations of explanations for their results than those who try to weave results they do not really understand into "models" that no one can possibly understand. I mean only that during my working life there was a polarity in my subject between those who laboured to construct "models" for cognitive processes without considering whether these made any predictions precise enough to be tested and those who used experimental task analysis, but recognized, ruefully, that they could only interpret the phenomena that they discovered in terms of theoretical constructs that, while they were quite limited in their application at least, provoked further experimental questions that revealed unsuspected and interesting new phenomena.

In the wistful retrospections characteristic of deep retirement I find an omen in the title of the first scientific talk I gave, at a tiny, sparsely attended research seminar in the Department of Experimental Psychology in Cambridge. I called it "Five experiments in search of a theory". Only one member of the audience enthusiastically recognized, and appreciated, my predicament, and went out of his way to assure a very timid junior researcher that he did so – but I am glad to remember that he was the doyen of UK experimenters, Christopher Poulton, then beginning a long, undeserved eclipse by the shadows of many more than five otiose theories in hopeless search of experimental predictions.

I now argue that Chris Poulton's, Jim Birren's, Alan Welford's and my own plight as experimenters, and Donald's plight as a brilliant architect of free-floating intellectual edifices, represent different reactions to the predicament of our subject between the mid-1950s and the mid-1990s: the meagre information that we could obtain from behavioural tasks with the primitive technologies then available. We were all sustained by the same hope that persistence in accumulating behavioural data must, eventually, lead to understanding brain function. This is what Chris, Alan, Jim and I tried to do. I believe that this obstinate persistence has nevertheless been useful.

Much has been written about failures of interpretation and promulgation of fatuous hype in attempts to understand the increasingly rich data that brain imaging technologies now provide. The difficulties are enormous, but at least we begin to recognize what they are, and need no longer spend entire careers deriving models for a speculative future neuropsychology derived from inadequate and ill-understood behavioural data gathered for quite other purposes. At least we avoided the dismal, reverse-Rumplestiltkin task preferred by our contemporaries: spinning the gold of reliable experimental data into the straw of incoherent "models".

At the close of my play in this excellent game I realize that the idea that a useful "model" far less a "theory", of cognitive ageing can be derived solely from behavioural data was always an expedient fantasy. Like the best, useful and inspiring delusions, it sustained me and scores of excellent colleagues through decades of intensely interesting work, fostered encounters with brilliant and heart-warmingly kind colleagues and, best of all, provided me with far more than my fair share of fun.

References

Broadbent, D. E. (1954). The role of auditory localization in attention and memory span. *Journal of Experimental Psychology, 47*(3), 191–196.

Broadbent, D. E. (1956). Successive responses to simultaneous stimuli. *Quarterly Journal of Experimental Psychology, 8*(4), 145–152.

Broadbent, D. E. (1984). Modules in models of memory. *Behavioral and Brain Sciences,* 7(1), 86–94.

Poulton, E. C. (1953). Two-channel listening. *Journal of Experimental Psychology, 46*(2), 91–96.

Index

Note: **Bold** page numbers refer to tables and *italic* page numbers refer to figures.

For Product Safety Concerns and Information please contact our
EU representative GPSR@taylorandfrancis.com Taylor & Francis
Verlag GmbH, Kaufingerstraße 24, 80331 München, Germany